Innovation and China's Global Emergence

Innovation and China's Global Emergence

Edited by
Erik Baark, Bert Hofman and Jiwei Qian

NUS PRESS
SINGAPORE

© 2021 Erik Baark, Bert Hofman and Jiwei Qian

Published by:

NUS Press
National University of Singapore
AS3-01-02, 3 Arts Link
Singapore 117569

Fax: (65) 6774-0652
E-mail: nusbooks@nus.edu.sg
Website: http://nuspress.nus.edu.sg

ISBN 978-981-325-148-9 (paper)

National Library Board, Singapore Cataloguing in Publication Data

Name(s): Baark, Erik, editor. | Hofman, Bert, editor. | Qian, Jiwei, 1976- editor.
Title: Innovation and China's global emergence / edited by Erik Baark, Bert Hofman and Jiwei Qian.
Description: Singapore : NUS Press, [2021] | Includes bibliographical references and index.
Identifier(s): OCN 1240294794 | ISBN 978-981-325-148-9 (paperback)
Subject(s): LCSH: China--Economic policy--2000- | Technological innovations--Economic aspects--China. | China--Foreign economic relations.
Classification: DDC 338.951--dc23

Typeset by: Ogma Solutions Pvt Ltd
Printed by: Integrated Books International

Contents

List of Tables

List of Figures

1

Introduction: Innovation and China's Global Emergence

Bert Hofman, Erik Baark and Jiwei Qian

The International Implications of Innovation in China

The US-China trade war has called attention to China's transition to a "new normal" economy driven by innovation and productivity growth. The global implications of this transition will be large, as China's economy has become the second largest in the world and is deeply integrated into world trade and global value chains. China's rapid economic growth during the last four decades has lifted large segments of the Chinese population into middle-income international levels, with the average Chinese citizen's purchasing power now about a quarter of that of the average American. This achievement was grounded in the mobilisation of labour, capital and foreign direct investment that provided technological upgrading and generated export-led growth. The recent slowdown of economic growth is related to the decline in productivity growth experienced as the previous strategy of cheap labour and high rates of savings and investment ran its course, and this has prompted observers to predict that China may risk entering the middle-income trap (Zeng and Fang 2014). The concept of a middle-income trap was launched in 2007 and the factors leading countries to fall into—or to avoid—such a trap have been debated ever since (for example, Cai 2012; OECD 2013; Doner and Schneider 2016). Regardless of such predictions, China's leadership has recognised the need for a transition to high value-added production, institutional reform, and innovation as drivers for the next phase of economic development.

Consequently, China in 2019 invested 2.2 per cent of its GDP in research and development (R&D) and China's total R&D expenditure is the second highest in the world after the United States (Guojia tongji ju 2020). The number of patents filed by Chinese companies and individuals has risen sharply since 2010, domestically as well as internationally. The number of patents filed overseas expanded five-fold from 2010 to 2017, and China's "total citation count" (number of patents times forward citations) increased from 4 per cent to 7 per cent of that of the US. Over the same period, the number of foreign patents filed by US companies in China increased by 50 per cent. The number of Chinese patents filed overseas is expected to triple by 2025, which would make China the fourth-largest filer after the United States, Japan and Germany. The sharp rise in China's patent count was in part due to multinationals that offshored R&D to China: the R&D expenditure of US multinationals' foreign affiliates in China grew fourfold between 2004 and 2014 (Branstetter et al. 2019). Co-invented and Chinese-invented patents assigned to multinational firms made up well over half the patent count until the end of the last decade. This contrasts with the experience in Japan and Korea, where most patents were filed by domestic firms during their take-off of R&D investment. In addition, the number of R&D personnel in China has almost doubled during the ten-year period, with the full-time equivalent headcount growing from 2,291,252 in 2009 to 4,381,443 in 2018 (OECD 2019). The number of STEM (science, technology, engineering and mathematics) graduates in China has also grown exponentially, as more than 40 per cent of Chinese university students major in STEM subjects, thus adding 4.7 million new STEM graduates in 2016– the year that US universities graduated 568,000 new STEM graduates (World Economic Forum 2016). Moreover, China has benefitted from the flow of returnees that have received advanced training overseas, a "brain gain" that is analysed in Chapter 5 by Cong Cao and Denis Simon.

These data are indicative of China's new global status as a rising technology power.[1] Despite this rise, overseas sources of technology and international linkages to technology, investment and markets remain crucial for China's technological system. In this volume, the global implications of emerging technological capabilities and the continued dependence on international linkages in China are addressed in particular by the six chapters in Part One. These chapters include discussions of the conflict between the US and China, but they also address the role of international linkages in research cooperation, improvement of human talent and China's efforts to upgrade its indigenous innovative capabilities.

Despite the increase in R&D spending and patent count, China's growing innovative capabilities have not, or not yet translated into higher productivity growth. In fact, productivity growth as measured by Total Factor Productivity (TFP) shows a drop since the global financial crisis (World Bank and Development Research Center 2019; Dieppe et al. 2020). This observation is based on micro data from China's enterprise surveys and confirmed in macroeconomic data (Brandt et al. 2020). The slowdown in productivity growth is a worldwide phenomenon, but the pattern of TFP trends during the last decade in China appears related to the negative impact of institutional constraints and capital reallocation favouring state-owned enterprises over the private sector in the economy (Qian 2020; Wu 2020). Moreover, profitable opportunities in real estate also acted to crowd out investments in corporate TFP growth. This trend affected the state-owned enterprise (SOE) sector in particular, with a less significant effect in the private sector (Lu et al. 2019).

Engagement in a Global Value Chain (GVC) is useful to improve the growth of productivity at the firm level. In a recent OECD report, firms that are initially less productive or smaller are likely to improve their productivity faster than others when they are connected to key players in the production networks (Criscuolo and Timmis 2018). The GVC became a valuable route to upgrading technology for Chinese firms, particularly after China's access to the WTO, as China's share of global manufacturing value-added increased from 7 per cent in 2000 to about 27 per cent in 2015 (World Bank and Development Research Center 2019). This also provided opportunities for rapid expansion based on innovation, as Yuqing Xing shows in Chapter 11. Nevertheless, China still relies to a large extent on imports of some core technologies, such as semiconductors, software, among others, and it is likely that a potential de-coupling of the US and Chinese economies will upset these sources of essential inputs.

In order to raise productivity through a transition to high-value economic activities, China has developed a range of new industrial policies. China has had a long tradition of economic planning and industrial policy, with mixed results. The reforms since 1978 emphasised the development of markets and promotion of the private sector, but industrial policy never fully disappeared, and since the middle of the 2000s saw a revival. A stronger role of the state has emerged since the ascent of Xi Jinping to the leadership in 2012, and with it a renewed emphasis on industrial policy. With decoupling threatening to cut off China from critical technologies, such emphasis is only likely to grow. This raises again the challenges of the role, design and implementation of industrial policies in China's future development. This is the theme of the four chapters in Part Two of this volume, where individual chapters analyse respectively the relation of industrial policies to state investment allocation, the role of intangible assets in the *Made in China 2025* policy, local policies to promote cloud computing, and innovation in global value chains in mobile phone production.

In particular, the *Made in China 2025* policy issued in 2015 has been controversial in international circles, in part because of China's size and the potential spillovers of such a policy to the rest of the world. Furthermore, there has been confusion on the nature of the policy, which some argued was China's attempt at massive import substitution, and even dominance of world markets in particular industries. This confusion is in part based on a working group document that identified the share of imports that China could, *if needed,* supply itself (Zenglein and Holzman 2019). Communicating these numbers as targets has been damaging to the policy as it created a negative perception abroad.

China's targeting of new or emerging industries for its industrial policy can be seen as a means to move up the value chain, while avoiding sectors and industries in which other countries already have established abundant Intellectual Property (IP), and therefore collect most of the rents. The debate on industrial policy itself has seen a revival both internationally and in China (Aiginger and Rodrik 2020). Industrial policies have been defined as a set of policies imposed by governments to protect industries with favourable subsidies and tax breaks from competition with products from other countries (Aghion et al. 2015). It is different from trade policy, even if overlap may occur between policy objectives and effect. The EU and various member countries have each defined specific industrial policies, and Germany's "Industrie 4.0" is said to have been an example for China's *Made in China 2025* policy. Authors such as Mariana Mazzucato (2015) have re-evaluated the role of the state in major technological developments in the West. She argues for "mission-driven" industrial policy, as opposed to industry specific policy. Dani Rodrik (2004) and others consider industrial policy particularly important for achieving economic growth and moving up the value chain, though the tools increasingly appear to be generic policies such as competitive exchange rates and tax incentives, rather than industry specific subsidies. These emerging views contrast with previous mainstream views alleging that governments cannot pick winners and that industrial policy invites rent seeking to the point where net benefits turn negative.

In China, industrial policies have shifted towards more generic development of essential infrastructure and integration of initiatives in various sectors, where national policies function more as signalling devices for priorities and guideposts for coordinated state and private investments, more in line with the ways that promotion of industrial and economic development is implemented internationally (Filipe 2015; Dadush 2016). Part of the reason may be leadership recognition of the need for incentives for private actors to follow the policies, especially since private firms dominate the key industries subject to those policies. *Made in China 2025* is a case in point: the policy document maintains broad scope and generalised aims and does not contain specific financial commitments—though these were included in subsequent documents. Moreover, the policies are shaped by the decentralised nature of the implementation of industrial policy in China: most are implemented by local governments, which may have slightly different priorities than the central government.

Much of the financial support for innovation is channelled through the financial sector: government provides seed funding for the industrial guidance funds for new industries or strategic sectors which is leveraged with state and non-state financial sector capital. The amount of the government industrial guidance fund was set to increase to over RMB 10 trillion by the end of June 2019, compared to about RMB 5.8 trillion in 2018 (Xinhua 2019).

After the international critique of *Made in China 2025*, it was de-emphasised by China. Instead, a long-term plan for the industrial policy, announced by the National Development and Reform Commission (NDRC) and another 14 departments, highlights an ambition to deeply integrate the development of the manufacturing industry with the promotion of a modern service industry. According to the document, a group of deeply integrated enterprises and platforms will be built by 2025 (NDRC 2019).

Innovation, Globalisation and Competition: The Evolution of the US-China Tech War

From our perspective, the progress of innovative capabilities in the Chinese economy has been driven mainly by a combination of the domestic need for economic development and the new geopolitical strategy adopted under Xi Jinping's leadership. But they have also challenged established global powers over technological competitiveness and generated strong reactions internationally. The US-China Trade War was launched in 2018 with the US imposing tariffs on imports from China with the stated aim to reduce the trade deficit with China and create manufacturing jobs in the US. This triggered several rounds of retaliation from China and an escalation of tariffs from the US side. Behind the conflict over the balance of trade, there were very serious grievances from the US side regarding Chinese practices that in their view distorted competition, technology transfer and intellectual property (White House Office of Trade and Manufacturing Policy 2018).

Furthermore, China was increasingly seen as a strategic competitor and potential adversary (White House 2021). Thus, the current controversies over trade, investment and technology are only one part of a much larger rivalry between competing systems and worldviews, and the standoff over tariffs was only the first skirmish in what seems certain to be a protracted and difficult conflict (Boustany and Friedberg 2019; Kwan 2020). The dispute over the competition in technology and a potential decoupling of innovative systems between China and the US have consequently become the main battleground of the conflict (Capri 2020b). This conflict was not resolved by the Phase One US-China Economic and Trade Agreement signed in January 2020. This agreement addressed some issues relating to trade but hardly resulted in mitigation of rivalry over Chinese support to innovation and technology (Hofman 2020). To some extent, the linked US-China trade, technology and geopolitical conflicts have precipitated a new Cold War, as both powers are aiming for strategic advantage in an increasingly bitter contest to determine which of them will be the pre-eminent power of the 21st century (Dupont 2020).

Most of the actions taken by the US up to 2020 focused on undermining the efforts of innovative Chinese firms, in particular Huawei, to capture global markets for telecommunications systems such as the 5th generation mobile network (5G) infrastructure (Lee 2020). The actions against Huawei have come as a combination of several measures. These included erecting export restrictions for semiconductors or advanced design equipment from the US, and placing Huawei and 70 affiliates on the so-called Entity List that restricts business dealings with foreign firms that pose a national security risk for the US. Moreover, the US has attempted to persuade governments overseas to exclude Huawei from participating in the development of their national 5G infrastructure (Dupont 2020). In addition, the US-China tech war spilled over into restrictions of the US-based operation of popular Chinese mobile apps such as TikTok and WeChat. US restrictions in China's access to semiconductors that are essential for the development of advanced artificial intelligence (AI) systems have also challenged Chinese firms in the sector, exposing strategies that lacked advanced fundamental research capabilities and relied chiefly on their ability to exploit huge data sets (Ernst 2020).

While a trade war between the US and China could find a solution over time, resolving the strategic competition in technological innovation or the fundamental political philosophies between the two powers will be far harder. Both sides are driven by techno-nationalism and devote their resources to long-term objectives, witnessing a new symbiosis of state interventionism and private sector activism in defence of strategic and competitive advantages (Capri 2020a). However, there are crucial differences in the world-views of political elites and social actors in China and the US, and with its new status, China will challenge the liberal world order created under western influence in the 20th century, regardless of whether a new willingness to cooperate and adjust generates a political compromise (De Graff and van Apeldoorn 2018).

The prospects of a new Cold War in security and technology, and a decoupling of the Chinese and US economies are likely to be highly damaging for the two countries involved as well as the rest of the world. As discussed in Chapter 2, by Gary Jefferson, a transition towards a more cooperative system, based on a new balance, would provide long-term stability in economic and technological relations between China and advanced industrialised countries. On the other hand, even the mere threat of a new Cold War has induced China to allocate more resources to promote domestic innovation and technology development, and it is evident that the 14th Five Year Plan (2021–25) reflects this trend (Hofman 2021).

Industrial Policies for the New Economy

We see many new developments taking place in China's promotion of innovation as fundamentally related to the leadership's commitment to furthering the digital economy. One area of innovation in which China has already been quite successful is the digital economy. Platforms for e-commerce, financial technologies (fintech) and increasingly networks for e-health and online education have developed rapidly in China, coupled with extensive efforts to build digital infrastructure such as 5G communications. New key technologies such as AI have supported these developments, and have benefited from the data the digital economy generates.

Xi Jinping underlined the importance of "the data-oriented digital economy" at the second collective study session of the Politburo in 2017, thus emphasising the role of the digital economy as a new driving force for high-quality growth in China (Xinhua 2017). In China as elsewhere, the criterion for measurement of "high quality" economic growth is the improvement of total factor productivity (Qian 2020). Some recent empirical evidence supports the view that advances in digital technology can improve productivity in both the manufacturing and service sectors (Dieppe et al. 2020: 228).

Given the leadership's ambition to transform the Chinese economy into a data-driven digital economy, both central and local governments have subsequently released action plans for the development of different areas in the digital economy including cloud computing, artificial intelligence (AI) and the industrial internet. The overall strategy was provided in the *Made in China 2025* plan that underscored China's ambitions to develop intangible assets and capture new value-added in the global economy, as described in Chapter 9 by Anton Malkin. It can be argued that these efforts are creating a new context for industrial policy and indeed transforming innovation policy instruments.

With economic shocks such as the US-China trade war and COVID-19, promoting investment in data infrastructure is considered a major policy initiative to stabilise economic growth (Xinhua 2020). The 2020 government work report saw the first mention of the term "New Types of Infrastructure" which included data infrastructures such as 5G, big data storage centres, AI and industrial internet. It is noteworthy that while previous five-year plans in China have involved ambitious construction of transport and energy-supply infrastructure, the 14th Five-Year Plan (2021–25) is emphasising new infrastructure that will enable the new drivers of economic growth. This includes information-based infrastructure such as 5G base stations; converged infrastructure supported by the application of the internet, big data and artificial intelligence; and innovative infrastructure that supports scientific research, technology development and product development (Stern and Xie 2020).

The contributions in this volume suggest that China's industrial policies are transitioning to a new paradigm that is heavily influenced by innovation theory and competition in R&D, while also taking into account the role of the new economy based on data-driven development. These policies are often designed to facilitate and promote developments with new investment, facilitating development in the private as well as the public sector and following up on emerging strengths, as illustrated by the analysis of cloud computing by Bai Gao and Yi Ru in Chapter 10. Policies may enhance existing private industry investment with selective central and local funds, as indicated by Carsten Holz (Chapter 8), instead of creating new industries relying exclusively on centralised investment in state-owned enterprises. In the new approach, policy makers are showing more awareness of the impact of intellectual property rights and similar intangible assets, as shown in Chapter 9 by Anton Malkin.

Overview of Chapters

The first part of this volume explores the global implications of China's rise as an innovative nation in terms of international tensions and the prospects for future cooperation. Given the recent US-China trade war, the discussion is naturally shaped by the way that a conflict that initially appeared to be a trade dispute has morphed into a broader rivalry. Clearly, the interpretation of China's rise as an economic and technological power calls for a better understanding of the internal forces of change, such as the policies enacted by the state and the response of public and private sectors, as well as the changing external environment and policy directions of other countries, the background against which China's policies are evolving.

The US-China technology war has brought new challenges for the Chinese leadership and many of the leading innovative firms, and this is addressed in the theoretical analysis by Gary Jefferson in Chapter 2. He argues that the relationship will follow a trajectory similar to that of the Kuznets "inverted U" curve, where the incentives for cooperation dominate the first stage of asymmetrical innovative capabilities, while the incentives for conflict arise in the second stage of rising Chinese capabilities and China threatening to overtake the lead. A third stage of parity could bring back cooperation, as with the relationship that the US has with other industrialised countries. Jefferson explores two political scenarios for US actions—containment of China or transitioning towards a more cooperative system—and finds that the former is founded on a set of somewhat implausible assumptions, leaving the cooperation scenarios as being most likely to yield longer-term benefits to China, the US and the rest of the world.

Chapter 3, by Dan Prud'homme, focuses on contrasting discourses on China's intellectual property rights (IPR) regime and finds that an important contribution to the origins of the US-China trade war has been two contrasting sets of false myths about the Chinese IPR regime. The falsities include Chinese claims that aggressive forced technology transfer policies have not existed in recent years and that other aspects of China's IPR regime are not against free-trade norms. On the side of foreign observers, false myths claim, among other things, that China's longstanding Confucian culture prevents it from seriously protecting IPR, or that China's IPR regime is categorically weaker than the IPR regimes of developed nations. The debunking of these myths should help the scholarly, policy and practitioner communities in China and abroad to better understand the value of more constructively and truthfully engaging with each other in the future.

China's policies to promote indigenous innovation have also been subject to international controversy, and in Chapter 4, Erik Baark discusses a range of specific policy instruments that the Chinese government has employed, including public procurement of indigenous technologies and support for independent Chinese IPR and technical standards. It is proposed that the official promulgation of these policy instruments should be seen in the light of a legacy of self-reliance, where the inputs from domestic R&D have become increasingly vital for competitiveness and productivity. Furthermore, Baark argues that whether or not these policies challenge global incumbents, Chinese indigenous innovation may also contribute new, more competitive forms of innovative processes, and Chinese innovations may offer key technologies for a sustainable global future.

Given that international competition in innovation essentially boils down to a competition for human resources or talent, Cao Cong and Denis Simon argue in Chapter 5 that it is the contributions of scientists, engineers, other qualified professionals, as well as Chinese who possess business and legal knowledge and skills, that have propelled China to the global competitive position that it now occupies. China has developed various programmes to attract returnees among its overseas educated students and scholars, seemingly achieving some sort of "brain gain" and "brain circulation". However, China continues to face some serious challenges regarding its talent situation, just as the country did in the past. For example, not only is the quality of the returnees not completely satisfactory, various talent-attracting programmes may be merely a temporary solution to addressing China's critical talent challenges, while tensions between China and the US may cut off some of China's access to the most advanced technology. In their chapter, Cao and Simon argue that the key to meeting China's ultimate talent challenges lies in answering the "Qian Xuesen puzzle", specifically, that China has not yet been able to foster such values as independent thinking, tolerance of dissent and freedom of inquiry; these factors are essential for growing and nurturing truly innovative talent.

In Chapter 6 Denis Simon analyses China's evolving strategy, policies and practices regarding its international science and technology relations. By 2018, China had established S&T cooperation partnerships with 155 countries and regions and executed over 100 inter-governmental agreements on S&T cooperation. Simon highlights China's strategic posture and footprint in terms of its goal of becoming a player of influence in the international S&T system, including its relationships with several major S&T countries, comparing similarities and differences in terms of the depth and breadth of cooperation. Along with China's improvement in its S&T capacity and core competencies, China's role in international S&T cooperation is changing gradually from learner to partner and rule maker. Finally, the chapter concludes with a discussion of the changing landscape of the international S&T system, with a focus on the ways in which China's expanded participation might alter the evolving structure and operation of the system in the coming years.

Chapter 7, by Xiaolan Fu, Cintia Külzer-Sacilotto, Haibo Lin and Hongru Xiong, provides an analysis of the role and means of international innovation collaboration (IIC) in achieving radical innovation in China. Evidence from an in-depth case study of a leading Chinese technology company supports the suggestion that IIC can enable firms to become radical innovators, but that happens only with effective search and collaboration management. Opening up to international partners, combining problem-solving and blue-sky exploration, and sufficient internal inputs to facilitate absorption and integration are critical in ensuring that IICs become fruitful. Internal R&D capability, especially embedded in extramural R&D, strongly determines the transfer performance in making use of external knowledge or complementary resources, mainly due to the absorptive capacity and technology distance effects. However, most Chinese firms do not have the necessary infrastructure to search and manage IICs effectively. Policies strengthening the layout of the IIC network and facilitating international collaborations, such as the development of platforms and other tools to orchestrate international collaborations, are required to increase the chances of regular indigenous firms connecting with and managing external partners.

Part two contains contributions that address the Chinese experience with innovation in terms of industrial policies and global value chains. These chapters are primarily concerned with analysis of the significant features which distinguish how China implements its efforts to promote advanced technology sectors, and the role of public organisations and private firms in this process.

The discussion of China's industrial policies is opened up by Carsten Holz in Chapter 8, noting that these have attracted widespread attention lately. The 2015 policy of *Made in China 2025*, in particular, is widely viewed as creating an invincible economic powerhouse. Underlying such interpretations is the assumption that Chinese industrial policies have a decisive effect on resource allocation. The findings of this chapter suggest that this assumption is not valid. Six sets of industrial policies enacted since 2004 are introduced and their impact on the patterns of investment growth in the industry is examined. Further analysis considers sector, administrative subordination, funding and ownership patterns of investment. The evidence suggests that industrial policies have little or no effect on investment outcomes in the industry. At least through 2015, investment was driven primarily by profitability considerations. When industrial policies appear to have an effect, changes in investment patterns precede industrial policy.

In Chapter 9, Anton Malkin focuses on the less-understood aspects of *Made in China 2025*, namely intangible asset commercialisation and the promotion of automation, and explains why this part of the plan conforms to, rather than distorts, the emerging logic of globalisation. This logic is defined by growing competitive pressures to amass defensive and strategic intangible assets by means of IP commercialisation, public investment in emerging technologies and government-encouraged mergers and acquisitions. The potential for Chinese firms to earn revenues from their IP is growing rapidly, as seen most vividly in Chinese firms' growing appetite to register their patents as "standard-essential", giving them rights to negotiate technology licensing arrangements with global firms that utilise technology that includes the standards they had helped set in the first place. This echoes what is argued in Chapter 5, that China's role is transforming into a rule maker in the context of international S&T cooperation. The chapter examines a Chinese state-owned semiconductor design firm's efforts to catch up through both joint ventures and outbound acquisitions, but indicates the risks that this approach entails, suggesting that the goals of *Made in China 2025* will need to be revamped to reconcile the duality of China's industrial upgrading approach.

In Chapter 10, Bai Gao and Yi Ru examine the impacts of Chinese industrial policy on the digital economy in relation to private entrepreneurship, considering whether Chinese industrial policy is different from that practised by governments in other countries. This discussion is based on an analysis of the development of the cloud computing industry in Hangzhou and Shenzhen, focusing on Alibaba and Tencent. Contrary to the stereotype of the heavy-handed Chinese state, Gao and Ru argue that the market-facilitating state in the digital economy focuses on enhancing factor endowment, building infrastructure, reducing transaction costs, creating market demand, encouraging industrial clusters and promoting corporate rivalries. The primary goal of industrial policy practised by the market-facilitating state is to build an effective market, identify technological frontiers and lure private investments towards them. Such an industrial policy is often informed by private entrepreneurship and constrained by the dominance of private companies in the digital economy. The policy's effectiveness is often determined by private companies' willingness to follow the state's guidance.

Global Value Chains (GVC) provide a new channel of innovation for firms participating in value chains or utilising the value chain strategy to grow. Chapter 11, by Yuxing Xing, provides an analysis of the Chinese firms involved in the value chain of the iPhone and shows that the Chinese mobile industry has climbed up the ladder of the iPhone value chain and performed relatively sophisticated tasks beyond simple assembly. In addition, by examining foreign value added and technology embedded in the smartphones of OPPO, Xiaomi and Huawei, Xing argues that Chinese smartphone vendors primarily follow a non-linear model of innovation, jumping directly to brand development before acquiring sufficient technology capacity. They have been focusing on incremental innovations and product differentiation by taking advantage of available technology platforms. This value chain strategy has enabled them to overcome a technology deficiency effectively and has provided a short-cut to catch up with foreign rivals and to evolve into leading smartphone makers in both domestic and foreign markets. However, the US-China trade war indicates that the golden era of these GVC strategies may be over.

Concluding Discussion

Developments in 2020 suggested that China-US competition in technology will continue for some time. This book suggests that China has benefited significantly from international collaboration in innovation and new opportunities for accessing the global market and new sources of technology. Further, industrial policies have been used to promote productivity for the sake of achieving high quality growth. Both policies (that is, international collaboration and industrial policy) are likely to continue in the new geopolitical context because China has embarked on a trajectory founded on new capabilities and with a domestic market that supports demand for more advanced technologies and competition in both the private and public sectors. The concept of supporting a dual circulation with both a domestic economy and the international economic system that has set the tone for China's 14th Five-Year Plan reveals that the Chinese leadership acknowledges the risk of decoupling led by the US and therefore needs to rely on strengthening domestic innovative capabilities. This book provides insights into the challenges and driving forces of this evolution, and hopefully contributes to a better framework for policy makers in China and overseas to identify ways to reach a new equilibrium.

Note

[1] A more detailed cross-country comparison of China's catchup in technology can be found in Jiang, Shi and Jefferson (2019).

References

Aghion, Philippe et al. 2015. "Industrial Policy and Competition", *American Economic Journal: Macroeconomics* 7, 4: 1–32.

Aiginger, Karl and Dani Rodrik. 2020. "Rebirth of Industrial Policy and an Agenda for the Twenty-First Century", *Journal of Industry, Competition and Trade* 20: 189–207.

Boustany, Charles W. and Aaron L. Friedberg. 2019. *Answering China's Economic Challenge*. NBR Special Report no. 76. Available at https://www.nbr.org/publication/answering-chinas-economic-challenge-preserving-power-enhancing-prosperity/ [accessed 4 Sept. 2020].

Brandt, Loren et al. 2020. *China's Productivity Slowdown and Future Growth Potential*. Policy Research Working Paper 9298. Washington, DC: World Bank Group.

Branstetter, Lee G., Britta Glennon and J. Bradford Jensen. 2019. "The IT Revolution and the Globalization of R&D", *Innovation Policy and the Economy* 19, 1: 1–37.

Cai Fang. 2012. "Is There a 'Middle-income Trap'? Theories, Experiences and Relevance to China", *China & World Economy* 20, 1: 49–61.

Capri, Alex. 2020a. *Techno-nationalism: The US-China Tech Innovation Race*. Hinrich Foundation. Available at https://www.hinrichfoundation.com/research/wp/tech/us-china-tech-innovation-race/ [accessed 10 Sept. 2020].

_____. 2020b. *Strategic US-China Decoupling in the Tech Sector*. Hinrich Foundation. Available at https://www.hinrichfoundation.com/research/wp/tech/us-china-decoupling-tech/ [accessed 4 Sept. 2020].

Chen Ling and Barry Naughton. 2016. "An Institutionalized Policy-making Mechanism: China's Return to Techno-industrial Policy", *Research Policy* 45, 10: 2138–52.

Criscuolo, Chiara and Jonathan Timmis. 2018. "The Changing Structure of Global Value Chains: Are Central Hubs Key for Productivity?", *International Productivity Monitor* (Ottawa Centre for the Study of Living Standards), 34: 64–80.

Dadush, Uri. 2016. *Industrial Policy: A Guide for the Perplexed*. Policy Brief PB-16/05. Rabat: OCP Policy Center. Available at https://ideas.repec.org/p/ocp/ppaper/pb-16-05.html [accessed 9 Dec. 2020].

De Graff, Naná and Bastiaan van Apeldoorn. 2018. "US–China Relations and the Liberal World Order: Contending Elites, Colliding Visions?", *International Affairs* 94, 1: 113–31.

Dieppe, Alistair, Sinem Kilic Celik and Gene Kindberg-Hanlon. 2020. "Global Productivity Trends", *Global Productivity: Trends, Drivers, and Policies*, ed. Alistair Dieppe. Washington, DC: World Bank, pp. 5–38.

Doner, Richard F. and Ben Ross Schneider. 2016. "The Middle-Income Trap: More Politics than Economics", *World Politics* 68, 4: 608–44.

Dupont, Alan. 2020. *New Cold War: De-risking US-China Conflict*. Hinrich Foundation. Available at https://www.hinrichfoundation.com/research/wp/us-china/new-cold-war/ [accessed 7 Sept. 2020].

Ernst, Dieter. 2020. *Competing in Artificial Intelligence Chips: China's Challenge amid Technology War*. Waterloo: Centre for International Governance Innovation. Available at https://www.cigionline.org/publications/competing-artificial-intelligence-chips-chinas-challenge-amid-technology-war [accessed 10 Sept. 2020].

Filipe, Jesus, ed. 2015. *Development and Modern Industrial Policy in Practice*. Cheltenham: Edward Elgar.

Guojia tongji ju [National Bureau of Statistics], 2020. *Zhonghua renmin gongheguo 2019 nian guomín jingji he shehui fazhan tongji gongbao* [Statistical Communiqué of the People's Republic of China on the 2019 National Economic and Social Development]. Available at http://www.stats.gov.cn/tjsj/zxfb/202002/t20200228_1728913.html [accessed 5 Sept. 2020].

Hofman, Bert. 2020. *The Fallout of Phase One: What the Trade Agreement between the United States and China Means.* EAI Commentary No. 8. Available at https://research.nus.edu.sg/eai/wp-content/uploads/sites/2/2020/06/EAIC-08-20200131.pdf [accessed 28 Aug. 2020].

————. 2021. *China's 14th Five-Year Plan: First Impressions.* EAI Commentary No. 26. Singapore: National University of Singapore. Available at https://research.nus.edu.sg/eai/wp-content/uploads/sites/2/2021/03/EAIC-26-20210311-1.pdf [accessed 18 March 2021].

Jiang Renai, Shi Haoyue and Gary H. Jefferson. 2020. "Measuring China's International Technology Catchup", *Journal of Contemporary China* 29 (124): 519–34.

Kwan Chi Hung. 2020. "The China–US Trade War: Deep-Rooted Causes, Shifting Focus and Uncertain Prospects", *Asian Economic Policy Review* 15: 55–72.

Lee, Nicol Turner. 2020. *Navigating the US-China 5G Competition.* Washington, DC: Brookings Institution. Available at https://www.brookings.edu/wp-content/uploads/2020/04/FP_20200427_5g_competition_turner_lee_v2.pdf [accessed 28 Aug. 2020].

Lewin, Arie Y., Martin Kenney and Johann Peter Murmann, eds. 2016. *China's Innovation Challenge: Overcoming the Middle-income Trap.* Cambridge: Cambridge University Press.

Lu Bing, Tan Xiaofen and Zhang Jinhui. 2019. "The Crowding Out Effect of Booming Real Estate Markets on Corporate TFP: Evidence from China", *Accounting & Finance* 58:1319–45.

Mazzucato, Mariana. 2015. *The Entrepreneurial State: Debunking Public vs. Private Sector Myths.* London: Anthem Press.

National Development and Reform Commission (NDRC). 2019. *Guanyu tuidong xianjin zhizao ye he xiandai fuwu ye shendu ronghe fazhan de shishi yijian* [Implementation Opinions on Promoting the Deep Integration Development of Advanced Manufacturing and Modern Service Industry]. Available at http://www.gov.cn/xinwen/2019-11/15/content_5452459.htm [accessed 9 Dec. 2020].

Organisation for Economic Co-operation and Development (OECD). 2013. *The People's Republic of China – Avoiding the Middle-income Trap: Policies for Sustained and Inclusive Growth.* Paris: OECD.

OECD. 2019. *Main Science and Technology Indicators.* Paris: OECD.

Qian Jiwei. 2020. "Chinese Economy in 2019: Structural Reforms and Firms' Behaviour amid Growing Uncertainties", *East Asian Policy* 12, 1: 5–18.

Rodrik, Dani. 2004. *Industrial Policy for the Twenty-First Century.* Harvard Kennedy School KSG Working Paper RWP04-047.

Stern, Nicholas and Xie Chunping. 2020. *China's 14th Five-Year Plan in the context of COVID-19: Rescue, Recovery and Sustainable Growth for China and the World.* London: Grantham Research Institute on Climate Change and the Environment, London School of Economics and Political Science.

White House. 2021. Remarks by President Biden at the 2021 Virtual Munich Security Conference. 19 Feb. 2021. Available at https://www.whitehouse.gov/briefing-room/speeches-remarks/2021/02/19/remarks-by-president-biden-at-the-2021-virtual-munich-security-conference/ [accessed 18 March 2021].

White House Office of Trade and Manufacturing Policy. 2018. *How China's Economic Aggression Threatens the Technologies and Intellectual Property of the United States and the World.* Washington, D.C.: The White House, https://www.whitehouse.gov/wp-content/uploads/2018/06/FINAL-China-Technology-Report-6.18.18-PDF.pdf [accessed 27 Nov. 2018].

World Bank Group; Development Research Center of the State Council, The People's Republic of China. 2019. *Innovative China: New Drivers of Growth.* Washington, DC: World Bank.

World Economic Forum. 2016. *Human Capital Report 2016.* Geneva: World Economic Forum.

Wu, Harry X. 2020. "In Quest of Institutional Interpretation of TFP Change—The Case of China", *Man and the Economy* 6, 2: 1–22.

Xinhua. 2017. *Xi Jinping zhuchi zhonggong zhongyang zhengzhi ju di er ci jiti xuexi bing jianghua* [Xi Jinping hosting and giving speech at the second collective study meeting of the Political Bureau of the CPC Central Committee]. Available at http://www.gov.cn/xinwen/2017-12/09/content_5245520.htm [accessed 5 Sept. 2020].

_____. 2019. *Woguo zhengfu yindao jijin mubiao guimo chao 10 wan yi yuan yi daowei zijin chao 4 wan yi yuan* [The target size of the Chinese government's guidance fund exceeds 10 trillion yuan, and the funds in place exceed 4 trillion yuan]. Available at http://www.xinhuanet.com/finance/2019-10/25/c_1210326949.htm [accessed 9 Dec. 2020].

_____. 2020. *Liaowang: xin jijian shi da zhanlüe fangxiang* [Ten major strategic directions for new infrastructure]. Available at http://www.xinhuanet.com/2020-04/30/c_1125929139.htm [accessed 5 Sept. 2020]

Zeng Jin and Fang Yuanyuan. 2014. "Between Poverty and Prosperity: China's Dependent Development and the 'Middle-income Trap'", *Third World Quarterly* 35, 6: 1014–31.

Zenglein, Max and Anna Holzman. *Evolving Made in China 2025: China's Industrial Policy in the Quest for Global Tech Leadership.* 2019. Mercator Institute for China Studies (MERICS) Paper on China No. 8, 2 July 2019. Available at https://merics.org/sites/default/files/2020-04/MPOC_8_MadeinChina_2025_final_3.pdf [accessed 9 Dec. 2020].

Part One

Implications of China's Innovation Emergence

This first part of the volume contains analysis of the challenges presented by China's new technology and innovation policies in the global context. These policies have caused significant modifications in China's relations with the US as well as other industrialised countries. The chapters in this section discuss the new developments from different angles, including "the US-China technological rivalry", the shaping of conflicts by myths surrounding China's intellectual property regime, the reactions to China's promotion of indigenous innovation, the challenges of human resources and international talent flow, together with the continued need for international collaboration.

2

China and the US:
Technology Conflict or Cooperation?

Gary H. Jefferson

"If you know the enemy and know yourself, you need not fear the result of a hundred battles. If you know yourself but not the enemy, for every victory gained you will also suffer a defeat. If you know neither the enemy nor yourself, you will succumb in every battle".

Sun Tzu, *The Art of War*, 5th Century BCE

Introduction

During the first 35 years of China's economic reform, the US and China maintained a largely harmonious and seemingly mutually beneficial cooperative economic relationship, including the exchange and utilisation of US-sourced technologies. Recently, particularly during the Trump Administration, this harmonious relationship has changed dramatically as the US has at one and the same time imposed tariffs on Chinese imports and taken steps to block both the access of China's high-tech sector to American technology and access by the American market to Chinese technology.

The thesis of this chapter is that the technology relationship between two countries, one a technology leader, in this case the US, and the other a technology follower, China, with the potential to match or exceed the science and technology capabilities of the former, depends on the technological distance between the two countries. Specifically, the proposition is that the China-US policy relationship will likely, but not necessarily, follow a trajectory similar to that of the Kuznets "inverted U" curve. That is, when the US enjoys an undisputed lead, as it did with China during the last decades of the 20th century and when in the future the two countries have achieved relative technological parity, the incentives to avoid disengaging technologically and instead to jointly engage in a relatively open, cooperative technology relationship will be powerful. However, China's transition from technological novice to partial catch-up to technological proximity or parity is deeply problematic for both countries for a variety of reasons. As an aggressive follower with the resources and determination to match or exceed the technological prowess of the US, China is increasingly perceived in the US as a threat to the established leadership and security of the country. At the same time, by virtue of the passage of time and practice, the US assumes that it is entitled to continued technological hegemony. Moreover, the established rules and practice that have distributed asymmetric advantages to the two sides are viewed by China as unfair and malleable and by the US as sacrosanct to the economic and technology lifeline of the country.

The prevailing analysis suggests two broadly possible strategies and outcomes. The first is the containment of China leading to a fragmentation, or uncoupling, of the world's innovation and technnological systems sustained by two separate operating systems. From the perspective of this chapter, whether or not the US achieves some degree of containment, it is very unlikely to obstruct China's rise to achieve economic and technological parity or superiority. The second policy option involves transitioning towards a more cooperative system in which China more closely adheres to the global "rules of the game", while the US accepts the role of shared technological leadership. In order to compensate for the growing US scale disadvantage and the problem of unilateral credibility, the success of this approach depends fundamentally on the ability of the US to engage effectively with other Organisation for Economic Cooperation and Development (OECD) countries to create and present a united front to China. While the exchange of certain security-related technologies may be limited, when virtual technological parity has been achieved, such that disruptive behaviour by one country can be effectively matched by the other side, the breach of known standards is likely to result in mutually-assured disruption.

The following section surveys China's transition from technological backwardness to becoming a major technology actor on the global scene. Section 3 describes the advent of China's rise and the emergence of policy conflict, including the decisive role of China's official report, *Made in China 2025*. Section 4 describes the the US policy response and perceptions regarding the nature of the threat. Section 5 formulates a theoretical perspective in which the technology distance between a rising technology power and an incumbent power creates conflict; we map this perspective into distance-conflict space. The section then seeks to lay out two general policy scenarios as they relate to our theoretical perspective. Section 6 attempts to identify the key assumptions underlying each of the contending policy scenarios with implications for their respective feasibility. Section 7 offers conclusions and related issues for discussion.

From Imitation to Innovation

During the 25 years following China's reform initiative in 1979, virtually every major American manufacturer established a footprint in China. As a result, supply chains proliferated, labour costs fell, profits rose and shareholders benefitted; corporate America enjoyed access to rapidly growing Chinese and overseas markets; and the American consumer enjoyed substantial cost savings. On the Chinese side, technology and capital flowed to joint ventures and Chinese-owned companies; employment surged, with tens of millions of workers migrating to higher-paying jobs and with falling poverty; exports surged, and a fast-growing middle-class prospered.

During these years, is was widely known and accepted that China aggressively imitated foreign technologies, engaging in a variety of manoeuvres to acquire certain technological capabilities of foreign-invested companies. The officially mandated principle of these policies—Technology in Exchange for Markets (*jishu huan shichang*)—required that as a condition of foreign investment, or sometimes of the renewal of a registration, foreign companies would share certain technologies with a Chinese counterpart. In many instances, such exchanges were undertaken through joint research initiatives involving both Chinese and foreign nationals, thus enabling the transfer of new R&D capabilities as well as specific technologies. According to Jiang et al. (2019a), these collaborative research projects, notably those granted United States Patent and Trademark Office (USPTO) approvals, resulted in patent quality outcomes that were at once significantly above the patent quality achieved by Chinese-engineered patents, but also significantly lower in quality than patents from domestic US research collaboration. At least until recently, much of this technology transfer transpired well inside the international technology frontier.

In the four years following China's accession to the World Trade Organisation in December 2001, Chinese exports doubled as a share of GDP. In 2004, the volume of China's high-tech exports surpassed that of the US and nine years later rose to four times the volume of US high-tech exports

(Naughton 2018: 363ff). While exports were classified as "high tech", spanning computers, smartphones and various types of equipment, in fact many of the exports consisted largely of assembled imported components. Moreover, within China, the vast majority of these exports were manufactured and exported by foreign-invested firms. For example, laptops assembled by Taiwanese firms in China came to account for 90 per cent of the world's laptop production (Naughton 2018: 376). This surge in high tech exports led to two interrelated pathways.

The first concerned China's technology policy. In 2006, this heavy dependence on foreign technology, foreign-owned companies, exports with foreign brands and foreign-controlled supply chains motivated a deep rethinking of China's science and technology development strategy. This reassessment of China's technological relationship with the rest of the world culminated in the Medium and Long-Term Plan (MLP) (2006–20). With a view towards reducing China's reliance on the near monopoly of foreign invested firms controlling the technology, manufacture and sale of "high-tech" exports, the MLP set forth "the guiding principles for our S&T undertakings over the next 15 years". These included an emphasis on "indigenous innovation, leapfrogging in priority fields, enabling development, and leading the future" (The State Council 2006: 9). Among the "frontier technologies" emphasised in the plan were biotechnology, information technology, advanced materials technology, advanced manufacturing technology, advanced energy technology, marine technology, laser technology and aerospace technology, which considerably overlapped with the OECD definition of "high-tech" and "medium high-tech" industries.[1]

After 2001, the growing reliance on foreign-invested firms for the technology content of the export surge led to discomfort and determination to achieve greater technological autonomy. However, the second implication of the surge in high tech exports after this date was a substantial widening of China's export base, including the technologies incorporated in its growing range of high-tech exports. Notwithstanding the troubling condition of deepening reliance on foreign-owned technology and foreign invested firms, the FIE-domestic collaborations were critical for enabling the Chinese research enterprise to transition primarily from imitation to increasing degrees of innovation and from the lower rungs of the technology ladder to the mid- and upper-level. During the first decade of the 21st century, China began to achieve a substantial degree of technology catch-up in a number of fields. As documented by McKinsey & Co in their report, *The China Effect on Global Innovation* (2015), when measured by exports as a share of home industry output, and with the exception of railroad equipment, China's performance was relatively weak in the broad categories of science and engineering-based industries. The strength of the export sector was concentrated in customer-focused and efficiency-driven industries, including wind and solar-powered equipment, household appliances, generic pharmaceuticals and electronic equipment. Within a decade of joining the WTO, China had begun to make substantial progress in its move up the global technology ladder.

China's Rise: *Made in China 2025*

A decade after the presentation of the MLP, Prime Minister Li Keqiang in 2015 launched *Made in China 2025* (MIC 2025), which set forth explicit and ambitious goals for modernising China's industrial capabilities. The report both represented and precipitated a transformative understanding of China's S&T capabilities. Focusing on intelligent manufacturing to secure China's position as a global powerhouse, the 10-year comprehensive strategy conveyed China's ambition to move up the value-added chain, repositioning itself from a low-cost manufacturer to a direct competitor with technologically advanced OECD economies, including South Korea, Japan and Germany—and the US (Institute for Security & Development Policy 2018). Drafted by the Ministry of Industry and Information Technology (MIIT) with extensive input from 150 experts from the China Academy of Engineering, MIC 2025 lays out a set of wide-ranging goals, strategies and policies for achieving its ambitions. In contrast with the more uncoordinated approach of the US, *Made in China 2025* resembles Germany and Japan's systematic approach to government planning and policy.

Clear goals of MIC 2025 are to make Chinese companies more competitive across the board, to localise production of components and final products and to have Chinese firms move up the value-added chain in production and innovation networks so as to achieve greater international brand recognition. In addition, the plan calls for Chinese firms to ramp up their efforts to invest abroad by becoming more familiar with overseas cultures and markets, while strengthening investment and risk management.

Underlying the enormous indigenous endowment of an evolving supply of STEM-trained labour, an enormous and fast-growing consumer market and unequaled collaboration with a range of technology-driven foreign invested firms, China's S&T policy was becoming increasingly focused and ambitious. If the MLP represented the take-off stage for China's S&T, the *Made in China 2025* industrial policy report represented a kind of coming of age, with respect to China's ambition and confidence, resulting in a certain disregard for the impact of its aggressive intentions on the sensibilities of the heretofore-leading technology powers, especially the US. By flagging its ambitions and seemingly defying the established hegemony, *MIC2025* provoked widespread public and official response, particularly within the US.

Those reacting with alarm might not have been so surprised had they been attentive to the achievements of China's S&T programme over the previous 15 years. These include:

- A surge in the growth of Chinese investment in research and development, having increased to around 2.3 per cent of GDP, a proportion comparable to that of the large OECD countries;
- The ability to produce substantially more patent filings than any other country in the world.[2] That is, during the first two decades of the current century, China dramatically increased the sheer volume of production of intellectual property. The quality and management of that intellectual property warrant deeper attention.
- The production, circa 2010, of more science and engineering PhDs than the US, a proportion that has grown steadily over the past decade (McKinsey & Company 2015).

Clearly, there are significant quality differences in the nature of R&D, with China's R&D significantly more focused on development and less focused on basic research. Likewise, the average Chinese patent represents fewer claims and citations than counterpart US patents and the surge in investment in China's higher education has likely compromised quality. Nonetheless, these proportions are shifting rapidly towards quality improvements in China's favour.

However, product capabilities and their implications were the most unsettling for many American observers. Thomas Friedman, the *New York Times* correspondent, captured many of these in a 2019 op ed piece (Friedman 2019). According to Friedman, so long as China's technological capabilities were limited to "T-shirts, tennis shoes, and toys", China functioned more as a complement than as a competitor to the technology hegemony of the US. However, China has begun to make and sell to the rest of the world the same high-technology tools that the US and Europe sell, for example, smartphones, artificial intelligence systems, 5G infrastructure, electric cars and robots. Furthermore, as characterised by Friedman, certain of these products incorporate "deep technologies" that can become embedded in the US economy and social systems, thereby rendering many within the US sceptical and insecure about networking with Chinese technology within or accessible to these systems. As Friedman asserts, "the absence of trust and shared values" also matters.

In addition to the issues of cybersecurity and "shared values" raised by Friedman, the US Council on Foreign Relations opened its report, "Is 'Made in China 2025' a Threat to Global Trade?", with the following (McBride and Chatzky 2019):

> The Chinese government has launched "Made in China 2025", a state-led industrial policy that seeks to make China dominant in global high-tech manufacturing. The program aims to use government subsidies, mobilise state-owned enterprises, and pursue intellectual property acquisition to catch up with—and then surpass—Western technological prowess in advanced industries.... For the United States and other major industrialized democracies... these tactics not only undermine Beijing's stated adherence to international trade rules but also pose a security risk.

While some focused on issues of cybersecurity and the methods of China's S&T programmatic initiatives, the Trump Administration was at once more inclusive and ambiguous, also stressing these cybersecurity and IPR issues, but seemingly equally alarmed by the prospect of China matching or eclipsing US technological capabilities. China's dramatic advances along several product lines were particularly concerning for the Trump Administration. The most problemmatic included China's advances in 5G, which have arguably surpassed those in the US, which, in turn relies on Ericsson, Nokia and other overseas sources for 5G components as alternatives to China's Huawei, ZTG and other Chinese 5G suppliers. As Scott Kennedy (2019) recounted in his report, given that *Made in China 2025* pushes China to become a leader not just in aerospace, but also in sectors like telecoms equipment and phones and 5G, AI, semiconductors, automobiles and medical products, "the goal is to comprehensively upgrade Chinese industry, making it more efficient and integrated so that it can occupy the highest parts of global production chains". With respect to 5G, China has achieved that goal.

Andrew Kennedy and Darren Lim (2018) outline the principal means through which China has pursued its ambitious S&T goals. They summarise these as "making, transacting, and taking". While many of the activities and policies have been adopted by rising economies, including Japan, South Korea, and the US during its eclipse of UK technological dominance, with the propagation of the WTO, the various intellectual property treaties,[3] and other treaties and international rules and guidelines, the Chinese strategy pushes boldly against international norms. Kennedy and Lim summarise these Chinese initiatives:

- *Making*: The *Made in China 2025* industrial policy seeks to use subsidies, regulation, and government acquisition to spur Chinese innovation and technological advancement in emerging technology sectors, including electric cars and other new energy vehicles, next-generation information technology (IT) and telecommunications, and advanced robotics and artificial intelligence.

- *Transacting*: As well as outright commercial transactions with foreign entities that result in the transfer of key technology, the China approach to transacting continues to link the ability to do business in China to the precondition of technology transfer, "jishu huan shichang".
- *Taking* means acquiring existing technology from foreign states and companies without paying for it. This objective can be realised through legal means, such as collecting open-source material like published scientific papers or sending Chinese students to study abroad, or through illegal means, such as the cyber-theft of intellectual property from foreign governments and competitors.

Arguably, these are the methods that many developing economies, the four Asian Miracle economies, (notably South Korea, Taiwan, Hong Kong, and Singapore), and Germany and Japan employed to achieve their industrial rise. This claim invites two rejoinders. The first is that the methods used by these other economies were not as extensive during their own industrial transitions. If for no other reason, China is likely to utilise the range of technology-augmenting measures due to the scale of its economy and population that both enable it to leverage concessions from foreign enterprises and also create the opportunities for greatly decentralised measures by lower-level provincial and municipal governments and state-owned enterprises beyond the purview of the central government. The second rejoinder is that with the WTO, TRIPS and other IP-related treaties (see "Treaties-Intellectual Property"), the rules of the game have substantially evolved, with more enforcement provisions from those which applied in the earlier 20th century, when many of these provisions were being established. While China's economy has evolved in an era of far greater global vitality with respect to trade and technology transfer, the protections afforded to the owners and originators of these goods and services, largely sited in OECD countries, have become more detailed and rigorously managed.

As well as the US, EU leaders have long complained about both Chinese subsidies that distort the global economy, and restricted market access for European firms and the lack of protection for their intellectual property. Like the US, the EU has filed complaints against China at the WTO and imposed anti-dumping measures on many products.

The US Council on Foreign Relations reported that Chinese officials, wary of international blowback and realising that some of the language in MIC2025 raised alarms, have increasingly framed the plan as aspirational and unofficial. They have begun to reduce their allusions to it as Western leaders have voiced concerns. In the opening session of the 2019 National People's Congress, Premier Li Keqiang did not mention *China 2025* at all; it was the first time he left the programme out of his annual report to the congress since it was first introduced. On 16 August 2020, the *New York Times* headlined an article, "With Trump on the Attack, China Softens Its Tone in Hopes of Truce". (Hernández 2020). The article suggested that in order to substantially mitigate the conflict, China would need to offer "concrete proposals". Given that President Trump might have believed that his toughening stance towards China was an important selling point of his 2020 reelection campaign, any mutual softening and negotiation were highly unlikely until 2021.

The US Response: Nature of the Threat?

A 2019 US Congressional Research Service study (Congressional Research Service 2019) outlines the key issues aggravating China-US economic relations. While this study and subsequent events underscore the critical role of the trade deficit, by far the largest US bilateral trade imbalance, and forms of tariff retaliation undertaken by the Trump administration, we focus here on issues addressed by the CRS that are most relevant for the present and future US-China technology relationship:

- *Intellectual Property Rights (IPR) and Cybertheft.* US firms cite the lack of effective IPR protection as one of the biggest impediments to conducting business in China. The report notes that "A May 2013 study by the Commission on the Theft of American Intellectual Property estimated that China accounted for up to 80% (or $240 billion) of U.S. annual economic losses from global IPR theft". In November 2018, FBI Director Christopher Wray asserted, "No country presents a broader, more severe threat to our ideas, our innovation, and our economic security than China".[4]
- *Industrial Policies.* The report notes: "Major Chinese government practices of concern to US stakeholders include subsidies, tax breaks and lowcost loans given to Chinese firms; foreign trade and investment barriers; discriminatory intellectual property (IP) and technology policies; and technology transfer mandates". Recently issued economic plans, including the *Made in China 2025* plan, "appear to indicate a sharply expanded government role in the economy".
- *Foreign Direct Investment (FDI).* Chinese FDI flows to the United States, the report notes, were "facing enhanced scrutiny by the Trump Administration,

which contends that the Chinese government seeks to obtain US cutting-edge technologies and IP in order to further its industrial policy goals". The enactment of the Foreign Investment Risk Review Modernization Act of 2018 upgrades the ability of the Committee on Foreign Investment in the United States (CFIUS) to expand the types of in-coming investment subject to review, including certain non-controlling investments in "critical technology". In April 2018, US intelligence agencies said that Chinese recruitment of foreign scientists, its theft of US intellectual property and its targeted acquisitions of US firms constituted an "unprecedented threat" to the US industrial base (Capaccio 2018).

- *Advanced Technology Issues.* The report notes that "the Trump Administration has raised national security concerns over global supply chains of advanced technology products, such as information, communications and telecommunications (ICT) equipment", where China is a major global producer and supplier. China is the largest foreign supplier of ICT equipment to the United States. Citing a "national emergency", President Trump, on 15 May 2019, issued an executive order 13873, stating that "US purchases of ICT goods and services from 'foreign adversaries' posed a national security risk to the United States" and authorised "the Federal government to ban certain ICT transactions deemed to pose an 'undue risk'". On the same day, the US Commerce Department announced that it would add Chinese telecommunications firm Huawei and 68 of its non-US affiliates to the Department's Bureau of Industry and Security Entity List, which would require an export license for the sale or transfer of US technology to such entities.

While the CRS study helps to provide a quasi-objective assessment of the sources of conflcit, it does not represent the range of measures available to the US government to counter many of these concerns. The principal legal avenue through which prior Administrations and the Trump Administration have devised and justified economic and trade actions against other countries is Section 301 of the 1974 Trade Act. Section 301 sets out three categories of acts, policies or practices of a foreign country that are potentially actionable: (i) trade agreement violations; (ii) acts, policies or practices that are unjustifiable (defined as those that are inconsistent with US international legal rights) and that burden or restrict US Commerce; and (iii) acts, policies or practices that are unreasonable or discriminatory and that burden or restrict US commerce.

Furthermore according to the CRS: "Prior to the Trump Administration… the United States has used Section 301 authorities primarily to build cases and pursue dispute settlement at the WTO…. However, President Trump has been more willing to act unilaterally under these authorities to promote what the Administration considers to be 'free', 'fair' and 'reciprocal' trade…pointing to alleged weaknesses in WTO dispute settlement procedures and the inadequacy or nonexistence of WTO rules…".

On 14 August 2017, President Trump issued a memorandum directing the Office of the United States Trade Representative (USTR) to determine if China's policies on IPR protection and forced technology requirements "may be harming American intellectual property rights, innovation, or technology development", and thus warranted a Section 301 investigation. Following the investigation, on 22 March 2018, President Trump signed a Memorandum on the Actions by the United States Related to the Section 301 Investigation. It listed four IPR-related policies that justified US action, including China's forced technology transfer requirements, cyber-theft of US trade secrets, discriminatory licensing requirements and attempts to acquire US technology to advance its industrial policies (such as the *Made in China 2025* initiative). These investigations, findings and similar memoranda have established the rationale and legal basis for the number of tariff and techology restrictions that were proposed and enacted in the following years.

A Theoretical Perspective

At this point, a theoretical perspective may be helpful for anticipating the possible outcomes of the rising China-US technology conflict. This perspective is founded on a key proposition, that the current conflict needs to be viewed within a larger context of a longer evolution of China-US relations. As such, according to this proposition, the current situation is at the coincidence of three stages, one of which is past, the second is now evolving; the third can only be speculative. The stages are:

- Stage I: 1980–2010: Based on a clear set of comparative and mutual benefits, China and the US enjoyed a generally harmonious open and cooperative technology exchange with market access.
- Stage II: 2010 to the indefinite near future: As China achieved substantial economic and technological catchup with the US, thereby challenging the US in sensitive areas, the comparative advantage is transitioning into competitive conflict, and concomitant US efforts of containment.
- Stage III: China and the US achieve virtual technological parity. The two countries, facilitated by the role of other OECD economies, acknowledge the mutual benefit of a more open science and technology system than the fragmentation and rule-breaking during Stage II. Outside of certain fields

of defence and cybersecurity, key innovations beome readily accessible and commercially exchanged. In the areas of both defence and cybersecurity, China and the US have achieved the stabilising condition of mutually assured disruption.

Figure 2.1 shows an inverted "U" curve, which generally follows the shape of the trajectory proposed by Simon Kuznets in which income inequality within countries tends to be relatively limited when countries are low income and largely agrarian in nature. As economies evolve with industrialisation and deeper economic integration with other nations, and attracting new technologies and investment to certain areas, new development results in poverty reduction, but also in rising income inequality. Measures of inequality, namely the Gini coefficient, rise. Finally, as economies transition to the more uniformly high-income, product, labour and capital markets become more mature and efficient, while governments spend more widely for health, education, old-age support and various forms of insurance. A growing middle-class emerges, resulting in falling inequality and declining measures of poverty. This characterisation of the pattern of rising, then declining, income inequality resulting in the inverted "U" curve shown in Figure 2.1 has also been extensively applied to the tendency for the environmental degradation of individual countries to rise and fall. Following industrialisation and the proliferation of chemical use in agriculture and industry, and as living standards rise, demands for clean air and clean water, combined with a shift from heavy industry to the services sector and with greater environmental regulations result in a decline in environmental degradation, thereby tracing out a pattern of change similar to that of income inequality and economic development, that is, that of an inverted "U" curve.

In this chapter, Kuznets' metaphor of the inverted "U" curve is borrowed to underscore the evolution of bilateral conflicts as the technological distance between the two countries evolves. Initially, when a clear division of labour exists between a technology-rich, high-income country and a technology-backward low-income country with low-cost labour and a large, growing consumer market, the comparative advantage is deep and compelling. As the low-income country benefits from technology spillover and technology upgrading, facilitated by foreign investment, scale and the diversity of its expanding economy, the original comparative advantage erodes, becoming replaced by expectations by the rising country of parity, resulting in fear within the heretofore hegemonic country of burdensome competition, and of possibly being overtaken in key industries. The original comparative advantage transforms to intensifying competition; conflict emerges.

Figure 2.1: Kuznets "Inverted U" Curve: Technology Policy Conflict vs. Technology Distance

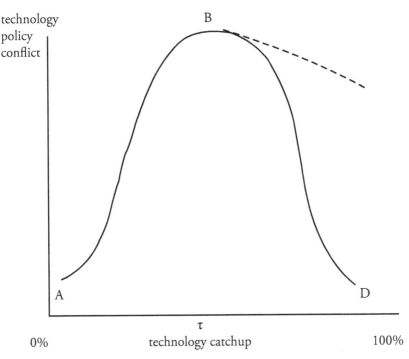

Generalising, Graham Allison (2017) characterises this condition as Thucydides's Trap, based on the Greek historian's account of the Peloponnesian War. According to Thucydides: "It was the rise of Athens and the fear that this instilled in Sparta that made war inevitable". As Allison explains, "The past 500 years have seen 16 cases in which a rising power threatened to displace a ruling one. Twelve of these ended in war".

Modern analysts generally do not expect the evolving conflict between China and the US to result in bloodshed. While some observers contend that the conflict may be "existential", with technology as a metaphor for the wider military, economic, political and cultural supremacy that may be at stake, the "instruments of war" are likely to be limited to a collection of economic and technological skirmishes, focused more on the disengagement of competing resources than a fight to the finish.

Again, this formulation is highly speculative; however, it is intended to bring some order to the discussion that has a wide range of starting points, suppositions and possible outcomes. In Figure 2.1, the axis of "technology catchup" may serve as a useful baseline for understanding a key nature of the conflict, as the Trump Administration attempted to freeze or expand the technology distance between the US and China, while China's leadership and S&T establishment aggressively seek to narrow the technology distance, as for example by staking out space on the global technology frontier.

Given the formulation of the technology-conflict Kuznets curve shown in Figure 2.1, it may be assumed that the analysis will identify that segment of the curve representing the current state of the China-US struggle. It matters if the struggle lies to the left or right of the peak, or if the struggle is, in fact, peaking at this moment. The research by Jiang et al. (2019a and 2019b) suggests that China's overall technology remains substantially distanced from that of the US, though our analysis is limited largely to China's overall relative technology position, using patent data that extend only to 2017, likely some years behind China's advancing capabilites. A brief summary of key findings includes:

- While China's domestic patent office processes far more patents than any other country's, in terms of patent approvals and total citations in international patent offices, and while China has matched France and the UK, it continues to lag behind Germany and South Korea and is far behind Japan and the US;
- China shows large variation in patent quality. In key areas, such as telecommunications, semiconductors and optics, China's average USPTO patent quality, in terms of claims and citations lags significantly behind the US and other (but not all) major OECD economies.
- China's USPTO patent production is dramatically concentrated in just three cities—Beijing, Shanghai and Shenzhen—representing two-thirds of the patent grants originating with less than five per cent of the country's population.[5] This result shows both the challenge for China to diversify its centres of innovation, and the immense potential China enjoys for expanding the scale of its high-end innovative capabilites.

Notwithstanding these findings, within discrete technology categories and at the firm level, elements of Chinese S&T are in break-out mode at or near the global frontier, including 5G equipment and networking, electric vehicles, defence and cybersecurity. At the same time, investments in AI, aerospace, including commercial aircraft, and biomedical research are rapidly advancing. The MIC2025 emphasis on "comprehensive" competitive engagement with the advanced OECD economies suggests rapid movement along the "technology distance" axis. As such, the alarm engendered by China's S&T push may be as much, and perhaps more, a result of the speed of China's technological advance, as of alarm occassioned by the actual extent of the current closure of the technology gap.

Possibility and Feasibility

While there are many possible paths involving initiative and consequences, which meet with different degrees of feasibility, arguably they can be condensed into two. Meijer (2016), for example, distills the possibilities into the "Control Hawks" group which believes that exporting technologies to competitors is a security risk, and the "Run Faster" advocates who believe that exports are essential for keeping technology industries competitive and able to innovate.

In this section, we simply distinguish the approaches as the "containment strategy" and the "cooperation strategy".

Containment: The containment assumption is based on several key assumptions. All assume a unilateral approach, similar to that initiated by the Trump Administration. These assumptions include:

- That the US has the methods that it can deploy sucessfully to deny US technology and markets to Chinese suppliers;
- That other countries cannot and will not substitute the US in supplying either technologies or markets that enable China to outpace the development and use of the key technologies and markets that are particularly concerning to the US.
- Assuming that many of the individual initiatives that constitute the containment policy succeed, China will not have the resources in the longer run to achieve the technological and economic capabilities to match and overtake the US; in the longer term, that is, the containment policy fails.
- That the US can manage the overall situation, so that it will not get "out of hand", entailing the serious loss of US markets, prestige or armed conflict overseas resulting in the loss of American life.

These appear to be the most general assumptions underlying the US administration's "public" policy. For the most part, thus far the policy has been *ad hoc* and piecemeal without an open, thoughtful discussion of this largely unilateral containment strategy. Part of the problem is that, at the time of the writing of this chapter, the US was in the midst of an electoral contest culminating in November 2020. As a result, and even with the transition to the Biden administration in 2021, it is difficult to distinguish most near-term motivations. Is, for example, the "China threat" an election issue simply, or a well-conceived sustainable, public policy option for the US?

Cooperation: As with the containment strategy, the strategy of establishing a comparatively open, cooperative technology system with China is based on a deep set of assumptions. Most of these are contrary to those underlying the containment strategy. They include:

- The US is unable to achieve its objective with respect to China unilaterally; China's economy is too large; its population and core S&T capabilities, combined with the central roles of science and techology in its educational and political/cultural systems, make it impossible to "contain" China in any meaningful sense. Goodman and Ratner (2018) argue that attempts to cut off technology will simply speed China's determination and domestic capacity to develop and diversify critical technologies.
- Many aspects of technology are essentially public goods making them highly accessible to Chinese researchers. Such conditions include the requirement, embedded in US and international patent law, that patent applications contain sufficient information for the invention to be replicated, while not being used for commercial purposes, as well as reverse engineering and outright theft, as needed.
- Efforts to motivate China to better conform with international law and norms regarding its economic and technological relations with the rest of the world cannot be achieved by the US unilaterally, at least not through negative incentives. Goodman and Ratner (2018) further explain that while many countries share Trump's desire to combat Chinese hi-tech mercantilism, Trump divided allies rather than unifying them to confront China.
- Such unilateral initiatives will ultimately serve to isolate the US as both China and the rest of the world either view both China and the US as unworthy of their support or single out the US as simply being unwilling to share its hegemonic position with China or any other country.
- The US is likely to diminish or exhaust itself in a battle with China. Any success is likely to be transitory, resulting in a Pyrrhic victory.

A central difference between the containment strategy and the cooperation strategy may be the time horizon over which the respective strategies are intended to be implemented and sustainable. The cooperation strategy appears to be more focused on a longer time-horizon than that of the containment advocates, with respect to its sustainability as well as the time required for its implemenation. The central assumption of the advocates of cooperation is that even if the objectives of the containment advocates and the cooperation advocates are identical with respect to China, the objectives cannot be obtained unilaterally. An alliance, such as the G7, the largest of the high-income OECD economies, is required. Arguably, the alliance is not addressing issues of sheer scale, which over time is likely to tilt to the disadvantage of the US; the alliance approach is critical for two additional reasons. Both have to do with perceptions.

The first is that unilateral initiatives by the US, which has evolved as the world's economic and technology hegemon over the past century, have been and will continue to be viewed by China's leadership, its intelligensia and general population as attempts by the world's bully to suppress China's rise. The critical issue is not China, but the weakness and insecurity of the US. The second reason is basically that much of the rest of the world will also view the problem in these terms. Section 301 of the 1974 Trade Law is ambiguous. Not only does it have force for violations of international or US law, in addition, as shown in President Trump's memorandum to the US Trade Representative, Section 301 provides a window for punitive action against countries with which the US incurs a trade deficit or with which trade or investment has resulted in the diversion of American jobs.[6] Seemingly, simply as a result of the deficits and job loss resulting from commercial relations with the US, any US trading partner can fall within the crosshairs of Section 301; this is particularly so when the US finds itself engaged in "strategic competition" with a rising power.

Together, if China strongly adheres to this view, and the rest of the world follows, the legitimacy of the US effort is seriously eroded, resulting in its isolation. The second, more central vulnerability of the unilateral approach is that it will divert attention from what should be the focus of consternation, namely, China's persistence in not adhering to agreements regarding trade, foreign investment and intellectual property rights, and the legitimate concern regarding the misuse of cyber techniques to compromise the security of various countries and their citizens.

In any event, these two strategy alternatives do not necessarily dictate the shape of the trajectory shown in Figure 2.1. If the emphasis is on punishing China, through either the containment or the cooperation strategy (in which success is limited to cooperation with OECD allies to change China's behaviour), and with China remaining unresponsive, the trajectory could transition from B to C in Figure 2.1, not B to D. The analysis above suggests that given the circumstances of comparable scale and the limitations of single-country advocacy, the second approach is likely to be more feasible, while imposing fewer costs in terms of American resources and reputation. However, to the extent that the cooperation scenario is successful, its success is more likely to rely less on decoupling and the preservation of the singular role of US economic and technological dominance. Its focus, feasibility and success would more likely result in greater clarity regarding the global "rules of the game" and

China's compliance with those rules. The cooperation scenario has more upside potential than the containment strategy.

For the US, the potential benefits of the cooperation strategy are considerable. These include:

- The ability to play a leading role in renegotiating, reaffirming and reinforcing a set of international rules and treaties that effectively engage China;
- Having access to a critical R&D endowment shortage, that of skilled labour supplied by Chinese researchers, many of whom would be trained in US universities.
- Access to advanced Chinese technology, for example the 1,000 mile electric vehicle battery, and markets for US innovations, for example a cure for Alzheimer's.
- More openness and transparency for Chinese technology, making it feasible to achieve a state of *mutual assured disruption*, the reciprocal ability to use remote techniques to disrupt communication, technology and energy systems, thereby limiting the likelihood of hostile disruptive measures.

If these potential benefits once recognised by the US do materialise between China and the US, and across the international system with Chinese-US support, then the predictions of the Kuznets "Inverted U" curve at D, corresponding with 100 per cent or virtual catch up, are more likely to materialise.

Conclusions and Discussion

This chapter begins with a reference to Sun Tzu's dictum: "If you know the enemy and know yourself, you need not fear the result of a hundred battles". We enlist this dictum in support of a somewhat optimistic perspective on the eventual resolution of the current China-US tensions. Fundamentally, we view this conflict as resulting from the accumulation of destabilising change in the relative economic and technological stature of the world's two largest economies. Reminiscent of the outlines of Thucydides's Trap, the economic and technological rise of one economy is challenging to the established hegemony of an established economic power.

From a policy perspective, the principal reason for not wanting to quarantine or decouple from Chinese technology is that it is unlikely that the containment strategy will work; moreover, it creates numerous risks for the US while not promising compensating benefits. The containment strategy is likely to fail even more in the medium term and still more in the long run. In terms of sheer economic scale and technology capability, it is very likely that time is on China's side. The US should use this limited interval to move from its hardball containment strategy, thereby legitimising the approach for China as it acquires more leverage; this may be the last opportunity for the US to take a leadership role in forging an OECD or G7 consensus that effectively engages China in a global consensus regarding the management of technology in the global economy.

Looking forward, US policy is unlikely to substantially affect China's long-run economic and technological advance. Efforts to block the transfer of technologies, thus voiding the trend towards specialisation and comparative advantage, are most likely to motivate China to undertake a more determined, comprehensive and aggressive technology development strategy. It is highly likely that the best way to limit troubling outcomes, including destructive technologies such as nuclear arms, cyber-attacks and rogue gene editing, is through international engagement and collaboration. The most likely way to encourage this condition is through technology cooperation and competition. Clearly, in order to achieve technology cooperation, shown at the far right side of the Kuznets Curve, China has to change. A key precondition for such change is likely to be the country acquiring the indigenous appetite and need for IPR protection. In *The Spies Who Launched American's Industrial Revolution*, Klein (2019) documents the acquisition of the means through which, as Doron S. Ben-Atar notes, "the United States emerged as the world's industrial leader by illicitly appropriating mechanical and scientific innovations from Europe" (Ben-Atar 2004: xxi). This appropriation created the platform for its indigenous innovation capabilities that evenually allowed it to emerge as the world's foremost advocate for intellectual property rights and guarantees. China is advancing along this track. Nonetheless, China needs to advance its ability to demonstrate to the world and its own population its understanding that S&T leadership entails a commitment to the open exchange of ideas, people and technologies.

A key change for the US is to renew its commitment to behaving like the world's S&T leader by investing in basic R&D for next generation technologies and opening its doors to aspiring and successful scientists, engineers and entrepreneurs. A race is on for various countries to emerge as the leader in next generation technologies including 5G, medical and health care innovations, measures to mitigate global warming, space exploration and other fields. The US must renew its commitment to science and its innovative applications. In doing so, in the process of cooperating and competing with the rest of the world, China included, the US can hopefully restore its confidence that it can compete successfully in a global economy with an open exchange of ideas, people and technologies.

Acknowledgements

The author appreciates the contribution to the formulation of this chapter of the lively discussion at the International Conference on Innovation and China's Global Emergence, organised by the East Asian Institute, National University of Singapore, 25–26 July 2019, as well as to colleagues at the Institute who have assisted with revisions.

Notes

[1] The OECD classifications, in some cases different from those used in the MLP, are *High-technology industries*: aircraft and spacecraft, pharmaceuticals, office, accounting and computing machinery; radio, TV and communications equipment; medical, precision and optical instruments. *Medium-high-technology industries* include: electrical machinery and apparatus, motor vehicles, trailers and semi-trailers, *chemicals* excluding pharmaceuticals, railroad equipment and transport equipment, machinery and equipment. (See OECD Directorate for Science, Technology and Industry 2011.)

[2] See the WIPO "country statistical profiles" for China and the US at the World Intellectual Property Organisation website, https://www.wipo.int/portal/en/.

[3] For a representative sampling, please see "Treaties--Intellectual Property" on the Tarlton Law Library, Jamail Center for Legal Research website.

[4] The Report of the US Trade Representative (OUSTR 2018: 8, Table 1.1) includes a list of China IPR commitments: "China's Bilateral Commitments Relating to Technology Transfer, 2010–2016 Agreements".

[5] According to Jiang et al. (2019b), China's concentration is significantly higher than the US' for which the comparably scaled proportion of the population accounts for 21 per cent of US patent production.

[6] See, for example, the Executive Office of the US President 14 August 2017 memorandum which reads: "China has implemented laws, policies, and practices and has taken actions related to intellectual property, innovation, and technology that may encourage or require the transfer of American technology and intellectual property to enterprises in China or that may otherwise negatively affect American economic interests. These laws, policies, practices, and actions may inhibit United States exports, deprive United States citizens of fair remuneration for their innovations, divert American jobs to workers in China, contribute to our trade deficit with China, and otherwise undermine American manufacturing, services, and innovation".

References

Allison, Graham. 2017. "The Thucydides Trap", *Foreign Policy OBSERVATION DECK*, 9 June. Available at https://foreignpolicy.com/2017/06/09/the-thucydides-trap/ [accessed 10 Nov. 2020].

Atkinson, Robert D. 2020. "How Nine Flawed Policy Concepts Hinder the United States From Adopting the Advanced-Industry Strategy It Needs", Information Technology and Innovation Foundation (ITIF), 10 August 2020. Available at https://itif.org/publications/2020/08/10/how-nine-flawed-policy-concepts-hinder-united-states-adopting-advanced [accessed 10 Nov. 2020].

Ben-Atar, Doron S. *Trade Secrets: Intellectual Piracy and the Origins of American Industrial Power.* New Haven, CT: Yale University Press.

Capaccio, Tony. 2018. "China's 'Thousand Talents' Called Key in Seizing U.S. Expertise", *BNN Bloomberg Online.* Available at https://www.bnnbloomberg.ca/china-s-thousand-talents-called-key-in-seizing-u-s-expertise-1.1097112 [accessed 12 Feb. 2021].

Congressional Research Service [CRS]. 2019. *U.S.-China Trade Issues. Updated, June 23, 2019.* Available at https://crsreports.congress.gov/product/pdf/IF/IF10030/43 [accessed 10 Nov. 2020].

_____. 2020. *Section 301 of the Trade Act of 1974, Updated January 27, 2020.* Available at https://www.wita.org/atp-research/section-301-trade-act-1974/ [accessed 10 Nov. 2020].

Executive Office of the US President August 14, 2017 Memorandum. "Addressing China's Laws, Policies, Practices, and Actions Related to Intellectual Property, Innovation, and Technology". Available at https://www.federalregister.gov/documents/2017/08/17/2017-17528/addressing-chinas-laws-policies-practices-and-actions-related-to-intellectual-property-innovation [accessed 10 Nov. 2020].

Friedman, Thomas L. 2019. "The World-Shaking News That You're Missing: The U.S.-China Divide isn't Just about Trade", *The New York Times* Online. 26 Nov. 2019. Available at https://www.nytimes.com/2019/11/26/opinion/united-states-china.html [accessed 17 Dec. 2020].

Goodman, Matthew P. and Ely Ratner. 2018. "A Better Way to Challenge China on Trade: Trump's Harmful Tariffs Aren't the Answer", *Foreign Affairs,* 22 March.

Hernández, Javier C. 2020. "As Relations with U.S. Sink, China Tones Down 'Hotheaded' Nationalism", *The New York Times,* 15 August 2020. Available at https://www.nytimes.com/2020/08/15/world/asia/china-us-nationalism.html [accessed 10 Nov. 2020].

Institute for Security & Development Policy. 2018. *Made in China 2025 Backgrounder,* June 2018. Available at http://isdp.eu/content/uploads/2018/06/Made-in-China-Backgrounder.pdf [accessed 10 Nov. 2020].

Jiang Renai et al. 2019a. "The Role of Research and Ownership Collaboration in Generating Patent Quality: China-U.S Comparisons", *China Economic Review* 58, issue C.

Jiang Renai, Gary H. Jefferson and Shi Haoyue. 2019b. "Measuring China's International Technology Catchup", *Journal of Contemporary China* 29, 124: 519–34.

Kennedy, Andrew B. and Darrren J. Lim. 2018. "The Innovation Imperative: Technology and US–China Rivalry in the Twenty-first Century", *International Affairs* 94, 3 (2018): 553–72.

Kennedy, Scott. 2015. *Made in China 2025*.Washington DC: Center for Strategic and International Studies, 1 June 2015. Available at https://www.csis.org/analysis/made-china-2025 [accessed 17 Dec. 2020].

Klein, Christopher. 2019. *The Spies Who Launched America's Industrial Revolution*, The History Channel Online, 10 Jan. 2019. Available at https://www.history.com/news/industrial-revolution-spies-europe [accessed 17 Dec. 2020].

McBride, James and Andrew Chatzky. 2019. *Is 'Made in China 2025' a Threat to Global Trade?* Council on Foreign Relations,13 May 2019. Available at https://www.cfr.org/backgrounder/made-china-2025-threat-global-trade [accessed 10 Nov. 2020].

McKinsey & Company. 2015. *The China Effect on Global Innovation*. Available at https://www.mckinsey.com/~/media/McKinsey/Featured%20Insights/Innovation/Gauging%20the%20strength%20of%20Chinese%20innovation/MGI%20China%20Effect_Full%20report_October_2015.ashx [accessed 12 Nov. 2020].

Meijer, Hugo. 2016. *Trading with the Enemy: The Making of US Export Control Policy toward the People's Republic of China*. Oxford: Oxford University Press.

Naughton, Barry. 2018. *The Chinese Economy: Adaptation and Growth*, Cambridge, MA: MIT Press, 2018.

OECD Directorate for Science, Technology and Industry, Economic Analysis and Statistics Division. 2011. *ISIC Rev. 3 Technology Intensity Definition*. Available at https://www.oecd.org/sti/ind/48350231.pdf [accessed 11 Feb. 2021].

OUSTR [Office of the United States Trade Representative, Executive Office of the President]. 2018. *Findings of The Investigation into China's Acts, Policies, and Practices Related to Technology Transfer, Intellectual Property, and Innovation Under Section 301 of The Trade Act of 1974*. 22 March. Washington, D.C.

Roberts, Anthea, Henrique Choer Moraes and Victor Ferguson. 2019. "Toward a Geoeconomic World Order", *Journal of International Economic Law* 22, 4: 655–76.

The State Council, the People's Republic of China. 2006. *The National Medium- and Long-Term Program for Science and Technology Development (2006–2020) An Outline*. Beijing.

"Treaties--Intellectual Property". The Tarlton Law Library, Jamail Center for Legal Research, the University of Texas at Austin. Available at https://tarlton.law.utexas.edu/c.php?g=457743&p=3129119 [accessed 10 Nov. 2020].

3

The US-China Trade War and Myths about Intellectual Property and Innovation in China

Dan Prud'homme

Introduction

China's intellectual property (IPR) regime has been increasingly criticised for poorly protecting IPR, "forcing" transfer of technology (FTT) and enabling outright IPR "theft" (for example, Navarro and Autry 2011; CTAIP 2013, 2017; USTR 2018a,b; OTMP 2018). These complaints have contributed to one of the largest trade wars in modern history—the US-China trade war starting in 2018—consisting of a barrage of tariffs, export restrictions and other punitive measures by the US government against Chinese entities (for example, Prud'homme and Cohen 2019). More generally, the complaints have directly and indirectly contributed to current initiatives to decouple US economic activity from that in China, upending global value chains (GVC) in the process (for example, Schell and Shirk 2019; Lovely and Liang 2018). How did we get here? I offer a somewhat counter-intuitive explanation in this chapter. Specifically, I argue that a notable portion, albeit certainly not all, of the US-China trade war is attributable to two major conflicting myths about China's IPR regime borne in scholarly, government and business circles.

The word "myth" is derived from Ancient Greek but its modern definition evolved in the seventeenth and eighteenth centuries to mean a story that creates misconceptions (Segal 2015). Myths embed themselves in the fabric of human discourse in multiple ways. One way is for them to be strategically planted. Another is misunderstanding due to information asymmetries and faulty analysis. As mentioned in passing later in this chapter, both of these mechanisms help explain the origins of the current myths about China's IPR regime.

In terms of methods for this chapter, I identified myths about China's IPR regime by juxtaposing my understanding of the realities of China's IPR regime with perspectives presented by others. Although an important risk receiving increased attention recently, I consider cyber-intrusions/hacking a separate issue not primarily governed by China's IPR regime. To identify myths about China's IPR regime, a large body of literature was reviewed, including scholarly works, government reports and practitioner and press articles in English and Chinese. My understanding of China's IPR regime is built on in-depth phenomenological study in the country, including by working on IPR issues as an employee in several private-sector institutions and at an IPR office;[1] conducting numerous interviews with IPR professionals, academics and government officials in China; conducting legal research on IPR regimes in China and elsewhere in the world; and reviewing a range of literature in English and Chinese. This analysis resulted in the identification and debunking of two major myths and seven subsidiary ones about China's IPR regime. To be sure, while the analysis in this chapter builds on other recent work of mine pointing out three myths about China's IPR regime (see Prud'homme 2019c), this chapter offers a much more detailed explanation about those myths and other falsities circulating about China's IPR regime and how they collectively contributed to the ongoing US-China trade war.

The myths discussed in this chapter all involve the ability of China's IPR regime to protect IPR owned by private businesses (especially, but not only foreign ones), rather than the social optimality of the regime (its contribution to societal welfare). With this in mind, when evaluating the "strength" or "quality" of China's IPR regime in this chapter, I rely on the framework developed in Prud'homme (2019a) of the "business friendliness" of an IPR regime. That framework considers, from the perspective of a generic IPR-intensive business, an IPR regime that has fewer (in number and magnitude) suboptimal constraints on appropriability and on entrepreneurial opportunities, as well as fewer (in number and magnitude) excessive transaction costs to be more business-friendly.

I make two main contributions within this chapter. First, I identify and debunk two major conflicting myths about China's IPR regime that appear to have contributed to the current trade war. This is a somewhat counter-intuitive explanation, vis-à-vis conventional wisdom, for the tense state of global affairs.

The first major myth—which originates from Chinese stakeholders and is supported by two subsidiary myths—indicates that China's IPR regime is more business friendly than it is in actuality. This falsity created significant frustration among foreign stakeholders, leading to the trade war. The second major myth—which originates from foreign stakeholders and is supported by five subsidiary myths—indicates that China's IPR regime is less business-friendly than it is in actuality. This falsity created misunderstandings and overzealousness among foreign stakeholders, also leading to the trade war. Second, I offer general suggestions about how the scholarly, policy and practitioner communities can make use of this much needed "reality check".

Major Myths about China's IPR Regime

Myths Originating from Chinese Stakeholders

Chinese scholars and the Chinese state appear responsible for knowingly spreading the myth that China's IPR regime is more business friendly than it is in actuality. Much of this falsity has taken the form of *denial* about a range of concerns, many legitimate, involving risks that China's IPR regime poses to foreign multinational corporations (MNCs). Alternatively, sometimes Chinese authorities have promised reform but strategically do not deliver on it until much later in order to provide local firms the chance to engage in uninhibited technological learning and acquire market share (Prud'homme et al. 2018; Prud'homme and von Zedtwitz 2018, 2019). In addition, a range of Chinese stakeholders, including local scholars, firms and government officials have contributed to this myth by not proactively addressing IPR infringement targeted against foreign MNCs on the ground in China.

Within this major myth, the first subsidiary myth propagated by Chinese stakeholders is that China has not aggressively exerted pressure on foreign-Sino technology transfer arrangements in the recent past. I have heard this myth repeated multiple times by Chinese state media, knowledgeable Chinese IPR scholars and Chinese government officials over the years. A typical example is the following quote in Chinese state media:

> China promises not to use technology transfer as a prerequisite for foreign market access ... [there is] no reliable evidence that China has violated this commitment .... China's requirements for joint ventures...are in line with China's commitment to join the WTO. This is the approach adopted by most countries and has nothing to do with compulsory technology transfer (Xinhua 2018).

I have even heard otherwise highly informed Chinese scholars go as far as to deny the existence of controversial technology transfer provisions in Chinese law (for example, those in China's *Technology Import-Export Regulations* as well as China's *Rules for New Energy Auto Manufacturing Companies and Products*), down to the article number and exact text. (See Chapter 4 of Prud'homme and Zhang [2019] for a detailed account of these provisions.) In a more cautious, yet nonetheless clear denial of the aggressiveness of China's foreign–Sino technology transfer policies, Zhang Xiangchen, China's Ambassador to the WTO, as recently as 2018, stated that "the fact is, nothing in these regulatory measures [regarding technology transfer in China that US firms have complained about] requires technology transfer from foreign companies …[these complaints are] pure speculation" (Miles 2018).

I suspect that these narratives have circulated partially due to strategic denial by the Chinese authorities, partially as a knee-jerk reaction to the perceived-to-be accusatory tone in which discussions on related issues often take place, and partially due to genuine ignorance. Whatever the reasons, the idea that China has not instituted aggressive technology transfer policies—including preconditioning market access on technology transfer in a likely WTO-inconsistent way and sometimes coercing technology transfer via other WTO-incompliant means—is false. Table 3.1 outlines some of the most aggressive technology transfer policies in place in China as of 2018. When I use the term "policy" I mean both written documents and systematic, de facto practices. The policies falling into the "no choice" category in the table can arguably be legitimately labelled as "forced" technology transfer (FTT) policies. Further, although the policies falling outside the "no choice" category do not actually "force" technology transfer, they are nonetheless highly aggressive, not commonly found in developed nations and in some instances are arguably even WTO inconsistent.

Table 3.1:   Typology of Aggressive Technology Transfer Policies in China

Category	Mechanism behind technology transfer	Examples
Lose the market	Foreign firms should transfer technology in line with the policy or lose market access	• Perhaps the best-known requirements imposed on foreign firms to transfer their technology to a foreign-Sino joint venture (JV) as a precondition for market access (for example, a business license) and/or access to state support (for example, public procurement and

Table 3.1 (*cont'd*)

Category	Mechanism behind technology transfer	Examples
		other financial resources) in China were in the traditional auto industry and high-speed trains industry. Similar requirements were reported in other industries such as the big-power-generation turbines industry, aircraft industry, and, most recently, the new energy vehicles (NEV) industry.[2] • Other state policies were reported to, directly or indirectly, require transfer of technology as a precondition for market access, such as (the now revised) local content requirements for operating and winning government procurement contracts in the wind turbine industry, among other foreign investment restrictions.[3]
No choice	Foreign firms do not have a reasonable choice about whether or not to transfer technology because the state interprets the letter of the law governing such transfer in a highly dubious way/ one that is clearly unreasonable vis-à-vis what is written.	• Requirements to excessively disclose trade secrets directly to the state or to experts on state-organised panels as a precondition for receiving regulatory approvals (for example, in the pharmaceuticals, chemicals and other industries). Such disclosure should not be necessary to grant regulatory approvals; worse, the confidential business information disclosed is sometimes leaked to competitors.[4] • Unfair court rulings involving intellectual property that favour local firms.
Violate the law	Foreign firms should choose to transfer technology in line with the written policy/law (which itself may be ambiguous or burdensome but	• Several provisions of China's Technology Import-Export Regulations (for example, a provision requiring that subsequent improvements in technology developed in contractual relationships are owned by the party making the improvements and a provision mandating that foreign

(*cont'd overleaf*)

Table 3.1 (*cont'd*)

Category	Mechanism behind technology transfer	Examples
	nonetheless can at least generally be planned around) in order to be cautious and avoid potentially being subject to administrative or judicial actions enforcing that policy/law.	technology licensors bear liability for any accusation of infringement that may be brought against a technology importer in relation to the use of licensed technology). • Several provisions in recent measures governing IPR and anti-trust, and several governing IPR and technical standards (for example, burdensome standard-essential-patent disclosure requirements and dubious licensing terms). • Provisions in the foreign-Sino Equity Joint Venture Regulation "generally" restricting technology contracts in foreign-Sino equity JVs to a duration of ten years and requiring that the technology-importing party in the JV should be granted the right to use such technology "continuously" after the contract expires.

Sources: Prud'homme (2012), Prud'homme et al. (2018), Prud'homme and Zhang (2019), Prud'homme and von Zedtwitz (2019), USTR (2018a).

One may wonder why, if these technology transfer policies were really as aggressive as foreign firms said they were, they remained in China for any prolonged period of time. The answer reflects a number of important phenomena. Previously, some foreign MNCs did not support WTO complaints because they feared that they could be targeted for reprisals. Some FTT policies were targeted at specific industries in which there was oligopolistic competition, and therefore there would be little secret about who was behind the complaints about such policies (Prud'homme and von Zedtwitz 2019). And some foreign firms viewed their home government diplomats as heavy-handed in their tactics and not always presenting as united a front as industry associations (Prud'homme and von Zedtwitz 2019). However, as foreign MNCs became further embedded in the Chinese market due to increasing investment there alongside the globalisation of value chains, and as Chinese rivals became more capable, the transaction costs, appropriability risks and broader threats to competitiveness that a number of Chinese technology transfer policies posed to MNCs became more acute (Prud'homme and von Zedtwitz 2018, 2019). This is a major reason, alongside political changes in the US and Europe, why it was not until 2018 that WTO cases against a range of Chinese technology transfer policies were brought. In other words, although many of these policies have been around for years, it has not been until recently that many foreign MNCs have felt it worth the risk to support a WTO case against them (Prud'homme et al. 2018; Prud'homme and von Zedtwitz 2019). In my opinion, there is legal merit to at least portions of the WTO cases brought by the US and Europe in 2018 against a range of Chinese technology transfer policies (see WTO 2018a, b for details of the cases).

Moreover, arguably as a tacit admission of guilt, in 2018 and 2019 the Chinese government rapidly instituted an incredible number of reforms to the majority of the policies listed in Table 3.1 (which include most of the same policies mentioned in the US' and Europe's 2018 WTO complaints, as well as broader concerns about China's technology transfer regime). I critique these changes in depth in Prud'homme and Zhang (2019) and provide a short summary of them in Prud'homme (2019b).

The second subsidiary myth propagated by Chinese stakeholders is that various other aspects of China's IPR regime (beyond FTT policies) present at the start of the trade war are not against free-trade norms. Some of the most prominent examples of this myth, taken from high-level meetings between foreign rights holders and the Chinese authorities that I participated in while working in China, include denial by certain Chinese authorities of the dubiousness of certain court rulings regarding co-existence of local trademarks and foreign trademarks, an unwillingness to recognise the export of infringing goods produced by Chinese original equipment manufacturers (OEMs) as trademark infringement (just because the final products were not sold domestically) and questionable approaches to adjudicating likelihood of confusion and bad faith matters involving trademarks (Prud'homme and Zhang 2019). Other examples of this phenomena could be given, although further discussion about this relatively straightforward myth would be superfluous.

Myths Originating from Non-Chinese (Foreign) Stakeholders

In contrast to Chinese stakeholders, I believe that a number of foreign stakeholders, some knowingly and others more unknowingly, have contributed to the myth that China's IPR regime is less business friendly than it is in actuality. The most strategic propagators of this myth may range from foreign defence hawks looking to build an anti-China narrative to support a harder military stance against the country to certain foreign MNCs facing incredible competition from newly innovative Chinese firms. In other cases, these myths likely start out as hyperbole rather than concerted lies, or result from sampling bias (for example, only speaking with parties that feel most aggrieved by China's IPR regime due to their bad experiences, which may indeed have been deplorable but nonetheless do not represent the current norm, about the inadequacy of China's IPR regime to protect IPR). They then morph from there.

In many cases, however, myths about China's IPR regime have been derived from the conflation of legitimate grievances about very real IPR infringement with gripes about the quality of China's IPR institutions (that is, state mechanisms for protecting IPRs, which I interchangeably call the "IPR regime"). No mistake should be made: IPR infringement is certainly a major problem in China. In fact, China experiences the highest rates of counterfeiting and piracy in the world (European Community 2017). Further, Chinese courts are home to the greatest numbers of patent litigation cases in the world (Global IPR Project 2014) and even more copyright and trademark infringement cases (Supreme People's Court 2017).[5]

At the same time, while significant rates of IPR infringement can be an indicator of insufficient IPR institutions in a country, there is often what I call a "temporal gap" between institutional change and its effectiveness, that is, the inevitable lag between the time IPR and other complementing institutions (including but not limited to formal educational and public awareness systems) are reformed and when their full deterrent effects on IPR infringement can be realised. And this gap may be more pronounced in larger economies, such as China's, with significant heterogeneity in terms of subnational institutional development – what the insightful IPR law scholar Peter Yu calls "crossing over points" (Yu 2009, 2013). Yet other factors may also help explain this temporal gap in China (Prud'homme 2019a) and the inter-related but more complex phenomena of "institutional disconnects" (Prud'homme, Tong and Han 2021). If we roughly estimate the temporal gap in China to be around 5–10 years, we can understand how it is paradoxically possible for there to be significant IPR infringement in the country even though the country's IPR institutions are of a reasonable level of quality. Lack of understanding of this paradox has helped fuel the myth that China's IPR regime is worse than it is in actuality.

The first subsidiary myth propagated by foreign stakeholders is that China's longstanding Confucian culture prevents the country from seriously

protecting IPR. This myth is rooted in a number of scholarly works, perhaps the most seminal of which is Harvard law professor William Alford's treatise, which argued that China's Confucian values have embedded deep in Chinese culture an imitation-approach to learning, and in fact a respect for emulation of elders and certain others, and this will perpetuate a culture of IPR infringement in the country (Alford 1995). Alford's argument was largely based on a phrase he attributed to Confucian thought "窃书不算偷" (originally translated as "to steal a book is an elegant offence", but in my opinion is better translated as "theft of a book doesn't count as stealing") (Alford 1995). International business scholars, among others, have repeated this line of argumentation in recent years (for example, Zimmerman and Chaudry 2009; Zimmerman 2013).

However, in reality, violations of IPRs in modern China are rarely explained by Confucian-value narratives (Shi 2008; Yu 2015). There are several reasons for this. While elements of Confucian values are still present in some form in modern China, the value-system no longer exists at anywhere near the level it did prior to the 1900s. The "新文化运动" ("new culture movement"), which started around the collapse of the Qing dynasty and continued till the 1920s was instrumental in rooting out a significant portion of Confucian values from Chinese society and replacing them with modern scientific inquiry (Furth 1983). Mao Zedong's Anti-Confucian Campaign from 1973–75, at the tail end of the Cultural Revolution, also further diluted Confucian values in mainland China (Gregor and Chang 1979). Further, the phrase "to steal a book is an elegant offence [theft of a book doesn't count as stealing]" has in fact long been misattributed: Confucius never uttered the phrase, rather it much later emerged in the popular fiction book, *Kong Yiji* (孔乙己), published by well-known novelist Lu Xun in 1919, which attempted to parody traditional values through the life of a character with the same surname as Confucius (Shi 2008: 458).[6]

Looking outside mainland China further helps illustrate that violations of IPRs in modern China are rarely explained by Confucian-value narratives. Japan and South Korea have retained more Confucian values than mainland China, yet they highly respect IPRs (Shi 2008). Also, regions such as Taiwan (Chinese Taipei) (Dimitrov 2009), Hong Kong SAR and Singapore, with significant proportions of culturally-Chinese inhabitants, highly respect IPR (Peng et al. 2017a, b).

None of this is to say that there are not Chinese cultural attributes that influence the design of China's IPR regime and the willingness of Chinese citizens to respect IPRs. Nor is it to say that there is not a strong culture based on tradition and collectivism in China—there surely is one. However, the influence of domestic culture on China's IPR institutions is arguably much more closely linked to so-called "Chinese pragmatism": a cultural characteristic embedded in Chinese society that values pragmatic actions and is reinforced by the country's political system (Pan 2011; Pye 1995).[7]

The second subsidiary myth propagated by foreign stakeholders is that because China is not a Western-style liberal democracy, its governing institutions will never reasonably respect firms' IPR. Some prominent international business scholars have recently suggested that China's non-democratic, non-liberal, political system significantly undermines the rule of law which in turn facilitates large-scale IPR infringement and a generally "weak" IPR regime in the country (for example, Brander et al. 2017: 908, 912; Li and Alon 2020).[8] The definition of a "weak" IPR regime here obviously means one that offers unreasonable/insufficient protection of IPR, especially for foreign firms, although beyond this the exact parameters are left undefined (for example, Brander et al. 2017; Li and Alon 2020). This proposition that "only Western-style liberal democracies can provide reasonable protection of IPRs" has also previously been put forth in different forms by other prominent scholars from different disciplines. For example, William Alford offers a more tempered view, but nonetheless an antecedent, by arguing that "political culture [in China] … is unlikely to be able to protect their [Chinese citizens'] property rights, which in turn means that it will be even less likely to protect the highly sophisticated property interests [including IPRs] of foreigners" (Alford 1995: 120).

Before I proceed to debunk this myth, an important caveat is warranted. A discussion about how China's political culture vis-à-vis that in Western liberal democracies protects all rights in all situations is far beyond the scope of this chapter. In fact, it is worth mentioning up front to avoid misinterpretation that I, like many others, strongly believe that liberal democracies are better suited to provide robust protections, defined in any number of ways, for individual socio-cultural rights. Further, I fully recognise that debate is warranted into how China's communist and socialist political ideologies and legal origins shape the letter and practice of law in the country. These factors obviously limit real property rights. And such a political economy perspective may indeed be useful for partially understanding why state objectives reflected in certain IPR and technology-related policies, IPR administration and IPR enforcement, still sometimes supersede fair treatment of foreigners and certain Chinese firms vis-à-vis Chinese firms with closer government relationships (for example, Palmer 2001; Prud'homme 2012, 2019c; Prud'homme and von Zedtwitz 2018). Scholars of Chinese law have provided one broad frame to start thinking about these issues, debating the differences between the concepts of "法制" and "法治" (and therein "rule by law"/"legal institutions" vs. "rule of law") and the interrelated issue of the influence of Communist Party choices on those made by Chinese courts (for example, Li 2003; Wang 2010).

All this being said, I believe that degree matters: I do not believe that China's lack of adopting a liberal democratic political system, per se, will relegate the country's IPR regime to being *generally* "weak". I have three reasons for this belief. First, some countries that are not liberal democracies respect the rule of economic law needed to protect IPR just as well, if not better than liberal democracies. For example, Singapore, which is not a "liberal" democracy (Allison 2015), has one of the best reputations globally for respecting IPR, foreign IPR included (Ramcharan 2006; US Chamber 2018: 35–6). Further, if extending our discussion to a central behaviour that IPR regimes are supposed to incentivise—innovation—we find that Singapore is widely recognised as one of the most innovative countries in the world (Global Innovation Index 2019).

Second, having a liberal democratic political system does not actually ensure state compliance with the rule of international economic law, despite its clearer ability to safeguard sociocultural rights. In fact, some iconic liberal democracies frequently violate international legal norms by discriminating against foreign businesses. For example, there appears to be a persistent anti-foreign bias in IPR litigation in Canada (Mai and Stoyanov 2019). There is also potential discrimination against foreigners during the patent examination processes at the European Patent Office, Japanese Patent Office (Webster et al. 2014), and patent offices in other liberal democracies (Yang 2019; deRassenfosse et al. 2019). More generally, if adjudicated violations of WTO law are used as a crude benchmark of adherence to rule of international economic law, one finds that the most iconic Western liberal democracies perform poorly. The US and EU, not China, are by far the world's leading defendants/respondents in WTO cases[9] and, according to some estimates, the US and EU have the worst records out of any WTO members in terms of timely and fully complying with all the WTO judgments against them (Reich 2017:18–21).

Third, there are counterexamples to the proposition that Chinese institutions, in particular, categorically do not protect IPRs as well as those in liberal Western democracies. After conducting extensive research about the workings of the many components of China's current IPR regime experienced by both domestic and foreign entities and comparing them to regimes elsewhere in the world, I believe that it is inaccurate to call China's IPR regime categorically "weak", even though there are still areas where the regime deserves improvement (for example, Prud'homme and Zhang 2017; Prud'homme 2019a; Prud'homme and Zhang 2019; Prud'homme, Tong and Han 2021). Moreover, as explained in more detail in the context of the fourth myth propagated by foreign stakeholders, in some ways China's IPR regime actually offers both domestic and foreign rights holders more appropriability at less cost than the IPR regimes of Western liberal democracies such as the US and those in Europe. Meanwhile, the Chinese government, led by the Communist Party, has integrated a number of important national mechanisms in China's legal system that act as checks and balances in IPR law-making and enforcement similar to those one would expect in Western liberal democracies.[10] Yet none has required that China becomes a Western-style liberal democracy.

The third subsidiary myth propagated by foreign stakeholders is that "forced" technology transfer (FTT) is ubiquitous in China. This perception about FTT in China is evident in a variety of government, think-tank and scholarly research that has emerged in recent years (for example, Navarro and Autry 2011; CTAIP 2013, 2017; USTR 2018a, b). These works clearly state, with few if any caveats (although some works are more cautiously worded than others), that the Chinese government is "forcing" technology transfer through a wide range of means across the country, implying that it is nothing short of ubiquitous.

However, while interviewing and surveying multinational executives in China, I have found that the most egregious Chinese policies coercing technology transfer do not appear to have been commonly faced by foreign firms in recent years (Prud'homme et al. 2018; Prud'homme and von Zedtwitz 2019). Moreover, the most commonly cited examples of less egregious policies, which more transparently mandate technology transfer for market access, have usually been confined to a handful of industries (Prud'homme et al. 2018; Prud'homme and von Zedtwitz 2019). Further, the rest of China's controversial technology transfer policies, while problematic in terms of transaction costs, typically do not result in unmanageable losses of value incurred by foreign firms (Prud'homme and von Zedtwitz 2019; Prud'homme and Zhang 2019). In other words, although there certainly were technology transfer policies in China at the start of the trade war that violated free-trade norms, they were not as widespread or always as consequential as many assume (Prud'homme 2019c). All this helps explain why only 8 per cent of respondents to a foreign industry association survey in the lead up to the trade war reported that expectations of technology transfer in China were a top IPR challenge for them (AmCham 2018). "Theft" of IPR by employees and cyber-hacking, behaviour which is distinguishable from FTT policies, may also be more sporadic than many assume: 13 per cent and 8 per cent, respectively, of respondents on a recent foreign industry association survey reported that they faced these issues in China (AmCham 2019).

Moreover, in 2018 and 2019—clearly in response to the trade war —the Chinese government rapidly instituted a number of significant reforms to the majority of its most controversial technology transfer policies (Prud'homme 2019b). Recent reforms have also been made to China's IPR court infrastructure that should help mitigate the effects of discriminatory treatment of foreign IPR in local courts, a type of FTT policy (Cohen 2019).

More generally, what have often been characterised by businesses, government officials and scholars as "forced" technology transfer policies, in fact do not always appear to technically "force" technology transfer—if the common definition of "force" is used, that is, being compelled by threats (physical or otherwise), violence or an utter lack of alternatives (Prud'homme and Zhang 2019; Prud'homme and von Zedtwitz 2019). Instead, with the important exception of "no choice" policies (mentioned in Table 3.1 in the context of the first subsidiary myth propagated by Chinese stakeholders), foreign firms are allowed some flexibility to decide whether or not they want to comply with China's so-called "FTT" policies. In this sense, "forced" may not be the most accurate word to describe many controversial technology transfer policies in China. This being said, as also mentioned in the context of the first subsidiary myth propagated by Chinese stakeholders, the choice not to comply with the policies most often considered to "force" transfer of technology in/to China is always met with consequences, some significant, and many of these policies appear to be WTO inconsistent.

The fourth subsidiary myth propagated by foreign stakeholders is that China's IPR regime is categorically weaker, and therefore less business-friendly, than the IPR regimes of developed nations. This myth has been explicitly or implicitly stated by numerous sources, scholarly and practitioner-oriented. For example, even recent scholarly international business literature—working within the overly-reductionist conceptualisation of countries as having either "weak" or "strong" IPR regimes—considers China's IPR regime to be "weak" (for example, Berry 2017; Brander et al. 2017).

Reforms are unquestionably still needed to China's IPR regime in order to make it more conducive to innovation; however, with some important exceptions, the quality of China's regime is generally comparable in many aspects (IPR laws and regulations, IPR administration and IPR enforcement) to those in developed nations (Prud'homme and Zhang 2019). Moreover, and perhaps surprising to many, in some ways China's IPR regime is actually more friendly (that is, poses less risks and costs) for IPR-intensive businesses— including, and sometimes especially, foreign businesses—than the IPR regimes in prominent developed nations. Table 3.2 provides some examples of these aspects of China's IPR regime.

Table 3.2:   Aspects of China's IPR Regime Currently Making it Friendlier than the IPR Regimes in Prominent Rich Nations to IPR-intensive Businesses

Component of IPR regime	Examples (non-exhaustive)
IPR laws and regulations	• Business method patents (BMPs) are more accessible in China than the US and Europe • Certain biotechnology and software are protectable in China but not in the US • Non-Compete Agreements allowed in China but not in some US states (for example, California)
IPR administration	• Faster invention patent pendency (time to grant patents) in China than at the European Patent Office and US Patent & Trademark Office • Certain subject matter is protectable in China but not in the US (see above) • Invention patent examination is of higher quality in China than at some offices in Europe
IPR enforcement[11]	• Lower attorney and court costs for IPR litigation than the US and some other jurisdictions† • Faster IPR trials in China than other key markets • "Local administrative enforcement" route offers more enforcement options than available in developed nations • Foreigners win most of their IPR cases in China† • Chinese courts more strictly enforce non-competes than courts in some US states • Specialised IPR courts and a specialised IPR appeals court in the Supreme Court are available in China yet not always present in the same form elsewhere • Arguably less risk of patent trolls in China than in the US

Table 3.2 (*cont'd*)

Component of IPR regime	Examples (non-exhaustive)
Other IPR policies/ measures	• Special campaigns to limit infringement of foreign IPR in particular* • Blacklist for repeat IPR infringers and those engaging in other "dishonest" behaviour related to IPRs • Aspects of several other programmes and policies (for example, state-established licensing platforms)

Notes: † Indicates that instrument/phenomenon may not always be intentionally designed/orchestrated by the state, but nonetheless makes China's IPR regime more business-friendly (often for foreign businesses in particular) than the regimes in many developed nations. *Reflects clear efforts to protect foreign IPR, although may be unnecessary if there were less IPR infringement in China.

Sources: Prud'homme (2019a, c), Prud'homme and Zhang (2019).

The fifth subsidiary myth propagated by foreign stakeholders is that China's formal and informal institutions create Chinese firms that are merely copycats rather than innovators. This myth, rooted in Abrami et al. (2014) and other literature, combines elements of the previously mentioned myths. But it deserves to be debunked on its own since it discusses not only institutions protecting IPR, but also the connection between such institutions and innovation.

There are several ways to debunk this myth. At the most macro level, one could note that there does not appear to be a causal link between democratic institutions and greater amounts of, or the quality of, innovations (Taylor 2016; Gao et al. 2017). But continuing along this line of argumentation would obviously require scrutinising the relationships between more specific Chinese institutions and innovation, which is outside the scope of this chapter. Meanwhile, however, a more straightforward way to debunk the myth is to assess the extent to which Chinese firms are actually innovating, whether because of or despite Chinese institutions. Chinese firms are already seriously innovating in China in a range of industries and will become even more competitive in the future (for example, Prud'homme and von Zedtwitz 2018; Greeven et al. 2019). For example, Tencent and Baidu are innovating in Internet business models, Haier is highly competitive in innovative consumer goods/white goods, DJI is engineering high-quality drones, Huawei and Xiaomi are producing high-quality and affordable telecommunications equipment, Huawei is a leader in 5G standards setting, Alibaba is offering popular and inexpensive cloud data services, BYD is making competitive NEVs, BGI is advancing in genome sequencing and Cloudwalk is developing advanced artificial intelligence facial recognition technology (Prud'homme and Cohen 2019). Even in industries built upon decades of Western talent and research, where Western firms have sizeable experience curves and lead-time advantages, Chinese firms are making headway. For example, HiSilicon, owned by Huawei, is making competitive smartphone semiconductor chips, and Cambricon and Horizon Robotics are making competitive artificial intelligence (AI) chips.

Implications for Scholars, Policymakers and Practitioners

The debunking of the two main myths and seven subsidiary myths discussed in this chapter provides a much-needed reality check for scholars, policymakers and practitioners. There are two overarching implications that can be drawn from this reality check. First, it should help foreign and Chinese stakeholders understand the value of more constructively and truthfully engaging with one another in the future. The Chinese side should recognise how foot-dragging and denial about certain problems in China's IPR regime, alongside coordination and capacity problems, contributed to the bubbling up of foreign stakeholders' frustrations about Chinese institutions. This ultimately erupted in the form of a trade war. It would behoove the Chinese side to avoid this outcome again in the future if possible. Meanwhile, on the non-Chinese/foreign side, those stakeholders should realise that constructive engagement with the Chinese authorities about IPR reform based upon established facts is ultimately in their long-term interest.

Moving forward, this mutual understanding should allow both groups of stakeholders to better focus time and resources on addressing genuine problems with China's IPR regime. In terms of enforcement, it could benefit, for example, from more systematically awarding higher damages in practice, improving procedures for collecting evidence and enforcing court orders, and further reducing local protectionist judgments (see Chapters 7 and 9 of Prud'homme and Zhang 2019). In terms of laws and regulations, China could benefit from a number of revisions to those governing plant varieties, unfair competition/trade secrets, trademarks, copyrights, patents and integrated circuits (see Chapters 2 and 9 of Prud'homme and Zhang 2019). In terms of IPR administration and other IPR measures, China could benefit from several reforms (see Chapters 3, 4, 6 and 9 of Prud'homme and Zhang 2019; Prud'homme and Song 2016). As this chapter was being finalised, judicial interpretations and other measures were in the works to help address some of these issues.

Second, the reality check provided in this chapter should help foreign stakeholders understand that neither China's IPR system nor the trade war will seriously restrain Chinese innovation or Chinese entities' usage of IPR in the long run. As mentioned, innovation in China has taken off in recent years. Further, despite the trade war, there will be considerable temptation for some Western firms to engage in co-opetition or otherwise collaborate with increasingly capable Chinese firms and research organisations to advance next-generation technologies that no one dominates at present, ranging from various applications of AI to new energy vehicles. In addition, the trade war has already emboldened a heighted sense of nationalism in the form of a feverish quest for technological "自力更生" ("self-reliance") in China contributing to faster mobilisation of state and private resources that might enable Chinese firms to catch up to foreign counterparts in a range of industries, both emerging and more mature (Prud'homme and Cohen 2019). Additionally, even if the trade war further fragments global markets, it will not prevent innovative Chinese firms from being both domestically and internationally competitive nor prevent them from filing more and more of their own IPRs (Prud'homme and von Zedtwitz 2018; Prud'homme and Cohen 2019). Chinese firms will inevitably leverage their growing presence, not just in China but in other emerging markets, which have accounted for almost two-thirds of world economic growth and more than half of new consumption over the last fifteen years (MGI 2018). And China's Belt and Road Initiative (One Belt, One Road) might help secure these important sources of future demand (Scheve and Zhang 2016) and even serve as a canvass on which Chinese IPR and other norms may be rolled out (Prud'homme 2019a).

In response, foreign firms and governments will need to improve their own innovation and IPR management capabilities in order to compete with Chinese rivals in global markets. Hiding behind the walls of protectionism erected by the current trade war will not ensure their survival in the long term.

Conclusions

In this chapter, I have attempted to explain why the United States and China have become embroiled in one of the greatest trade wars in modern history. A notable portion, albeit certainly not all, of the US-China trade war is attributable to two major myths about China's IPR regime borne in scholarly, government and business circles. This is a somewhat counter-intuitive explanation, vis-à-vis conventional wisdom, for this tense state of global affairs.

The first major myth, which originates from Chinese stakeholders, indicates that China's IPR regime is more business-friendly than it is in actuality. This falsity is supported by two subsidiary myths, namely that (1) aggressive forced technology transfer policies have not existed in recent years in China; and (2) various other aspects of China's IPR regime in place at the start of the trade war have not violated free-trade norms. These myths created significant frustration among foreign stakeholders, leading to the trade war. The second major myth, which originates from foreign stakeholders and contrasts sharply with the one arising from Chinese stakeholders, indicates that China's IPR regime is less business-friendly than it is in actuality. This falsity is supported by five subsidiary myths, namely that (1) China's longstanding Confucian culture prevents it from seriously protecting IPR; (2) because China is not a Western-style liberal democracy its governing institutions will never reasonably protect IPR; (3) "forced" technology transfer is ubiquitous in China; (4) China's IPR regime is categorically weaker than the IPR regimes of developed nations; and (5) China's formal and informal institutions create Chinese firms that are merely copycats rather than innovators. These myths created misunderstandings and overzealousness among foreign stakeholders, also leading to the trade war.

The debunking of these myths should help the scholarly, policy and practitioner communities in China and abroad to better understand the value of more constructively and truthfully engaging with one another in the future. It should also help foreign stakeholders to better understand that neither China's IPR system, nor the trade war will seriously restrain Chinese innovation or Chinese entities' usage of IPR in the long term.

Notes

[1] I reflect on my experiences gained by working full-time in China as a consultant at an international law firm's office in Beijing, a division manager at a boutique consulting firm in Beijing, as manager of the IPR and R&D working groups at the European Union Chamber of Commerce in China based in Shanghai, and as a policy advisor/technical expert at the European Union Intellectual Property Office (EUIPO)'s Beijing-based EU-China "IP Key" division. In those roles, I worked closely with a wide range of multinational corporations on IPR and innovation management issues and managed relations with central and subcentral Chinese government officials, as well as European and US government officials engaged with China.

[2] The policy in the new energy vehicles (NEVs) industry started in 2009 and was tightened in 2017. The 2009 policy required "mastering" of one of three core NEV technologies within a foreign-Sino JV in order to receive an NEV production licence and access to government procurement and subsidies. The 2017 policy required mastering

of all (not just one of three) core NEV technologies. As of early 2019, the measure still appeared to be in effect; however its effects on foreign MNCs appear largely nullified due to changes in 2018 to China's investment requirements in the NEV industry.

3 For example, some foreign MNCs have been required to set up an R&D centre in China as a precondition for entering a JV in industries in which a JV was the requisite mode of entry. By way of another example, foreign firms have complained about provisions in Chinese law requiring data servers to be localised in China as a precondition for receiving and maintaining certain business licenses.

4 For further details see: Prud'homme 2012: 101.

5 This being said, when considering patent litigation cases per capita, the US and Germany experience the most patent litigation in the world. (Source: calculations based on data from Darts-IPR (Global IPR Project 2014) and population figures from the World Bank).

6 More generally, one might also note that the idea of legitimately being able to use a copyrighted work without paying for it (in some capacity without committing infringement) is reflected, to varying degrees, in exceptions to copyright exclusivity found in many countries.

7 A related overarching value worth mentioning that permeates China's political economy is the notion that "实践是检验真理的唯一标准" ("Practice is the sole criterion for testing truth").

8 Among other passages explaining this reasoning, see, for example: "We criticize the argument that China will endogenously improve IPR protection due to internal pressures from its domestic IPR sector as the United States and some other countries did in the past. China's governance institutions are very different from those of the liberal Western democracies, past and present, as China has a weak internal rule of law, a fragmented governance system and cultural traditions that favor collective over individual rights" (Brander et al. 2017: 908); and "It [IPR protection] … is a particular problem in China due to the lack of checks and balances that exist in Western liberal democracies" (Brander et al. 2017: 912).

9 Figures based on Reich (2017) and WTO statistics collected by the author. These figures are both in terms of absolute numbers of cases and when the numbers of cases are adjusted according to the number of years which each party has been a member of the WTO. This being said, as mentioned previously, there has historically been reluctance to bring WTO cases against China for fear of reprisals against foreign firms operating in the country. And, as discussed elsewhere in this article, WTO complaints specifically about IPR have been brought against China.

10 For example, the process of drafting commercial laws and regulations, and sometimes even economic policies, in China—including those governing IPR—is relatively open for public comments. I can attest to the relative openness of this process as on many occasions I worked with foreign stakeholders to provide comments on draft IPR measures directly to the Chinese government. Based on my discussions with the authorities, I believe that they took all the comments they received seriously, especially those from powerful organisations (both foreign and domestic). (Although, as in the

West, there is certainly a fair bit of sausage-making behind the scenes when it comes to finalising and approving the drafts.) In the area of enforcement, the Supreme People's Court has instituted "guiding cases" which while not formally setting precedent, as China is a civil law, not a common law, country, can serve as an example of best practice for encouraging judges to adopt less-protectionist judgements (Long and Wang 2015). Numerous other institutional mechanisms, some of which are discussed in this chapter, have been adopted in China to further reduce local protectionist tendencies in IPR judgements or otherwise act as checks or balances in the country's IPR regime.

[11] One might also point to what seems to be a higher rate of granting injunctions in IPR cases in China (see the figures in RPX [2018]) relative to the US (for example, see the figures in Hines and Preston [2013]). But further research, based on more up-todate statistics and analysis of the reasons for granting/not granting the injunctions, is warranted before firm conclusions can be drawn.

References

Abrami, Regina M., William C. Kirby and F. Warren McFarlan. 2014. "Why China Can't Innovate", *Harvard Business Review*.

Alford, William P. 1995. *To Steal a Book is an Elegant Offense: Intellectual Property Law in Chinese Civilization*. Stanford: Stanford University Press.

Allison, Graham. 2015. "Singapore Challenges the Idea that Democracy is the Best Form of Governance", *World Post*. Available at https://www.hks.harvard.edu/ publications/singapore-challenges-idea-democracy-best-form-governance [accessed 10 Aug. 2019].

AmCham China. 2018. *AmCham China 2018 Business Climate Survey*. Beijing.

_____. 2019. *AmCham China 2019 Business Climate Survey*. Beijing.

Berry, Heather. 2017. "Managing Valuable Knowledge in Weak IPR Protection Countries", *Journal of International Business Studies* 48: 787–807.

Brander, James, Victor Cui and Ilan Vertinsky. 2017. "China and Intellectual Property Rights: A Challenge to the Rule of Law", *Journal of International Business Studies* 48: 908–921.

Cohen, Mark. 2019. "A Federal Circuit with Chinese Characteristics? – The Launch of China's National Appellate IPR Court", *China IPR*.

CTAIP [Commission on the Theft of American Intellectual Property]. 2013. *The IP Commission Report*. May. Washington: National Bureau of Asian Research.

_____. 2017. *Update to the Commission Report: Reassessments of the Challenge and United States Policy*. February. Washington: National Bureau of Asian Research.

deRassenfosse, Gaétan et al. 2019. "Are Foreigners Treated Equally under Trade-Related Aspects of Intellectual Property Rights Agreement?", *Journal of Law and Economics* 62: 663–85.

Dimitrov, Martin K. 2009. *Piracy and the State: The Politics of Intellectual Property Rights in China*. Cambridge: Cambridge University Press.

European Community [Europol and the EU IPO]. 2017. *Situation Report on Counterfeiting and Piracy in the European Union.* Available at https://www.europol. europa.eu/publications-documents/2017-situation-report-counterfeitingand-piracy-in-european-union [accessed 10 Nov. 2018].

Furth, Charlotte. 1983. "Intellectual Change: from the Reform Movement to the May Fourth movement, 1895–1920", in *Republican China 1912–1949, Part 1. The Cambridge History of China*, ed. J. Fairbank. Cambridge: Cambridge University Press, pp. 322–405.

Gao Yanyan et al. 2017. "Does Democracy Cause Innovation? An Empirical Test of the Popper Hypothesis", *Research Policy* 46: 1272–83.

Global Innovation Index. 2019. *Global Innovation Index Report.* Available at https://www.globalinnovationindex.org/gii-2019-report [accessed 30 Nov. 2020].

Global IPR Project. 2014. *Annual Global Patent Litigation Report.* Darts IPR. Available at https://www.darts-ip.com/newsletter/201508/AnnualGlobalPatentLitigationReport2014.pdf [accessed 10 Nov. 2018].

Greeven, Mark J., George S. Yip and Wei Wei. 2019. "Understanding China's Next Wave of Innovation", *MIT Sloan Management Review* Spring: 75–80.

Gregor, A. James and Maria Hsia Chang. 1979. "Anti-Confucianism: Mao's Last Campaign", *Asian Survey* 19: 1073–92.

Hines, Doris Johnson and J. Preston Long. 2013. "The Continuing (R)evolution of Injunctive Relief in the District Courts and the International Trade Commission", *Finnegan.* Available at https://www.finnegan.com/en/insights/articles/the-continuing -r-evolution-of-injunctive-relief-in-the-district.html [accessed 10 Nov. 2019].

Li Buyun. 2003. *Cong 'fazhi' dao 'fazhi' ershi nian gai yi zi* (From 'rule by law' to 'rule of law': change of one word in 20 years). *Fali Tansuo* (The Exploration of Jurisprudence). Changsha: Hunan Renmin Chubanshe.

Li Shaomin and Ilan Alon. 2020. "China's Intellectual Property Rights Provocation: A Political Economy View", *Journal of International Business Policy* 3: 60–72.

Li Yahong. 2017. "Introduction", in *Patents and Innovation in Mainland China and Hong Kong: Two Systems in One Country Compared*, ed. Yahong Li. Cambridge: Cambridge University Press, pp. 1–26.

Long, Cheryl Xiaoning and Jun Wang. 2015. "Judicial Local Protectionism in China: An Empirical Study of IPR Cases", *International Review of Law and Economics* 42: 48–59.

Lovely, Mary E. and Liang Yang. 2018. *Trump Tariffs Primarily Hit Multinational Supply Chains, Harm US Technology Competitiveness.* Peterson Institute for International Economics Policy Brief. Available at https://www.piie.com/system/files/documents/pb18-12.pdf [accessed 30 Nov. 2019].

Mai, Joseph and Andrey Stoyanov. 2019. "Anti-foreign Bias in the Court: Welfare Explanation and Evidence from Canadian Intellectual Property Litigations", *Journal of International Economics* 117: 21–36.

McKinsey Global Institute (MGI). 2018. *Outperformers: High-growth Emerging Economies and the Companies that Propel Them.* Available at https://www.mckinsey.

com/~/media/mckinsey/featured%20insights/innovation/outperformers%20
high%20growth%20emerging%20economies%20and%20the%20companies%20
that%20propel%20them/mgi-outperformers-full-report-sep-2018.ashx [accessed
30 Nov. 2019].

Miles, Tom. 2018. "U.S. and China Clash over 'Technology Transfer' at WTO", *Reuters.*
Available at https://www.reuters.com/article/us-usa-trade-china/u-s-and-china-clash
-over-technology-transfer-at-wto-idUSKCN1IT11G [accessed 30 Nov. 2019].

Navarro, Peter and Greg Autry. 2011. *Death by China: Confronting the Dragon – A
Global Call to Action.* Upper Saddle River, NJ: Pearson Prentice Hall.

OTMP (White House Office of Trade and Manufacturing Policy). 2018. *How China's
Economic Aggression Threatens the Technologies and Intellectual Property of the United
States and the World.* White House Office of Trade and Manufacturing Policy.
Available at https://www.whitehouse.gov/wp-content/uploads/2018/06/FINAL-
China-Technology-Report-6.18.18-PDF.pdf [accessed 30 Apr. 2019].

Palmer, Scott J. 2001. "An Identity Crisis: Regime Legitimacy and the Politics of
Intellectual Property Rights in China", *Indiana Journal of Global Legal Studies* 8:
449–77.

Pan Junwu. 2011. "Chinese Philosophy and International Law", *Asian Journal of
International Law* 1: 233–48.

Peng, Mike W. et al. 2017a. "History and the Debate over Intellectual Property",
Management and Organization Review 13: 15–38.

——————. 2017b. "An Institution-based View of Global IPR History", *Journal of
International Business Studies* 48: 893–907.

Prud'homme, Dan. 2012. *Dulling the Cutting Edge: How Patent-related Policies and
Practices Hamper Innovation in China.* European Union Chamber of Commerce
in China.

——————. 2019a. "Re-conceptualizing Intellectual Property Regimes in International
Business Research: Foreign-friendliness Paradoxes Facing MNCs in China", *Journal
of World Business* 54: 399–419.

——————. 2019b. *Reform of China's 'Forced' Technology Transfer Policies.* University of
Oxford Law Faculty, Oxford Business Law Blog [OBLB]. Available at https://www.
law.ox.ac.uk/business-law-blog/blog/2019/07/reform-chinas-forced-technology-
transfer-policies [accessed 30 Nov. 2020].

——————. 2019c. "3 Myths about China's IP Regime", *Harvard Business Review.*
24 Oct. Available at https://hbr.org/2019/10/3-myths-about-chinas-ip-regime
[accessed 30 Nov. 2020].

Prud'homme, Dan and Mark Cohen. 2019. "Overlooked Strategies for Surviving
the US-China Trade War", *The World Financial Review.* Available at https://
worldfinancialreview.com/overlooked-strategies-for-surviving-the-us-china-trade-
war-and-possibly-others/ [accessed 30 Nov. 2020].

Prud'homme, Dan and Hefa Song, ed. 2016. *Economic Impacts of Intellectual Property-
Conditioned Government Incentives.* Singapore: Springer.

Prud'homme, Dan and Max von Zedtwitz. 2018. "The Changing Face of Innovation in
China", *MIT Sloan Management Review* 59: 24–32.

_____. 2019. "Managing 'Forced' Technology Transfer in Emerging Markets: The Case of China", *Journal of International Management* 25: 1–14.

Prud'homme, D. and Zhang Taolue. 2017. *Evaluation of China's Intellectual Property Regime for Innovation*. Report commissioned by the World Bank.

_____. 2019. *China's Intellectual Property Regime for Innovation: Risks to Business and National Development*. Cham, Switzerland: Springer.

Prud'homme, Dan et al. 2018. "'Forced Technology Transfer' Policies: Workings in China and Strategic Implications", *Technological Forecasting & Social Change* 134: 150–168.

Prud'homme, Dan, Tony Tong and Nianchen Han. 2021. "A Stakeholder-based View of the Evolution of Intellectual Property Institutions", *Journal of International Business Studies*.

Pye, Lucien W. 1995. "Chinese Politics in the Late Deng Era", *The China Quarterly* 142: 573–83.

Ramcharan, Robin. 2006. "Singapore's Emerging Knowledge Economy: Role of Intellectual Property and its Possible Implications for Singaporean Society", *The Journal of World Intellectual Property* 9: 316–43.

Reich, Arie. 2017. *The Effectiveness of the WTO Dispute Settlement System: A Statistical Analysis*, European University Institute Department of Law Working Paper. Available at http://cadmus.eui.eu/bitstream/handle/1814/47045/LAW_2017_11.pdf?sequence=1 [accessed 30 Nov. 2020].

RPX. 2018. *A Quantitative Analysis of Chinese Patent Litigation*. Available at https://www.rpxcorp.com/intelligence/blog/a-quantitative-analysis-of-chinese-patent-litigation/ [accessed 30 Nov. 2020].

Schell, Orville and Susan L. Shirk. 2019. "Course Correction: Toward an Effective and Sustainable China Policy", *Task Force Report*. Available at http://china.ucsd.edu/_files/2019-CourseCorrection.pdf [accessed 30 Nov. 2020].

Scheve, Kenneth and Ruxi Zhang. 2016. *One Belt One Road: Chinese Strategic Investment in the 21st Century*. Harvard Business Review Case Studies.

Segal, Robert A. 2015. *Myth: A Very Short Introduction*. Oxford: Oxford University Press.

Shi Wei. 2008. "The Paradox of Confucian Determinism: Tracking the Root Causes of Intellectual property Rights Problem in China", *The John Marshall Review of Intellectual Property* 7: 454–68.

Supreme People's Court of China (SPC). 2017. *Outline of the Judicial Protection of Intellectual Property in China (2016–2020)* (in Chinese). Available at http://www.court.gov.cn/ [accessed 11 Apr. 2019].

Taylor, Mark Zachary. 2016. *The Politics of Innovation: Why Some Countries are Better than Others at Science & Technology*. Oxford: Oxford University Press.

US Chamber of Commerce Global IPR Center. 2018. *US Chamber International IPR Index*, Sixth Edition. Available at https://www.theglobalipcenter.com/ipindex2018/ [accessed 30 Apr. 2019].

USTR [United States Trade Representative]. 2018a. *Findings of the Investigation into China's Acts, Policies, and Practices Related to Technology Transfer, Intellectual Property, and Innovation under Section 301 of the Trade Act of 1974.* Office of the United States Trade Representative, available at https://ustr.gov/sites/default/files/Section%20 301%20FINAL.PDF [accessed 30 Apr. 2019].

_____. 2018b. *Update Concerning China's Acts, Policies and Practices Related to Technology Transfer, Intellectual Property, and Innovation.* Office of the United States Trade Representative. Available at https://ustr.gov/sites/default/files/ enforcement/301Investigations/301%20Report%20Update.pdf [accessed 30 Apr. 2019].

Wang Chengwang. 2010. "From Rule of Man to the Rule of Law", in *China's Journey toward the Rule of Law: Legal Reform, 1978–2008*, ed. Dingjian Cai and Chenguang Wang. Leiden: Brill, pp. 1–50.

Webster, Elizabeth, Paul H. Jensen and Alfons Palangkaraya. 2014. "Patent Examination Outcomes and the National Treatment Principles", *The RAND Journal of Economics* 45: 449–69.

World Trade Organization (WTO). 2018a. *US' WTO Request for Consultations Regarding Certain Measures on the Transfer of Technology in China.* Available at https://www.wto.org/english/tratop_e/dispu_e/cases_e/ds542_e.htm [accessed 30 Nov. 2019].

_____. 2018b. *EU's WTO Request for Consultations Regarding Certain Measures on the Transfer of Technology in China.* Available at https://www.wto.org/english/ tratop_e/dispu_e/cases_e/ds549_e.htm [accessed 30 Nov. 2019].

Xinhua. 2018. *Zhishi chanquan zen neng chengwei maoyi baohu de da bang?* (How can IPR become a big stick for trade protectionism?). Available at http://opinion.people. com.cn/n1/2018/0409/c1003-29914793.html [accessed 30 Nov. 2019].

Yang Deli. 2019. "National Treatment, Institutions, and IPR Uncertainties: An Analytics of Compliance, Change and Comparability", *International Business Review* 28: 101585.

Yu, Peter K. 2009. "Global Intellectual Property Order and Its Undetermined Future", *WIPO Journal* 1: 1–15.

_____. 2013. "Five Oft-repeated Questions about China's Rise as a Patent Power", *Cardozo Law Review De Novo* 78: 81–8.

_____. 2015. "Intellectual property and Confucianism", in *Diversity in Intellectual Property: Identifies, Interests, and Intersections*, ed. Irene Calboldi and Srividhya Ragavan. Cambridge: Cambridge University Press, pp. 247–72.

Zimmerman, Alan. 2013. "Contending with Chinese Counterfeits: Culture, Growth, and Management Responses", *Business Horizons* 56: 141–8.

Zimmerman, Alan and Peggy E. Chaudhry. 2009. "Protecting Intellectual Property Rights: The Special Case of China", *Journal of Asia-Pacific Business* 10: 308–25.

4

Global Implications of China's Policies on Indigenous Innovation

Erik Baark

Introduction

The first official political support for indigenous innovation by the Chinese government was launched at the Fifth Plenary Session of the 16th Central Committee in October 2005 (*Shiliu* 2005). Subsequently, the concept was used repeatedly in the announcement of the Medium and Long-term Program for Science & Technology (MLP) launched in 2006, which specifically announced that indigenous innovation products would receive preference in public procurement (State Council 2006: Section 8, point 3).

The MLP identified 11 priority areas and a number of key megaprojects in selected areas of engineering and science to be developed over the next decade and a half, and which were to be provided with substantial government funding (Cao et al. 2006; Serger and Breidne 2007). It also outlined a number of concrete policy instruments, including public procurement favouring indigenous innovation, and strategies for developing Chinese intellectual property rights (IPR) and Chinese technology standards. Such policy instruments reflect an international trend in innovation theory that underscores the vital importance of supporting the demand for innovation in society in addition to the traditional emphasis on the supply of new knowledge, such as funding public or private R&D (Bloom et al. 2019).

The Chinese literature on indigenous innovation developed rapidly after the concept was launched in the 2000s. A review of papers published during

2003–12 revealed that around 500 articles were concerned with the policies supporting indigenous innovation, while 150 addressed the ways in which indigenous innovation was implemented (Yang and Liu 2014). Chinese authors were mostly concerned with the balance between domestic and foreign sources of technology, and how policies could reduce the dependency on foreign technology transfer. Discussions of Chinese policies on indigenous innovation published in Western languages have also addressed such issues, but have been primarily concerned with the political and international implications, especially for the United States of America (US).

This chapter reviews the policy instruments introduced in China to promote indigenous innovation, considering international reactions and contexts (see also Baark 2019). This leads to two key arguments: Firstly, the promotion of indigenous innovation is an integral feature of China's long-term ambitions for self-reliance; in this sense, it is not a "new" policy but rather a concretisation of the general principle, through policy instruments that have become more prominent internationally. Secondly, while Chinese ambitions to build national capabilities for indigenous innovation are likely to challenge other countries that fear technological competition, they may also provide an important platform for introducing new modes of innovation and perhaps offer innovations which are significant contributions to future global development.

The Definition of "Indigenous Innovation"

The terms "indigenous innovation" or "independent innovation" are the English translations of the Chinese term *zizhu chuangxin,* with the literal meaning independent, or autonomous, innovation. The literal meaning thus underscores sovereignty, that is, the need for China to be able to exert control and ownership over the innovation. The concept of indigenous innovation was defined in the MLP in the following terms (State Council 2015, "Guiding Principles" [Section 2, point 1]):

> Indigenous innovation means strengthening original innovation, integrated innovation, and re-innovation based on the assimilation and further development of imported technology, in order to enhance national innovative capabilities.

The meaning of original innovation is similar to the concept of originality used when evaluating the patentable nature of an invention internationally, which is that the invention should be completely new in the world. However, in the MLP definition, originality also implied the sense of domestic Chinese origin. Integrated innovation relies on the innovative combination and enhancement of existing technological components in order to generate a new product or process (Sun and Jiang 2017). This type of innovation has a meaning that resembles what W. Brian Arthur has called the "combinatorial evolution of technology", where new technologies are put together from parts, assemblies, modules, that are themselves already existing technologies (Arthur 2009). The MLP concept of re-innovation is closer to the international concepts of incremental innovation, that is, significant improvements that result in a new design or a more efficient production process.

The key requirement for all indigenous innovations is that a major part of the intellectual property should be owned by domestic Chinese organisations or people. Many publications simply designate technologies developed with a domestic research and development (R&D) input as indigenous innovation, in contrast to technology developed with overseas R&D and owned by overseas firms. The definition of indigenous innovation has thus been presented in somewhat ambiguous terms. In the following, the MLP definition represents a main reference point, but authors quoted may also have used a straightforward definition of indigenous innovation as innovation performed by Chinese actors on the basis of domestic R&D inputs.

At the same time, it is important to emphasise that the rationale for the MLP and other policies that promoted indigenous innovation was also to establish or enhance indigenous capability for innovation at the national and local levels. According to the State Council's MLP guiding principles (State Council 2006: Section 2, point 1): "This calls for placing the strengthening of indigenous innovation capability at the core of S&T undertakings.... If our country wants to take the initiative in the fierce international competition, it has to enhance its indigenous innovation capability, master core technologies in some critical areas, own proprietary intellectual property rights, and build a number of internationally competitive enterprises". In this view, it was at least as important for Chinese policies to build dynamic *indigenous innovation capability—zizhu chuangxin nengli*—as it was to create new Chinese products or processes. Such capability could secure continued innovation in China in the future and reduce dependency on overseas sources of technology.

International Perspectives on China's Indigenous Innovation Policies

While there were initially few international reactions to the publication of the MLP, foreign businesses in China began to be concerned with the promotion of indigenous innovation in public procurement towards 2010. This happened after the adoption of a State Council circular on accreditation of indigenous innovation products in 2009, and promulgation of a range of provincial guidelines and catalogues on local government procurement of such products (Morrison 2018a). As a result, the US International Trade Commission launched a so-called 332 Investigation in 2010 of China's indigenous innovation policies, including policies on IPR (USITC 2010). In an attempt to address US concerns, China pledged at the May 2011 session of the US-China Strategic and Economic Dialogue that the government would eliminate all its national catalogues for certification of indigenous innovation products. Nevertheless, many provincial and municipal governments continued to refer to local catalogues of accredited indigenous innovation products in their public procurement tender announcements.

US views on indigenous innovation emphasised that all policy initiatives launched under the MLP were in contravention of international practice. Thus, it was argued that the funding of scientific and engineering megaprojects, public procurement regulations, and subsidies for patenting by Chinese firms were simply examples of a "web of industrial policies" designed to favour national champions and disadvantage foreign firms (McGregor 2010). State funding for research and development projects is a common feature of innovation policies in virtually all countries, including the US, Europe and Japan. Therefore, the criticism levelled at China for its state-sponsored funding for large research and engineering development projects in various high-tech fields and energy systems quickly lost its momentum.

a. *Procurement*

Instead, China's priorities for procurement and support for Chinese intellectual property became the main focus of international criticism. The chief objection was that the criteria for including products in the indigenous innovation procurement catalogue stipulated a bias in favour of domestic Chinese products.

It is important to recognise that public procurement has been used by advanced industrialised nations as a policy instrument to promote innovation, and this policy instrument has been implemented largely in accordance with the guidelines and requirements of international conventions (Georghiou et al. 2014; Lember et al. 2014; Edquist et al. 2015; OECD 2017; Chicot and Matt 2018). In fact, government procurement by the US Defense Advanced Research Projects Agency (DARPA) was instrumental in the development of key advanced innovations in the Post-War period, including military and civilian aircraft, the Internet and the Global Positioning System (Mowery 2010; Weiss and Thurbon 2006). Thus, despite the fierce American rhetoric vis-à-vis China and other countries, the US continues to employ discriminatory government procurement in its own industrial policies and as a trade weapon (Block 2008). The role of the US as an entrepreneurial state, with its extensive government procurement of the results from public and private R&D, has been essential in the development of major advanced technologies and their commercial success. Many of the technologies utilised, for example, for the development of the iPhone launched by Apple in 2007 were created on the basis of such projects (Mazzucato 2013:113–38).

The Chinese system for public procurement was initiated in the 1990s, and legislation was accelerated in connection with negotiations related to China's membership of the WTO in 2001, but this legislation did not address the issues of procurement for innovation until 2006 with the MLP and then in 2007 with an amendment of the Law of the People's Republic of China on Progress of Science and Technology which explicitly favoured indigenous or independent innovation (Chen and Cheng 2014).

The Chinese criteria for including indigenous innovation products in these catalogues were that they should be produced by an enterprise with full ownership of the intellectual property in China; have a trademark that is owned by a Chinese company and is registered in the PRC; feature a "high degree" of innovation; and be of dependable quality (O'Brien 2010: 55). During the assessment of bids in a tender, a bid containing certified indigenous innovation products can be 5–10 per cent more expensive in a price competition, or should be provided with a 4–8 per cent higher score for a combined technical evaluation (Caizheng Bu 2007: Section 3).

Much of the US argument rested on an interpretation of Chinese commitments to the World Trade Organization (WTO) when China joined in 2001. Legal scholars have argued that the accreditation system for public procurement for central and local governments is potentially in conflict with the country's WTO obligations (An and Peck 2011; Boumil 2012). Other legal scholars have argued that China has no technical obligation to provide open access to its government procurement market, since it has not acceded to the most relevant international regulation, the WTO Government Procurement Agreement (GPA). Nevertheless, even these scholars have argued that China should ensure that procurement measures are consistent with the WTO's "fundamental principles of free trade and non-discrimination" (Ahrens 2010; Chow 2013). China has offered to join the GPA six times since 2007. An offer was rejected by members of the GPA in 2014, largely due to international objections to the role of state-owned enterprises in the Chinese economy, proposed Chinese exclusions related to military procurement and other concerns with preference for domestic firms.

A recent analysis (Li and Georghiou 2016) of the use of procurement in connection with Chinese policies on indigenous innovation indicated that the role of procurement guides in signalling future demand for innovations was at least as effective in benefitting Chinese firms as the local government's efforts to certify indigenous innovation products in catalogues. Although the Chinese framework for procurement represented a maze of legal documents and government actors, several case studies demonstrated that Chinese firms had responded successfully to develop innovations that fulfilled a local demand. An issue has been that local protectionism has tended to reduce the coherence of policy initiatives to promote indigenous innovation through procurement (Li 2017: 441–2). Nevertheless, the Chinese experience has fostered new efforts among Chinese firms to enhance innovation much in the same way that this policy instrument functions in advanced economies (Uyarra et al. 2020).

A study based on interviews in 2011 with R&D executives and US officials in the information and communication technology industry furthermore indicated that US multinational corporations' R&D strategies in China had not been significantly affected by the indigenous innovation policies. According to the respondents, policy implementation varies among central ministries and especially local governments, making it necessary for the corporations to work with many actors in order to thread a path through the complex innovation policies, but they remained committed to doing business in China (Dedrick et al. 2012: 77).

b. *Made in China 2025*

After the controversies related to procurement of indigenous innovation products receded somewhat following the Chinese government's revision of its national guidelines and certification of indigenous innovation products in 2011, a new international uproar subsequently developed over the "Made in China 2025" (MIC 2025) plan that was announced in 2015 (Wübbeke et al. 2016). The MIC 2025 policy was inspired by the German initiative "Industry 4.0" aiming at advanced digitalisation and manufacturing technologies, but the MIC 2025 addressed a much broader scope in terms of industrial upgrading (State Council 2015; Li 2018). The announcement outlined strategic priorities for ten industrial sectors including aerospace, robotics and power equipment, together with various support mechanisms that would ensure the development of smart manufacturing and a digitised economy towards 2035 and make China a leading industrial superpower by 2049. In addition, a technical roadmap proposed specific market share percentages for Chinese products in several sectors (Zenglein and Holzmann 2019: 9).

The US administration perceived *Made in China 2025* as a state-directed and state-sponsored top-down policy for import substitution, intended to reduce China's dependence on foreign technology while supporting Chinese firms to become dominant global players and creating unfair competition for incumbent overseas firms (Morrison 2018b). To a considerable extent, this assessment of MIC 2025 has been shared by European Union analysts and commercial associations (European Union Chamber of Commerce in China 2017). While European concerns regarding Chinese restrictions on foreign investment and market access, protection of intellectual property rights and subsidies for state-owned corporations were similar to those of the US, the actual European strategies vis-à-vis China have focused more on using multilateral frameworks such as reformed WTO rules and bodies that govern the global trading system to counter China's initiatives (Buysse and Essers 2019: 18).

US criticism of MIC 2025 provided a launching pad for the US-China trade war in 2018. MIC 2025 was seen as a key component of a portfolio of Chinese policies alleged to support state-sponsored IP theft, forced technology transfer from foreign companies, economic coercion through export restraints on critical raw materials, information harvesting, and state-backed, technology-seeking overseas Chinese investment (White House Office of Trade and Manufacturing Policy 2018). Such policies were the essential point of the "technology for market access" approach used in developing joint ventures with multinational corporations in the 1990s. At present, China is employing a range of policies to support access to advanced foreign technology. The implementation of these policies in strategic emerging industries has been seen as helping Chinese firms to gain unfair advantages vis-à-vis international business (Prud'homme et al. 2018). The debate about these assertions regarding theft of intellectual property became highly politicised and dominated by myths propagated in both Chinese and overseas media, as discussed in Dan Prud'homme's chapter in this volume.

The implementation of the MIC 2025 initiatives has been steered by a large number of individual action plans, roadmaps, opinions, guidelines, notices, etc. issued by Chinese authorities and think tanks (Wang et al. 2020). Nevertheless, the Chinese leadership has emphasised the need for public-private partnerships and the important role of private entrepreneurship in achieving a new level of technological sophistication. The experience already gained in the fields of artificial intelligence (AI) and cloud computing demonstrates the success of mobilising private firms such as Alibaba, Tencent, Baidu and others in building indigenous R&D strength. This development reflects a longer-term trend for Chinese innovation policies to position the government as a facilitator rather than as an active participant in the commercialisation of new technology (Băzăvan 2019). MIC 2025 also takes into account the emergence of advanced digitalised services and manufacturing in the Chinese economy and the extent to which supply chains are being transformed by platform economics, in which private sector firms have become dominant (Lüthje 2019).

These trends towards the Chinese state as a facilitator and the private sector as the main driving force behind the creation of indigenous innovation capabilities tend to weaken the argument that the MIC 2025 initiatives are unfair international competition generated by state-owned enterprises. There is no doubt that Chinese government authorities at both the national and local levels are eagerly pursuing opportunities to support R&D and innovation, but the nature of industrial policy in an era of a digital economy, Internet Plus and Industry 4.0 has shifted the emphasis to facilitation and building infrastructure, rather than direct participation by the state in production. In addition, given the importance of MIC 2025 as a vital element of China's effort to avoid the "middle-income trap" through reforms of the economic structure and new gains in productivity, it appears unlikely that the current government will abandon the initiative (Liu 2018: 320).

c. *Intellectual Property Rights*

Promotion of indigenous Chinese innovation and the development of domestic intellectual property were core priorities for MIC 2025 (Jiang and Huang 2011). Accordingly, the technical roadmaps published as a follow-up included more substantial objectives concerning the extent to which production should come to rely on Chinese indigenous intellectual property. In essence, MIC 2025 represents an extensive effort to upgrade Chinese industry on the basis of commercialisation of intangible assets such as strategic Chinese patents, as discussed in Anton Malkin's chapter in this volume.

At the core of the indigenous innovation policies lie the Chinese priorities linked to intellectual property rights (IPR), in particular, the extent to which patented innovations are owned by Chinese actors. China has indeed witnessed a surge in patenting, but the evidence available indicates that much of the surge is related to new patentees and is not directly correlated with strong innovation results (Hu et al. 2017). In particular, the extensive subsidies offered by the Chinese state encourage applications for patent rights on a questionable basis; approximately 30 per cent of new patents granted in China are estimated to be low quality patents connected to subsidies (Dang and Motohashi 2015: 151). The quantitative growth of patents in China is thus generally an outcome of extensive public incentives and support, and a study of the impressive Chinese nanotechnology patent record shows that few of these patents actually result in commercial innovations (Huang and Wu 2012: 979–80). Nevertheless, the issues with ensuring higher quality of Chinese patents remain a systemic feature of IPR in China (Prud'homme 2012).

China has continued to improve its system for protection of intellectual property rights, including several updates of the patent law and the establishment of specialised IPR courts in major cities (Huang 2017). Prud'homme and Zhang (2019) found that China's IP regime for innovation has improved notably over time, and therefore is more conducive to innovation than many believe, but that it still poses a range of risks. The presence of these risks may, to varying degrees, negatively influence the innovation activities of both foreign and domestic firms, as well as of other actors participating in the innovation process. In turn, this poses a larger set of risks to China's national development. It has been argued that China is only following the path that the US led when it was catching up with European technology in the late 19th century (Peng et al. 2017: 32). On the other hand, an argument has been made that, at that time, the US had not signed international agreements, while today China has acceded to the TRIPS agreement (Brander et al. 2017: 914).

d. *Technical Standards*

A major objective of China's indigenous innovation activities has been to develop standards that will create a technological platform beneficial to Chinese interests (Ernst 2011). In a sense, the Chinese government has wished to transform the country from a "standards taker'" to a "standards maker" through the development of unique Chinese technology standards. Standards are increasingly recognised as crucial components to innovation and competitiveness (Blind 2016). Accordingly, Chinese industries in the information and communications technology (ICT) sectors have felt compelled to follow international standards which are increasingly built on intellectual property. This is related to the problem that Chinese ICT manufacturers have witnessed: the cost of licences to foreign IP cutting into their slim profits. The Chinese leadership has also wished to obtain "secure and controllable" networks of communication, and the role of standards for achieving this objective has only increased in recent years.

A prime example of efforts to engage in international standards setting and to capture significant shares of the intellectual property related to the platform is China's attempt to develop and commercialise its indigenous 3rd generation mobile communication standard TD-SCDMA (Gao et al. 2014). This standard was based on R&D carried out in 1997 by the Datang Group—a commercial offshoot of the China Academy of Telecommunications Technology—together with a consortium of foreign equipment producers including Siemens (Gao 2014). Chinese producers have been estimated to own almost 50 per cent of the patents related to TD-SCDMA. This has apparently helped Chinese mobile communications vendors to negotiate lower licence fees for the use of ICT standards in their systems (Breznitz and Murphree 2013: 2). TD-SCDMA was recognised as one of three 3G international standards by the International Telecommunications Union in 1999 and was adopted by China Mobile in 2008. Although it has not been deployed commercially outside China, the indigenous innovation capabilities derived from participation in its development have provided major Chinese telecommunications firms with a basis for their development of successful 4th generation (LTE) systems.

In trying to develop its own indigenous standards, however, China faces many challenges, both internationally from powerful multinational corporations and from domestic enterprises that have vested interests in supplying the international markets (Wang et al. 2014: 860–1). In any case, a closer link between standards in ICT and other high technology fields, patenting and economic development makes it imperative for latecomer countries to engage in international standardisation (Ernst et al. 2014: 855–6).

China's leadership has been equally concerned with security issues related to standardisation. For example, the Chinese encryption Wireless LAN Authentication and Privacy Infrastructure (WAPI) standard for wireless Internet connections was developed to ensure secure access for the Chinese authorities to all wireless communication, normally compliant with the international 802.11 standard (Kim et al. 2014). The decision to make this standard mandatory for all Wi-Fi equipment forced both Chinese and overseas producers to obtain licences from the developers of WAPI. The decision encountered strong objections from US producers of Wi-Fi related chips. After the US government officially protested to the Chinese authorities, China agreed in 2004 to postpone the implementation of the standard indefinitely. Nevertheless, most of the equipment sold in China today has been made WAPI compatible. Still, from a US point of view, the standard has been introduced as one of many Chinese efforts at trade protectionism (Cromer 2005). The issues of standards in Chinese cyber security priorities are still the basis for many international concerns and appear to have intensified during recent years (Gierow 2014: 6).

During the last decade, the Chinese leadership has been eager to reform and rationalise the national and local governance of standardisation, reorganising the formulation and implementation of technical standards, centralising decisions on mandatory standards and introducing a new category of "market-based" standards set by industrial associations, similar to the procedures practised in advanced industrialised countries (Seaman 2020: 16–7). This reform is motivated by the needs both to address some contradictions between national and local standards, removing some superfluous existing standards, and to facilitate trade internally in China. As mentioned above, the Chinese efforts at standardisation have also increasingly been directed by the need to support the development of indigenous innovation and influence over the process of development of international standards. These efforts would reduce payment of licence fees to foreign owners of IP embedded in international standards and hopefully embed Chinese IP in international standards for advanced technologies. This has increased the Chinese participation in international standardisation organisations, together with an effort to internationalise Chinese standards through the Belt and Road Initiative (Rühlig 2020: 24–7).

This culminated in the launch of a major research programme carried out by the Standards Administration of China and the Chinese Academy of Engineering in 2018 with the aim to formulate a national China Standards 2035 Strategy by the end of 2020. This strategy will strengthen the system for developing Chinese standards in advanced, high value-added manufacturing and service industries like 5G communications, the Internet of Things (IoT), and artificial intelligence. Furthermore, the strategy will coordinate standardisation efforts between civil and military sectors and will enhance China's role in international standards setting and the internationalisation of Chinese standards (Seaman 2020: 20–3). To a large extent, the use of standardisation to promote innovation can be considered a continuation of the policies for improving indigenous innovation and the Made in China 2025 Plan.

Consequently, the China Standards 2035 initiative has raised concern among international observers (Morrissey and Givens 2020; Arcesati 2019). Chinese efforts have been particularly aimed at generating new IP for standards in advanced technologies such as 5G and artificial intelligence, where competition for new innovations is particularly strong (Ding 2020). Ultimately, the Chinese ambition through state-supported efforts to reshape the international standardisation order is a challenge to existing systems such as that of the US, which depend to a much larger degree on private self-regulation (Rühlig 2020). This challenge has led to calls for the US to work with its allies to counter the Chinese initiatives envisaged under China Standards 2035 (Gorman 2020).

e. *Challenges of Technological Competition with the United States*

The emergence of China as a nation with growing technological capabilities and ambitious policies to promote further development of domestic ownership of innovations raises important questions about the country's global role. There is little doubt that international actors, such as the United States, see it as a challenge to their own role on the global stage of advanced innovation. Some emphasise the mercantilist aspect of China's indigenous innovation policies as an expression of techno-nationalism (for example Segal 2008: 425; Kennedy 2013).

Perhaps it is more fruitful to see the current issues as a result of technological imperatives and their consequences for innovation competition on the global level (Kennedy and Lim 2018). In this view, China and other nations are responding to technological imperatives to secure sustainable economic development. The consequence of such imperatives is to encounter a rivalry for prominence in innovation between a dominant and rising state. The technological imperative that drives the need to acquire and develop new technology in the rising state challenges the dominant state with two negative externalities. The dominant state experiences negative security externalities where its strategic global position is challenged by, for instance, the transfer of dual-use technologies with potential military applications; in addition, the dominant state can experience negative order externalities when the rising state challenges an international system and rules, such as the international IPR regime, that reflect the interests of the dominant state.

Although the immediate conclusion of this analysis is that China and the United States are destined to get caught in Thucydides's Trap (Allison 2017), the question remains whether it will benefit the US if China's efforts at indigenous innovation are confined to China alone. Given the possibility that China may become a leading innovation nation in the future, it can be argued that there will be opportunities for foreign firms in strategic coupling, or recoupling, with emerging Chinese leading innovative firms (He et al. 2017). In many ways, the new environment of Chinese innovation is already reflected in the strategies that the multinational corporations are adopting for their R&D and business in China (Prud'homme and von Zedtwitz 2018).

Indigenous Innovation: Legacies and Contemporary Role

The preceding discussion of the policies devoted to indigenous innovation represents initiatives introduced after 2006, but these policies represent a continued Chinese ambition to become less dependent on foreign sources of technological development. Thus, indigenous innovation in the sense of competitive assets based on domestic R&D, intellectual property rights and standards was pursued long before the policies launched with the MLP. In fact, this priority can be traced back to self-reliance campaigns during the 1950s and the Cultural Revolution in the 1960s (Sigurdson 1980). Studies that have analysed the outcome of indigenous innovation often predate the launch of the explicit policy of the MLP in 2006 and generally contrast the differences between relying on either domestic innovation or foreign technology transfer.

For example, Xiaolan Fu shows that the consistent policy emphasis in China on the development of indigenous innovation capabilities has resulted broadly in substantial total factor productivity (TFP) growth during more than a decade in industries of low- and middle-level technology, while helping a number of firms in the high technology sectors to reach innovation frontiers (Fu 2015: 135–6). One of the key reasons for this is that indigenous R&D is complementary to foreign technology transfer, raising a domestic firm's absorptive capacity, and because indigenous technology often is more appropriate in a middle-income country (Fu et al. 2011). Indigenous innovation is enhanced in the long run by complementary assets provided through cooperation with foreign partners and sources of technology (Tian and Li 2017: 1287–8). Fu's study (2015: 135–6), based on data from the 10th Five-Year Plan (2001–05), argues that government-sponsored high technology industrialisation projects had significant positive impacts on private small and medium-sized private enterprises in terms of approved patents and new technologies, while there was no impact on large, state-owned enterprises (Zheng and Zhou 2015). A UNIDO study using data from the same period examined the effects of knowledge derived from in-house R&D, foreign technology imports and purchasing domestic technology, respectively, on the innovation capability of Chinese state-owned enterprises in high tech industries. The results show that foreign technology imports alone did not improve innovation performance in terms of new patents, but had a positive effect when combined with indigenous R&D, especially in more advanced firms. In contrast, technology transfer from domestic R&D institutes had a significant impact only on less advanced firms (Li 2008: 20–1).

Another interesting report analyses the process of indigenous innovation through four stages of learning and output to arrive at its impact on private firm performance (Howell 2018). The study finds that learning-by-doing is an important element of capturing learning spillovers throughout the process of innovation. During the later stages of innovation, learning spillovers positively increase firms' innovation output as well as their performance; this is especially so for firms with high absorptive capacity (that is, indigenous R&D efforts). A similar point has been made in a paper that analysed whether international technology in-licensing by Chinese firms, compared with domestic technology in-licensing, contributed to indigenous innovation in the 2000s. It found that

Chinese firms that in-licensed international technologies performed better with regard to indigenous innovation than those that mainly in-licensed domestic technologies, even though the national innovation policy suggests otherwise (Li-Ying and Wang 2015: 131–2).

The role of indigenous innovation and foreign technology transfer has also played out differently in different regions of China. Thus, indigenous innovation has played a positive and significant role in improving the economic growth of the eastern and central regions, but it has not shown a significant role in promoting the western region. In contrast, foreign technology imports and domestic technology transfer contributed to the economic growth efficiency of the central and western regions, but had little effect on the efficiency improvement in the eastern region (Ding 2018). In a similar manner, foreign direct investment had a significant spillover effect on indigenous innovation in the inland provinces, but less effect in coastal areas with access to factor inputs such as finance and high quality human resources (Ren and Ding 2020).

An analysis based on China's provincial panel data (Huang et al. 2019: 282–3), covering 30 provinces over the period of 2000–2014, indicated that the impacts of indigenous R&D on TFP are larger than those of technology spillovers coming from FDI. This study also indicated that the imports had increased TFP, while exports tended to decrease it, thereby indicating that China's indigenous R&D inputs play a more important role in increasing TFP compared to the technology spillovers coming from openness. This study observed that a larger share of SOEs was improving TFP up to a certain threshold, but there was a negative effect beyond this threshold.

This brief survey of some of the evidence of China's achievements in promoting indigenous innovation reveals that: (1) the official recognition of indigenous innovation in 2006, and the explicit national policies promoting it were, in fact, only enhancements of a decade-long ambition by both state and private actors to gain their own innovative capabilities; (2) while state-owned enterprises were important in some of the Chinese efforts, the entrepreneurship of private firms was frequently decisive, especially in the high tech sectors; and (3) foreign technology sources remain important for the absorption, integration and re-invention elements of the process contributing to Chinese indigenous innovation, but these overseas inputs were particularly significant in the inland regions.

Elements of New Innovation Trajectories

If China continues to invest heavily in R&D and innovation and pursues strategies for indigenous innovation that address some of the country's most pressing issues, its diverging path of innovation is likely to be able to contribute significantly to progress at the global technological frontier (Schmitz and Altenburg 2015: 461). Such contributions could include innovations that have not been adequately pursued by other nations, governments or industries, such as new technologies to reduce climate change or to develop applications using biotechnology and/or artificial intelligence that enhance human health.

Indeed, China has been expanding investments in low-carbon innovations, including renewable energy from wind and solar power, together with new generations of nuclear power. So far, most of these areas have generally demonstrated the capabilities of Chinese producers to catch up with existing technological systems through assimilation and incremental innovation, with few examples of Chinese indigenous innovation that would move the technological frontiers forward. It may be too early to declare China a clean-tech superpower, but data from 2019 shows the country now produces most of the world's solar panels, wind turbines, electric vehicles and lithium-ion batteries (Temple 2020). The Chinese leadership has expressed a firm commitment to achieving a transition to a low-carbon economy. China's Doubling Plan aimed to double the governmental and/or state-directed investment in clean energy research and development as part of its contribution to Mission Innovation from RMB25 billion in 2015 to RMB50 billion (roughly 7.6 billion dollars) by 2020 (Zhang et al. 2018). Nevertheless, a major transition to low-carbon energy supply will require major shifts in public and private investments in new technology and R&D, together with a massive reform of the institutions regulating and providing incentives for cleaner technology—a process that is likely to take many years to complete (Andrews-Speed and Zhang 2019: 266–70). China has also increasingly recognised the potential benefits of intellectual property protection and has embarked on a drive to utilise the national and international IPR systems to protect its technologies to the greatest extent possible. This process would ensure that the results of Chinese indigenous innovation will become available for worldwide benefit.

A momentous aspect of China's emergence on the global innovation frontiers through indigenous innovation is that Chinese firms have made new progress in innovating the process of innovation itself. In particular, Chinese producers have taken important steps forward in terms of achieving greater efficiency and effectiveness in the discovery and development of potential new technologies and—perhaps most significantly—in implementing these quickly in society. Observers have already noted that Chinese firms have advanced their capabilities to develop and implement process and management innovations to cut costs in production and value chains. It seems likely that Chinese innovators and entrepreneurs will continue to excel in these aspects of innovation, and perhaps be able to enhance their approach with more advanced R&D and/ or artificial intelligence, creating a powerful Chinese mode of innovation that could come to dominate international competitiveness.

Chinese researchers of indigenous innovation focus mostly on the role of the state as the key component of a Chinese model of innovation. In particular, the support for strategic emerging industries has been seen as providing substantial policy benefit, raising the technological levels and innovative capabilities of industries such as high-speed railways, aeronautics and nuclear power (Wei et al. 2017). The development of high-speed railways has been considered one of the key successes in the development of indigenous technology, combining the stringent procurement criteria of the Ministry of Railways with the establishment of technological alliances with multinational producers of high-speed rail, and strengthened by scores of R&D projects under the MLP (Sun 2015). Case studies of specific industrial sectors or particular technologies in China also provide greater insight into the achievements of the Chinese efforts to promote indigenous innovation. These efforts have generally been more successful than the policy on "technology for market access" that guided much of the government's interaction with multinational corporations during the 1990s and early 2000s (Zhou et al. 2016).

However, it may be more interesting to look for the features of a Chinese mode of innovation beyond the confines of state support and explore the behaviour of Chinese firms that have succeeded in disruptive innovation by moderating, integrating or reforming the process of innovation. It is here, in the strategies pursued by firms regardless of top-down state support or interference, that the strengths of a Chinese mode of innovation are most likely to be found. Moreover, given that the most dynamic firms that contribute significantly to value-added in the Chinese economy belong to what may be called the private sector and function in a market economy, Chinese authors have increasingly argued that policies should shift from "selective industrial policy" to "strategic industrial policy" (Zheng and Shen 2018: 50).

In their study of the development of electronic industries in three Chinese cities, Breznitz and Murphree (2013) identified rapid commercialisation as crucial for the approach to innovation. They found that Chinese firms are concentrating on the D in R&D, and remain better at developing and improving existing products than at inventing new ones. The competitive edge of these firms is achieved by developing quickly enough to remain at the cusp of the global technology frontier without actually advancing the frontier itself. Similar points were made in McKinsey's study of the strength of Chinese performance in four archetypes of innovation: customer-focused, efficiency-driven, engineering-based and science-based. The study found that Chinese industries have established strength in efficiency-driven and customer-focused innovation, based on the extensive manufacturing ecosystem with networks of suppliers and availability of labour and infrastructure. China still lags in science- and engineering-based innovation, although advantages in Government-created local demand and rapidly increasing, low-cost R&D capabilities are creating new opportunities to catch up with international levels (Woetzel et al. 2015).

The Chinese knack for cost innovation has also been emphasised by Zeng and Williamson (2007), who provide case studies of Chinese firms that indicate creative ways which deliver high technology, variety and customisation at minimal price premiums, and which redirect niche offerings towards volume segments. Another study points to the ways that Chinese firms have been able to reengineer established innovation processes to further speed up the completion of projects, exploiting modularisation and simultaneous engineering, cycling rapidly through "Launch-Test-Improve" in pilot markets, and combining vertical hierarchy with horizontal flexibility (Williamson and Yin 2014: 29–30).

Similar points emerge from the study conducted by Greeven and Yip (2021), which shows that Chinese enterprises have often followed several different paths of innovation, sequentially or in combination. For example, they have ascended from incremental improvements based on basic technological capabilities in the early years, gradually arriving at a level of more radical product innovations, predominantly focusing on what the customer wants rather than what the technology could potentially provide. Chinese companies used the competitive process to continuously upgrade technological capability, relying on experimentation and learning from failures, facilitated by an agile and responsive organisational structure, and leveraging resources outside the company as much as possible to embed themselves in local ecosystems. In addition, Shen et al. (2020: 6–9) argue that, in the new economic era, a Chinese-style innovation has emerged with characteristics that include striving for simplicity, attention to speed, focus on low cost and "learning from failure", and they believe that this will have beneficial implications internationally. The consensus is emerging that new developments provide a China model in the development of strategic emerging industries (Wei et al. 2017).

The key point is that there may be both positive and negative implications of the Chinese ambition to promote indigenous innovation. On the one hand, Chinese technologies may become available globally to address global problems, for example in priority areas such as low-carbon innovation or advanced digital processing and communication; and Chinese innovations in the management of innovation have already demonstrated new abilities to cut costs and reduce time to market. On the other hand, these innovations may challenge foreign competitors and incumbents in global markets, with potential negative consequences for competitiveness in overseas economies and for their national security.

Concluding Remarks

An important purpose of this chapter has been to review some controversial aspects of the Chinese policy on indigenous innovation and international reactions to it. The MLP definition of indigenous innovation (sometimes translated "independent innovation") in a Chinese context is rather broad, covering both original innovation, the integration of various technologies in a new way and what has been called re-innovation of assimilated technology from overseas. All these forms should include Chinese ownership of intellectual property. Moreover, it is emphasised that Chinese policies aim to strengthen the capabilities of Chinese organisations to develop indigenous innovations. The policies are implemented by a range of policy instruments that are familiar to observers of innovation policy elsewhere, such as financial support for high priority R&D projects, public procurement of innovative products, promotion of national technical standards and the securing of nationally-owned intellectual property. At the same time, such policy instruments have appeared questionable in an international context, primarily because they are pursued in a country with strong state control and with economic institutions and structures that aim to support Chinese self-reliance and indigenous innovation capabilities.

The policies have been pursued in various forms, including the *Made in China 2025* initiative, since the concept of indigenous innovation was launched officially in 2006. It is important to note, however, that the roots of this latest Chinese effort to become autonomous derive from a decade-long, or perhaps more accurately century-long, ambition to increase Chinese independent ownership and control over new technologies. The results of this continued endeavour have been mixed, where the best outcomes have materialised after the Open-Door Policy, and in particular after China joined the WTO in 2001. Recent research has thus shown that it is most often the combined inputs of domestic and foreign R&D which have provided competitive new technologies for Chinese business. In fact, spillovers from FDI and international linkages are vital for indigenous innovation: the country's own R&D and foreign knowledge inputs are complementary. In other words, Chinese participation in the global networks of technological innovation is essential, and it would be a mistake to hold on to a dogmatic belief that the purpose of the indigenous innovation policy is to achieve complete Chinese technological autonomy, a belief that paradoxically sometimes is voiced by observers in both China and the US.

References

Ahrens, Nathaniel. 2010. *Innovation and the Visible Hand: China, Indigenous Innovation, and the Role of Government Procurement*. Asia Program, Number 114, Carnegie Endowment for International Peace. Available at https://carnegieendowment. org/2010/07/07/innovation-and-visible-hand-china-indigenous-innovation-and-role-of-government-procurement-pub-41125 [accessed 12 Nov. 2020].

Allison, Graham. 2017. *Destined for War: Can America and China Escape Thucydides's Trap?* Boston: Houghton Mifflin Harcourt.

An Siyuan and Brian Peck. 2011. "China's Indigenous Innovation Policy in the Context of Its WTO Obligations and Commitments", *Georgetown Journal of International Law* 42: 375–447.

Andrews-Speed, Philip and Zhang Sufang. 2019. *China as a Global Clean Energy Champion*. Singapore: Palgrave Macmillan.

Arcesati, Rebecca. 2019. *Chinese Tech Standards Put the Screws on European Companies*. Mercator Institute for China Studies (MERICS) Short Analysis, 19 Jan. 2019. Available at: https://merics.org/en/analysis/chinese-tech-standards-put-screws-european-companies [accessed 17 Dec. 2020].

Arthur, W. Brian. 2009. *The Nature of Technology: What It Is and How It Evolves*. New York: Free Press.

Baark, Erik. 2019. "China's Indigenous Innovation Policies", *East Asian Policy* 11, 2: 5–12.

Băzăvan, Adrian. 2019. "Chinese Government's Shifting Role in the National Innovation System", *Technological Forecasting & Social Change* 148: 1–11.

Blind, Knut. 2016. "The Impact of Standardisation and Standards on Innovation", in *Handbook of Innovation Policy Impact*, ed. J. Edler, P. Cunningham, A. Gök, and P. Shapira. Cheltenham: Edward Elgar, pp. 423–49.

Block, Fred. 2008. "Swimming Against the Current: The Rise of a Hidden Developmental State in the United States", *Politics & Society*, 36, 2: 169–206.

Bloom, Nicholas, John Van Reenen and Heidi Williams. 2019. "A Toolkit of Policies to Promote Innovation", *Journal of Economic Perspectives* 33, 3: 163–84.

Boumil, S. James, III. 2012. "China's Indigenous Innovation Policies Under the TRIPS and GPA Agreements and Alternatives for Promoting Economic Growth", *Chicago Journal of International Law* 12, 2: 755–81.

Brander, James A., Victor Cui and Ilan Vertinsky. 2017. "China and Intellectual Property Rights: A Challenge to the Rule of Law", *Journal of International Business Studies* 48: 908–21.

Breznitz, Dan and Michael Murphree. 2011. *The Run of the Red Queen: Government, Innovation, Globalization, and Economic Growth in China*. New Haven: Yale University Press.

_____. 2013. *The Rise of China in Technology Standards: New Norms in Old Institutions*. US-China Economic and Security Review Commission, 16 Jan. 2013. Available at https://www.uscc.gov/sites/default/files/Research/RiseofChinain TechnologyStandards.pdf [accessed 12 Nov. 2018].

Buysse, K. and D. Essers. 2019. "Cheating Tiger, Tech-savvy Dragon: Are Western Concerns about 'Unfair Trade' and 'Made in China 2025' Justified?" *NBB Economic Review* (September 2019): 47–70. Available at https://www.nbb.be/doc/oc/repec/ecrart/ecorevii2019_h3.pdf [accessed 17 Dec. 2020].

Caizheng Bu [Ministry of Finance]. 2007. *Caizheng bu guanyu yinfa 'zizhu chuangxin chanpin zhengfu caigou pingshen banfa' de tongzhi* (Announcement by the Ministry of Finance on the issuance of the "independent innovation products in government procurement assessment approach"). *Cai Ku* 30. Available at http://www.gov.cn/ztzl/kjfzgh/content_883671.htm [accessed 23 Nov. 2018].

Cao Cong, Richard P. Suttmeier and Denis F. Simon. 2006. "China's 15-year Science and Technology Plan", *Physics Today* 59, 12: 38–43.

Chen Jin and Cheng Chunzi. 2014. "The Legislation of Public Procurement Policy for Innovation in China", in *Public Procurement, Innovation and Policy*, ed. Veiko Lember, Rainer Kattel and Tarmo Kalvet. Berlin: Springer, pp. 93–108.

Chicot, Julien and Mireille Matt. 2018. "Public Procurement of Innovation: a Review of Rationales, Designs, and Contributions to Grand Challenges", *Science and Public Policy* 45, 4: 480–92.

Chow, Daniel C. K. 2013. "China's Indigenous Innovation Policies and the World Trade Organization", *Northwestern Journal of International Law & Business* 34 :81–124.

Cromer, Zia K. 2005. "China's WAPI Policy: Security Measure or Trade Protectionism?" *Duke Law & Technology Review* 4: 1–13.

Dang Jianwei and K. Motohashi. 2015. "Patent statistics: A Good Indicator for Innovation in China? Patent Subsidy Program Impacts on Patent Quality", *China Economic Review* 35: 137–55.

Dedrick, Jason, Tang Jian and Kenneth L. Kraemer. 2012. "China's Indigenous Innovation Policy: Impact on Multinational R&D", *Computer* 45, 11: 70–8.

Ding Feng 2018. "Zizhu chuangxin, jishu yinjin yu jingji zengzhang" [Indigenous innovation, technology introduction and economic growth], *Guanli xiandaihua* [Management modernization] 5: 42–45.

Ding, Jeffrey. 2020. *Balancing Standards: US and Chinese Strategies for Developing Technical Standards in AI*. NBR Commentary. Available at https://www.nbr.org/publication/balancing-standards-u-s-and-chinese-strategies-for-developing-technical-standards-in-ai/ [accessed 30 August 2020].

Edquist, Charles, et al., ed. 2015. *Public Procurement for Innovation*. Cheltenham: Edward Elgar.

Ernst, Dieter. 2011. *Toward Greater Pragmatism? China's Approach to Innovation and Standardization*. Institute on Global Conflict and Cooperation, Brief No. 18. Available at http://dx.doi.org/10.2139/ssrn.2742918 [accessed 12 Nov. 2018].

Ernst, Dieter, Lee Heejin and Kwak Jooyoung. 2014. "Standards, Innovation, and Latecomer Economic Development: Conceptual Issues and Policy Challenges", *Telecommunications Policy* 38, 10: 853–62.

European Union Chamber of Commerce in China. 2017. *China Manufacturing 2025: Putting Industrial Policy Ahead of Market Force.* Beijing. Available at http://www.europeanchamber.com.cn/en/china-manufacturing-2025 [accessed 12 Nov. 2018].

Fu Xiaolan.2015. *China's Path to Innovation.* Cambridge: Cambridge University Press.

Fu Xiaolan, Carlo Pietrobelli and Luc Soete. 2011. "The Role of Foreign Technology and Indigenous Innovation in the Emerging Economies: Technological Change and Catching-up", *World Development* 39, 7: 1204–12.

Gao Ping, Yu Jiang and Kalle Lyytinen. 2014. "Government in Standardization in the Catching-up Context: Case of China's Mobile System", *Telecommunications Policy* 38, 2: 200–9.

Gao Xudong. 2014. "A Latecomer's Strategy to Promote a Technology Standard: The Case of Datang and TD-SCDMA", *Research Policy* 43: 597–607.

Georghiou, Luke, et al. 2014. "Policy Instruments for Public Procurement of Innovation: Choice, Design and Assessment", *Technological Forecasting and Social Change* 86: 1–12.

Gierow, Hauke J. 2014. *Cyber Security in China: New Political Leadership Focuses on Boosting National Security.* Mercator Institute for China Studies (MERICS) China Monitor No. 20. Available at https://merics.org/en/report/cyber-security-china-new-political-leadership-focuses-boosting-national-security [accessed 17 Dec. 2020].

Gorman, Lindsay. 2020. "The U.S. Needs to Get in the Standards Game—With Like-Minded Democracies", *Lawfare*, 2 April 2020. Available at https://www.lawfareblog.com/us-needs-get-standards-game%E2%80%94-minded-democracies [accessed 14 Nov. 2020].

Greeven, Mark J. and George S. Yip. 2021. "Six Paths to Chinese Company Innovation", *Asia Pacific Journal of Management* 38: 17–33.

He Shaowei et al. 2017. "Towards a New Wave in Internationalization of Innovation? The Rise of China's Innovative MNEs, Strategic Coupling, and Global Economic Organization", *Canadian Journal of Administrative Sciences* 34: 343–55.

Hospers, Gert-Jan. 2005. "Joseph Schumpeter and his Legacy in Innovation Studies", *Knowledge, Technology, & Policy* 18, 3: 20–37.

Howell, Anthony. 2018. *Innovation and Firm Performance in the People's Republic of China: A Structural Approach with Spillovers.* ADBI Working Paper 805. Tokyo: Asian Development Bank Institute. Available at https://www.adb.org/publications/innovation-and-firm-performance-prc-structural-approach-spillovers [accessed 17 Dec. 2020].

Hu, Albert G.Z., Zhang Peng and Zhao Lijing. 2017. "China as Number One? Evidence from China's Most Recent Patenting Surge", *Journal of Development Economics* 124: 107–19.

Huang Can. 2017. "Recent Development of the Intellectual Property Rights System in China and Challenges Ahead". *Management and Organization Review* 13, 1: 39–48.

Huang Can and Wu Yilin. 2012. "State-led Technological Development: A Case of China's Nanotechnology Development", *World Development* 40, 5: 970–82.

Huang Junbing et al. 2019. "Technological Factors and Total Factor Productivity in China: Evidence Based on a Panel Threshold Model", *China Economic Review* 54: 271–85.

Jiang Yuhong and Huang Yong. 2011. "Zizhu chuangxin, zhishi chanquan he jingzheng zhengce de xietiao" [Indigenous innovation, intellectual property and coordination of competition policy]. *Dianzi zhishi chanquan* [Electronic Intellectual Property] 4: 43–8.

Kennedy, Andrew B. 2013. "China's Search for Renewable Energy: Pragmatic Techno-nationalism", *Asian Survey* 53, 5: 909–30.

Kennedy, Andrew B. and Darren J. Lim. 2018. "The Innovation Imperative: Technology and US–China Rivalry in the Twenty-first Century", *International Affairs* 94, 3: 553–72.

Kim Dong-hyu et al. 2014. "China's Information Security Standardization: Analysis from the Perspective of Technical Barriers to Trade Principles", *Telecommunications Policy* 38, 7: 592–600.

Lember, Veiko, Rainer Kattel and Tarmo Kalvet, ed. 2014. *Public Procurement, Innovation and Policy*. Berlin: Springer.

Li Ling. 2018. "China's Manufacturing Locus in 2025: With a Comparison of 'Made-in-China 2025' and 'Industry 4.0'", *Technological Forecasting & Social Change* 135: 66–74.

Li Xibao. 2008. *External Technology Purchase and Indigenous Innovation Capability in Chinese Hi-Tech Industries*. Research and Statistics Branch Working Paper 05/2008, Vienna: UNIDO.

Li Yanchao. 2017. "Assessing Public Procurement of Innovation as a Cross-Domain Policy: A Framework and Application to the Chinese Context", *Review of Policy Research* 34, 3: 421–46.

Li Yanchao and Luke Georghiou. 2016. "Signaling and Accrediting New technology: Use of Procurement for Innovation in China", *Science and Public Policy* 43, 3: 338–51.

Li-Ying, Jason and Wang Yuandi. 2015. "Find Them Home or Abroad? The Relative Contribution of International Technology In-licensing to 'Indigenous Innovation' in China", *Long Range Planning* 48: 123–34.

Liu, Kerry. 2018. "Chinese Manufacturing in the Shadow of the China–US Trade War", *Economic Affairs* 38, 3: 302–24.

Lüthje, Boy. 2019. "Platform Capitalism 'Made in China'? Intelligent Manufacturing, Taobao Villages and the Restructuring of Work", *Science, Technology & Society* 24, 2: 199–217.

Mazzucato, Mariana. 2013. *The Entrepreneurial State: Debunking the Public vs. Private Myth in Risk and Innovation*. London: Anthem.

McGregor, James. 2010. *China's Drive for 'Indigenous Innovation' – A Web of Industrial Policies*. Washington, DC: US Chamber of Commerce.

Morrison, Wayne M. 2018a. *China-U.S. Trade Issues*. Washington DC: Congressional Research Service. Available at https://fas.org/sgp/crs/row/RL33536.pdf [accessed 17 Dec. 2020].

_____. 2018b. "The Made in China 2025 Initiative: Economic Implications for the United States", *In Focus* no. 7-5700. Washington, DC: Congressional Research Service.

Morrissey, William and John Givens. 2020. "The Measure of a Country: America's Wonkiest Competition with China", *War on the Rocks*. Available at https://warontherocks.com/2020/08/the-measure-of-a-country-americas-wonkiest-competition-with-china/ [accessed 17 Dec. 2020].

Mowery, David C. 2010. "Military R&D and Innovation", in *Handbook of the Economics of Innovation, Volume 2*, ed. Bronwyn H. Hall and Nathan Rosenberg. Amsterdam: Elsevier, 1219–56.

O'Brien, Robert D. 2010. "China's Indigenous Innovation, Origins, Components and Ramifications", *China Security* 6, 3: 51–65.

OECD. 2017. *Public Procurement for Innovation: Good Practices and Strategies*. Paris: OECD.

Peng, Mike W. et al. 2017. "History and the Debate Over Intellectual Property", *Management and Organization Review* 13, 1: 15–38.

Prud'homme, Dan. 2012. *Dulling the Cutting Edge: How Patent-Related Policies and Practices Hamper Innovation in China*. European Union Chamber of Commerce in China, MPRA Paper No. 43299. Available at https://mpra.ub.uni-muenchen.de/43299/ [accessed 25 Nov. 2020].

_____ et al. 2018. "'Forced technology transfer' policies: Workings in China and Strategic Implications", *Technological Forecasting and Social Change* 134: 150–168.

Prud'homme, Dan and Max von Zedtwitz. 2018. "The Changing Face of Innovation in China", *MIT Sloan Management Review* 59, 4: 4–32.

Prud'homme, Dan and Zhang Taolue. 2019. *China's Intellectual Property Regime for Innovation*. Cham: Springer.

Ren Penglei and Ding Lizhai. 2020. "FDI, zizhu chuangxin dui jingji zengzhang yingxiang de quyu yi zhi xing: Yanhai yu nei lu shijiao" [Regional heterogeneity of the impact of FDI and independent innovation on economic growth: coastal and inland perspectives], *Jinrong fazhan yanjiu* [*Financial Development Research*] 7: 68–72.

Rühlig, Tim N. 2020. *Technical standardisation, China and the Future International Order: A European Perspective*. Brussels: Heinrich-Böll-Stiftung.

Schmitz, Hubert and Tilman Altenburg. 2016. "Innovation Paths in Europe and Asia: Divergence or Convergence?" *Science and Public Policy* 43, 4: 454–63.

Seaman, John. 2020. "China and the New Geopolitics of Standardization", *Notes de l'Ifri*. Paris: Ifri.

Segal, Adam. 2008. "Autonomy, Security, and Inequality: China, India, the United States, and the Globalization of Science and Technology", *Technology in Society* 30: 3–4: 423–8.

Serger, Sylvia Schwaag and Magnus Breidne. 2007. "China's Fifteen-Year Plan for Science and Technology: An Assessment", *Asia Policy* 4: 135–64.

Shen Zhifang, et al. 2020. "Chinese-Style Innovation and Its International Repercussions in the New Economic Times", *Sustainability* 12, 5: 1859–76.

Shiliu jie wu zhong quanhui: "Zizhu chuangxin" zhanlue zui fu xinyi [The Fifth Plenary Session of the 16th Central Committee: The "Independent Innovation" Strategy is the most innovative]. 2005. Available at http://www.chinanews.com/news/2005/2005-10-18/8/639462.shtml [accessed 13 Jan. 2021].

Sigurdson, Jon. 1980. *Technology and Science in the People's Republic of China: An Introduction.* Rpt. (e-book) 2013. Amsterdam: Elsevier.

State Council. 2006. *Guojia zhongchangqi kexue he jishu fazhan guihua gangyao (2006–2020)* [National Guidelines on Medium and Long-term Programme for Science and Technology Development (2006–2020)]. Available at http://www.gov.cn/jrzg/2006-02/09/content_183787.htm [accessed 27 July 2020].

————. 2015. *Guowuyuan guanyu yinfa "zhongguo zhizao 2025" de tongzhi* [State Council on issuing the announcement of "China Manufacturing 2025"]. Available at http://www.gov.cn/zhengce/content/2015-05/19/content_9784.htm [accessed 25 Nov. 2020].

Sun Mei and Jiang Hongbiang. 2017. "Innovating by Combining: A Process Model", *Procedia Engineering* 174: 595–9.

Sun Zhe. 2015. "Technology Innovation and Entrepreneurial State: the Development of China's High-speed Rail Industry", *Technology Analysis & Strategic Management* 27, 6: 646–59.

Temple, James. 2020. "China: Clean-tech Superpower", *MIT Technology Review* 123, 5: 22–3.

Tian Longwei and Li Yuan. 2017. "Double-edged Sword Effect of Independent Innovations and Foreign Cooperation: Evidence from China", *Journal of Technology Transfer* 42: 1276–91.

USITC [US International Trade Commission]. 2010. *China: Intellectual Property Infringement, Indigenous Innovation Policies, and Frameworks for Measuring the Effects on the US Economy* (Investigation No. 332-514), USITC Publication 4199, Nov. 2010. Washington, DC: USITC.

Uyarra, Elvira et al. 2020. "Public Procurement, Innovation and Industrial policy: Rationales, Roles, Capabilities and Implementation", *Research Policy* 49, 1: 1–10.

Wang Jian, Wu Huiqin and Chen Yan. 2020. "Made in China 2025 and Manufacturing Strategy Decisions with Reverse QFD", *International Journal of Production Economics* 224: 1–22.

Wang Ping, Kwak Jooyoung and Lee Heejin. 2014. "The Latecomer Strategy for Global ICT Standardization: Indigenous Innovation and its Dilemma", *Telecommunications Policy* 38: 933–43.

Wei Jieyu, Xue Lan and Zhou Yuan. 2017. "Zhongguo zhanlüexing xinxing chanye chuangxin moshi yanjiu" [Research on China's Strategic Emerging Industry Innovation Model], *Zhongguo Keji* [*Chinese S&T*] 6: 47–52.

Weiss, Linda and Elizabeth Thurbon. 2006. "The Business of Buying American: Public Procurement as Trade Strategy in the USA", *Review of International Political Economy* 13, 5: 701–24.

White House Office of Trade and Manufacturing Policy. 2018. *How China's Economic Aggression Threatens the Technologies and Intellectual Property of the United States and the World*. Washington, DC: The White House. Available at https://www.whitehouse.gov/wp-content/uploads/2018/06/FINAL-China-Technology-Report-6.18.18-PDF.pdf [accessed 14 Nov. 2018].

Williamson, Peter J. and Eden Yin. 2014. "Accelerated Innovation: The New Challenge from China", *MIT Sloan Management Review* Summer Magazine: 27–34.

Woetzel, Jonathan et al. 2015. *The China Effect on Global Innovation*. McKinsey Global Institute. Available at: https://www.mckinsey.com/~/media/McKinsey/Featured%20Insights/Innovation/Gauging%20the%20strength%20of%20Chinese%20innovation/MG20China%20Effect_Full%20report_October_2015.ashx [accessed 14 Nov. 2020].

Wübbeke, Jost et al. 2016. *Made in China 2025: The Making of a High-tech Superpower and Consequences for Industrial Countries*. Papers on China No. 2. Berlin: Mercator Institute for China Studies (MERICS). Available at https://www.merics.org/sites/default/files/2018-07/MPOC_No.2_MadeinChina2025_web.pdf [accessed 14 Nov. 2020].

Yang Jianjun and Liu Linbo. 2014. "Guonei zizhu chuangxin zuixin yanjiu dongtai yu pingshu: Yige xin kuangjia de tichu" [Review of the Recent Indigenous Innovation Research in China: A New Framework], *Keji guanli yanjiu* [Science and Technology Management Research] 6: 1–4, 21.

Zeng Ming and Peter J. Williamson. 2007. *Dragons at Your Door*. Cambridge, MA: Harvard Business Review Press.

Zenglein, Max J. and Anna Holzmann. 2019. *Evolving Made in China 2025: China's Industrial Policy in the Quest for Global Tech Leadership*. (Mercator Institute for China Studies) MERICS Paper on China No. 8, 2 July. Available at https://www.merics.org/en/papers-on-china/evolving-made-in-china-2025 [accessed 14 Nov. 2020].

Zhang, Jia, Fang Lv and Honghua Xu. 2018. "Analysis of Clean Energy Development in China on Mission Innovation to Face the Global Climate Change". IOP Conference Series: Materials Science and Engineering 394 (2018) 042064: 1–5.

Zheng A. and Shen K. 2018. "Zizhu chuangxin, chanye zhengce yu jingji zengzhang" [Independent innovation, industrial policy and economic growth], *Caijing kexue* [Finance and Economics] 6: 39–52.

Zheng Shilin and Zhou Li'an. 2015. "Zhengfu zhuanxiang xiangmu tizhi yu zhongguo qiye zizhu chuangxin" [Government special project system and indigenous innovation in Chinese enterprises], *Shuliang jingji jishu jingji yanjiu* [Research on Quantitative Economics and Technical Economics] 12: 73–89.

Zhou Yu, William Lazonick and Sun Yifei ed. 2016. *China as an Innovation Nation*. Oxford: Oxford University Press.

5

China's Talent Challenges Revisited

Cong Cao and Denis Fred Simon

Introduction

Today, the heightened intensity of international competition essentially boils down to a competition for human resources, or talent. This is no exception for China. In fact, the China story in the reform and open-door era is essentially a story of talent recruitment and development, deployment and utilisation. It is the contributions of scientists, engineers, other qualified professionals, as well as Chinese who possess business and legal knowledge and skills that have propelled China to the global competitive position that it occupies now. The evolving state of China's talent pool will continue to shape the country's future economic and technological trajectory in important ways.

This recognised, China also continues to face some serious challenges regarding its talent situation, just as the country did in the past. This chapter is developed around this theme of talent challenges—past, present and future. These challenges are in turn manifested in the "Qian Xuesen puzzle": why has China not turned out larger numbers of people with outstanding talent?[1] The chapter starts by revisiting the four propositions regarding China's talent challenges put forward in our co-authored book published some ten years ago (Simon and Cao 2009) to examine how the key issues have been addressed in recent years. It then assesses various programmes that the Chinese government has launched to attract the return of those with foreign study and advanced research experience. Presumably, a lack of high-end talent has challenged and will continue to challenge the on-going effort to develop China into an innovation-oriented nation and a world leader in science and technology (S&T). The chapter ends with a discussion on what the "Qian Xuesen puzzle" means for China's overall talent development over the next decade or so.

China's Multifaceted Talent Challenges

Despite possessing an impressive S&T talent pool and having an extensive human resource pipeline, China continues to face serious talent issues as it seeks to sustain domestic economic growth and promote rapid technological advance. In 2009, we suggested that four factors were responsible for explaining China's talent challenges in the early twenty-first century (Simon and Cao 2009: 22–56). First, the after-effects of the Cultural Revolution were still being felt; during the ten years between 1966 and 1976, higher education was disrupted and professionals were prosecuted and deprived of the right to carry out their work, thus leading to a dearth of well-educated specialists in all areas. Second, the "brain drain" of talents abroad after China opened its door in the late-1970s constrained the domestic availability of "the best and brightest minds". Third, the qualitative improvement of the talent pool had been sacrificed amid the quantitative expansion of higher education since the late-1990s, causing various structural mismatches, especially in terms of geographic demand and supply. And finally, China was fast approaching an "aging society", which would have significant implications for the supply and utilisation of talent over the coming decades.

Some ten years have passed and it certainly is an appropriate time to revisit these propositions to see how things have evolved. First, apparently, the lingering effects of the Cultural Revolution are mostly gone. Almost all of the so-called "worker-peasant-soldier" college students (*gong-nong-bing xueyuan*) have retired, with only very few who remain active in leadership positions having made up their educational deficiencies through advanced education at home and/or abroad. For example, the former President of the Chinese Academy of Sciences (CAS), Bai Chunli, studied at Peking University during the Cultural Revolution but furthered his studies with a doctorate at the CAS before conducting post-doctoral research at the California Institute of Technology.[2] Moreover, the generation of scientists and professionals receiving higher education during the initial phases of the reform and open-door era is more than coming of age. In fact, a significant number of them have retired or soon will retire. Those who were born in the 1960s or 1970s now occupy many of the key leadership positions in science and technology and the 1980s generation is entering its most productive age.

Second, the "brain drain" challenge still exists, although the situation is not as severe as it was ten years ago. China's central and local governments and different institutions have launched various returnee-attraction programmes to tackle this challenge. Consequently, China has witnessed the return of a growing number of its scientists, engineers, entrepreneurs and other professionals with foreign study and/or work experience. The growing availability of new and better opportunities also has attracted Chinese and non-Chinese experts to China. While the majority of Chinese PhDs still desire to travel abroad, either to make up for the lack of international experience or to meet the requirements for promotion as stipulated by their employers, most plan to pursue professional careers in their homeland. However, among the growing number of returnees are not only the academically competent and experienced "sea turtles" (*haigui*), who clearly are warmly welcomed, but also "seaweed" (*haidai*), who struggle professionally because a significant number of them spent only a year or two overseas and did not accumulate much meaningful foreign work experience (Zweig and Han 2010). In recent years, Chinese students have gone overseas at a younger age, some even attending foreign high schools. For example, at the turn of the twenty-first century, 80 per cent of the 60,000 Chinese students in American universities were at the postgraduate level. A decade later, the number of Chinese students in the United States rose to 158,000, but those at the graduate level dropped to below 50 per cent for the first time (48.8 per cent). In the 2017/18 academic year, Chinese students enrolled in American universities reached 373,000, with those at the graduate level accounting for only 36.8 per cent (IIE, various years). The prospects for members of the group who start their undergraduate studies abroad to become "sea treasure" (*haibei*), who are generally better prepared for global success, are uncertain as changes in the domestic environment and political tensions between China and the US and other Western countries could re-orient or re-shape their career planning and mobility. The new "brain drain" situation is discussed later in the chapter.

Third, China still faces a demonstrable mismatch challenge. Some aspects of this challenge are a result of the rapid expansion of higher education in China in the late 1990s as human capital accumulation just intrinsically takes a long time, first to expand the quantity then to upgrade the quality. For one thing, China simply did not have enough qualified faculty to teach the growing number of new university entrants. But other aspects have been caused by a variety of critical structural problems, which are difficult to solve, and therefore this overall challenge will not be mitigated any time soon. For example, graduates strongly prefer to work in first-tier cities such as Beijing,

Shanghai, Guangzhou and Shenzhen, often causing geographical mismatches. There are also mismatches between supply and demand, between knowledge acquired through education and skills required by jobs, and between the types of positions to be filled and the availability of quality and capable talent to fill the positions.

Finally, the "aging society" challenge is only getting more serious. In our book, we used data from the Population Division under the United Nations Department of Economic and Social Affairs and China's National Bureau of Statistics to predict a crossover of the group attending colleges (18 to 22 year olds) and the group approaching retirement (55 to 60 year olds) between 2015 and 2017, meaning that there would be more retiring S&T personnel than college-bound young people (Simon and Cao 2009: 266–68). In recent years, the number of students sitting for national college entrance examinations (*gaokao*) has been declining. While some of this decline may derive from the fact that more students are preparing to study abroad and are thus not taking *gaokao*, the diminishing pool of college-age youngsters indicates that the aging effect may have kicked in earlier than expected. The government's recent loosening of the one-child policy—from allowing families to have a second child if both parents were an only child, to if one parent was an only child, and to allowing all families to have two children—is probably too late to address current problems. Indeed, this corresponds with the Chinese saying, "it takes ten years to grow a tree but one hundred years to educate/nurture a person" (*shinian shumu, bainian shuren*). It definitely will take time and perhaps prove impossible for China to reverse the trend of becoming a rapidly aging society. The implications of the aging population in China vis-à-vis its ambition to become an innovation-oriented nation could be quite negative, though advances in technologies such as artificial intelligence will likely alter the degree of severity in some areas.

There also are particular areas of deficiency, such as lack of creativity, constraints on initiative-taking behaviour and a continued "cultural" aversion to risk-taking. There remains low tolerance for failure to support technological entrepreneurship and innovation, as well as a lack of critical "soft skills", including but not limited to management and communications. Finally, graduates still lack ample international exposure and cross-cultural awareness. Improvements in these key areas have been slow to materialise and the existing deficiencies within the education system will take time to repair. Even among those who have been educated abroad, many actually have had more of a "Chinese experience" at an overseas university and have not embraced much in the way of foreign cultures and values.

More fundamentally, lingering challenges seem to point to the relevance of a remark made by Qian Xuesen, a returnee from the United States in the mid-1950s and one of the most important contributors to China's missile and space programme (Cao 2014). In 2005, Qian told then visiting Chinese Premier Wen Jiabao that one important reason that China has not produced outstanding talent is that the nation does not have even one university that genuinely follows the model of nurturing scientific and creative talent and encouraging unique innovation. Qian made his remark towards the end of his life and did not elaborate on what he meant by his ideal model for universities, thus leaving much room for interpretation, speculation and even debate. Nonetheless, it is indeed a key challenge for China to develop ways to nurture innovative and creative talent.

Is a "Brain Drain" Still Looming?

The "brain drain" challenge is neither a China specific nor a recent phenomenon. The Royal Society of London coined the term in the 1960s to describe the exodus of professionals from the United Kingdom to North America, especially the United States. The situation has been spread to different countries, especially developing countries across Asia and other parts of the globe. Thereafter, economists have come up with different theories or strategies for ameliorating, if not completely getting rid of, the phenomenon. Jagdish Bhagwati (1976) proposed taxing the "brain drain". For Robert Lucas (2001), given the nature of international networks, through remittances and capital flows as well as the links between international trade, migration and technology transfers, immigrants from less developed countries help to stimulate the dynamics of economic growth and technological catch-up in their home countries so as to have the effects of "brain gain".

More recently, AnnaLee Saxenian, an economic geographer, has championed a theory of "brain circulation" in which migrants from India and China who studied in the US, and then worked in Silicon Valley and other high-tech areas, frequently brought technology and experience back to their home countries (1999). She has further developed a "new brain circulation" concept, whereby migrants not only bring home technology and experience, but also engage in entrepreneurial activities and list overseas-based start-ups, which do business in their home countries. With these new ventures having both overseas and home bases, circulation continues (Saxenian 2006). The collaborative knowledge networks forged by these types of "bi-cultural" and "multi-cultural" individuals have become the new vehicles for advancing global innovation as well.

The theoretical underpinnings described here have stimulated the Chinese government and organisations to take action to turn China's "brain drain" into a "brain gain" or at least a "brain circulation". Also, having realised that the talent shortage could have a significant negative impact on China's near-to-medium term growth and even jeopardise China's development transition, especially in terms of the development of innovative and technology-intensive sectors, China has initiated various programmes to proactively attract, retain and nurture talents, especially those at the high-end.

Efforts were first introduced in the early 1990s (Cao 2008). In 1994, the CAS rolled out a One Hundred Talents Program, targeting overseas Chinese talents, while the National Natural Science Foundation of China (NSFC) started to provide early returnees, as well as domestic scientists, with the National Science Fund for Distinguished Young Scientists (Cao and Suttmeier 2001). In 1998, with the substantial contribution from Li Ka-shing, a Hong Kong business tycoon, the Ministry of Education (MOE) set up a Cheung Kong Scholars Program, aimed at awarding returned scholars and attracting the return of overseas talent (Li and Tang 2019). But these programmes did not achieve the desired "brain gain"; at best, they created an academic "brain circulation". Among structural and cultural impediments, political constraints, prevailing income disparities and differing living conditions between China and developed countries, along with schooling issues for children and spousal employment challenges have discouraged overseas Chinese scholars and students from seriously considering pursuit of a long-term career in China. Of course, the lack of an adequate environment conducive to innovation was implied in the "Qian Xuesen puzzle".

In December 2008, to further address the "brain drain" challenge and also take advantage of the global financial crisis that cost some ethnic Chinese scientists, researchers and professionals their jobs abroad, China's Central Leading Group for Coordinating Talent Work, under the Department of Organization of the Central Committee of the Chinese Communist Party, launched an Attracting Overseas High-End Talent Program, also known as the Thousand Talents Program. Pledging to attract some 2,000 expatriate Chinese scholars to their homeland within five to ten years, the programme initially targeted full professors at well-known foreign institutions of learning, experienced corporate executives and entrepreneurs with core technologies under 55 years of age to support leapfrogging China's scientific research, high-tech entrepreneurship and economic development. In return for their permanent return and services, the central government offered a resettlement subsidy of RMB1 million tax free and a significant amount of funding for research or entrepreneurship, while local governments and employers matched these incentives with additional funding, housing benefits and a salary close to the returnees' overseas level (Simon and Cao 2011).

The Thousand Talents Program did not occur in isolation from other key reforms and new initiatives in the R&D system. During this period, China launched its 15-year Medium-to-Long Term Plan for the Development of Science and Technology (2006–20) along with a series of structural reforms regarding S&T policy to help advance China's attempts to become a serious player in international S&T affairs. In addition, during this same period, China began to increase its annual R&D expenditures substantially, with the goal of having its R&D expenditure reach 2.5 per cent of its growing GDP by the year 2020 (Appelbaum et al. 2018). At a time when R&D monies were becoming more constrained in the US and elsewhere, the availability of ample funding in China seemed to provide a good enticement for many aspiring S&T personnel.

The Thousand Talents Program attracted several very prominent academics to come back to China. They included Wang Xiaodong, the first US-bound mainland Chinese student in the open-door era who was elected as a member of the US National Academy of Sciences (NAS) at age 41 and a Howard Hughes Medical Institute (HHMI) investigator at the University of Texas Southwestern Medical Center; Shi Yigong, a chaired professor and also an HHMI investigator at Princeton University who is presently President of the new Westlake University in Hangzhou; and most recently, Xie Xiaoliang, the first mainland Chinese in the open-door era to hold a tenured full professorship at Harvard University, who is also a fellow of the American Academy of Arts and Sciences and a member of the NAS. There are many other such scholars from China who were appointed to the world's leading institutions of learning (see, for example, LaFraniere 2010). However, quite a significant number of awardees have been unable or unwilling to return to China permanently for various reasons, which ran counter to the core objectives and the initial goals of the programme (Wang 2011; Zweig and Wang 2013; Zweig, Kang and Wang 2020). Therefore, the government had to add a component for those who wanted to commit to only a couple of months of part-time work. Given the complicated nature of these part-time arrangements, the government never has made the entire list of Thousand Talents Program awardees public because revealing the broad array of special arrangements would likely cause embarrassment and problems to some of the part-timers. In 2019, the special incentives and provisions used to attract people into the Program, Chinese and foreign, became a major political issue in the US as a number of scholars began to be viewed with suspicion by the FBI due to intellectual property rights protection and related national security concerns (discussed later in the chapter).

In December 2010, the Central Leading Group for Coordinating Talent Work approved the addition of a component for emerging young scholars, the Young Thousand Talents Program, to the Thousand Talents Program. Administered by the NSFC, the Program aimed at attracting some 400 promising young talents annually between 2011 and 2015 from overseas, and turning them into innovative leaders in academia or high-tech entrepreneurship with moral character, outstanding professional ability and comprehensive quality. Meanwhile, the NSFC and MOE also added components to their respective programmes for emerging outstanding young scholars in 2012 and 2015 (Table 5.1 provides the number of returnees who benefited from the various programmes).

Table 5.1: China's Talent-Attracting Programmes and the Number of Returnees Benefited, 1994–2018

Programme	Agency in charge	Year initiated	Total number affected
Hundred Talents Program	CAS	1994	n.a.
National Science Fund for Distinguished Young Scholars	NSFC	1994	3454
Chunhui Program	MOE	1996	n.a.
Cheung Kong Scholar Program	MOE	1998	2948
111 Program	MOE & SAFEA	2005	n.a.
Thousand Talents Program	CLGCTW	2008	n.a.
Young Thousand Talents Program	CLGCTW	2010	3535
Science Fund for Emerging Distinguished Young Scholars	NSFC	2011	2398
Ten Thousand Talents Program	CLGCTW	2012	3454
New Hundred Talents Program	CAS	2014	n.a.
Young Cheung Kong Scholar Program	MOE	2015	440

Notes: CAS – Chinese Academy of Sciences; NSFC – National Natural Science Foundation of China; MOE – Ministry of Education; SAFEA – State Administration of Foreign Expert Affairs; CLGCTW – Central Leading Group for Coordinating Talent Work.
Source: Cao et al. 2020.

Each of the programmes targets different age groups of returnees, mostly the young or middle-aged. These titles—endowed professorship and grantees—carry significant academic honours in the Chinese context. The NSFC programmes provide funding for research, and their grantees are likely supplemented with a salary from the institutions; while non-NSFC programmes do not provide money for research, the awardees likely receiving matching funds from local governments and institutions for research. Chinese universities and research institutes compete fiercely for titled scientists as their numbers are valued in the official institutional rankings in China.

Alongside the return of some of the leading scientists and scholars from abroad has been an increase in the overall return of Chinese students, driven by a combination of both domestic pull and international push factors. By 2018, of the 5.86 million Chinese studying abroad during the reform and open-door era, 3.65 million had returned to China, registering an overall rate of return of 62.3 per cent. In 2017, 608,000 Chinese went abroad as students, and 481,000 returned upon finishing their overseas studies, with a rate of return in the year of 79.1 per cent. Looking at these statistics, one could conclude that China is no longer experiencing a "brain drain".[3]

However, several sources point to critical questions about the overall quality of the returnees, including those returning under the various programmes mentioned above. Of some 470,000 returnees seeking certification for their foreign educational credentials between 2008 and 2014 at the Chinese Service Center for Scholarly Exchange, under the Ministry of Education (2016: 35–91), 62.56 per cent had a master's degree, 29.8 per cent had a bachelor's degree, and only 6.2 per cent had a doctorate. The 29,341 doctorate-holding returnees received their degrees from more than 2,000 institutions in 67 countries in various disciplines (Tables 5.2 and 5.3). Specifically, the top eleven schools awarding 12.1 per cent of the doctorates included universities from Singapore (National University of Singapore, Nanyang Technological University), Japan (Tokyo, Kyushu, Tohoku, Nagoya, Hokudai, Kyoto, and Tsukuba) and the UK (Nottingham and Manchester). Top American universities whose graduates had sought their degree certification included the Illinois Institute of Technology, University of Illinois Urbana-Champaign, the University of Southern California, Columbia University, University of Illinois Chicago, Northeastern University, Missouri State University, Ohio State University, Boston University and the University of Maryland College Park; but most of their graduates were in master's programmes and only a small number were awarded PhDs.

Table 5.2: Chinese Returnees Who Sought Certification for Their Foreign PhD Degrees, 2008–14

Country	Number	%
US	8,228	28.04
Japan	6,140	20.93
UK	3,266	11.13
Korea	2,094	7.14
Germany	1,981	6.75
France	1,499	5.11
Singapore	1,240	4.23
Australia	823	2.81
Canada	767	2.61
Russia	586	2.00
Others	2,717	9.25
Total	29,341	100.00

Source: Chinese Service Centre for Scholarly Exchange 2016.

Table 5.3: Disciplines in which Chinese Returnees Received Their Foreign PhD Degrees, 2008–14

Discipline	Number	%
Engineering	10,601	36.13
Science	7,303	24.89
Medicine	3,280	11.18
Literature	1,779	6.06
Economics	1,528	5.21
Law	1,482	5.05
Management Science	1,394	4.75
Education	859	2.93
Others	1,115	3.80
Total	29,341	100.00

Source: Chinese Service Centre for Scholarly Exchange 2016.

Meanwhile, between 2006 and 2016, a total of 50,439 Chinese nationals received PhD degrees from American universities (National Center for Science and Engineering Statistics 2018: Table 26).[4] In 2015, 22 per cent of the 464,000 foreign born science and engineering (S&E) doctorate holders in the US were Chinese. Between 2012 and 2015, the vast majority of the S&E doctorate recipients in the US from China (83 per cent) reported plans to stay in the US, and approximately half of these individuals reported accepting firm offers for employment or postdoc research in the US. By country of citizenship at the time of degree conferment, China, the country that was the source of more S&E doctorate recipients than any other foreign country, had the highest 5- and 10-year stay rates. For the Chinese who received their doctorates in 2005, the 10-year stay rate was 90 per cent; for those receiving their American doctorates in 2010, the 5-year stay rate was 85 per cent, while the 5-year and 10-year stay rates for all the S&E Chinese PhDs from the US were both 70 per cent in 2015 (US National Science Board 2018: 3–138).[5]

Nevertheless, returnees, along with the overseas Chinese scholars, have contributed to the Chinese S&T system. By tracing the addresses of the authors with publication records in China, the United States, and the 28 member states of the European Union, Cao and his collaborators found that in recent years over 12 per cent of mainland China's total number of publications were published by scientists with overseas experience. The share of high-impact publications by these scientists is considerably higher than that of their colleagues who remained in China throughout their scientific careers, as might be expected. Moreover, the impact of publications by overseas Chinese is higher than those of researchers in China who have no overseas experience (Figure 5.1). This could be possibly interpreted as showing that the quality of output from China-based scholars still needed to improve and catch up with that of other scholars who first published in China but later moved abroad. However, more published Chinese researchers moved to the US, Europe and other developed countries over the study period (Figure 5.2), thus also suggesting that China may not yet be able to attract or retain its best scientists (Cao et al. 2020). Of course, many factors—not just talent—influence the quality and impact of publications. But most important is the quality of China's research environment, which though improving, may still be less conducive to the high-impact science that China would like to produce (Cao 2008).

Indeed, the deference shown to S&T talent has grown considerably. The Chinese R&D system no longer suffers from inadequate funding and an antiquated infrastructure. In addition, as suggested, there is now an ample number of high-quality graduates being produced by PRC universities in S&T

Figure 5.1: Share of High-impact Publications (top 10%, fracFWCI) by Returnees above Chinese Average; for Overseas Chinese it is Much Higher

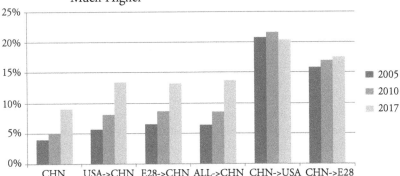

Notes: fracFWCI – fractional field-weighted citation impact.
CHN – Publications by China-based scientists with only China publication experience; USA->CHN – Publications by those who first published in the US and then in China; E28->CHN – Publications by those who first published in the 28 European Union states and then in China; All->CHN – Publications by all those who first published outside China and then in China; CHN->USA - Publications by those who first published in China and then in the US; CHN->E28 – Publications by those who first published in China and then in the 28 European Union states.
Source: Cao et al. 2020

Figure 5.2: Numbers of Mobile Chinese Scientists in China, the EU and US

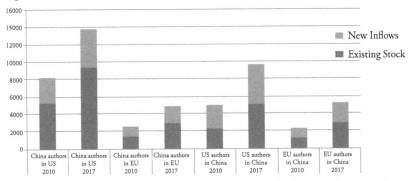

Notes: China authors in the USA – Authors who first published in China and then in the US; China authors in EU – Authors who first published in China and then in the EU; US authors in China – Authors who first published in the US and then in China; EU authors in China – Authors who first published in China and then in the EU.
Source: Cao et al. 2020.

at the undergraduate and graduate levels. The situation, overall, continues to improve, albeit at a much slower pace than desired by the scientific and political leadership. The key questions revolve around the difficulties associated with bringing what sociologist Talcott Parsons called "an achievement-oriented culture" (1951), or what sociologist Robert K. Merton called "universalism" (1942) into existence as the guiding philosophy for evaluation, promotion and support of talent. Again, the "Qian Xuesen puzzle" is relevant.

One other factor that has somewhat changed the situation has been the emergence of several high calibre joint venture universities in China such as Duke Kunshan University and the University of Nottingham Ningbo China, with which both authors have been affiliated. A significant number of ethnic Chinese has found it appealing to secure full-time employment at these types of institution because they believe there is an overriding commitment to academic freedom that is not yet present at most PRC universities. These new institutions also do not suffer from some of the legacy issues such as seniority and excessive bureaucracy that are still present in a traditional Chinese academic environment. Moreover, as these younger institutions build up their own research capabilities, local authorities have exhibited a strong commitment to support the recruitment of a new cadre of scientists and engineers whose work might help support local economic goals and objectives. It remains to be seen whether the environment nurtured at such institutions will eventually proliferate beyond their campuses.

The Impacts of Sino–US Tensions on Chinese Talent

Since the late 1970s, China has established strong collaborative and cooperative relations in science, technology and education with all the developed countries. Such relationships have helped enormously in advancing China's S&T enterprise. The Sino–US collaboration in S&T has been one of the most comprehensive, to which Chinese scientists have contributed significant efforts and from which Chinese scientists have benefitted enormously. Under the administration of then President Donald Trump, the tensions between the two countries escalated and China was labelled an economic threat and "strategic rival". There was the possibility that much of the collaboration and cooperation would be reduced if not discontinued. Unless bilateral relations greatly and swiftly improve under President Joe Biden, a real slow down is likely as the Chinese scientists involved in such collaboration and cooperation will find it more and more difficult to find willing partners on the US side (Suttmeier 2020). The irony, of course, is that just as the US-China relationship is shifting from one of asymmetry to greater parity, the US seems to want to disengage precisely when the idea of "mutual benefit" has potentially acquired some real meaning.

The national security concerns from both countries have generated adverse consequences already. For example, the US government has turned down the visa requests of a number of Chinese scientists desiring to visit the US or attend international conferences there, and has even denied or revoked visas to Chinese social scientists working on Sino–US relations, the South China Sea and cyber security, over fears of spying. For the same national security reasons, the Chinese government has likewise rejected the visas of some American scholars. The growing level of uncertainty engendered in this current period of political name-calling has produced anxieties about new collaborations on both sides of the Pacific.

Under the then Trump administration, rising domestic political pressure forced the Department of Energy, National Institutes of Health (NIH) and National Science Foundation (NSF), among others, to start investigating whether ethnic Chinese working at American institutions of learning and within the high-tech sector are illegally leaking technology and knowhow to China. China's returnee talent-attraction programmes, especially the high-profile Thousand Talents Program, aimed at recruiting high-end talent globally and from the US in particular, have caused further suspicion among American politicians and science administrators. In response, the Program's organiser stopped publicising recruits to it and ordered Chinese organisations to take the information of the recruits offline for fear that it would damage their careers elsewhere, especially in the US. In fear of losing US government funding, some US universities have been forced to withdraw their Chinese students' participation.

Most recently, after requests by the NIH, the MD Anderson Center at the University of Texas ousted three of the five scientists suspected of working with China without proper disclosure and authorisation. The Center also suspended at least one more scientist. All of these scientists are ethnic Chinese (Hvistendahl 2019). The Baylor College of Medicine, also in Texas, carried out an audit of the foreign affiliations of every faculty member with current NIH funding, numbering roughly 500 of its 3,500 scientists. Preliminary investigations have found that three ethnic Chinese scientists failed to disclose their concurrent appointments at Chinese universities. Baylor did not discipline them, but corrected the record with the NIH (Mervis 2019a). Overall, a year-long investigation by the NIH identified 180 scientists at more than 60 US research institutions which the NIH believes have violated the confidentiality of its peer review system or failed to disclose financial ties to foreign organisations (Mervis 2019b). Meanwhile, the NSF revealed that all but two of the 16 to 20 cases investigated for violating rules on the disclosure of foreign ties involved ties to China, although a majority of the scientists are US citizens and are not ethnically Chinese (Silver 2020). Those who left their positions in the US soon secured decent positions in China. For example, Xifeng Wu was Director of the Center for Public Health and Translational Genomics and the Betty B. Marcus Chair in Cancer Prevention at the MD Anderson Center until she was forced to resign in January 2019. Two months later, she became Dean of the School of Public Health at Zhejiang University.

It remains to be seen how other American universities and government agencies will deal with similar cases. Such a hostile environment may lead to a large exodus of Chinese-origin scientists, including part-timers of the Thousand Talents Program, from the US. As noted, every year over the last decade or so, American universities have graduated 4,000 to 5,000 Chinese PhDs, of whom about 90 per cent have expressed intentions to stay upon receiving their degrees; at least 70 per cent remained in the US five to ten years later. This occurred amid an overall increasing return of Chinese from overseas, as mentioned. The current hysteria is highly reminiscent of the McCarthyism in the 1950s and carries with it strong "racist" overtones. In the 1950s, a vociferous campaign against alleged communists in the US government, universities and other organisations drove Qian Xuesen, the famous rocket scientist at the California Institute of Technology, back to China where he eventually helped develop the PRC's strategic weapons programme (Chang 1996).

Meanwhile, as noted, over 363,000 Chinese nationals are currently enrolled at different levels of education in the US. Since the summer of 2018, Chinese students in the American programmes of robotics, aviation, engineering and high-tech manufacturing, among other sensitive fields, have faced tighter scrutiny in the visa application and renewal process. In May 2020, the Trump Administration decided to ban graduate students from seven military-affiliated Chinese universities from pursuing further education in the US, impacting about 3,000 to 4,000 Chinese students (Redden 2020).[6] Most of these visiting scholars and students did not actually break any laws or commit any crimes; the few who had obscured their affiliations were cited for visa fraud, but nothing else of a more nefarious nature.

Arising from such developments, on 3 June 2019, China's Ministry of Education held a press conference during which an MOE official pointed out that the restrictions on visas issued to Chinese students had affected Chinese students' and scholars' completion of their studies in the US, and warned them to assess the risk and prepare for worst case scenarios (China State Council Information Office 2019). Indeed, continued tensions between the US and China may further decrease the number of Chinese students pursuing studies in the US, thus damaging not only the American education and science systems that depend upon Chinese students for tuition and research staffing, but also the academic exchanges between the two countries and the development of Chinese talent, some of whom will eventually return to China. It also remains to be seen whether the decoupling from the US will adversely affect the pace and scope of China's S&T upgrading. Again, the irony of this situation is that education and S&T cooperation were once seen as the bedrock of the bilateral relationship, allowing the two countries to continue to engage even in times of political difficulties between Beijing and Washington, DC. However, these once "neutral" areas are now the source of some of the most intense conflicts and disagreements.

The level of US concern is most clearly reflected in two documents issued by the US government in March 2018 and November 2019. In the 2018 document entitled *China: The Risk to Academia*, the Federal Bureau of Investigation (FBI 2018: 1) highlighted the belief that among the 1.4 million international students and scholars enrolled at US institutions of higher education, there were state-directed actors who "seek to illicitly or illegitimately acquire US academic research and information to advance their scientific, economic, and military development goals". The document goes on to state that "the Chinese government [poses] a particular threat to US academia for a variety of reasons". The FBI suggested that these reasons include: China does not play by the rules of academic integrity; the Chinese government sponsors economic espionage and some Chinese scholars and students are being employed as "non-traditional collectors of intellectual property". Finally, the report indicated that "the Chinese government uses a 'whole-of-society approach' to advance its economic development, achieve generational advances in research and development, and save money" (FBI 2018: 5).

In the November 2019 report, *Threats to the U.S. Research Enterprise: China's Talent Recruitment Plans*, China is accused of operating a series of surreptitious programmes designed to acquire American know-how by illegal or illicit means. Sponsored by the US Senate Permanent Subcommittee on Investigations (2019), it specifically cited the Thousand Talents Program as a kind of "trojan horse" whereby US intellectual property derived from US government-funded research is being leaked into Chinese hands and exploited to advance Beijing's technological aspirations. Published in the midst of the unresolved, so-called "US-China trade war" and the dramatic demonstrations occurring in Hong

Kong during the fall of 2019, the report further undermined the ability of the two countries to proceed with not only the existing government-to-government programmes, but also many people-to-people, non-governmental forms of cooperation involving universities, research institutes and think tanks. Many US universities received substantial funding from the NIH, DOD and the Department of Energy, and are unwilling to jeopardise this important funding to cooperate with new or existing Chinese counterparts. Obviously, both reports aim to provide a rationale for cutting China's technological and talent ties with the US. Unfortunately, the situation in the aftermath of the Covid-19 outbreak has further complicated matters, and additional accusations have flown across the Pacific, leading to a further deterioration in the Sino–US S&T and education relationship.

Thinking Outside the Box?

Putting these international considerations aside for the moment, as suggested earlier, a domestic environment conducive to and sustainable for turning out qualified talent is critical for continuous economic progress. However, the key question remains whether China can become an innovation-oriented nation without becoming more open to different ways of thinking and creating a different type of culture within its research environment. This is more than a philosophical question. While innovation has been elevated to a very high status in China, and on the surface Chinese researchers and entrepreneurs are encouraged to think outside the box, equally important are the other ingredients of a true innovation culture, namely, autonomy, free access to the flow of information and especially dissent, both scientific and political, which at present are not adequately applauded or tolerated. Indeed, there is an international consensus that tolerance is as critical as talent and technology in driving creativity and growth (Florida 2002).

This leads to our thoughts on the "Qian Xuesen puzzle", alluded to above. No one knows exactly what Qian's remark meant. However, given his thorough understanding of China's education and research system from his vantage point, as well as his formative personal and professional life experience in the US—he had studied and worked at the Massachusetts Institute of Technology and the California Institute of Technology for 20 years before being expelled in the mid-1950s amid the McCarthyism zeal—Qian Xuesen was likely emphasising the importance of such values as independent thinking, tolerance of dissent and freedom of inquiry.

Indeed, answers to Qian's puzzle may have significant implications for China's goal to become an innovation-oriented nation amid the internationalisation of China's human resources. Globalisation has brought China various practical benefits and advantages. However, greatness in terms of science and innovation is not taken for granted. The development of a high-quality talent pool is relatively easy to attain in technical terms. The most difficult and important part to the Qian puzzle is to nurture independent thinking and freedom of inquiry; its widespread absence in China has limited the pool of academic talent and stultified imagination and innovation. The *gaokao* testing culture makes rote memorisation, rather than critical thinking, much more valued. Therefore, to make China's talent pool more responsive to an increasingly challenging global environment, the state needs to go beyond mere pragmatism, to treasure and uphold such universal values underlying science and innovation. The presence of joint venture universities, with their more open academic culture, might hold one of the keys to helping China break through some of the existing systemic constraints. Joint venture universities could serve as mechanisms to diffuse critical thinking and enhance risk-taking inside the Chinese education world. Only by driving ahead in terms of greater openness and critical thinking will China be able to turn out truly world-class graduates from world class universities with majors in world-class disciplines and have its talent leapfrog to the international frontiers of research, as its scientific and political leadership has envisioned. The decision to bring in the Sino–foreign joint venture universities represents a step in the right direction, but only if these unique types of institution are allowed to engage in pedagogical practices that truly nurture critical thinking, risk taking and independent debate.

The bottom line is that allowing "blooming and contending" are more critical than purely worshiping innovation as a new "religion".[7] If the former are not allowed to prosper, the potential success of China's innovation strategy will run into talent-related system-wide roadblocks. It is in this vein that China's innovation pursuits may be in conflict with the government's other goals, namely to maintain social stability and construct a harmonious society, as innovation often requires swimming against the tide rather than simply going with the flow.

Conclusion

This chapter has discussed various issues surrounding China's evolving talent challenges. By revisiting the four decade-old propositions put forward in our previous research on Chinese talent, this chapter concludes that the Cultural Revolution challenge no longer exists, while the challenges in the other three areas—the "brain drain," various structure-related mismatches and the aging society—are still having an appreciable impact, although the level of severity varies. Specifically, in recent years there has been a larger number of returnees among its overseas educated students and scholars, thus seemingly achieving some sort of "brain gain" and "brain circulation", thanks to a booming economy that has created exciting new opportunities for scholars and entrepreneurs. Added to this is the attention that the leadership has been paying to science, technology and innovation. Reforms continue to be introduced into the S&T sector, though they are often under tighter political controls. Therefore, it is not surprising that the efforts that the government and related organisations have made in attracting high-end talent from overseas have met with some success. However, not only is the quality of the returnees not completely satisfactory, the various talent-attracting programmes that have been launched may be merely a temporary solution to addressing China's critical talent challenges.

The tensions between China and the United States have not only been prolonged, but have also extended from the trade area to research and talent. On the one hand, these tensions have already cut off some of China's access to the most advanced and sophisticated technology because Chinese students are sometimes banned from studying these subjects in American universities, and Chinese scholars may lose the opportunity, at least temporarily, to collaborate with their American counterparts. This could be particularly damaging in fields such as artificial intelligence and quantum computing, fields in which China hopes to play a leading role on a global scale. On the other hand, the deepening tensions also could drive some of the more established Chinese-American scholars out of the US. While it is too early to tell whether the current political conditions will cause some ethnic Chinese to return to China, it does remain a distinct possibility. Indeed, this complex reality poses a real dilemma for China, which seems to have re-asserted its commitment to global engagement in order to maintain access to the frontiers of research and education.

While it is difficult to assess whether China's talent-attracting policies have truly provided more than a formal/superficial approach to solve the underlying talent issues, we would argue that the key to meeting China's ultimate talent challenges lies in answering the "Qian Xuesen puzzle". What Qian meant to suggest may actually be that there needs to be more importance attached to such values as independent thinking, tolerance of dissent and freedom of inquiry; these factors are essential for growing and nurturing truly innovative talent. If this is the case, the recent increases in investment in S&T and education, while obviously necessary, are not sufficient to enable China to meet its goals. China needs to continue not only improving and making its environment more conducive to creative expression, innovative thinking and talent development but also reducing the shocks caused by "structured uncertainty" across its system (Breznitz and Murphree 2011).

Acknowledgements

Research for this paper was partially supported by a grant from the National Natural Science Foundation of China (#71774091). We also benefitted from comments and suggestions made by participants during presentations at Duke Kunshan University, the University of the Chinese Academy of Sciences, the East Asian Institute (EAI) at the National University of Singapore and Nottingham University Business School.

Notes

[1] Qian Xuesen (1911–2009) was a US-trained and based rocket scientist who returned to China in 1955 to lead China's missile and space programme.

[2] Bai stepped down as CAS President in November 2020.

[3] The data on the overall stock and flow of Chinese students overseas and the return rate is from China's Ministry of Education (2019) and National Bureau of Statistics (2018), Table 21-10 Statistics on Postgraduates and Students Studying Abroad, respectively.

[4] Table 26 is entitled, "Doctorates Awarded for 10 Largest Countries of Origin of Temporary Visa Holders Earning Doctorates at US Colleges and Universities, by Country or Economy of Citizenship and Field: 2006–16".

[5] For a particular graduating cohort of foreign-born non-citizen S&E doctorate recipients, the proportion who report living in the US for a given number of years after receiving their degrees is an indicator of the cohort's long-term stay rate.

[6] These seven universities are Northwestern Polytechnical University, Harbin Engineering University, Harbin Institute of Technology, Beihang University (formerly known as Beijing University of Aeronautics and Astronautics), Beijing Institute of Technology, Nanjing University of Science and Technology, and Nanjing University of Aeronautics and Astronautics, directed by China's Ministry of Industry and Information Technology.

[7] "Blooming and contending" is from what Mao Zedong said in the mid-1950s, "let a hundred flowers bloom, let a hundred schools of thought contend", to stimulate the activities of scientists, artists and other intellectuals to participate in socialist construction.

References

Appelbaum, Richard P. et al. 2018. *Innovation in China: Challenging the Global Science and Technology System.* Cambridge, UK: Polity.

Bhagwati, Jagdish N. 1976. "Taxing the Brain Drain", *Challenge* 19, 3 (July/August): 34–8.

Breznitz, Dan and Michael Murphree. 2011. *Run of the Red Queen: Government, Innovation, Globalization, and Economic Growth in China.* New Haven, CT: Yale University Press.

Cao Cong. 2008. "China's Brain Drain and Brain Gain: Why Government Policies Have Failed to Attract First-Rate Talent to Return?", *Asian Population Studies* 4, 3:331–45.

————. 2014. "The Universal Value of Science and China's Nobel Prize Pursuit", *Minerva* 52, 2: 141-60.

Cao Cong and Richard P. Suttmeier. 2001. "China's New Scientific Elite: Professional Orientations among Distinguished Young Scientists", *The China Quarterly* 168: 959-83.

Cao Cong et al. 2020. "Returning Scientists and the Emergence of China's Science System", *Science and Public Policy* 47, 2: 172–83.

Chang, Iris. 1996. *Thread of the Silkworm.* New York: Basic Books.

China Ministry of Education. 2019. *Statistics on the Situation of Overseas Chinese Students in 2018* (in Chinese). Available at http://www.moe.gov.cn/jyb_xwfb/gzdt_gzdt/s5987/201903/t20190327_375704.html [accessed 4 Oct. 2019].

China National Bureau of Statistics. 2018. *China Statistical Yearbook 2018.* Beijing: China Statistical Press.

Chinese Service Center for Scholarly Exchange. 2016. *Report on the Certification of Educational Credentials Received from Institutions Outside China* (in Chinese). Beijing: People's Education Press.

China State Council Information Office. 2019. *The Ministry of Education Issued at a Press Conference the No. 1 Foreign Studying Early Warning in 2019* (in Chinese). Available at http://www.scio.gov.cn/xwfbh/xwbfbh/wqfbh/39595/40624/index.htm [accessed 4 Oct. 2019].

Florida, Richard L. 2002. *The Rise of the Creative Class. And How It's Transforming Work, Leisure and Everyday Life.* New York: Basic Books.

Hvistendahl, Mara. 2019. "Exclusive: Major US Cancer Center Ousts Asian Researchers after NIH Flags Their Foreign Ties", *Science* (19 April). Available at https://www.sciencemag.org/news/2019/04/exclusive-major-us-cancer-center-ousts-asian-researchers-after-nih-flags-their-foreign [accessed 4 Oct. 2019].

Institute of International Education (IIE), various years. *The Open Doors Report on International Educational Exchange.* Washington, DC: IIE.

Kerr, William R. 2018. *The Gift of Global Talent: How Migration Shapes Business, Economy & Society.* Stanford, CA: Stanford Business Books.

LaFraniere, Sharon. 2010. "Fighting Trend, China is Luring Some Scientists Home", *New York Times*, 6 Jan. At https://www.nytimes.com/2010/01/07/world/asia/07scholar.html?ref=asia [accessed 3 Feb. 2021].

Li Feng and Tang Li. 2019. "When International Mobility Meets Local Connections: Evidence from China", *Science and Public Policy* 46, 4: 518–29.

Lucas, Robert E. B. 2001. *Diaspora and Development: Highly Skilled Migrants from East Asia* (an Institute for Economic Development Working Paper prepared for the World Bank). Boston, MA: Boston University.

Merton, Robert K. 1942 [1973]. "The Normative Structure of Science", in *The Sociology of Science: Theoretical and Empirical Investigations*, ed. Norman W. Storer. Chicago, IL: University of Chicago Press, pp. 267–78.

Mervis, Jeffrey. 2019a. "US Universities Reassess Collaborations with Foreign Scientists in Wake of NIH Letters", *Science* (26 April). Available at https://www.sciencemag.org/news/2019/04/us-universities-reassess-collaborations-foreign-scientists-wake-nih-letters [accessed 4 Oct. 2019].

_____. 2019b. "Details Revealed on NIH Probe of Foreign Ties", *Science* 365, 6448: 14.

National Center for Science and Engineering Statistics, Directorate for Social, Behavioral and Economic Sciences. 2018. *2016 Doctorate Recipients from U.S. Universities* [NSF 18–304]. Alexandria, VA: US National Science Foundation.

Parsons, Talcott. 1951. *The Social System*. Glencoe, IL: Free Press.

Redden, Elizabeth. 2020. "New Restrictions for Chinese Students with Military University Ties", *Inside Higher Education* (May 29). Available at https://www.insidehighered.com/news/2020/05/29/us-plans-cancel-visas-students-ties-universities-connected-chinese-military [accessed 1 Aug. 2020].

Saxenian, AnnaLee. 1999. *Silicon Valley's New Immigrant Entrepreneurs*. San Francisco, CA: Public Policy Institute of California.

_____. 2006. *The New Argonauts: Regional Advantage in a Global Economy*. Cambridge, MA: Harvard University Press.

Silver, Andrew. 2020. "US Agency Reveals How It Is Tackling Foreign Influence", *Nature* 583, 7816: 342.

Simon, Denis F. and Cao Cong. 2009. *China's Emerging Technological Edge: Assessing the Role of High-End Talent*. Cambridge and New York: Cambridge University Press.

_____. 2011. "Human Resources: National Talent Safari", *China Economic Quarterly* 15, 2: 15–19.

Suttmeier, Richard P. 2020. "Chinese Science Policy at a Crossroads", *Issues in Science and Technology* 36, 2: 58–63.

US Federal Bureau of Investigation (FBI). 2018. *China: The Risk to Academia*. Washington, DC: FBI.

US National Science Board, 2018. *Science & Engineering Indicators 2018*. Alexandria, VA: US National Science Foundation.

US Senate Permanent Subcommittee on Investigations. 2019. *Threats to the U.S. Research Enterprise: China's Talent Recruitment Plans* (a Staff Report). Washington,

DC: U.S. Senate Permanent Subcommittee on Investigations, Committee on Homeland Security and Governmental Affairs.

Wang Huiyao. 2011. "China's New Talent Strategy: Impact on China's Development and Its Global Exchange", *SAIS Review* 31, 2: 49–64.

Zweig, David and Han Donglin. 2010. "'Sea Turtles' or 'Seaweed'? The Employment of Overseas Returnees in China", in *The Internationalization of Labour Markets*, ed. Christiane Kuptsch. Geneva, Switzerland: International Institute for Labour Studies, International Labour Organization, pp. 89–104.

Zweig, David and Kang Siqin. 2020. *America Challenges China's National Talent Programs*. Occasional Paper Series no. 4. Washington, DC: Center for Strategic and International Studies.

Zweig, David, Kang Siqin and Wang Huiyao. 2020. "'The Best are yet to Come': State Programs, Domestic Resistance and Reverse Migration of High-level Talent to China", *Journal of Contemporary China* 29, 125: 776–91.

Zweig, David and Wang Huiyao. 2013. "Can China Bring Back the Best? The Communist Party Organizes China's Search for Talent", *The China Quarterly* 215: 590–615.

6

China's International S&T Relations: From Self-Reliance to Active Global Engagement

Denis Fred Simon

"Only if core technologies are in our own hands can we truly hold the initiative in competition and development. Only then can we fundamentally ensure our national economic security, defence security and other aspects of security ... On the traditional competition field of international development, the rules were set by other people ... To seize the great opportunities in the new scientific-technological revolution and industrial transformation, we must enter early on while the new competition field is being built, and even dominate some of the construction of the competition field, so we become a major designer of the new rules of competition and a leader in the new field".

PRC President Xi Jinping, Speech to the Chinese Academy of Sciences/
Chinese Academy of Engineering, Beijing, June 2014

Introduction

The above statement by Chinese President Xi Jinping could not have been more prescient as just three short years later, China found itself embroiled in both a deleterious "trade war" and destructive "technology war" with the United States and several of America's allies. Under the former administration of President Donald Trump, the US attempted to constrain Chinese access to America's advanced technological know-how and even to limit the access of PRC students and scholars to American universities and research institutes. While China has sought to maintain its commitment to global engagement and the open policy launched under Deng Xiaoping in the late 1970s, the US—on both a unilateral and a multilateral basis—has sought to disengage with China and in essence slow down the pace of Chinese technological advance. These developments underscore the concerns expressed by President Xi at the CAS/CAE gathering that the once rather "user friendly" international environment has become increasingly challenging in terms of welcoming expanded cooperation and collaboration with the People's Republic of China. Little did President Xi recognise just how challenging that environment would become by mid-2020.

The 21st century represents a new, dynamic period in world history in terms of the conduct of international S&T affairs. One might even designate it a "new era of science diplomacy" (Ruffini 2017), though reference was made to the idea of leveraging the role of science and technology in foreign policy back in the 1970s when Henry Kissinger served as the US Secretary of State (Lord 2019). The idea of science diplomacy refers to "the use and application of science cooperation to help build bridges and enhance relationships between and amongst societies, with a particular interest in working in areas where there might not be other mechanisms for official engagement at an official level" (Turekian 2009). While for much of the 1980s and 1990s, China was a "target" for science diplomacy, with the West and Japan using S&T cooperation as a mechanism to bring China more into the mainstream of international relations, by the early 21st century, China itself started to embark on its own course of pro-active science diplomacy to enhance its image, visibility and reputation across different parts of the world, especially in the 60+ so-called "Belt & Road" (BRI) countries.

Of course, the ability of science diplomacy to thrive has been aided by the onset of globalisation. This phenomenon has enabled the almost unimpeded movement of people, products and services, and knowledge across borders and cultures. China has been one of its major beneficiaries, utilising access to the world's most advanced corporations, best universities, most dynamic research institutes, and government and non-governmental international organisations and scholarly bodies as a way to support and advance its own modernisation efforts (Samuelson 2018). For most of the last 40 years, China has had increasingly unencumbered access to these critical repositories of know-how and information, though Chinese leaders also have felt steadily more and more anxious about the degree to which the openness of the world economy would continue to work in China's favour (Zukus 2017). In fact, we likely also have entered an era in which the forces of globalisation are increasingly being threatened by the rise of "techno-nationalism" across the globe.

This chapter analyses China's evolving strategy, policies and practices regarding its international science and technology relations. It highlights China's strategic posture and footprint in terms of its goal of becoming a player of influence in the international S&T system. It examines the PRC's relationships with several major S&T countries, comparing similarities and differences in terms of the depth and breadth of cooperation. Finally, the chapter concludes with a discussion of the changing landscape of the international S&T system, with a focus on the ways in which China's expanded participation might alter the evolving structure and operation of the system in the coming years.

China's Evolving Global S&T Footprint

China's engagement in international S&T affairs began with the founding of the PRC in 1949, when the CPC formulated and implemented a bilateral S&T cooperation agreement with the former Soviet Union (*yi bian dao*), a relatively short-lived arrangement that was followed by the policy of self-reliance (*zi li geng sheng*) in response to Moscow's termination of technology assistance in 1960. The relationship between Moscow and Beijing had been highly asymmetrical as China was very dependent on the USSR for massive inflows of industrial equipment and managerial know-how to jump-start the Chinese economy after the end of the civil war with the Kuomintang in 1949. In the late 1970s, following the turmoil of the Cultural Revolution and beginning with Deng Xiaoping's Reform and Opening Up policy, China's leadership shifted its focus to rapid economic and S&T development. In terms of China's international S&T relations, guidelines were adopted to lay the foundation for expanded global engagement and a more pro-active international involvement, including a significant growth in the level of international S&T cooperation. By the end of the 20th century, China had achieved full-scale implementation of an international S&T cooperation system focused on acquiring foreign technology and fostering cooperative arrangements with leading international scientific institutions.

With the open policy and general abandonment of the policy of self-reliance, China joined numerous international and regional S&T organisations, and promoted foreign plant, equipment and technology imports. During the first two decades of the 21st century, the government pushed for more mutually beneficial international S&T cooperation, developing better-articulated programmes in an effort to achieve greater symmetry of results and better-defined mutual benefit. Currently, China is playing an increasingly active role in international organisations, encompassing major global science and engineering programmes, while at the same time strengthening technical assistance to developing countries (Cheng 2008). Since 2012, China has sought to plan and promote innovation with what it now characterises as a global vision, embodied in various key national policies.[1]

At present, China is in the process of transforming itself from primarily a technology importer to a technology importer and exporter, as it pursues its strategy of promoting an indigenous innovation strategy alongside global engagement (CPC 2016). Central to its efforts to move from imitator and copy-cat to an innovation-driven nation are a series of policies and initiatives associated with becoming a central player in international S&T affairs (Xie, Zhang and Lai 2014). By 2020, China had established S&T cooperation partnerships with 166 countries and regions and executed over 100 inter-governmental agreements on S&T cooperation. In addition, the PRC has joined over 200 inter-governmental international S&T cooperation and research organisations. It has appointed 144 S&T diplomats for its 70+ overseas offices in 47 countries. And, at the beginning of 2018, over 400 Chinese scientists held office in international S&T-related NGOs, including approximately 30 as chairman and 50 as vice-chairman. Among the world's 48 major cross-border big science programmes and projects, four have been initiated by China and 17 have China's official participation; China also serves as an observer in three programmes. This all demonstrates that China's presence in the structure and organisation of global S&T governance is becoming more meaningful and steadily expanding.

The Administrative Structure of China's International S&T Policies and Engagement

The S&T governance structure of China's international S&T engagement is composed of a number of key state agencies and organisations. There are multiple ministries and commissions, central and local government entities, and academic institutions involved in this sphere of activity. While aspects of this structure continue to evolve as a result of organisational changes first introduced at the 19th Party Congress and the "Liang Hui" meetings in March 2018, the basic fabric remains the same (Liu et al. 2011). Three organisations have emerged as the most important in organising and managing China's international S&T relations: the Ministry of Science and Technology (MOST), the Chinese Academy of Sciences (CAS) and the China Association for Science and Technology (CAST).[2]

The Ministry of Science and Technology (MOST)

The Ministry of Science and Technology is the predominant entity that plans and implements China's overseas S&T activities, providing the overarching framework for international S&T cooperation and exchanges at different levels and by increasingly diverse actors. Since its mission is to foster economic growth and technological advance, MOST coordinates basic research, frontier technology research and the development of key and advanced technologies. It is mandated also to formulate policies on international S&T cooperation and exchanges through bilateral and multilateral channels, guiding relevant departments and local governments in international interactions, appointing and supervising S&T diplomats and facilitating assistance to and from China. MOST's Executive Office is responsible for drafting and formulating important policies and handling tasks assigned by the State Council.

A number of other departments play key roles in China's S&T development, commercialisation and foreign relations. The Department of International Cooperation (DIC) is without question the most important of these, as it bears responsibility for China's international S&T cooperation. The department reports to one of the MOST vice-ministers who manages the international S&T portfolio. The DIC drafts policies on international S&T cooperation and exchange, providing guidance for the international S&T affairs of relevant agencies and local governments. For example, the department organises inter-governmental innovation dialogues and bilateral and multilateral S&T cooperation agreements and exchanges; tracks country-specific deployment of key S&T programmes; conducts technology forecasts; and promotes the construction of international S&T cooperation bases.

In March 2018, the State Administration of Foreign Experts Affairs (SAFEA) was placed under the oversight of MOST. SAFEA, heretofore, had been responsible over several decades for bringing to China a broad range of experienced scientific and technical experts to assist their Chinese counterparts with various developmental problems and issues. It also has sent many PRC delegations abroad, especially to the US, Western Europe and Japan for training in management and an assortment of technical fields.

As part of the same change, the China National Natural Science Foundation (NNSFC) was also moved under the direct oversight of MOST. The NNSFC oversees support for much of the research in basic science that occurs within China. Its creation was modelled after the US National Science Foundation; the onset of serious peer review in the submission and awarding of grants helped improve the reliability and credibility of the funding system. The NNSFC has developed extensive links with top scientists around the world and has included members of the international S&T community in the periodic reviews of its operational performance.

An important affiliated agency under MOST is the China Science and Technology Exchange Center (CSTEC). CSTEC has been assigned many important responsibilities, such as managing science and technology programmes/projects involving foreign elements related to research, implementation and training activities; managing science and technology representative offices in foreign countries; overseeing the experts exchange programme; and managing the programme to attract global scientific talents. The current workforce of CSTEC numbers more than 100, of which 20 are representatives of overseas scientific and technological offices. As a non-profit public service organisation, since its inception (more than 40 years ago), all its operating expenses have been granted by the state budget equivalent to more than one billion USD annually.

The Chinese Academy of Sciences (CAS)

The Chinese Academy of Sciences, until recently directed by President Bai Chunli,[3] is structured as a comprehensive, integrated R&D network. It is the nation's high-end think tank, a merit-based learned society as well as a system of higher education and has long functioned as the linchpin of China's national and global S&T ambitions. As of 2018, there were 124 institutions directly under CAS, with 104 research institutes, three universities, 12 branch academies, 11 supporting organisations in 23 provinces and 25 affiliated legal entities. CAS is constantly undergoing reform and change, with mergers and consolidation of institutes becoming more and more common. The size of the overall staff is 67,900, with 56,000 serving as professional researchers.

Since its inception, CAS has made significant progress in fostering international S&T cooperation relationships (Bai 2017a). It has succeeded in developing extensive and diverse partnerships with research institutes and scientists across the globe, and is well positioned to play a central role in shaping China's S&T diplomacy from a substantive point of view (Poo and Wang 2014). To take some recent examples, CAS has accomplished the following:

- establishment of 20 collaborative groups with the German Max Planck Society in areas including astronomy, life sciences and materials science;
- implementation of several talent programmes (such as the CAS Fellowship for Senior and Young International Scientists), attracting over 1,000 foreign scientists and engineers to conduct R&D activities at its institutes;
- initiation in 2016 of a BRI action plan calling for international S&T cooperation, training and cultivating more than 1,800 S&T management and high-tech personnel for relevant countries; and

- plans to become the spearhead and central hub for an Asia-Pacific, Eurasia and Asia-Africa collaborative innovation network system (Bai 2017b).

The structure and organisation of CAS are well developed, with a number of departments responsible for managing domestic R&D programmes and international S&T cooperation. The Bureau of International Cooperation's responsibilities are the most central to the international mission; its mandate includes formulating strategies, plans, rules and regulations for CAS international cooperation and exchanges; coordinating academy-level international cooperation affairs; initiating and managing key cooperative programmes and fellowships; and maintaining links with related agencies of international organisations in China.

The China Association for Science and Technology (CAST)

Founded in 1958, the China Association for Science and Technology (CAST) is under the direct jurisdiction of the Secretariat of the CPC's Central Committee. Its role includes promoting S&T exchanges and indigenous innovation, protecting and advancing the interests of scientific workers, organising S&T professionals to participate in formulating national S&T policies, and facilitating non-governmental international S&T exchanges and cooperation through developing liaisons with foreign S&T associations and scientists.

CAST is made up of national scientific and professional societies and local S&T associations. Among the national societies, 42 are in the natural sciences, 73 in engineering, 15 in agriculture, 26 in medical sciences and 23 in interdisciplinary scientific fields. Local associations—totalling around 3,000—include those organised by provinces, autonomous regions and municipalities directly under the central government, cities and counties. Among its various departments, the Bureau of International Liaison is mainly responsible for international S&T affairs. It is responsible for working out annual plans and advice for CAST bilateral communications, conducting research and summarising experiences on S&T exchanges, and exploring and developing partnerships with S&T associations in key countries and regions.

China's International S&T Policies: Continuity and Change

Since Deng Xiaoping's opening up and reform, the Chinese government has been consistent in both encouraging Chinese organisations to engage abroad to better leverage international S&T resources and formulating a series of policies to guide its S&T engagement with other countries (Bound et al. 2013).

Today, these policies reflect the growing emphasis on strengthening indigenous innovation, especially in view of the impact of the so-called US-China trade/tech war on PRC access to advanced technologies. From China's standpoint, indigenous innovation is necessarily coupled with an outward-looking strategy that calls for S&T partnerships and international collaborations. International S&T relations are thus best understood as constructed to serve China's goal of becoming a global innovation leader, especially in key technologies such as clean energy, artificial intelligence and life sciences (Cao and Suttmeier 2017).

China's state-led efforts to achieve indigenous innovation have not been well received by Western rivals (Atkinson, Cory and Ezell 2017). The 15 Year Medium-to-Long-term Plan for Science and Technology (MLP; Ministry of Science and Technology 2006), for example, was roundly denounced in a US Chamber of Commerce-sponsored report bearing the title, *China's Drive for Indigenous Innovation: A Web of Industrial Policies* (McGregor 2010; Ministry of Science and Technology 2016b). The report accused China of "hunkering behind the 'techno-nationalism' moat", switching "from defense to offense" in light of its economic ascendance as well as its fear of foreign domination (McGregor 2010). The MLP, according to the report, "is considered by many international technology companies to be a blueprint for technology theft on a scale the world has never seen before". The report obviously contains a great deal of hyperbole; nonetheless, the MLP's policies did provoke a strong reaction from China's major trade and technology partners that has not dissipated over time. Given that innovation capability and talent increasingly drive competition among countries, China's leaders recognise that a strong domestic S&T capacity has become the core requirement for meaningful and productive bilateral and multilateral S&T cooperation (Simon and Cao 2009b). For China, the emphasis on indigenous innovation, however, no longer meant self-reliance as was the case in the 1960s. Rather, it has been seen as a pathway to strengthen China's leverage in the international technology market.

Budgetary allocations for international S&T cooperation have grown apace with domestic S&T spending, especially at the local level (OECD 2014). As suggested above, China's emphasis on indigenous innovation should not obscure the fact that the government has spared no efforts to deepen and enlarge bilateral and multilateral S&T partnerships. The 13th Five-Year S&T Plan,[4] in contrast to its predecessors, designates tasks and goals that serve Beijing's current strategy of science diplomacy, transforming itself from passive recipient to active donor.

China's international S&T cooperation strategy is carefully differentiated according to a categorisation of partners into developed, developing and neighbouring countries. The Plan calls for increased openness of China's national S&T programmes, including offering governmental support to overseas experts who are expected to take the lead, or at least participate in, national S&T programme strategic research. It also calls for deepening international cooperation on an equal basis with international partners (a claim which has been met with some scepticism). To achieve its goals, China has initiated and organised significant international S&T programmes and projects; has become more actively involved in helping to set global S&T agendas; has accelerated the sharing of global large-scale scientific research information; and has begun active participation in global S&T governance, including the formulation of international S&T cooperation rules. Chinese scientists have increased their participation in scientific exchange programmes and sought official positions in major international scientific and technological organisations. China's most recent, and clearly most dramatic, diplomatic move in the science field is the BRI S&T cooperation network, which calls for promoting technology transfer and assisting countries in training young scientists, a clear indication that China plans to play a central role in the international S&T landscape as a technology exporter as well as importer (Zou 2018).

In January 2018, President Xi presided over the second round of the Leading Group for Comprehensively Deepening Reform of the central government. One important resolution called for actively initiating and organising international Big Science programmes and projects, another for strengthening regulations in IPR protection. Despite comments from foreign critics that the PRC appears to be becoming more techno-nationalistic, China clearly continues to look outward—out of both conviction and necessity—as it plans its S&T future.

China's International S&T Relations with Major Countries

Under its government-to-government bilateral arrangements, numerous scientists and engineers have participated in a broad array of collaborative projects with their counterparts abroad. Since the mid-1990s, however, China has greatly expanded its international S&T engagements. More and more activities are now occurring outside the government bilateral accords and now include a rapidly expanding number of university-to-university ties, corporate linkages and cooperation with think tanks. Most recently, China's provincial and local S&T organisations also have become increasingly involved in orchestrating overseas S&T ties; many Chinese provinces and municipalities are leading the charge to find new, dynamic international S&T cooperation partnerships.

Although China is extending S&T cooperation partnerships with an increasing number of countries globally, its focus is still on working with the major developed states, based on national recognition of the prevailing technology gaps.

China–US S&T Relations

The 1979–89 period featured the inception of China–US S&T cooperation. The 1979 agreement on science and technology has functioned as the overall framework under which the two governments have promoted S&T cooperation in various forms and through a large number of channels. The two countries also concluded an accord to allow for student and scholar exchanges. From 1978 to 1987, the number of students and visiting scholars sent by the Chinese government to the US reached 25,000. The China–US S&T relationship is overseen by a Joint Commission that meets on a scheduled basis to review existing programmes and identify new areas of cooperation. The membership on the Joint Commission reflects participation from the key government agencies tied respectively to China's State Council and the US Executive branch of government.

Bilateral S&T cooperation experienced rapid growth during the early years as it was new and exciting; the two parties invested significantly to support joint programmes. By 1987, there had been 27 signed cooperative agreements. That said, China–US S&T cooperation during this period also was constrained by a variety of political and financial factors and was largely asymmetrical and one-sided because China concentrated on utilising US-provided instruments and equipment, and experts from the US played the primary role in knowledge dissemination and personnel training. Nevertheless, it is important to bear in mind that the two sides also had quite different objectives. The US intended to counter the former USSR by developing rapport and trust with China, and the US technical community was interested in the distinctive natural and social phenomena in China. The Chinese side, however, assumed that engagement with the international science and technology system, especially with the US, would be a useful vehicle for promoting economic construction and catching up with world's leading powers (Suttmeier 2014).

From 1990 to 1999, bilateral S&T relations witnessed some apparent decline, followed by a resumption of activity. Due to the events in Tiananmen Square on 4 June 1989, many programmes were curtailed, including China–US space cooperation. The US also terminated high-level political exchanges and postponed meetings of the Joint Commission, which dealt a heavy blow to

S&T cooperation. Gradual resumption of bilateral S&T cooperation began in 1994, when the two parties decided to restore the Joint Commission Meeting (JCM). With China's accession to the World Trade Organisation in 2001 and the smooth transition to the next generation of Chinese leaders—Jiang Zemin to Hu Jintao—the possibilities for new growth began to appear (Suttmeier and Simon 2014).

From 2000 to 2015, China–US relations were characterised by comprehensive and rapid development. Then President Hu Jintao remarked in 2012 at the 14th meeting of the Joint Commission that S&T cooperation had become an important driving force for Sino–US relations, and a critical component of people-to-people exchange. This cooperation fell into six main areas: energy and physics, health and life science, ecology and environmental science, agriculture and food science, science education, and metrology. It is worth noting that beginning in 2006, when the MLP was launched, the agenda for bilateral S&T cooperation reflected a heightened awareness of the urgent need to explore interdisciplinary research themes, frontier science and international hot issues such as global warming, new and clean energy, carbon capture and aggregation. In other words, the rising salience of these global issues altered the context for both sides to think about how S&T cooperation might proceed. A series of new initiatives were taken that were based on high-level political commitments. The Strategic Economic Dialogue (SED) that came into place in 2006 and later the Strategic and Economic Dialogue (S&ED) produced an enormous expansion of activities and functions. The latter launched the Ten-Year Framework on Energy and Environment Cooperation in 2008, designating clean water, clean air, clean vehicles and energy efficiency as key areas with high priority for cooperation. By 2011, China had risen to become the top collaborating partner of the US, outpacing the UK, Japan and Germany, nations that have been long-time partners of the US in science (Suttmeier 2014). By the end of the decade, in jointly authored scientific papers, Chinese scientists claimed first authorship much more frequently than US counterparts (Wagner, Bornmann and Leydesdorff 2015).

One of the key elements of these new dialogues was the initiation of the China–US Innovation Dialogue, which began in 2008 as part of a discussion about how the Chinese side could improve performance of its own innovation system. The Innovation Dialogue had great potential when it started because it might have served as a useful vehicle for exchanging meaningful information about the evolving requirements for successful innovation in the twenty-first century. Unfortunately, the Innovation Dialogue ended up being neither a real dialogue nor about innovation. On the US side, growing disenchantment with China in the US Congress led to constraints being placed on the White House Office of Science and Technology Policy (OSTP) about expansion of S&T cooperation; funding was tightly controlled. Moreover, the innovation agenda was hijacked by the Office of the US Trade Representative (USTR) and made to focus on extracting concessions from the Chinese side on pressing trade matters. The bulk of discussions ended up concentrating on dismantling Chinese policies regarding the promotion of indigenous innovation. On the Chinese side, the prize still remained in sight, though their side also was often distracted from the core innovation-related issues that they expected to drive the Innovation Dialogue.

The Trump administration took a number of major steps to alter the essential dynamics of the overall China–US S&T relationship. Certain things have become clear as the two countries attempt to find a way around their on-going trade war—which essentially has been centred on technology issues. First, with the general weakening of the OSTP, the S&T relationship lacks a major policy advocate on the US side. Second, Congress remains reluctant to provide any substantial funding for growing the relationship in new areas. This is unfortunate because with China making real progress in terms of its S&T capabilities, there is now more opportunity than ever to take advantage of the greater symmetry in the relationship (Perez 2017). Third, because of tensions over trade, technology transfer, North Korea and the South China Sea, the political environment does not support maintaining the status quo let alone an expanded relationship. In fact, the newest bilateral S&T agreement (2018) did not experience a smooth renewal process during the most recent negotiations; the final decision to renew the agreement was done under the shadow of darkness and given a very low profile from both governments. The decision by the Trump Administration in March 2018 to invoke special legislation under the US Section 301 laws concerning trade and investment with China brought on the beginning of "a trade war" with China with technology theft and other related IPR issues positioned at the centre of American concerns (USTR 2017). Even as the two countries seemed to have arrived at an initial agreement over their trade issues by the end of 2019, not much real progress was made. Even under the new Biden administration, Washington and Beijing still remain at loggerheads over several delicate issues regarding technology, national security and IPR issues past and present (OECD/EUIPO 2016).

And finally, the growing reality is that non-government exchanges and cooperation regarding the private sector, universities and think tanks have far surpassed the level of government-to-government cooperation. This was the main thrust, albeit implicit, of comments made by former Vice-Premier Liu

Yandong during her Fall 2017 visit to the US where she highlighted the need for greater emphasis and support for people-to-people diplomacy in the area of China–US science and cooperation. It also became the focal point of critical comments by the Director of the Federal Bureau of Investigation in early 2018 when he warned American higher education institutions about the vulnerability of their institutions to "non-traditional" collectors coming from China of critical scientific and technical information. The onset of the COVID-19 virus in Wuhan in early 2020 and its transition into a major global pandemic further exacerbated the tensions between the Trump administration and the Chinese leadership under President Xi Jinping. Finger-pointing, accusations about blame and lack of transparency, and even racism, etc. have travelled across the Pacific in both directions, thus further damaging the possibilities for rekindling the kind of relationship that existed in the past.

China–Russia S&T Relations

China–Russia S&T relations should be divided into three phases—Phase One: close China–Soviet S&T cooperation (1949–60); Phase Two: the Sino–Soviet Split (1961–90); and Phase Three: renewed China–Russia S&T cooperation in the post-Cold War era (1991–present). Relations today between the two countries under Russia's Vladimir Putin and China's Xi Jinping respectively seem to be on the verge of a golden era, as they both see expanded opportunities for re-building their bilateral S&T relationship.

During Phase One, the Soviet Union transferred a variety of technologies to China that helped lay the foundation for the renewal of industrial production, assisted China with formulating a 12-year plan for S&T development, established S&T research and design institutes, developed scientific research and industrial technology and cultivated S&T talent (Jersild 2014). That said, the over-dependence on the Soviet Union for technology introduction and implementation ultimately proved to have a negative impact when Moscow suddenly withdrew its experts and terminated all assistance in 1960 due to rising political tensions between the Communist Party organisations in the two countries.

Several agreements were critical in terms of laying the initial overall framework for S&T cooperation between Moscow and Beijing. The 1954 Sino–Soviet Agreement on Science and Technology Cooperation ushered in Moscow's 156 technical aid projects, mostly in industrial production and equipment, as well as the establishment of a special joint committee that administered and oversaw S&T cooperation between the two countries.

Moscow provided Beijing with a significant amount of technical data and documents, such as design data for power plants, coal mines, machinery, teaching outlines and technical standards. Most of the projects were located in China's old industrial northeast region. In 1956, Moscow sent S&T experts to Beijing to help China formulate its "12-Year Plan for Science and Technology Development", which was a milestone for setting in place China's S&T efforts under Mao Zedong. Both the development of the plan and the development of China's entire post-1949 S&T system were heavily shaped by Russian influence, and it took major reform efforts under Deng Xiaoping after 1978, lasting till the start of the 21st century, to come out from under the heavy weight of that Soviet influence.

Soviet assistance in S&T talent cultivation was conducted in three ways: China sent experts and outstanding S&T professionals to the USSR, either as interns or researchers, to work and gain knowledge in areas that were seen as most urgent for economic and industrial development. These professionals would return to establish the foundation of critically needed technologies for growing the Chinese economy. In some instances, China would directly recruit Soviet experts to help set up scientific research institutes within CAS and relevant departments and promote comprehensive cooperation with the Chinese S&T community. Large groups of Chinese professionals were organised to receive training by Soviet experts already in China to support ongoing development projects. Training in the USSR helped to spearhead the development of China's computer industry in the 1950s; the majority of the first cadre of computer scientists in China were all trained there.

Apart from S&T support in the civilian sector, Moscow also provided technologies that were of great importance for developing China's military capability and national defence. In 1954, Khrushchev agreed to assist China in developing atomic energy for peaceful purposes, in exchange for Mao's political support. This was the first step in China's research and production effort in nuclear weapons (Lewis and Xue 1991). In 1956, the Eastern Atomic Energy Institute was established in Dubna (a designated "science town" in the Moscow *oblast*). China shouldered 20 per cent of the costs for construction and operation; Moscow, 50 per cent. To a certain degree, this joint endeavour helped lay the theoretical and personnel foundation for the Chinese nuclear weapons programme. In 1958, a heavy water reactor, cyclotron, and a scientific nuclear research facility were completed in Tuoli, a suburb southwest of Beijing, which enormously improved research conditions for China's nuclear physics programme. Sophisticated technology and equipment were provided to support the research, design and production of China's first atomic bomb and missile delivery systems.

Needless to say, this brief period of close China–Soviet technology cooperation reflected Moscow's *Realpolitik*, even if much of it was couched in terms of a Communist brotherhood (Shen and Xia 2012). Khrushchev's decision to assist China in developing nuclear energy for peaceful purposes occurred within the framework of a post-Stalin power struggle in which Mao's support was critical for strengthening his political status within the former Soviet government. Moscow's support for China's nuclear programme subsequently expanded to include weapons-related technologies in 1957, after Mao expressed his support for Khrushchev, who was under threat of being overthrown in Moscow by a senior group who objected to his programme of "de-Stalinisation". Mao, however, soon became disenchanted with Khrushchev's de-Stalinisation campaign and let his dissatisfaction be known. Predictably, the flow of Soviet nuclear aid to China became increasingly limited in pace, scope and depth when Khrushchev's position was firmly secure (Shen and Xia 2012). In addition, as China fell into the turbulence and radicalism of the Cultural Revolution (1966–76), the Russians had become increasingly concerned about what was happening in China, about Mao's leadership and about security issues along the Sino–Soviet border.

Phase Two saw cooperation between the two countries come to a grinding halt. Military tensions about border issues along the Amur (Ussuri) River on the Chinese north-eastern border as well as the revolutionary posture of the Chinese Communist Party in its relations abroad made for difficult times. It was not until Gorbachev came to power and offered an olive branch to China that S&T cooperation could be restored. Gorbachev offered to work with China to build a railroad line linking Urumqi and Kazakhstan, to engage China in Russia's space programme and to resolve the navigation channel issues on the Amur River.

In Phase Three, the so-called "post-Cold War era", China–Russia S&T cooperation has strengthened and become increasingly institutionalised, the result of both traditional political ties and the practical need to maintain strategic coordination to balance the power and influence of the United States (Wilson 2014). Shortly after the collapse of the USSR, Beijing sent a vice-ministerial level S&T delegation to Moscow to establish inter-governmental S&T relations. In 1992, the two sides concluded the Agreement on China–Russia Science and Technology Cooperation, setting up the Standing Committee for S&T cooperation at the vice-premier level Sino–Russia Committee of Economic, Trade, and S&T Cooperation. More than 200 inter-governmental programmes were formulated during 1993–6, covering almost all aspects of socioeconomic development. The mechanism of regular meetings between

Chinese and Russian premiers was established in 1997, which was a historic milestone in the process of institutionalising bilateral S&T relations.

The 1998–2012 period can be categorised as a time of exploration for high-tech industry transformation and innovation cooperation. China and Russia signed a Memorandum of Understanding (MOU) for Innovation Cooperation, creating a working group to guide, supervise and facilitate joint R&D in such diverse areas as nuclear energy, telecommunications, shipbuilding, environmental protection, biotech, aeronautics and astronautics. The Sino–Russian Science and Technology Park in Changchun began operation in 2006 as a demonstration project for cooperation in wider areas.

From 2012 onward, Sino–Russia S&T cooperation has gradually shifted from short-term, small-scale to mid- to long-term cooperation on big projects. An MOU was initiated to direct joint efforts in priority areas including nanotechnology, materials science, life science, energy, and information and communication technology. The most recent important development is the first Sino–Russia Innovation Dialogue convened by MOST and Russia's Department of Economic Development in June 2017. The dialogue engages some 200 representatives from government, universities, research institutes, industry, investment institutions, technology transfer institutes and high-tech innovation enterprises. The two parties issued a joint statement that commits concerted bilateral efforts to coordinate national innovation policies and to strengthen communications over issues such as innovation strategy, trends, construction of national innovation systems, technology transfer, mass entrepreneurship, S&T finance and industry conglomeration. In addition, China and Russia will support cooperation between business incubators located in both countries, encourage young people to start their own businesses, strengthen cooperation between Chinese and Russian science parks and push for the establishment of a China–Russia technology industry cooperation platform.

China–Japan S&T Relations

S&T exchanges between China and Japan began in the 1960s, initially conducted largely by civil society organisations, with limited government participation.[5] In 1978, following the normalisation of relations six years earlier, the Japanese government established official cooperative S&T links with China; the principal participants were Japan's Ministry of Foreign Affairs (MOFA) and China's State S&T Commission (later Ministry of Science and Technology). Cooperation during this period was characterised largely by one-way technology transfer to China, which was then eager for the scientific knowledge and industrial technology it regarded as indispensable for building its basic science and research system and industrial base. The 1980 Agreement on China–Japan Science and Technology Cooperation marked the inception of the so-called "horizontal" cooperative mechanism that expedited cooperation and, more importantly, significantly expanded the forms, channels and participants involved in the cooperative S&T relationship.

Despite the often strained state of the bilateral relationship stemming from the unresolved issues associated with World War II, Sino–Japan S&T cooperation is increasing (Yahuda 2013). Expanded cooperation is conducted under the overall framework of several important agreements, including Agreements on China–Japan Science and Technology Cooperation, China–Japan Cooperation in Environmental Science, and China–Japan Nuclear Energy Cooperation; exchanges and cooperation through the Japan International Cooperation Agency (JICA); and direct cooperation between the S&T ministries and departments of each country. Personnel exchanges are witnessing a rapid increase, in that major Chinese government departments and research institutes have established regular and stable cooperative partnerships with Japanese counterparts.

The Joint Committee of Sino–Japan S&T Cooperation serves as an important organisation that oversees, administers and promotes exchanges and joint R&D programmes. The 10th annual meeting held in Tokyo in 2003 was of particular significance in that the parties pledged increased collaboration based on the principle of "equal status and mutual benefits". There was an emphasis on high-level exchanges, encouraging the active participation of universities, research institutes and industries. China and Japan agreed that the focus of cooperation in the future should be on biotech, life science (including agricultural and food technologies), IT, nanotechnology, energy and the environment. The last named has arguably proven to be the most effective, given its large scale and high level of personnel exchange, covering wide areas of cooperation. Beijing and Tokyo signed the first agreement on environmental protection in 1994, and the inter-governmental joint committee organised the first conference to designate a series of environmental protection programmes. In 1996 Japanese Prime Minister Takeshita Noboru initiated the China–Japan Friendship Environmental Protection Center through Japan's Office of Development Assistance (ODA). Currently, the centre plays an important role in pollution prevention technology, environmental monitoring, environmental information, environmental strategy and policy studies, personnel training, and environmental technology exchanges. Japan has been particularly concerned about the level of acid rain flowing across Northern Japan from the industrial pollution in China's northeast where many older factories still continue to produce goods using dated technology and energy sources, including burning China's notoriously dirty coal. Japan also is concerned about its coastal waters, given China's offshore drilling activity and the extensive Chinese fishing fleet in the area.

Apart from inter-governmental cooperation, non-governmental S&T exchange and cooperation also are playing increasingly important roles, as investments and R&D centres established by Japanese high-tech enterprises are rapidly growing. Demonstration projects have included Sharp Wuxi (LCD), SGNEC (chips), Shanghai Huahong NEC (semi-conductors), Shanghai Fanuc (robots), world telecommunications tycoon NTT Docomo (Internet), and Huawei and China Unicom (Internet of Things).

Japanese enterprises are seeking greater cooperation with Chinese universities to expand their business channels in China. For instance, Sumitomo and Shanghai Jiaotong University signed an agreement to foster joint R&D, personnel training, and co-funded technology development programmes with high potential. The establishment of the Daikin–Tsinghua R&D Centre marked the first S&T initiative in China by Japanese air-conditioner makers, intended to develop energy-saving technologies. Other Japanese industrial leaders have established overseas R&D centres in China, including Toshiba, Ricoh and Fujitsu (Zhang 2007). In addition, with the platform provided by MOST and the Japan Science and Technology Agency (JST), universities in both countries are able to cooperate on S&T innovation and other urgent S&T-related issues. In 2016, MOST and JST initiated a joint programme on the urban environment and energy with participation from Chinese universities (Tsinghua, PKU and Zhejiang) and Japanese universities such as the University of Tokyo, Tohoku University and Nagoya University (Embassy of the PRC in Japan 2016).

Notwithstanding these increases, Sino–Japan S&T relations occur within an overall framework of the political strains mentioned earlier stemming from historical conflicts, current territorial disputes and worsening security competition in East Asia (Newby 2018). In response to a unilateral move by Tokyo to nationalise the Senkaku/Diaoyu Islands in 2012, Beijing cancelled the annual meeting organised by the China–Japan S&T Cooperation Committee, which was not resumed until 2015. A highlight of the new engagement between the two countries involves energy conservation and environmental protection. The 2nd Sino–Japan Energy Saving and Environmental Protection Science and Technology Summit was held in Dongguan in December 2017, which facilitated the confirmation of multiple projects between Chinese and Japanese enterprises in energy saving and air pollution control.

The first "Sino–Japanese energy conservation and environmental protection technology summit forum" was held in Dongguan in 2016. The "China–Japan Energy Conservation and Environmental Protection Cooperation Pavilion" and the "China–Japan Energy Conservation and Environmental Protection Science and Technology Summit Forum" have been identified as the permanent activities of China (Dongguan) International Scientific and Technological Cooperation Week. China's energy-saving and environmental protection industry is developing rapidly with huge investments and a vast potential market; Japan has advanced technology and management experience that China requires (Swanström and Kokubun 2012). In 2017, the Guangdong Provincial Department of Science and Technology also released the Guidelines for Joint Innovation International Cooperation Projects, focusing on encouraging projects jointly supported by China and Japan in various fields for the purpose of moving new ideas into commercial production.

China's S&T Relations with the EU

S&T relations between China and the EU have undergone fast development since the normalisation of diplomatic ties in 1975.[6] The agreements between the EU and China exist in parallel with a host of bilateral S&T agreements that China now has in place with various EU members. With Brexit, the departure of the UK from the European Union, the Sino–UK S&T relationship will take on added importance for the two countries. The EU and China signed a formal Science & Technology Cooperation Agreement in 1999, implemented through a joint steering committee, which has since served as providing guidelines and an overall framework for cooperation. In 2008, the European Atomic Energy Community and the Chinese government signed an agreement that put in place R&D cooperation for peaceful uses of nuclear energy. In 2003, the EU–China Comprehensive Strategic Partnership was created and cooperation in a wide range of areas has been deepened and broadened, resulting in high interdependence today. The two parties adopted the EU–China 2020 Strategic Agenda for Cooperation and had the first High Level Innovation Cooperation Dialogue during the 16th EU–China Summit held in November 2013. Through regular meetings and a broad range of sectoral dialogues, the Strategic Agenda has been implemented under the cooperative umbrella set by the annual High Level Strategic Dialogue, the annual High Level Economic and Trade Dialogue and the bi-annual People-to-People Dialogue.

China has been recognised by the EU as a key partner on science, technology and innovation, with EU–China cooperation intensifying in recent years (EU

2015; Le Corre and Sepulchre 2016). China was the third most important international partner country under the Framework Programme 7 (FP7) that ran from 2007 to 2013, with 383 participants from Chinese organisations in 274 collaborative research projects and a total EU contribution of €35.24 million. Moreover, the well-recognised Marie Skłodowska-Curie Programme has included around 959 Chinese participants. China has been a key partner country in Horizon 2020 (H2020), the EU's special Framework Programme for Research and Innovation, running from 2014 to 2020. So far, 227 applications from China were presented in 187 eligible proposals, with 60 participations of Chinese organisations in 33 main listed projects (EU 2015).[7]

Among all EU Member States, China's S&T relations with Germany are perhaps the most stable and productive (Shambaugh and Sandschneider 2007). Germany has traditionally loomed large in the Chinese perception of the world S&T landscape due to the country's strong industrial competitiveness and R&D capabilities. During Premier Li Keqiang's 2017 visit to Germany, the two parties announced a "Plan of Action for Sino–German Cooperation: Shaping Innovation" which provides for a strategic high-tech project "Industry 4.0", a German initiative on urbanisation and industrialisation along with informatisation and agricultural modernisation, which are China's policy priorities. This is likely to result in increasing complementarity and coordination between "Made in China 2025" and "Industry 4.0", facilitating innovation and global standard setting in the field of smart manufacturing (State Council 2015). Germany's Federal Ministry of Education and Research (BMBF) issued its China Strategy in 2015, and China's MOST issued "Jointly Shaping the Future through Technology Innovation: Germany Strategy" in 2016, reflecting consensus on a shared responsibility to lead a new round of innovative industrial and economic change, one based on increased policy dialogue and enhanced S&T cooperation between the two countries.

There remain, however, some areas in which Germany shows little enthusiasm to cooperate, out of deep-seated concern that cooperation in some high-tech fields (for example, development of new automobile engines and solar panels) will erode its technologically competitive edge. The German government remains cautious in its approach to cooperation with China, given China's poor record regarding IPR protection (European Commission 2018). In dealing with China, Germany is trying to strike a reasonable political balance between protecting its own competitive interests regarding the China market and ensuring some sort of alignment with the US and its other NATO partners.

Main Outstanding Issues and Challenges

In spite of the overall progress China has made in institutionalising its international S&T cooperation structure and expanding its cross-border S&T relationships, numerous challenges remain. IPR protection has been, and will continue to be, a serious concern for foreign S&T partners in both public and private sectors. The rise of China as a more active player in global S&T affairs has reflected its strengthened S&T capabilities, thus reducing the S&T gap with developed countries and shifting its relative position from a poor under-developed country to an emerging technological superpower (Literature Research Office of the CCP's Central Committee 2016). This transition has significant implications for its S&T cooperation efforts. Technology imports shaped much of China's cooperative relations during the time when China was playing catch-up; many foreign firms were willing to indulge China even with its lax IP protections as the price of gaining entry to the world's largest and fast-growing market (Breznitz and Murphree 2011). Now that the "Chinese dream" is being realised, and China is increasingly viewed as a serious competitor, relations have become more difficult across a broad spectrum of areas (Friedberg 2020). For example, given China's plans for massive investments in the development of artificial intelligence, will Western countries be willing to collaborate with China and perhaps put their technology at risk? Along with the rise of China's position in the global innovation landscape, it has become increasingly difficult for the country to play the role of learner in its cooperation with developed countries. Clearly, China is in the process of redefining its role to one where it desires more of a co-equal partnership in terms of cooperation and contribution. This will require China to afford far greater IP protection for foreign partnerships; at present, PCT applications by China are roughly one third those of the US.[8]

Despite these challenges, some appreciable progress is being made. The US-China Clean Energy Research Center (CERC) provides one illustrative example. CERC is characterised by public–private consortia underpinned by a strong IPR protection agreement. A special IPR Annex is part of the founding protocol. According to CERC's 2012–13 annual report, projects under the Advanced Coal Technology Consortium yielded 17 patents, and projects under the Clean Vehicles Consortium projects resulted in 20 patents and invention disclosures in the US and 12 patents in China (US-China Clean Energy Research Center 2013). China's diminishing asymmetry also opens up broad new avenues for substantive bilateral and multilateral cooperation, as China becomes a more important contributor to the world's S&T literature, producing a growing number of top-tier cited refereed articles (Suttmeier and Cao 2006). In the framework of Horizon 2020, for example, the European Union and the Chinese government agreed to set up a joint project funding mechanism involving annual investments of roughly €100 million and 200 million RMB in support of joint projects between EU and Chinese agencies.

Over the past four decades, China has achieved significant gains from international S&T cooperation, spurred on by rapid economic development and its opening-up policy (Gewirtz 2019). China now sees international S&T cooperation as part of a new stage in its S&T development, in which there will be greater demand for international S&T cooperation at all levels and among public and private stakeholders. Along with China's improvement in its S&T capacity and core competencies, China's role in international S&T cooperation is changing gradually from learner to partner and rule maker. We expect to see increasing proactive participation by China in global S&T governance, as Chinese scientists hold a growing number of positions in major international S&T organisations, and as more Chinese-initiated "big science" projects and advanced research facilities attract scientists from all over the world.[9]

Under the specific reforms launched under the 13th Five-Year STI Plan and Strategy of Innovation-Driven Development (China STI 2016), China has put forth a strategic vision for future international S&T cooperation that includes very ambitious goals and innovative mechanisms (Ministry of Science and Technology 2016a). If reforms are successfully implemented, they should increase the openness of China's S&T programmes, resulting in growing demand for international cooperation. Through comprehensive reforms, some of the issues that have thus far hindered S&T cooperation, such as restrictions on travel abroad and the use of funds, might be resolved.

Nonetheless, the Chinese government needs a clearer definition of its key role, one that improves the quality of its services to China's major innovation actors. It is already reinforcing its international S&T cooperation strategy through such efforts as promoting innovation dialogues, expanding cultural and educational exchanges, upgrading the scale of communications and involving an expanded number of stakeholders such as universities, research institutes and private enterprises. The government also is setting up special funds and programmes, with different purposes and characteristics, to promote international S&T cooperation. More resources are being channelled and leveraged from not only central and local governments, but also the growing private sector. In the long run, China needs to develop a more coherent strategic plan and policy umbrella that will better guide its international cooperation activities and design more innovative mechanisms to better meet the country's changing needs. It clearly is an appropriate time to introduce additional reforms that will foster mutually beneficial international S&T cooperation; these reforms will have to provide more incentives to potential and existing foreign partners that will overcome the anxieties and uncertainties that up to now, too often, have constrained the growth of new activities.

The bottom line looking ahead is a simple one: there is no major international S&T-related issue whose meaningful solution will not require close cooperation and collaboration with China (Mammadov 2020). Climate change, clean energy, global pandemics, water and other such issues are central to China's future and mission, and critical for the world if it is to avoid major disasters in the coming years. China's decision in 2017 to step up on global climate change despite the US decision (under President Trump) to withdraw from the Paris Accord signed during the Obama Administration marks an important turning point in China's role in the international S&T system. Simply stated, China's willingness to take on a leadership role in this issue portends an expanded Chinese presence across multiple similar issue areas. Chinese behaviour is starting to re-shape the global S&T and innovation landscape. How countries such as the US, Japan and the EU nations will deal with this new Chinese posture remains one of the key challenges facing the international S&T system (Wagner 2020).

During the 19th CPC National Congress held in October 2017, and despite the sense among many foreign observers, the Party's General Secretary Xi Jinping indicated that China would continue to attach great importance to openness; Xi asserted that openness is critical for turning China into a true innovative country with global competitiveness. Under Xi's leadership, despite an obvious increase in nationalist spirit, China promises to become more and more open, will combine "bring in" and "go global", give priority to promoting the Belt and Road Initiative, and strengthen international cooperation to enhance its innovation capacity.

To achieve its goals, Beijing intends to make use of S&T comprehensively to advance major power diplomacy through strengthening and refining top-down designs for international S&T cooperation, deepening and expanding innovation dialogue mechanisms with major countries and S&T partnerships with developing countries, proactively initiating and coordinating international Big Science projects and programmes, and attracting high-end overseas S&T talent. There is a growing realisation among PRC leaders that China is steadily, albeit more gradually than desired, moving towards the centre of the global innovation stage, becoming one of the leaders in a number of important fields, and shifting from being a passive follower to achieving '*san pao bing cun*' (catching up, running neck and neck and becoming top runner at the same time) (Steinfeld 2010: 184). This is the underpinning for the widely discussed *Made in China 2025* initiative (Hsu 2017). Domestically, the major challenge facing Chinese society is people's increasing demand for high quality life versus unbalanced, insufficient development. By pressing harder to enhance the performance of the research sector, the leadership hopes that advances in its S&T innovation capabilities can offset current shortcomings facing the Chinese economy (He 2017).

At the so-called "Liang Hui" or "Two Sessions" held in March 2018, Chinese policy regarding S&T and innovation appears to have undergone even further changes. China's strategic high technologies are increasingly approaching the world frontier; the PRC has entered an historic stage of "running neck and neck, becoming top runner" while being in less of a "catching up" mode. Before his retirement as MOST minister, Wan Gang urged the Chinese S&T community to strengthen openness and cooperation so as both to proactively take part in international innovation and entrepreneurship, and to more efficiently leverage innovation resources both at home and abroad. China's S&T diplomacy will be further enhanced by creating new dialogue mechanisms within existing multilateral organisations such as the BRI summit, G20 and BRICS, expanding the country's S&T partnership network and diversifying prevailing methods of cooperation. The world's most advanced major S&T powers still will loom large in China's overall international S&T networks, especially when it comes to strategic emerging technologies like artificial intelligence and clean energy automobiles. In addition to upgrading the level of "mass entrepreneurship and mass innovation", the government plans to improve existing talent polices to expand green channels for foreign experts to work in China, and attract Chinese international students to engage in entrepreneurial activities.

At the same time, Beijing has announced plans to co-build S&T cooperation platforms with Belt and Road countries such as national laboratories and research centres, technology transfer centres, and technology demonstration and promotion bases. As part of its own new "science diplomacy", China has committed itself to building up the S&T capacity of developing countries both in hardware (research facilities) and software (knowledge and talent pools). This includes encouraging and supporting foreign scientists to initiate and participate in strategic research and in the formulation, implementation and evaluation of guidelines as well as strengthening the local talent pool to meet the demands of the new economic situation. As seen in comments in the Chinese media as well as the speeches of PRC officials, the government is determined to expand the channels for talent introduction, attract more high-end overseas Chinese and foreign experts, and promote Chinese scientists to high positions in international S&T organisations. This may help to explain why the former State Administration for Foreign Experts has been incorporated into the MOST organisation.

Equally important, Beijing has suggested that enterprises also will play a more active role in promoting the country's international S&T innovation cooperation. They will be absorbed into inter-governmental S&T cooperation mechanisms, and those in good financial condition will be supported to establish overseas R&D centres to carry out international industry-university-research institute cooperation. Also, foreign companies will continue to be encouraged by the Chinese government to set up R&D centres and labs in China. However, there remain two outstanding issues for Beijing. The first revolves around the immediate impact of the COVID-19 pandemic on the Chinese economic trajectory. At the May 2020 meeting of the "Liang Hui" (Two Sessions), it was announced that the national budget for science would be cut by 9.1 per cent; this stands in contrast to the 13 per cent increase that occurred in 2019 (Chen 2020). The gap is to be filled by local governments, so that the net result still will be a 3 per cent increase in public R&D expenditures. MOST Minister Wang Zhigang specifically noted that international cooperation would still be a major high priority.

The second issue deals with the impact of the COVID-19 experience on the prevailing structure and operation of the global supply chain and the evolving Chinese role in the global value chain. Many rumours have emerged about how Western firms will begin a significant retreat home as their degree of dependence on China and Chinese suppliers has come to be viewed as a high risk factor during the COVID-19 period. While initial indications from many multinationals are that there is much hyperbole surrounding many of the initial media reports, the fact remains that there are likely to be some pronounced shifts over the coming 2–3 years that could alter China's plans to become a high value-added manufacturer and new source of design and innovation in the near future. Xi Jinping's pronouncements in summer 2020 about China's need to pursue a so-called "dual circulation" strategy that gives greater attention to the Chinese domestic economy highlight the fact that China already is preparing for potential discontinuities, including the increased difficulties that it will have gaining access to advanced foreign know-how (Lelyveld 2020).

Looking ahead, given that the country aims to deepen engagement in global S&T innovation governance, we likely will see more Chinese efforts at agenda setting for the global innovation system and more emphasis on rule setting for key international S&T projects to address key global challenges including food security, energy security, environmental protection, climate change and public health. It remains unclear, however, whether the international S&T community will welcome an enhanced Chinese presence without a series of concomitant gestures from Beijing with respect to prevailing norms and values in areas such as internet freedom, cyber security, IPR protection, research ethics, etc. The verdict has not yet been decided about just how bumpy the road ahead will be for China's international S&T relations if present concerns are not addressed head on by Beijing.

Notes

[1] Examples are the "Opinions of the CPC Central Committee and State Council on Deepening S&T Reform and Speeding Up the Building of a National Innovation System" (CPC 2016), the 13th Five Year Science and Technology Plan, the Innovation-Driven Development Strategy and the Belt and Road Initiative on Building International S&T Cooperation Networks.

[2] Others include the Foreign Affairs Leading Group of the CPC, and the Inter-Ministerial Coordination Mechanism, which includes the Ministry of Agriculture (MOA), Ministry of Education (MOE), the international cooperation departments of local governments, the China Association for International Science and Technology Cooperation, and enterprises. MOST also commands some 20 affiliated agencies, including the Institute of Scientific and Technical Information of China, the High-Tech Research and Development Centre, the Intellectual Property Rights Centre, the Supervision Service Centre for Science and Technology Funds and the National Science and Technology Venture Capital Development Centre.

[3] Professor Bai was President until December 2020; the current (January 2021) President is Professor Hou Jianguo.

[4] See in particular the 13th Five-Year Plan Special Program on International S&T Cooperation (Beijing: MOST 2016).

[5] Information in this section on Japan and China S&T cooperation was mainly derived from assorted issues of the *JETRO China Newsletter*, 1980–2000 (Japan External Trade Organisation, Tokyo).

[6] Information in this section was largely drawn from the website of the Delegation of the European Union to China (https://eeas.europa.eu/delegations/China_en).

[7] For detailed facts and figures regarding priority areas of FP7 and H2020 as well as Chinese participation, refer to the European Commission's document "EU-China Research & Innovation Relations", available online.

[8] The Patent Cooperation Treaty (PCT) provides an international legal framework intended to ensure standard patenting procedures that provide IP protection.

[9] For a somewhat different conclusion, see Baark (2014), who argues that China does not yet possess the excellence that positions its scientific research institutions as world-

leading, even if research in key organisations may be able to support leading and original research achievements.

References

Atkinson, Robert D., Nigel Cory and Stephen J. Ezell. 2017. *Stopping China's Mercantilism: A Doctrine of Constructive, Alliance-Backed Confrontation*. Information Technology and Innovation Foundation (ITIF) (March). Available at https://itif.org/publications/2017/03/16/stopping-chinas-mercantilism-doctrine-constructive-alliance-backed [accessed 16 Nov. 2020].

Baark, Erik. 2014. *Is China Becoming a Science and Technology Superpower, and So What?* Discussion paper presented at conference entitled The Evolving Role of Science and Technology in China's International Relations, 3–4 April, Arizona State University, Tempe, AZ.

Bai Chunli. 2017a. *International S&T Cooperation Network Will Be Established by 2030*. National Natural Science Foundation of China. http://www.nsfc.gov.cn/publish/portal0/tab434/info68550.htm [unavailable as at 17 Nov. 2020].

————. 2017b. "ORI Network of International S&T Cooperation to Be Established by 2030". *Xinhua*. Available at http://news.xinhuanet.com/tech/2017-05/10/c_1120945651.htm [accessed 17 Nov. 2020; in Chinese].

Bound, Kirsten et al. 2013. *China's Absorptive State: Research, Innovation, and the Prospects for China-UK Collaboration*. London: National Endowment for Science, Technology and the Arts [Nesta].

Breznitz, Dan and Michael Murphree. 2011. *Run of the Red Queen: Government, Innovation, Globalization, and Economic Growth in China*. New Haven, CT: Yale University Press.

Cao Cong and Richard P. Suttmeier. 2017. "Challenges of S&T System Reform in China", *Science* 335: 1019–21.

Cao Cong, Richard P. Suttmeier and Denis F. Simon. 2006. "China's 15-Year Science and Technology Plan", *Physics Today* 59, 12: 38–43.

Cao Qing. 2014. "Insight into Weak Enforcement of Intellectual Property Rights in China", *Technology in Society* 38: 40–7.

CAS [Chinese Academy of Sciences]. 2017. *Report on the State of One Belt One Road S&T Cooperation* (9 May). CAS and Elsevier. [in Chinese] Available at http://www.cas.cn/sygz/201705/t20170509_4600090.shtml [accessed 17 Nov. 2020].

Chen, Stephen. 2020. "Two Sessions 2020: China Cuts Science Budget by 9 per cent but National R&D still Tipped to Grow". *South China Morning Post*, 22 May.

Cheng R. 2008. "China's International Science and Technology Cooperation Strategy and Policy Evolution in 30 Years" [in Chinese], *China S&T Forum* 7, 26: 7–11.

China STI. 2016. *The 13th Five-year National Plan for Science, Technology and Innovation of the People's Republic of China* (August).

CPC. 2016. CPC. *Outline of the National Strategy of Innovation-Driven Development*. Central Committee and State Council (May 20) [in Chinese]. Available at http://

www.scio.gov.cn/34473/Document/1478594/1478594.htm [accessed 17 Nov. 2020].

Embassy of the PRC in Japan. 2016. *Japan Science and Technology Agency and Ministry of Science and Technology China Initiate Joint R&D Projects* [in Japanese]. Available at http://www.fmprc.gov.cn/ce/cejp/jpn/sgxw/t1408125.htm [accessed 17 Nov. 2020].

EU. 2015. *EU–China Research and Innovation Relations*. Available at http://ec.europa.eu/research/iscp/pdf/policy/1_eu_CHINA_R_I.pdf#view=fit&pagemode=non [accessed 17 Nov. 2020].

European Commission. 2018. *China – Certain Measures on the Transfer of Technology Request for Consultations by the European Union*. Available at http://trade.ec.europa.eu/doclib/docs/2018/june/tradoc_156910.pdf.pdf [accessed 17 Nov. 2020].

European Union Chamber of Commerce in China. 2017. *China Manufacturing 2025: Putting Industrial Policy Ahead of Market Forces*. Available at http://docs.dpaq.de/12007-european_chamber_cm2025-en.pdf [accessed 17 Nov. 2020].

Friedberg, Aaron. 2020. "An Answer to Aggression: How to Push Back Against Beijing", *Foreign Affairs* (Sept/Oct.): 150–64.

Gewirtz, Julian B. 2019. "China's Long March to Technological Supremacy", *Foreign Affairs*, August 27 [full text available online to subscribers].

Ghafele, Roya and Benjamin Gibert. 2012. *Promoting Intellectual Property Monetization in Developing Countries*. Washington, DC: The World Bank.

Grimes, Seamus and Marcela Miozzo. 2015. "Big Pharma's Internationalization of R&D to China", *European Planning Studies* 23, 9: 1873–94.

He Huifeng. 2017. "Premier Li Keqiang's Innovation Push Proves No Miracle Cure for China's Economy", *South China Morning Post* (March 9). Available at http://www.scmp.com/news/china/policies-politics/article/2076391/young-take-lead-chinese-premiers-innovation-push [accessed 17 Nov. 2020].

Hsu, Sara. 2017. "Foreign Firms Wary of 'Made in China 2025,' but It May Be China's Best Chance At Innovation", *Forbes*, 10 March. Available at https://www.forbes.com/sites/sarahsu/2017/03/10/foreign-firms-wary-of-made-in-china-2025-but-it-may-be-chinas-best-chance-at-innovation/#2a17140624d2 [accessed 17 Nov. 2020].

Institute of International Education. 2015. "Top 25 Places of Origin of International Students, 2013/14–2014/15, *Open Doors Report on International Educational Exchange*. Available at http://www.iie.org/opendoors [accessed 17 Nov. 2020].

Jersild, Austin. 2014. *The Sino-Soviet Alliance: An International History*. Chapel Hill: University of North Carolina Press.

Le Corre, Philippe and Alain Sepulchre. 2016. *China's Offensive in Europe*. Washington, DC: Brookings Institution Press.

Lelyveld, Michael. 2020. "China Unveils New Strategy for Economic Growth", *The Eurasia Review*, August 22. Available at https://www.eurasiareview.com/22082020-china-unveils-new-strategy-for-economic-growth-analysis/ [accessed 17 Nov. 2020].

Lewis, John W. and Xue Litai. 1991. *China Builds the Bomb*. Stanford: Stanford University Press.

Literature Research Office of the CCP's Central Committee (comp.). 2016. *Excerpts of Xi Jinping's Speeches on Science, Technology, and Innovation* [in Chinese]. Beijing: Central Literature Publishing House.

Liu Feng-Chao, et al. 2011. "China's Innovation Policies: Evolution, Institutional Structure, and Trajectory", *Research Policy* 40, 7: 917–31.

Lord, Winston. 2019. *Kissinger on Kissinger: Reflections on Grand Strategy, Diplomacy and Leadership*. New York: St. Martin's.

Mammadov, Seymur. 2020. *China is Tapping into its Intellectual Potential*. GCTN, Beijing, 22 Aug.

McGregor, James. 2010. *China's Drive for 'Indigenous Innovation': A Web of Industrial Policies*. US Chamber of Commerce Global Regulatory Cooperation Project. Available at https://www.uschamber.com/report/china%E2%80%99s-drive-indigenous -innovation-web-industrial-policies [accessed 17 Nov. 2020].

Ministry of Science and Technology. 2006. *National Medium- and Long-Term Science and Technology Development Plan (2006–2020)* [in Chinese]. Available at http:// www.most.gov.cn/ztzl/gjzcqgy/zcqgygynr/1.htm [accessed 17 Nov. 2020].

_____. 2016a. *The Thirteenth Five-Year Plan for Science, Technology, and Innovation* (in Chinese). Available at http://www.most.gov.cn/mostinfo/xinxifenlei/gjkjgh/ 201608/t20160810_127174.htm [accessed 17 Nov. 2020].

_____. 2016b. *The 13th Five-Year Plan Special Program on International S&T Cooperation*. Available at http://fi.china-embassy.org/eng/kxjs/P02017102578185 1971820.pdf [accessed 17 Nov. 2020].

National People's Congress (NPC). 2016. *The 13th Five-Year Plan for the National Economic and Social Development of the People's Republic of China* [in Chinese]. Available at http://www.npc.gov.cn/wxzl/gongbao/2016-07/08/content_1993756. htm [accessed 17 Nov. 2020].

Newby, Laura. 2018. *Sino-Japanese Relations: China's Perspective*. London: Routledge.

OECD. 2014. *China Headed to Overtake EU, US in Science & Technology Spending, OECD Says*, 11 Dec. Available at http://www.oecd.org/newsroom/china-headed-to-overtake-eu-us-in-science-technology-spending.htm [accessed 17 Nov. 2020].

OECD/EUIPO. 2016. *Trade in Counterfeit and Pirated Goods: Mapping the Economic Impact*. Paris: OECD.

Perez, Bien. 2017. "China Closes Gap with US in Hi-Tech Breakthroughs, KPMG Finds", *South China Morning Post*, 6 March. Available at http://www.scmp.com/ tech/innovation/article/2076348/china-closes-gap-us-hi-tech-breakthroughs-kpmg-finds [accessed 17 Nov. 2020].

Poo Mu-ming and Wang Ling. 2014. "On CAS Pioneer Initiative – An Interview with CAS President Chunli Bai", *National Science Review* 1, 4: 618–22.

Ruffini, Pierre-Bruno. 2017. *Science and Diplomacy: A New Dimension in International Relations*. Paris: Springer International.

Samuelson, Robert J. 2018. "China's Breathtaking Transformation into a Scientific Superpower", *Washington Post*, 21 Jan. Available at https://www.washingtonpost. com/opinions/chinas-breathtaking-transformation-into-a-scientific-superpower/ 2018/01/21/03f883e6-fd44-11e7-8f66-2df0b94bb98a_story.html?utm_term=. bcadc1c526ed [accessed 17 Nov. 2020].

Shambaugh, David and Eberhard Sandschneider. 2007. *China-Europe Relations: Perceptions, Policies and Prospects*. London: Routledge.

Shen Zhihua and Xia Yafeng. 2012. *Between Aid and Restriction: Changing Soviet Policies toward China's Nuclear Weapons Program: 1954–1960*. Nuclear Proliferation International Project Wilson Center. Available at https://www.wilsoncenter. org/article/between-aid-and-restriction-changing-soviet-policies-toward-chinas-nuclear-weapons-program [accessed 16 Nov. 2020].

Simon, Denis F. and Cao Cong. 2009a. "Creating an Innovative Talent Pool", *China Business Review* 2 Nov. Available at http://www.chinabusinessreview.com/creating-an-innovative-talent-pool/ [accessed 17 Nov. 2020].

————. 2009b. *China's Emerging Technological Edge: Assessing the Role of High-End Talent*. Cambridge: Cambridge University Press.

State Council of the PRC. 2015. *Made in China 2025* [in Chinese]. Available at http:// www.gov.cn/zhengce/content/2015-05/19/content_9784.htm [accessed 17 Nov. 2020].

———— 2017. *China to Invest Big in 'Made in China 2025' Strategy*. Available at http://english.gov.cn/state_council/ministries/2017/10/12/content_28147590 4600274.htm [accessed 17 Nov. 2020].

Steinfeld, Edward S. 2010. *Playing Our Game: Why China's Rise Doesn't Threaten the West*. Oxford: Oxford University Press.

Sun Yifei, Max von Zedtwitz and Denis F. Simon, ed. 2008. *Global R&D in China*. New York: Routledge.

Sun Yutao and Seamus Grimes. 2017. *China and Global Value Chains: Globalization and the Information and Communications Technology Sector*. London: Routledge.

Suttmeier, Richard P. 2014. *Co-inventing the Future? Science Diplomacy and the Evolution of Sino–US Relations in Science and Technology*. Discussion paper presented at conference entitled The Evolving Role of Science and Technology in China's International Relations, 3–4 April, Arizona State University, Tempe, AZ.

Suttmeier, Richard P. and Cao Cong. 2006. *China–US S&T Cooperation: Past Achievements and Future Challenges*. US–China Forum on Science and Technology Policy. Available at http://china-us.uoregon.edu/pdf/CHINAUSST COOPERATIONForum.pdf [accessed 17 Nov. 2020].

Suttmeier, Richard P. and Denis Simon. 2014. "Conflict and Cooperation in the Development of US-China Relations in Science and Technology", in *The Global Politics of Science and Technology*, vol. 2, ed. Maximillian Mayer et.al. Berlin: Springer International, pp. 143–59.

Swanström, Niklas and Kokubun Ryosei. 2012. *Sino-Japanese Relations: Rivals or Partners in Regional Cooperation*. Singapore: World Scientific.

Turekian, Vaughan. 2009. "Science as a Tool for International Diplomacy", European Commission CORDIS. Available at https://cordis.europa.eu/article/id/30532-science-as-a-tool-for-international-diplomacy [accessed 17 Nov. 2020].

US–China Clean Energy Research Center. 2013. *Annual Report 2012–2013: Accomplishments from the Second Year of the US–China Clean Energy Research Center.* Available at https://cercbee.lbl.gov/sites/default/files/US-China_CERC_Annual_Report_2012-2013_0.pdf [accessed 17 Nov. 2020].

USTR [Office of the United States Trade Representative]. 2017. *Special 301 Report on Intellectual Property Rights.* Available at https://ustr.gov/sites/default/files/301/2017%20Special%20301%20Report%20FINAL.PDF [accessed 17 Nov. 2020].

Wagner, Caroline S. 2020. "The Trump Administration is Curtailing Visas for Chinese Scientists. That May Backfire", *Washington Post,* 26 June.

Wagner, Caroline S., Lutz Bornmann and Loet Leydesdorff. 2015. "Recent Developments in China–US Cooperation in Science", *Minerva* 53, 3: 199–214.

Walsh, Kathleen. 2003. *Foreign High-Tech R&D in China.* Washington, DC: Henry L. Stimson Center.

Wilson, Jeanne. 2014. *Strategic Partners: Russian–Chinese Relations in the Post-Soviet Era.* New York: Routledge.

Xie Yu, Zhang Chunni and Lai Qing. 2014. "China's Rise as a Major Contributor to Science and Technology", *Proceedings of the National Academy of Sciences* 111, 26: 9437–42.

Xinhua. 2016. "The Outline of the Thirteenth Five-Year Plan for the National Economy and Social Development of the People's Republic of China" [in Chinese], 17 March. Available at http://news.xinhuanet.com/politics/2016lh/2016-03/17/c_1118366322.htm [accessed 17 Nov. 2020].

_____. 2017. "Li Keqiang: Mass Entrepreneurship and Innovation Is Flourishing". *Xinhuanet* 12 Sept. Available at http://www.xinhuanet.com/english/2017-09/12/c_136603727.htm [accessed 17 Nov. 2020].

Yahuda, Michael. 2013. *Sino-Japanese Relations After the Cold War.* London: Routledge.

Zhang Tuosheng. 2007. "Despite Sticking Points, Relations Enter New Era", *China Daily,* April 11. Available at http://www.china.org.cn/english/wen/206810.htm [accessed 4 Feb. 2021].

Zhou Yu, William Lazonick and Sun Yifei. 2016. *China as an Innovation Nation.* Oxford: Oxford University Press.

Zhuo Wenting. 2017. "Shanghai Unveils Steps to Attract Foreign R&D Centers", *China Daily,* 17 Oct. Available at http://www.chinadaily.com.cn/business/2017-10/17/content_33352161.htm [accessed 17 Nov. 2020].

Zou Lei. 2018. *The Political Economy of China's Belt and Road Initiative.* Singapore: World Scientific.

Zukus, Jason. 2017. "Globalization with Chinehse Characteristics: A New International Standard", *The Diplomat,* 9 May. Available at https://thediplomat.com/2017/05/globalization-with-chinese-characteristics-a-new-international-standard/ [accessed 17 Nov. 2020].

7

How Does International Collaboration Lead to Radical Innovation in Latecomer Firms?

Xiaolan Fu, Cintia Külzer-Sacilotto, Haibo Lin and Hongru Xiong

Introduction

By following different paths, latecomer economies leverage international knowledge to grow and catch up with advanced economies. The "traditional" path is to acquire more advanced technologies and diffuse them internally. Most latecomer countries have taken this path, including China. They acquire, assimilate and adapt foreign technologies through imports, licensing and inward foreign direct investment (Fu et al. 2011). These mechanisms often lead to more incremental innovations, with firms potentially imitating the technologies available in advanced countries. Although this path has benefitted China during take-off and catch-up phases, it is not free from criticism, for example the lack of creativity and heavy dependence on foreign investment (Fu 2015). Another criticism refers to the limitations of foreign advanced technologies. Technologies are usually created to serve a particular environment, and this environment, for instance, in advanced countries, might be very different from those in emerging countries (Acemoglu 2002). Emerging economies are much more labour-intensive, hence the need for technologies that optimise the use of their resources.

The "unconventional" path is to co-create innovations leveraging international knowledge. In recent years, in its pursuit of the transition from

144

imitator to innovator, China has increasingly employed various unconventional knowledge-sourcing mechanisms. International innovation collaboration (IIC) is regarded as an essential channel for knowledge co-creation as innovation is frequently a collaborative, global undertaking. Can IIC help latecomer Chinese firms become radical innovators at the world technology frontier? There is no consensus on the definition of radical innovation (as discussed in Green et al. 1995). However, we agree that what distances incremental from radical innovation "is the degree of novel technological process content embodied in the innovation and hence, the degree of new knowledge embedded" (Dewar and Dutton 1986: 1423). In particular, we ask: how should the process be managed to ensure that IIC brings the promised benefits to enable leapfrogging in technology advancement for latecomer firms?

It is often argued that IIC provides significant benefits to innovation. It enables an innovator to tap into complementary capabilities (Beaver and Rosen 1979; Wagner and Leydesdorff 2005), access scarce or unique resources in other countries (Zhao et al. 2013) and increase the prestige or visibility of research (Narin et al. 1991; Sooryamoorthy 2009). However, language, cultural, institutional and geographic distances between collaborators may present significant barriers to the knowledge co-production process.

Despite several studies relating to collaboration and innovation behaviour (for example, Kafouros et al. 2015), the research on *how* collaboration impacts radical innovation is limited. Most literature has focused on international collaboration and innovation (for example, Hird and Pfotenhauer 2017; Criscuolo et al. 2010; Frenz and Ietto-Gillies 2009), and some relates to radical innovation in particular (for example, Enkel and Heil 2014; Leeuw et al. 2014). These studies used evidence from advanced countries predominantly, with two important exceptions: Jugend et al. (2018) who explored the impact of collaboration on radical innovation within Brazil; and Fu et al. (2020) who explored the impact of IIC on radical innovation in Chinese manufacturing firms. However, our understanding of how IIC impacts radical innovation in developing countries is still limited.

This chapter aims to fill this gap in the literature by exploring how IIC impacts radical innovation in latecomer economies. An in-depth case study of a leading Chinese technology company is employed to explore IIC management in successful Chinese firms in their pursuit of leapfrogging to the world technology frontier. This study supports previous evidence that IIC is associated with more radical innovation. However, such gains of collaboration for radical innovation come only with effective collaboration management. Opening up to international partners, combining problem-solving and blue-sky exploration and procuring sufficient internal inputs to facilitate absorption and integration of innovative technology are critical to ensure that IICs are fruitful.

This chapter's contributions to the literature are firstly to provide evidence concerning the selection of IIC partners and projects in attempts to achieve radical innovation in latecomer firms, and secondly to make the first exploratory analysis to understand how the process of IIC is managed in successful latecomer firms to ensure that the promised benefits are achieved.

Gains from International Collaboration and Radical Innovation: Received Wisdom

Gains from IIC

The transformation from imitation to innovation requires increasing radical innovation in latecomer economies. The launch of radical innovation involves extending the firm's knowledge base, namely, its knowledge breadth and depth (Zhou and Li 2012). Such an extension can be achieved by investing in internal R&D as well as by accessing external innovation resources and capabilities (Bao et al. 2012). One of the mechanisms for doing the latter is collaboration. External linkages with universities and research institutes (URIs), and along the value chain increase firms' innovation possibilities (Freeman and Soete 1997). Collaboration not only helps the firm acquire knowledge from outside its boundaries, but it also helps with combining different sources of knowledge to explore uncertain worlds (Belderbos et al. 2004), supporting exploratory research and radical innovation through open processes.

As innovation becomes more open, collaborative and global, it improves innovation performance (Criscuolo et al. 2010; Narula and Zanfei 2004). Application of knowledge production functions to a dataset of thousands of firms discovered that being globally engaged in innovation leads to higher productivity, mainly due to learning from more sources, such as suppliers and customers, universities and their intra-firm worldwide pool of information (Criscuolo et al. 2010). In addition to multinational-led global innovation generation, strategic technology partnering complements internal R&D-based innovation (Narula and Zanfei 2004). This stream of literature found that large firms choose strategic partnering because of their strong technological capabilities and absorptive capacity. That enables firms to keep up with technological frontiers (Cantwell 1995). On the other hand, Narula (2002) found that small firms rely on external sources due to their lack of human, technological and financial resources. They cannot perform all innovation stages, from research and development to commercialisation, to create and capture value within their borders. Small firms often exploit niche markets, and a larger pool of resources and markets helps them implement their specialisation strategy (Chesbrough 2010).

The internationalisation of innovation and the rise of the emerging economies have induced much R&D outsourcing activity from advanced to emerging economies. China and India have invested heavily in R&D, and both have reservoirs of low-cost high-skilled labour (Fu et al. 2011), which makes them particularly attractive partners. However, despite substantial investment in R&D and a large pool of educated scientists and engineers, firms in developing countries are frequently constrained from world-leading innovation performance (for example, Hobday et al. 2004; Dantas and Bell 2009). One salient reason is that universities in latecomer economies are often over-engaged in the diffusion, instead of the creation of knowledge, and this leads to domestic university-firm partnerships enhancing incremental innovation (Fu and Li 2016). Innovation through international collaboration is likely to break these constraints, nurturing more radical innovation and changing the technology trajectory of China.

Motivations and the Actual Gains from IIC for Radical Innovation

Firms collaborate with external partners, such as customers, suppliers and URIs, in a range of paradigm-shifting and technical problem-solving activities. The effect of innovation collaboration is shaped by the type of innovation nurtured by these interactions. For instance, Criscuolo et al. (2010) found that information flows from universities are critical for patenting, whereas flows from business contacts are important for other metrics of innovation performance. Indeed, collaborating with URIs can significantly enhance both a firm's entry to new technological fields and new product development (George et al. 2002; Perkmann et al. 2011; Mindruta 2013). It can also support paradigm-shifting projects, although Parida et al. (2012) showed that collaboration and integration with customers in the supply chain also positively influence radical innovation in high-tech sectors.

Due to the heterogeneity of knowledge across industries and locations, the supply of expertise in one specific field at a given site may be limited. This phenomenon induces firms to look for knowledge from external sources. Superior performance and assistance in unlocking greater innovation potential are some of the advantages of IICs in emerging economy enterprises (Kafouros et al. 2015; Lichtenthaler 2008; Peng et al. 2013). However, there are disadvantages in that differences in linguistic, cultural, institutional and geographical location challenge IIC effectiveness. Evidence from the UK and the Netherlands suggests that, despite these challenges, firms prioritise the quality of research over geographical proximity (Laursen et al. 2012). In China, location has not been deemed to be an essential factor in deciding international research collaboration in recent years (Zhou and Tian 2014). Once such social and cultural connectors have been allowed for, multinationals are likely to set up R&D labs close to collaborators (Castellani and Pieri 2013). Therefore, the gains from IIC are more substantial than the disadvantages caused by geographical distance.

To engage in collaborations, firms have to develop scanning capabilities to find the best external partners and projects (Kim and Park 2010). These capabilities are not often in place (Laursen and Salter 2014), particularly in the case of international collaborations, as latecomer firms often cannot leverage on their existing domestic network (Peng et al. 2013). Firms also face challenges in managing long-distance partnerships and securing value from them. On top of the technological, cultural and geographical distances, latecomer firms need to deal with coordination costs, different incentives and appropriability recurrent in all collaborative innovation projects but amplified in international ones. Literature suggests that firms particularly struggle to manage and control knowledge-sharing (Bouncken and Kraus 2013), although "sharing facilitates revolutionary and radical innovation that requires an extensive portfolio of resources" (Bouncken and Kraus 2013: 2063). To overcome such challenges, firms have to take a central role in their partnerships (Brunswicker and van de Vrande 2014), keeping relative control over resources and decisions to enforce commitment and align incentives in international collaborations.

The extent of collaboration depends on the firm's absorptive capacity, business objectives, type of partnership and the ability to search for and manage international collaborations. Talents and institutions with similar expertise tend to cluster together (Audretsch and Feldman 1996). In this context, if absorptive capacity is in place, cross border IICs are more likely to produce ground-breaking innovations due to a broader knowledge base and the input of leading researchers with world-class expert relevant knowledge. Some prior studies have proved that technology-sourcing is often linked to radical innovation performance for high-tech firms, whereas technology scouting is linked to incremental innovation performance (Katila and Ahuja 2002; Pittaway et al. 2004; Parida et al. 2012). A stronger orientation towards technology breakthroughs instead of problem-solving seems vital for a firm to have radical innovation outcomes from IIC.

IIC in China

Over the past four decades, China's innovation system has transitioned from being relatively isolated and un-integrated to being relatively open and market-oriented. China was believed to have the highest openness within the developing countries in terms of business, trade activities and relevant institutions (OECD 2008). More recently, China has begun to participate deeply in global innovation networks and international innovation governance. Promoting IIC to enhance indigenous innovation capability is regarded as one of China's innovation-driven development targets.

Policies Towards Supporting IICs

Policies towards supporting IICs have been proposed since the 1980s and have been evolving with the upgrading of innovation activities in China. Firstly, policy domains have expanded from mainly supporting basic research cooperation to applied research and industrial, technological collaboration. The relevant subjects gradually grow from joint manufacturing to joint R&D, designing, branding, talent training, cross-licensing as well as cross border technology acquisition. Secondly, the main beneficiaries extend from URIs to various forms of domestic enterprises, and from country-level science and technology (S&T) projects to multi-level innovation projects, platforms and research bases. Thirdly, the primary policy orientation has pivoted from inward open innovation to outward open innovation. Since 2012, renewed policy emphasis has accelerated the implementation of *going-abroad* strategies, making greater use of global innovation resources. In recent years, more policy emphasis has been placed on the combination of "bringing in" and "going global", taking a more proactive approach to integrating into the global innovation network, and building an open innovation mechanism at a higher level. Fourthly, the use of relevant policy tools has become diversified and more targeted. For instance, the preferential tax policy for R&D collaboration activities was strengthened in 2010. Additionally, in recent years, more cooperation funds and various R&D platforms have been established, together with deregulation and facilitation of cross-border innovation flows (or collaborative interaction). In 2017, the National Natural Science Foundation of China (NSFC) launched an initiative to increase collaboration agreements with countries along the "One Belt, One Road" (Chen et al. 2020). Fifth, the national R&D programme has been opening to the world, and taking the lead in organising international big science programmes, that is, large and complex scientist research programmes, as well as big science engineering programmes. From 2017 onwards, international scientific research institutes and other organisations alike may take the lead or participate in national strategic research (Chen et al. 2020).

Policies towards inward open innovation, or innovation exploration, have been particularly influential in China. International technology transfer and assimilation have been critical to supporting indigenous firms in implementing radical innovation and opening their innovation processes (Fu 2011). Other strategies in this direction are a collaboration with universities, equity in university spin-offs, overseas investment and acquisition. Policies towards outward open innovation, or innovation exploitation, have been implemented but not as extensively used as those regarding exploration (Fu 2011). These policies aim at promoting the external commercialisation of new technologies and are more associated with incremental innovation. Policies towards open innovation networks have been used by immediate innovation service institutions, science parks and incubators in the context of helping indigenous firms as well. The aim of these policies is to support market-oriented R&D systems centred around the firm, and to develop technology transaction markets where technology can be transferred, consulted, exchanged and mediated (Fu 2011).

IIC and Radical Innovation in Chinese Firms

According to the National Innovation Survey of 646,000 firms carried out by the National Bureau of Statistics of China in 2014, while around 130,000 (20.1 per cent) Chinese firms have engaged in collaborative innovation, the proportion is higher in the manufacturing sector (26.4 per cent). For those firms that have engaged in collaborative innovations, the majority were state-owned firms (61.3 per cent), while privately-owned firms engaged in university-industry collaboration stood at 38.8 per cent (National Bureau of Statistics 2017). Firms collaborate with various partners, including other firms within their company groups, suppliers, customers, competitors, consultants or private R&D institutes, URIs and commercial labs. URIs are the sector that registered the most significant number of collaborations, especially domestic URIs. Suppliers and customers also have many innovation collaborations. Collaboration with customers is the most popular pattern of innovation collaboration, with 45.4 per cent of all cases registered in this category, followed by suppliers, reported as 36.1 per cent of innovation collaboration.

Despite the fact that most of the collaborations are domestic, evidence shows that IICs are relevant and growing. Previous literature states that international cooperation is critical for China's scientific knowledge creation (for example,

Wang et al. 2013; Liu et al. 2015). Using data from the NSFC, Yuan et al. (2018) studied the prevalence and trends of international collaboration. Out of 326,000 grants between 2006 and 2016, 15,966 were assigned to 75 countries and 7,989 institutions. The majority of these collaborations were with G7 and Asia-Pacific countries, particularly with the US, the UK and Australia. However, collaborations are expanding into other countries in Europe and along the "One Belt, One Road".

Using the national innovation survey dataset of manufacturing firms, Fu at al. (2020) assessed the impact of IICs on radical innovation in China. The authors found evidence that firms with a greater extent of international collaboration introduce more radical innovation, measured as the percentage of new to the market innovation (regarded as ground-breaking at the world level). The authors reported a positive impact of IIC intensity and the moderating effects of R&D intensity on the relationship between international openness and radical innovation that a firm produces. The R&D intensity itself also exerts a significant positive impact on radical innovations. Moreover, firms in high-technology industries are more likely to develop radical innovation than firms do in traditional sectors. Exporters and firms that receive support from public research programmes are also more likely to create radical innovations.

Methodology and Data

We used an exploratory case study approach to analyse how IICs lead to radical innovations. C-Tech, a leading Chinese technology company, was selected for the study. C-Tech is admittedly an exceptional case: it is a private, competitive and internationalised company that has caught up technologically with its competitors in emerging and advanced countries. In 2010, C-Tech successfully implemented an initiative to systematically build and manage collaborative innovation, domestically and internationally. Since then, it has engaged in over 6,000 collaborations with more than 300 universities in 20 countries, many of them leading to ground-breaking innovations. Extensive and effective collaborative innovation is indeed an essential strategy of the firm, for incremental and radical innovation. As its founder, the President of C-Tech, stated, "C-Tech possesses an open innovation paradigm because blind exclusivism would make innovation sink into a closed system that leads to death".

As a successful latecomer, C-Tech is paving the way for the internationalisation and opening up of other indigenous firms in China. Understanding how C-Tech systematically manages IICs sheds light on how other high-tech indigenous firms can open their innovation processes, leverage international knowledge and co-create ground-breaking innovations with external partners. It also sheds light on critical inputs required by indigenous firms to effectively search for and manage IICs to inform managerial and policy implications.

We focussed on the C-Tech Innovation Research Program (IRP) and the unit of analysis of relevant R&D projects involved. To collect the primary data, we conducted several rounds of field interviews with C-Tech executives and staff from 2014 to 2018 and interviewed several external collaborators. Additionally, secondary data were used for identification and corroboration purposes. A statistical test was carried out on a random sample of IRP projects (100 domestic and 100 international from a pool of 6,000 collaboration projects) to examine whether there are significant differences in the novelty of the outputs between domestic and foreign projects.

An In-depth Case Study of a Leading Chinese Technology Firm

Is There a Difference between Foreign and Domestic Collaborations? Project-level Evidence from C-Tech

C-Tech began to build an open, collaborative framework for technology exploration and exploitation in 1999. In 2010, its S&T Fund was reshaped into the Innovation Research Program (IRP). The programme adopts a more systematic approach to allow C-Tech engineers to collaborate with researchers at top universities and other organisations, both domestic and foreign, to achieve technology breakthroughs or to solve complex technical problems. By the end of 2016, the IRP had supported more than 6,000 research projects. Academic institutions take a leading role in their research partnerships; URIs form nearly 60 per cent of the company's total research partners.

From the IRP's 6,000 collaborative projects' dataset, we randomly selected a sample of 200 projects. We examined the attributes of collaborative partners' geographic region (foreign vs. domestic) and Cooperation Type.[1] Table 7.1 shows the cross-tabulation of the novelty of the projects against the type of partner. The 100 projects with external partners comprised 62 Technical Research projects containing a high level of originality and 38 Technical Development projects, which mainly involved the development of existing technologies. The 100 projects involving domestic collaboration comprised only 44 Technical Research projects containing a high level of novelty and 56 Technical Development projects. We used a logistic regression test to confirm the significance of the differences between the two groups because the dependent variable is a binary variable which equals 1 for novel innovation-oriented research collaborations and 0 for incremental innovation-oriented technical development projects. Table 7.2 shows that the estimated coefficient of the "foreign" variable was 0.731 with an odds ratio of 2.077 and was statistically significant at the 5 per cent significance level. This evidence confirms that foreign and domestic collaborations differ in terms of the type of collaboration. Collaboration with external partners is linked to a more research-oriented project, potentially leading to more breakthrough innovations. Of course, this evidence suggests correlation instead of any causality going from international collaboration to radical innovation. The classification of outcomes may merely reflect the initial category from which the projects were funded. Therefore, caution is needed in drawing any conclusions regarding the impact of international collaboration based on this evidence.

Table 7.1: Randomly Selected Collaboration Projects with their Attributes (from C-Tech Global Collaboration Database)

	Foreign Collaboration	Domestic Collaboration	Total
Technical Research	62	44	
Technical Development	38	56	
Total	100	100	200

Table 7.2: Difference between Foreign and Domestic Collaboration: Logit Regression Results

	Coefficient	Odds Ratio	Std. Err.	p-value
Foreign Collaboration	0.731**	2.077	0.288	0.011
Constant	-0.241	0.786	0.201	0.231
Log Likelihood	-134.999			
N	200			

Note: Dependent variable: a dummy variable equals 1 for technical research and 0 for technical development. Foreign collaboration is a dummy variable that equals 1 for foreign collaboration projects and 0 for domestic collaboration projects.
Robust standard errors in parentheses *** $p<0.01$, ** $p<0.05$, * $p<0.1$.

How Does C-Tech Choose Innovation Collaborators? Opening Up to International Collaboration

While considering potential partners, C-Tech optimises technological distance over geographical proximity to ensure the best potential for novelty creation.

According to the literature, the greater the technological distance between the firm and an external collaborator, the higher the potential for novelty, but the lower the ability of the firm to absorb the knowledge (Nooteboom et al. 2007). Given C-Tech's high absorptive capacity, it can regard originality and technical leadership as the primary selection criteria. Indeed, the most crucial internal principle of technology cooperation is, as C-Tech interviewees mentioned, "tracing the source and choosing the best of best" despite the geographical distance. They generally start from "keeping abreast of the initial technical source, clarifying academic context, identifying the leading people, selecting the best and continuing to develop the Top 1 & 2 lab resources globally".

C-Tech emphasises persistent and mutual complementarity, as well as promoting long-term cooperation relationships with high-quality partners. The technical cooperation department also effectively coordinates the collaborative programmes with internal R&D by providing more resources to enhance the competitiveness of C-Tech itself. Moreover, C-Tech is continuously building a qualified collaborative partners list and implementing portfolio management in selecting potential partners. For example, all the existing collaborative projects and potentially relevant partners would be evaluated and classified routinely according to C-Tech's TQRDCS evaluation system (an initialism which refers to technology, quality, response, delivery, cost-effectiveness and social responsibility dimensions), and only the fittest will qualify. In general, comprehensive technological distance is the most critical factor in their selection of research partners. The higher the advanced technology level of the potential partner, the higher the cooperation probability. Experiences in collaboration with industrial partners are the second requirement. Geographical distance is taken into account only when comprehensive technology distances are the same.

Effective Collaboration Management: The Problem-Breakthrough-Integration Model

From a long-term perspective, C-Tech's IRP seeks a large variety of potential technological partners for radical innovation. There are three sub-programmes, Exploratory, Open and Flagship.[2] Each one has a "problem-breakthrough-integration" model to facilitate open radical innovations. C-Tech seeks technical cooperation in two categories of R&D projects: (1) those for which the technology and market fields have bright prospects but insufficient internal capabilities, and (2) those for which there is considerable uncertainty in technology or market prospects. The Flagship programme mainly serves category

(1), supporting research that will significantly impact technological capability. C-Tech's internal R&D staff participate in these programmes alongside partners. Most Open and Exploratory programmes belong to category (2). For instance, a unique feature of the IRP Open programme is funding projects that support novel and early-stage research ideas. C-Tech issues an annual "IRP Open Call for Proposals" that lists key topics of interest and solicits proposals for research subjects. These programmes not only increase blue-sky exploration, broadening C-Tech's existing technology horizons, but also constitute a source pool for long-term or strategic cooperation.

C-Tech has developed an effective management system to guide the dynamic cooperation process. To ensure clarity over the responsibilities of the different players, IRP and the internal technology department, which raised the demand for cooperation, are kept separate but mutually dependent. The technology department can make suggestions for potential partners in the cooperation management department. However, in order to prevent internal corruption, the technology department is prohibited from bypassing the cooperation management department and communicating directly with the partners.

Within collaborations, the IRP designs and executes a series of bonus systems and IPR-sharing systems to maximise the incentive effects for each high-quality partner. It also deploys a lean mission-oriented team, called "The Iron Triangle", to manage the operational business of each technology cooperation project in the programme. This team is generally involved with three key roles: the project manager (PM) who is in charge of general operations, the principal investigator (PI) who is focused on technical interaction and generally based in the host department and the local cooperation manager (LCM) responsible for managing the partnerships. The implementation of "The Iron Triangle" minimises potential conflict and maximises interaction efficiency, significantly reducing the potential obstacles brought about by geographical distances.

Taking the practice of an Optical Transmission System-related project as an example, the power consumption of high-capacity, long-distance systems is very challenging. The technical team worked with several incumbent collaborators, but all failed. Then they presented this as an IRP Open challenge. A German professor of wireless communication proposed a novel idea that introduced a method from wireless technology hitherto unknown to the optical transmission system experts. After initial exploratory efforts validated the assumption, an IRP Flagship project was set up to fully integrate the method with all the product details and to carry out rigorous testing. Both sides met monthly to discuss the current operations and jointly solve countless problems, both in theory and in engineering. Common goals led to a strong committed team, which included the professor and his best PhDs, who joined C-Tech to continue the research after the joint project. The collaboration team finally produced patentable breakthrough technologies that led to a marketable solution. Thus, it can be seen that the problem-breakthrough-integration model enables radical innovation.

The Importance of Internal R&D and Organisational Inputs

C-Tech's internal R&D and relevant R&D management inputs are important for radical innovation. On the one hand, radical innovations need the firm's absorptive capability and joint efforts to turn the ideas into practice. C-Tech has many engineers and continuously spends on R&D, which builds a strong base for knowledge absorption. Each year, C-Tech devotes more than 10 per cent of its revenue and almost half its employees to R&D, resulting in a portfolio of over 50,000 patents. The substantial long-term investment in R&D and a large engineering team help create absorptive capacity.

On the other hand, R&D management inputs such as the "IRP Open Call for Proposals", "Iron Triangle" and network-based knowledge communication flows are required for successful collaborative blue-sky exploration. The open call pushes the internal R&D team out of their comfort zone to interact with researchers and scientists with different expertise, challenging the internal team's ideas and driving out-of-the-box thinking towards blue-sky exploration. Among "Iron Triangle" coordination teams, the LCMs, mostly based in overseas R&D centres or institutes, play an indispensable role in promoting formal or informal communication between host R&D staff and overseas partners. This helps C-Tech not only to manage established collaborations, prevent and solve potential conflicts, but also to identify new projects and partners overseas. In the process of a joint research project, the department in charge will organise frequent cross-disciplinary discussions among the partners and internal research staff, to examine the validation platform of the pilot test team, together with the product development team, and there will also be input from customer demand, to gradually make the "pain points" clear.

Figure 7.1 represents the knowledge flows' network embedded in a typical IRP Project. In short, interactive flows are multidirectional and integrated between internal research, development and implementation departments (see solid lines). The initial research demand information towards the (external) partners is through an open call for proposals or invitations to selected potential partners. The research institute needs to rephrase the wording of the problems seeking solution into academic research questions so as to speed up the collaboration progress and facilitate the communication between industry and academia (see the connection between the Research Institute and Partners). Solutions provided by external partners are tested by the Validation Platform and the validated technical solutions are then passed on to the Product Line. Feedback is then provided to the Partners to finalise the collaboration outputs. Therefore, in addition to policy incentives, careful internal collaboration management is another factor that is crucial to ensuring the success of international innovation collaboration.

Figure 7.1:   Knowledge Flows Network Embedded in a Regular IRP Project

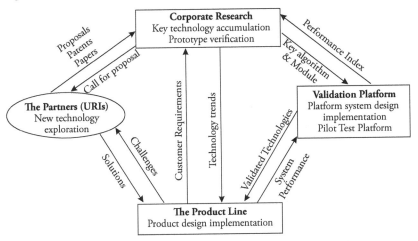

Conclusions and Policy Implications

This chapter examines the role and means of IIC in achieving radical innovation in China. Given that innovation is increasingly a collaborative task and that globalisation is driving more firms to adopt international collaboration, this chapter analyses how IIC can contribute to China's transformation from imitator to radical innovator. IICs are more likely to produce ground-breaking innovations due to a broader knowledge base and the input of interactive cooperation between leading researchers with different backgrounds.

Through an in-depth case study of C-Tech, this chapter has discussed how successful latecomers search and manage IICs, and how that leads to breakthrough innovations. In particular, C-Tech engages foreign partners for research-oriented collaborations. Comprehensive technology distance is the most crucial factor in their selection of research partners. The higher the advanced technology level of a potential partner, the higher the cooperation probability. To ensure international collaborations, C-Tech combines problem-solving with blue-sky exploration and sufficient internal inputs to facilitate absorption. Internal R&D capability, especially that embedded in extramural R&D, strongly determines the transfer performance in making use of external knowledge or complementary resources, mainly due to the absorptive capacity and technology distance effects. Latecomers need to increase their R&D intensity, both internally and externally, during open innovation processes. Integration capability is also vital for effective IICs. C-Tech created the IRP to search and manage international collaboration systematically. Within the IRP, C-Tech assigns a mission-oriented R&D team organised to manage the operational business of each IRP project.

The findings from this research have profound managerial implications. Radical innovation in Chinese firms is internationally collaborative. Technology is advancing at an unparalleled rate, so innovation cannot be limited to internal development alone. Enlarging the talent pool and collaborative networks is vital for fresh perspectives and new skills. To some extent, collaboration is a crucial conduit for innovation-related knowledge flows, both for firms that use R&D (either internally developed or externally acquired) and for those that are not R&D active. International collaboration plays a vital role by allowing firms to gain access to a broader pool of resources and knowledge at a lower cost with shared risks, integrated into global value chains. Thus, an organisation's disruptive or radical innovator strategy must actively seek international partners who can provide complementary assets to accelerate its innovation path.

Moreover, an open mind and a strategy for path-breaking innovation are required instead of path-following incremental innovation during the transition from imitative innovation to radical innovation. One of China's main development objectives is to make the economy become an innovation powerhouse in the world. This massive transition of the national innovation system requires high-level creative ideas and talents that are different from those necessary for imitative innovation. It involves vision in identifying the strategic direction and substantial investment for long-term R&D activities with partners to share risk, plus high-level, complex skills to carry out ground-breaking innovations. International collaborative innovation is, therefore, an effective mechanism to address these challenges for path-breaking radical innovations and achieve global innovation leadership.

In the increasingly global context, with innovators drawing on technologies and ideas from all over the world, innovations can be built on unique local and regional strengths. Policies should facilitate the development of enduring linkages and networks among researchers and innovators across countries

(OECD 2015). This focus is, in fact, a widely observed trend among OECD countries that have introduced a series of programmes to encourage and support international collaboration. More recently, specific open innovation policies have been discussed to improve the linkages between science and innovation, embrace uncertainty with the intersection of disciplines and sectors, increase private investment and help firms navigate a complex regulations environment to disrupt traditional industries (Bogers et al. 2018).

Some aspects are still preventing IICs and limiting their impact vis-à-vis boosting radical innovations. The lack of R&D expenditure, particularly basic research, which functions as the absorptive capacity for assimilation of technologies, prevents latecomer firms from using foreign advanced technology, competing with international firms in an open economy and engaging in radical innovations (Chen et al. 2020; Gao 2019). Remarkable progress has been made in addressing this deficit, but China still lags behind developed countries (Fu 2011; Chen et al. 2020). The lack of efficient global technology transaction markets and professional open innovation management expertise also prevents indigenous firms from engaging in IICs. Most firms do not have the necessary infrastructure to search and manage IICs effectively. Policies strengthening the layout of the IIC network and facilitating international collaborations, such as the development of platforms and other tools to orchestrate international collaborations, increase the chances of regular indigenous firms connecting with and managing external partners (Chen et al. 2020).

Although less direct, policies related to regulations and competitiveness are also supported by the evidence presented in this study. Policies help indigenous firms navigate regulations, such as those affecting IIC (for example, intellectual property sharing) or radical innovation (for example, barriers to enter highly regulated but impactful sectors). Policies are needed which promote not only cooperation but competition among indigenous firms to keep managers and shareholders motivated, willing to take risks and continue to innovate (Bogers et al. 2018).

This study has limitations that should be overcome by future research. The conclusion regarding how to manage IICs to lead to radical innovation is derived from a single in-depth case study. This study described how a private, internationalised and highly innovative firm effectively uses IIC to create radical innovations. Given the exceptionality of the case, it should not be directly generalised. Most indigenous firms are in entirely different situations. Therefore, although policies towards increasing absorptive and integration capacity in latecomer firms can be translated precisely to them, more studies are needed on how latecomer firms use and manage IICs to lead to radical innovations. Moreover, our empirical evidence suggests that firms may assign more technical research projects for international collaboration in comparison to technical development projects. It is still not clear how successful a latecomer firm can be in the creation of ground-breaking radical innovation through international collaboration. Future research needs to provide more accurate evidence on this potential gain, in particular on the size of the benefits. Caution is still needed not to over-state the benefits of international collaboration relative to collaboration with domestic partners.

Acknowledgements

The authors are grateful for helpful comments from Erik Baark, Bert Hofman, Jiwei Qian, Jizhen Li, two anonymous reviewers and workshop participants at the East Asian Institute, National University of Singapore. The literature review section of this chapter includes excerpts from a working paper written by some of the co-authors.

Notes

[1] We observed that different types of R&D projects often correspond to different types of collaboration. In C-Tech, one aspect of collaboration projects' classification is the Cooperation Type, which generally corresponds to the maturity of the deliverables. Within this attribute, we are particularly interested in two types, namely Technical Research and Technical Development. Generally, Technical Research projects are more fundamental and might need further development work to make them applicable to practical use, while Technical Development ones produce immediate results that show whether a technology can be applied in a product. Thus, we regard the former as being more fundamental, and the latter as being more application-oriented.

[2] *Exploratory* is event-driven and fast-moving for ideation and initial trials of innovation to set up the problem.

Open is a global call open to academia who are seeking breakthroughs across many ICT themes; it also welcomes wildcard proposals.

Flagship is by invitation only to resolve focused technical challenges, often in close collaboration.

References

Acemoglu, Daron. 2002. "Directed Technical Change", *Review of Economic Studies* 69, 4: 781–810.

Audretsch, David and Maryann Feldman. 1996. "R&D Spillovers and the Geography of Innovation and Production", *American Economics Review* 86, 3: 630–40.

Bao Yongchuan, Chen Xiaoyun and Kevin Zheng Zhou. 2012. "External Learning, Market Dynamics, and Radical Innovation: Evidence from China's High-tech Firms", *Journal of Business Research* 65, 8: 1226–33.

Beaver, D. D. and R. Rosen. 1979. "Studies in Scientific Collaboration: Part II. Scientific Co-authorship, Research Productivity and Visibility in the French Scientific Elite, 1799–1830", *Scientometrics* 1, 2: 133–49.

Belderbos, René, Martin Carree and Boris Lokshin. 2004. "Cooperative R&D and Firm Performance", *Research Policy* 33, 10: 1477–92.

Bogers, Marcel, Henry Chesbrough and Carlos Moedas. 2018. "Open Innovation: Research, Practices and Policies", *California Management Review* 60, 2: 5–16.

Bouncken, Ricarda B. and Sascha Kraus. 2013. "Innovation in Knowledge-intensive Industries: The Double-edged Sword of Cooperation", *Journal of Business Research* 66: 2060–70.

Brunswicker, Sabine and Vareska van de Vrande. 2014. "Exploring Open Innovation in Small and Medium-sized Enterprises", in *New Frontiers in Open Innovation*, ed. Henry Chesbrough, Wim Vanhaverbeke and Joel West. Oxford: Oxford University Press, 135–56.

Cantwell, John. 1995. "The Globalisation of Technology: What Remains of the Product Cycle Model", *Cambridge Journal of Economics* 19, 1: 155–74.

Castellani, Davide and Fabio Pieri. 2013. "R&D Offshoring and the Productivity Growth of European Regions", *Research Policy* 42, 9: 1581–94.

Chen Kaihua, Feng Ze and Fu Xiaolan. 2021. "International Innovation Collaboration in China". Forthcoming Book Chapter.

Chesbrough, Henry. 2010. "Open Innovation: a Key to Achieving Socioeconomic Evolution", *Economy, Culture & History Japan Spotlight* 29, 1: 13–5.

Criscuolo, Chiara, Jonathan E. Haskel and Matthew J. Slaughter. 2010. "Global Engagement and the Innovation Activities of Firms", *International Journal of Industrial Organisation* 28, 2: 191–202.

Dantas, Eva and Martin Bell. 2009. "Latecomer Firms and the Emergence and Development of Knowledge Networks: The Case of Petrobras in Brazil", *Research Policy* 38: 829–44.

Dewar, Robert D. and Jane E. Dutton. 1986. "The Adoption of Radical and Incremental Innovations: An Empirical Analysis", *Management Science* 32, 11: 1422–33.

Eisenhardt, Kathleen M. 1989. "Building Theories from Case Study Research", *Academy of Management Review* 14, 4: 532–50.

Eisenhardt, Kathleen M. and Melissa E. Graebner. 2007. "Theory Building from Cases: Opportunities and Challenges", *Academy of Management Journal* 50, 1: 25–32.

Enkel, Ellen and Sebastian Heil. 2014. "Preparing for Distant Collaboration: Antecedents to Potential Absorptive Capacity in Cross-industry Innovation", *Technovation* 34, 4: 242–60.

Freeman, Chris and Luc Soete. 1997. *The Economics of Industrial Innovation*. London: Pinter.

Frenz, Marion and Grazia Ietto-Gillies. 2009. "The Impact on Innovation Performance of Different Sources of Knowledge: Evidence from the UK Community Innovation Survey", *Research Policy* 38, 7: 1125–35.

Fu Xiaolan. 2011. "Open Innovation in China: Policies and Practices", *Journal of Science and Technology* 2, 3: 196–218.

_____. 2015. *China's Path to Innovation*. Cambridge: Cambridge University Press.

Fu Xiaolan and Li Jizhen. 2016. "Collaboration with Foreign Universities for Innovation: Evidence from Chinese Manufacturing Firms", *International Journal of Technology Management* 70, 2/3: 193–217.

Fu Xiaolan, Lin H. and Xiong H. 2020. "How Can Chinese firms Become Radical Innovators?: The Role of International Collaboration". Unpublished Working Paper. Technology and Management Centre for Development, University of Oxford.

Fu Xiaolan, Carlo Pietrobelli and Luc Soete. 2011. "The Role of Foreign Technology and Indigenous Innovation in Emerging Economies: Technological Change and Catch-up", *World Development* 39, 7: 1203–12.

Gao Xudong. 2019. "Approaching the Technological Innovation Frontier: Evidence from Chinese SOEs", *Industry and Innovation* 26, 1: 100–20.

George, Gerard, Shaker A. Zahra and D. Robley Wood. 2002. "The Effects of Business-university Alliances on Innovative Output and Financial Performance: a Study of Publicly-traded Biotechnology Companies", *Journal of Business Venturing* 17, 6: 577–609.

Green, S., M. Gavin and L. Aiman-Smith. 1995. "Assessing a Multidimensional Measure of Radical Technological Innovation", *IEEE Transactions on Engineering Management* 42, 3: 203–14.

Hird, Mackenzie D. and Sebastian M. Pfotenhauer. 2017. "How Complex International Partnerships Shape Domestic Research Clusters: Difference-in-difference Network Formation and Research Re-orientation in the MIT Portugal Program", *Research Policy* 46, 3: 557–72.

Hobday, Michael, Howard Rush and John Bessant. 2004. "Approaching the Innovation Frontier in Korea: the Transition Phase to Leadership", *Research Policy* 33: 1433–57.

Jugend, Daniel et al. 2018. "Relationships among Open Innovation, Innovative Performance, Government Support and Firm Size: Comparing Brazilian Firms Embracing Different Levels of Radicalism in Innovation", *Technovation* 74: 54–65.

Kafouros, Mario et al. 2015. "Academic Collaborations and Firm Innovation Performance in China: The Role of Region-specific Institutions", *Research Policy* 44: 803–17.

Katila, Riitta and Gautam Ahuja. 2002. "Something Old, Something New: A Longitudinal Study of Search Behavior and New Product Introduction", *Academy of Management Journal* 45, 6: 1183–94.

Kim Hyukjoon and Park Yongtae. 2010. "The Effects of Open Innovation Activity on the Performance of SMEs: the Case of Korea", *International Journal of Technology Management* 52, 3/4: 236–56.

Laursen, Keld and Ammon J. Salter. 2014. "The Paradox of Openness: Appropriability, External Search and Collaboration", *Research Policy* 43: 867–78.

Laursen, Keld, Francesca Masciarelli and Andrea Prencipe. 2012. "Regions Matter: How Localized Social Capital Affects Innovation and External Knowledge Acquisition", *INFORMS* 23, 1: 177–93.

Leeuw, Tim de, Boris Lokshin and Geert Duysters. 2014. "Returns to Alliance Portfolio Diversity: The Relative Effects of Partner Diversity on Firm's Innovative Performance and Productivity", *Journal of Business Research* 67, 9: 1839–49.

Lichtenthaler, Ulrich. 2008. "Open Innovation in Practice: An Analysis of Strategic Approaches to Technology Transactions", *IEEE Transaction on Engineering Management* 55, 1: 148–57.

Liu Weishu et al. 2015. "China's Global Growth in Social Science Research: Uncovering Evidence from Bibliometric Analysis of SSCI Publications (1978–2013)", *Journal of Informetrics* 9, 3: 555–67.

Mindruta, Denisa. 2013. "Value Creation in University-firm Research Collaborations: a Matching Approach", *Strategic Management Journal* 34: 644–65.

Narin, Francis, K. Stevens and Edith S. Whitlow. 1991. "Scientific cooperation in Europe and the Citation of Multinationally Authored Papers", *Scientometrics* 21, 3: 313–23.

Narula, Rajneesh. 2002. "Innovation Systems and 'Inertia' in R&D Location: Norwegian Firms and the Role of Systemic Lock-in", *Research Policy* 31: 795–816.

Narula, Rajneesh and Antonello Zanfei. 2004. "Globalisation of Innovation: the Role of Multinational Enterprises", in *The Oxford Handbook of Innovation*, ed. J. Fagerberg, D. Mowery and R. Nelson. Oxford: Oxford University Press, pp. 318–47.

National Bureau of Statistics [NBS]. 2017. *Report of Main Findings from National Innovation Survey.* Unpublished document.

Nooteboom, Bart et al. 2007. "Optimal Cognitive Distance and Absorptive Capacity", *Research Policy* 36: 1016–34.

OECD. 2008. *Open Innovation in Global Networks.* Paris.

_____. 2015. *The Innovation Imperative: Contributing to Productivity, Growth and Well-being.* Paris.

Parida, Vinit, Mars Westerberg and Johan Frishammar. 2012. "Inbound Open Innovation Activities in High-Tech SMEs: The Impact on Innovation Performance", *Journal of Small Business Management* 50, 2: 283–309.

Peng Xiaobao, Wei Song and Duan Yuzhen. 2013. "Framework of Open innovation in SMEs in an Emerging Economy: Firm Characteristics, Network Openness, and Network Information", *International Journal of Technology Management* 62, 2/3/4: 223–50.

Perkmann, Markus, Zella King and Stephen Pavelin. 2011. "Engaging Excellence? Effects of Faculty Quality on University Engagement with Industry", *Research Policy* 40:539–52.

Pittaway, Luke et al. 2004. "Networking and Innovation in the UK: A Systematic Review of the Literature", *International Journal of Management Reviews* 5, 3–4: 137–68.

Sooryamoorthy, Radhamany. 2009. "Do Types of Collaboration Change Citation? Collaboration and Citation Patterns of South African Science Publications", *Scientometrics* 81, 1: 177–93.

Wagner, Caroline S. and Loet Leydesdorff. 2005. "Network Structure, Self-organization, and the Growth of International Collaboration in Science", *Research Policy* 34, 10: 1608–18.

Wang Xianwen et al. 2013. "International Scientific Collaboration of China: Collaborating Countries, Institutions and Individuals", *Scientometrics* 95, 3: 885–94.

Yin, Robert K. 1994. *Case Study Research: Design and Methods.* Thousand Oaks, CA: Sage Publications.

Yuan Lili et al. 2018. "Who are the International Research Collaboration Partners for China? A Novel Data Perspective Based on NSFC grants", *Scientometrics* 116, 1: 401–22.

Zhao Xin-gang et al. 2013. "International Cooperation on Renewable Energy Electricity in China–A Critical Analysis", *Renewable Energy* 55: 410–16.

Zhou Changhui and Li Jing. 2012. "Product Innovation in Emerging Market-based International Joint Ventures: An Organizational Ecology Perspective", *Journal of International Business Studies* 39: 1114–32.

Zhou Ping and Tian Huibao. 2014. "Funded Collaboration Research in Mathematics in China", *Scientometrics* 99, 3: 695–715.

Part Two
Industrial Policy Challenges

In Part Two, various evaluations of industrial policy and developments in China are presented. Many of these policies have become controversial in the international debate, but detailed analyses of their actual focus and impacts are often missing. Therefore, the chapters examine issues such as: the extent to which actual investments in industrial sectors are directed by central government policies in China; the support for developing intangible assets as a key priority in the *Made in China 2025* policies; the role of local governments in policies to promote the digital economy and cloud computing, and the ways in which Chinese producers have exploited the opportunities for innovation based on global value chains to capture significant proportions of the Chinese mobile phone market.

8

PRC Industrial Policies Postdate Rather than Lead Economic Activity

Carsten A. Holz

Introduction

The industrial policies pursued in the People's Republic of China (PRC) have attracted widespread attention. The 2015 policy of *Made in China 2025*, in particular, is generally viewed as creating an invincible economic powerhouse. Underlying such interpretations is the assumption that the PRC's industrial policies have a decisive effect on resource allocation. The findings of this chapter suggest that this assumption is not valid.

Economists typically understand "industrial policy" to mean government measures "which attempt to speed the process of resource allocation among or within industrial sectors", occasionally with an additional purpose such as "correcting market distortions" (Rutherford 1992), gaining an early comparative advantage, or creating a "national champion". For the purpose of this chapter, industrial policy refers to sector-specific policies. These policies may incorporate elements of innovation policy, competition policy, growth policy or some other type of government economic policy.

Industrial policy is widely credited with having played a major role during East Asia's phase of rapid economic growth (for example Wade 1988 and 1990; Amsden 1994). The view that the government can "pick winners" has since given way to justifying government intervention with information and coordination externalities (for example Rodrik 2004); government coordination may be beneficial in the presence of not only market failures or market imperfections, but also of learning effects or other positive externalities.

Today's industrial policy has many dimensions, as Gao and Ru in this volume show, from resource mobilisation to infrastructure provision, research subsidisation, market protection and regulation. Subsidisation in the case of the PRC biotechnology industry includes loose rules around the sharing of medical information, state funding and centralised procurement processes that lower prices for generic drugs (Ballard 2019). An infant industry argument applies to PRC intellectual property rights as strategic industries are protected from global competition while themselves enjoying open, global markets (Li and Alon 2019).

The results of individual industrial policies in the PRC are mixed. For the shipbuilding industry, Barwick, Kalouptsidi and Zahur (2019) found that while industrial policy was successful in terms of boosting domestic investment in the industry, domestic entry and world market share, it also created large distortions, fragmentation, and underutilisation. For R&D inputs of large- and medium-sized firms, Eberle and Boeing (2019) found that subsidies crowd out private R&D investments (while overall R&D employment in firms increases) and increased investment rates for physical capital also reflect increased investment in residential buildings (not R&D). Soo and Jing (2019) documented the unsuccessful governmental attempts to establish a semiconductor industry going back to the 1990s and argued that the capability to reverse-engineer designs did not translate into the ability to innovate. Holz (2011) showed that the PRC does not strategically make use of positive externalities through linkage effects, in that the state does not channel state-owned enterprise activities into high-linkage sectors.

Implementation of industrial policy requires a capable administration. Prud'homme's (2016) analysis of provincial Strategic Emerging Industries programmes suggests that administrative decentralisation in the PRC may lead to sub-optimal implementation of industrial policies. While some provinces pursue their comparative advantages and specialise appropriately, other provinces do not and instead pursue new developments likely to fail. Wu, Zhu and Groenewold (2019) found that the PRC's five-year plans have significant impacts on the output growth of favoured industries, but only during the period of the five-year plan; political compliance with central directives and the availability of additional resources seem to be the leading drivers of policy implementation.

How success of industrial policy is measured varies across the literature. A regularly used criterion is output or productivity growth in the industry under consideration. For example, from 1998 to 2007, industrial policies directed at competitive sectors or fostering competition within a sector increased total factor productivity growth in the majority-private large- and medium-sized domestic firms, but this only held for subsidies and tax holidays, not for subsidised loans or tariffs (Aghion et al. 2015). From a macroeconomic point of view, a more appropriate criterion for the evaluation of industrial policy would be a measure of the *economy-wide* consequences of the policy, or a cost-benefit analysis for the particular application of government resources and government regulatory authority (suggesting the use of a computable general equilibrium model, an approach not taken in the recent literature).

This chapter bypasses the question of how to evaluate outcomes. It also does not focus on the different facets of industrial policies or on the individual means by which the government intervenes in the economy. Instead, it focuses on the one channel through which industrial policy is inevitably realised, investment, and examines the possible effects of industrial policies on investment. Whether the objective of industrial policy is innovation (product or process innovation) or economies of scale or consolidation, or any other objective, implementation will involve reallocation of capital, that is changes to investment patterns across sectors.

In the remainder of this chapter, six sets of industrial policies enacted since 2004 are introduced and their impact on the patterns of investment growth in industry is examined through regression analysis. Further analysis considers sector, administrative subordination, funding and ownership patterns of investment.[1]

Industrial Policies

Establishing investment priorities has long played an important role in the economic development of the PRC. In the second half of the 1950s, investment in 156 industrial projects established with the help of the Soviet Union laid the foundations of the PRC economy. In the Third Front Construction of the late 1960s and early 1970s, industrial investment was directed geographically according to military prerogatives. By the late 1980s, investment policy repeatedly assumed macroeconomic policy functions; for example, in the aftermath of the 2008 global financial crisis an aggregate investment push—which distinguished little between different types of projects—helped maintain economic growth.

A fundamental change in investment decision-making occurred in 2004. The State Council decreed that investment planning would morph into an investment approval procedure, transferring to the investing unit the investment initiative and extensive decision-making authority. Investment by non-state units became, in principle, no longer subject to government approval (State Council 2004).[2]

The government did not, however, fully surrender its influence over investment decisions. An appendix to the regulation listed restricted types of investment projects by sector that continued to require government authorisation. Direct government investment was still to occur in sectors where the market could not achieve an "effective allocation of resources". The government continued its practice of setting out its priorities in five-year plans. And it began to issue a number of industrial policy measures intended to channel investment and productive activities into government-favoured endeavours. The following sub-sections briefly describe six sets of industrial policy measures issued since the early 2000s.[3]

A. Industrial Policies 2004–09

Three types of industrial policies emerged after the relaxation of investment controls in 2004:[4]

(i)   Broad policies targeting more than one sector: priority investment catalogues for high-tech industries (2004, 2007, 2011) and foreign investors (2005, 2007), adjustment of the industrial structure (2005 and 2011), a Science and Technology Development Plan 2006–20, acceleration of service sector development (2007), technologies and products for import (2007, 2009, 2011) and industrial technology promotion (2009).

(ii)   Policies targeting individual sectors: the automobile industry (2004), machine-building industry (2006), nine traditional sectors for revitalisation (2009),[5] information technology industry (2009), logistics industry (2009) and culture (2009).

(iii) Sector-specific ministry five-year plans.

Many of these policies are extensive in their coverage. For example, the 2005 guidance catalogue for adjustment of the industrial structure lists approximately 500 "encouraged" types of investment projects such as "Construction of a National Agricultural Products Base" and "Development of Inter-Regional Power Grid Engineering Technology", 200 "restricted" types of projects and 400 types of projects to be "eliminated" (NDRC [National Development and Reform Commission], 2 Dec. 2015). The catalogue was revised in 2011 (NDRC 2013). A number of implementation instructions accompanied the catalogues, with later instructions reclassifying some projects.

B. Strategic Emerging Industries (2010)

In 2010, the State Council identified seven "strategic emerging industries" (*zhanluexing xinxing chanye*), with a target share in 2015 GDP of 8 per cent, and in 2020 GDP of 15 per cent (State Council 2010). The seven industries are: energy-saving and environmental protection technologies, next generation information technology, biotechnology, high-end equipment manufacturing, new energy, new materials and new energy vehicles. The document elaborates on each of these industries and then proceeds to list ways to support their development. Non-state (*minjian*) investment is explicitly encouraged.

These industries cannot be readily identified in the sector classification system because each cuts across the PRC's sector classification system as published by the National Bureau of Statistics (NBS). For example, the "new energy" industry touches more than one sector in the sector classification system, and the sector classification system does not distinguish between "old" and "new" within any one sector.

The catalogue of strategic emerging industries was revised in 2013 and then again in 2016. In 2016, "digital innovation" was newly added as an eighth favoured industry, and the eight industries were broken down into 174 "key directions" with 4,000 products and services (NDRC 2017).

C. Twelfth Five-Year Plan (2011–15)

One of the 60 sections of the 12th Five-Year Plan (2011–15) covers the strategic emerging industries without, however, going into any further detail than the 2010 State Council document does.[6] Another section of the Plan covers nine traditional industries: equipment manufacturing, shipping, automotive, iron and steel, non-ferrous metals, building materials, petrochemicals, light industry and textiles. Further elaboration suggests that it is not so much the sector itself that is favoured but specific projects within a sector. A particular sector thus may comprise favoured and non-favoured projects, with an ambiguous overall effect on investment in this sector.

A key topic of the 12th Five-Year Plan was "structural change", targeting a breakthrough for the strategic emerging industries and an increase in their share of the tertiary sector (that is, services) in GDP by four percentage points. The Plan also involved adjusting and "optimising" the investment structure, emphasised the important role of investment for domestic demand and encouraged non-state investment.

D. Supply-side Structural Reform (2015)

The "supply-side structural reform" agenda was first introduced by the Finance and Economics Leading Small Group of the Communist Party Central Committee in November 2015.[7] It comprises five elements, with the first three directly impacting investment: eliminating excess capacity, especially in steel and coal production; reducing stocks, mostly in real estate in second- and third-tier cities; de-leveraging across the economy; lowering costs, including those due to taxes, regulations and social security contributions; and a broad catch-all call for "strengthening weak points" (Naughton 2016).

The agenda does not involve draconian closure orders but represents a nod to publicly owned firms to merge and become more efficient, and the encouragement of local officials to implement environmental and other regulations and to eliminate the least desirable production capacities. A call to reduce excess capacity may also be a response to falling profitability and increasing losses at a time when prices for coal and steel were plummeting.

E. Made in China 2025 (2015)

On 8 May 2015 the State Council issued a circular titled *Made in China 2025*—the PRC version of Germany's 2012 "Industry 4.0"—which encouraged a fourth industrial revolution towards "smart factories".[8] Breakthroughs are to occur in ten priority industries: information technology, numerical control tools and robotics, aerospace equipment, ocean engineering equipment and high-tech ships, railway equipment, energy saving and new energy vehicles, power equipment, new materials, medicines and medical devices and agricultural machinery.[9] These ten priority industries dovetail with the 2010 seven strategic emerging industries, slightly rephrased, and the original "high-end equipment manufacturing" now reflected in several more narrowly defined categories.[10] A central leading group was set up and supporting documents were released.[11] Implementation of *Made in China 2025* follows traditional PRC policy patterns with pilot cities (Ningbo being the first), annual targets and tasks, and assignment of responsibility for implementation.

Beyond identifying ten priority industries, *Made in China 2025* does not favour certain sectors over others. Even in the case of the priority industries, investment need not increase for the sector in total but could shift between projects within a sector. An overall objective to become the leading manufacturing nation of the world in little more than thirty years suggests broad growth in manufacturing, with adjustments to how manufacturing is conducted within each sector rather than a drastic redirection of investment flows between sectors.

F. Thirteenth Five-Year Plan (2016–20)

The industry section of the 13th Five-Year Plan in three paragraphs lists comprehensive and industry-specific desirables.[12] The section elaborates in more detail on six sub-sectors and covers similar ground as the original seven strategic emerging industries (2010) and *Made in China 2025*:[13] acceleration of the development of high-tech industries, revitalisation of equipment manufacturing, optimal development of the energy industry, adjustment of the raw materials industry, an increase in the level of light industry and promotion of information technology.

Beyond these specifically listed industries, the coverage of the Plan is far-reaching, covering virtually every aspect of industry. Except for some raw materials industries singled out for a reduction in excess capacity, the Plan is not so much about promoting particular sectors as about various forms of upgrading within each sector.

Matching Industrial Policies into the Sector Classification System

The industrial policies represent a combination of broad exhortations and specific objectives that are difficult to match into the official sector classification system along which the official investment data are organised. Even when specific objectives are given, including for types of projects, the objectives may cut across sectors or shift the balance of projects within a sector. Table 8.1 presents an attempt to map the six sets of policies to the greatest extent possible into the sector classification system ("GB2011", the 2011 sector classification standard [*guobiao*]). For the various pre-2010 policies, a year is given in the table. For the subsequent five sets of policies, "x" denotes that this particular sector is covered (positively) by the policy and "(–)" that the policy constrains development in this sector.

Some examples illustrate the difficulty of matching industrial policies with sectors. The sector classification system includes a fourth-digit sector "biotechnology extension services" within the first-digit service sector "science" as the only potential counterpart to a policy promoting biotechnology. While there is a second-digit service sector "ecological protection and environmental management", none of its sub-sectors is an immediate counterpart to a policy targeting "environmental protection technology". There are no sector counterparts for policies on "new energy", "new materials" or "new energy vehicles" (none of the automobile manufacturing sub-sectors refers to new energy vehicles or electric vehicles).[14]

Table 8.1: Industrial Policy Summary

Sector Digit	Classification system (GB2011) Name	Policy	A	B	C	D	E	F
	Primary sector							
2	Fisheries	Fisheries			x			
	Secondary sector							
2	Mining and washing of coal	Coal; Energy development				(−)		(−)
3	Oil and natural gas exploration	Energy development						x
2	Mining and processing of ferrous metal ores	Steel; Raw material industry adjust.				(−)		(−)
2	Textile manufacturing	Textiles (high-tech, next generation)			x			
2	Textile and apparel	Light industry						x
3	Refined petroleum products manuf.	Petrochemical industry			x			
2	Chemical Raw Materials and Products	Raw material industry adjustment						(−)
2	Medicine manufacturing	Medicine; medical devices	2009				x	
3, 4	Glass fiber and ceramic products manufacturing (3); with sub-sectors (4)	Building materials (focus on glass, ceramics)			x			
2, 3	Smelting and pressing of ferrous metals	Iron and steel; Steel; Raw material adj.			x	(−)		(−)
2, 3, 4	Smelting and pressing of non-ferrous metals	Non-ferrous metals			x			
2, 3, 4	General purpose machinery (2); Special purpose machinery (2); Electrical machinery and apparatus (2); each with numerous sub-sectors (3, 4)	Machine building; High-end equipment manuf.; Equipment manuf. (twice); Numerical control tools & robotics	2006	x	x		x	x
4	Agricultural and sideline food processing equipment manufacturing	Agricultural machinery					x	

Table 8.1 (*cont'd*)

Sector Digit	Classification system (GB2011) Name	Policy	A	B	C	D	E	F
3	Special equipment manufacturing; Agriculture, forestry, animal husbandry, fishing special machinery manufacturing	Agricultural machinery					x	
4	Special instrument manufacturing; Agriculture, etc. special instrument manufacturing	Agricultural machinery					x	
4	Other motor-driven equipment manufacturing	Motor breakthrough			x			
3, 4	Motor manufacturing	Motor breakthrough			x			
3	Automobile manufacturing	Automobiles	2004, 2009		x			
3	Automobile manufacturing	New energy vehicles (twice); Energy saving and new energy vehicles		x	x			
3	Railway transportation equipment manuf.	Railway equipment					x	
2	Rail, shipbuilding, aerospace and other transportation equipment manufacturing; data on the aerospace sub-sector are missing	High-tech industries						x
3	Railway transportation equipment manuf.	Railway equipment					x	
3	Shipbuilding and related equipment manuf.	Ocean engineering equipment					x	
4	Electric light source manufacturing	Light industry			x			

(*cont'd overleaf*)

Table 8.1 (*cont'd*)

Sector Digit	Classification system (GB2011) Name	Policy	A	B	C	D	E	F
3	Household electric appliance manufacturing	Light industry			x			x
3, 4	Battery manufacturing (3); sub-sectors Lithium-Ion, Nickel-Hydrogen, and "Other" (4)	Battery technology			x		x	x
4	Thermal / hydroelectric / nuclear power gener.	Energy development						x
3	Electricity production	Power equipment					x	
3	Electricity supply	Energy development						x
2	Gas production and supply	Energy development						x
	Tertiary sector		2009					
1, 2	Transportation (1); sub-sectors include loading/unloading and warehousing (2)	Logistics	2009					
4	Ocean freight and passenger transportation	Logistics		x				
2	Environmental management	Environmental protection technologies		x	x			
1	Information technology (services)	Information techn.; Next-generation inf. techn. (twice); High-tech industry	2009	x	x		x	x
2	Air transport services	High-tech industries; Aerospace equip.					x	x
2	Water transport (services)	Ocean engineering equipment					x	
1	Real estate	Real estate				(–)		
1	Science	Same as information techn. (services)	2009	x	x		x	x
4	Biotechnology extension services	Biotechnology (twice); Light industry		x	x			x
1	Culture, sports, and entertainment	Culture	2009					

Table 8.1 (*cont'd*)

Note: The order of sectors follows the official sector classification system GB2011. Numbers in parentheses after sector labels denote the digit-level of the sector. Policies of two separate periods in one field are separated by a semi-colon. The symbol "x" means that the policy favours investment in this sector and "(–)" that the policy constrains investment in this sector.

A: pre-2010 industrial policies. B: Strategic Emerging Industries (2010). C: Twelfth Five-Year Plan (2011–15). D: Supply-side Structural Reform Program (2015). E: *Made in China 2025* (2015). F: Thirteenth Five-Year Plan (2016–20).

Source: See discussion of industrial policies in text.

The NBS in December 2012 issued a trial sector classification system for the strategic emerging industries to match the State Council's seven categories, further broken down into 30 sub-categories and 100 sub-subcategories, at which level a correspondence is being established with 359 sectors in the NBS's official sector classification system.[15] The NBS emphasises that the correspondence is not exact not only in that a particular aspect of the strategic emerging industries may be reflected in more than one sector of the official sector classification system (which its matching exercise captures), but also in that some sectors of the official sector classification system may contain both strategic emerging industry aspects and other aspects (an issue the NBS cannot address).[16] No such NBS regulations were issued in the case of *Made in China 2025*, possibly following the Party's recent attempts to downplay the policy.[17]

In 2013, in response to the 12th Five-Year Plan and to a guiding opinion of the State Council Office of 2011 on accelerated development of the high tech service sector, the NBS issued a trial sector classification scheme for high tech *service* industries (*gaojishu chanye* [*fuwuye*] [NBS 2013a]), followed by a separate document on high tech *manufacturing* industries, also of 2013 (NBS 2013b), in which the NBS identified six manufacturing categories as high-tech industries (pharmaceuticals, aviation, electronics and communication equipment, computer and office equipment, medical equipment, "information chemical" manufacturing [*xinxi huaxuepin zhizaoye*]) and matched them into 69 second through fourth-digit manufacturing sectors.[18]

Industrial Policies and Investment Growth

In this section, the question whether industrial policies affect sector investment patterns is addressed through regression analysis. Industrial policies are captured by dummy variables for each of the six policies identified above as well as for the NBS' identification of strategic emerging industries and, separately, high-tech manufacturing industries.

Investment is measured as "Fixed Asset Investment" (FAI, *guding zichan touzi*). FAI is the sum of all fixed asset investment spending by firms.[19] Detailed sector and ownership data are available for a significant but changing subset of FAI over time: (i) in 2003–10, urban investment (accounting for 82 to 88 per cent of FAI); and (ii) since 2011, "investment, except by rural households" (accounting for 97 to 99 per cent of FAI).[20] In the following, the label "urban" investment will be used for both of these (sequential) subsets, independent of whether these are data of the years prior to 2011 or since that year. Due to three statistical breaks between 2009/2010 and 2012, the investment data are best analysed separately for the periods before and after the statistical breaks.[21] The investment data are in nominal terms; sector-specific investment deflators are not available.[22]

Factors other than industrial policies may affect investment. A prime competing explanatory variable for the observed investment patterns is profitability. Investment and profitability data can be matched, sector by sector, for mining, manufacturing and utilities ("industry"). What is available for industry is (limited) balance sheet and profit and loss account data for the above-norm industrial enterprises, a set of enterprises that accounts for approximately 90 per cent of industrial value-added. Assuming that profitability of above-norm industrial enterprises in a particular sector is representative of the profitability of all industrial enterprises in that sector, and that investment in industry is exclusively conducted by industrial enterprises, the investment and industry datasets can be combined.[23] Fourth-digit sector industry data are available for 2012–16 *only* (while fourth-digit sector investment data are available for 2003–12 and 2014–17).[24] Given the 2010 and 2015 policy interventions, regression analysis is conducted separately for the two periods 2012–15 and 2015–17.

Profitability is measured by return on assets (RoA).[25] Several control variables are included: (i) Sales growth represents market demand, with changes in market demand potentially triggering changes in investment. (ii) Different ownership forms, measured by their share in investment, may come with different investment behaviour. (iii) Investment per employee controls for capital intensity; investment potentially shifts away from or towards sectors with high capital intensity. It is measured in CNY million per employee, while all other variables are measured in percentages.

For the first period (2012–15), due to data limitations, sales growth data are those of 2013.[26] RoA is also of 2013. Because fourth-digit sector investment data are not available for 2013, ownership shares are those of 2014—ownership shares are quite stable between adjacent years and the particular choice of year should have little effect—as are the data on investment per employee (2012 employment data are missing in the industry statistics). For the second period (2015–17), sales growth data are those of 2015 compared to 2013, while RoA, ownership shares and investment per employee are of 2015.

Table 8.2 reports the Ordinary Least Squares regression results for the first period (2012–15) across fourth-digit sectors plus those third-digit sectors for which no fourth-digit sector data are available.[27] Profitability has a significant positive impact on investment growth, as do sales growth and capital intensity (first column of Table 8.2). The investment share of state-owned and state-controlled units (SOSCUs) has a negative impact, while the shares of foreign-funded units (FFUs) and of Hong Kong, Macau and Taiwan units (HKMTUs) have no impact (second column); the omitted ownership group is entirely composed of non-state domestic units, for which no further breakdown is available.[28]

Of the six sets of industrial policies, only two have a significant effect (and with the expected signs): the supply-side structural reform programme of 2015 and *Made in China 2025*. Both effects occurred in the three years (2012–15) *before* the policy was initiated.

The NBS measure of strategic emerging industries (with a dummy variable for 236 fourth-digit sectors in industry identified by the NBS) shows no significant impact of this 2010 policy on the investment patterns of 2012–15.[29] The 62 high tech fourth-digit manufacturing sectors identified by the NBS in 2013 also have no significant impact.

Table 8.3 reports the regression results for investment growth between 2015 and 2017. Sales growth and ownership matter, as before. The share of investment by FFUs and at times by HKMTUs is now also significant, with a positive impact on investment growth. The coefficient of capital intensity is consistently significant but now with a negative sign, indicating investment growth away from high capital intensity sectors, in contrast to the previous period of 2012–15.

Profitability in 2015 consistently plays no role in explaining investment growth. Data problems led the NBS to stop publishing detailed industry data starting in 2017, indicating potentially increasingly problematic profitability data. If the lack of significance were to reflect a real world phenomenon of profitability having no impact on investment patterns, this would open wide the door to alternative explanations including industrial policies.

The supply-side structural reform programme of 2015 had a barely significant (negative) correlation with investment growth in 2015–17, indicating a possible policy effect, except that investment changes in the industries targeted by the supply-side structural reform programme had already been well underway for several years before the policy was issued and the policy may simply coincide with an ongoing trend established years earlier. *Made in*

Table 8.2: Explaining Investment Growth, 2012–15

	Dependent variable: growth rate of investment 2012–15 in %										
	(1)	(2)	(3)	(4)	(5)	(6)	(7)	(8)	(9)	(10)	(11)
RoA 2013	***2.75	***2.21	***2.12	***2.19	**2.10	**2.16	**2.16	***2.21	*1.87	**2.33	***2.20
	(0.75)	(0.80)	(0.81)	(0.81)	(0.82)	(0.80)	(0.80)	(0.80)	(0.82)	(0.81)	(0.80)
Sales growth 2013	***0.74	***0.64	***0.63	***0.64	***0.63	**0.62	***0.65	***0.64	**0.60	**0.62	**0.62
	(0.24)	(0.24)	(0.24)	(0.24)	(0.24)	(0.24)	(0.24)	(0.24)	(0.25)	(0.24)	(0.24)
SOSCU 2014 share in investment	***-0.83	***-0.83	***-0.87	***-0.84	***-0.85	**-0.77	***-0.84	***-0.83	***-0.83	***-0.88	***-0.84
	(0.31)	(0.31)	(0.31)	(0.31)	(0.31)	(0.31)	(0.31)	(0.32)	(0.32)	(0.31)	(0.31)
FFU 2014 share in investment	-0.22	-0.22	-0.20	-0.19	-0.13	-0.31	-0.34	-0.22	-0.49	-0.30	-0.55
	(0.92)	(0.92)	(0.92)	(0.93)	(0.93)	(0.91)	(0.91)	(0.92)	(0.95)	(0.92)	(0.95)
HKMTU 2014 share in inv.	0.14	0.14	0.07	0.14	0.14	0.08	0.32	0.13	-0.07	0.13	-0.14
	(1.29)	(1.29)	(1.29)	(1.2)	(1.29)	(1.29)	(1.29)	(1.29)	(1.31)	(1.29)	(1.30)
Investment / employee 2014	***9.69	***11.9	***11.9	***11.9	***12.0	***11.6	***11.8	***11.9	***11.3	***11.9	***12.0
	(2.74)	(2.86)	(2.86)	(2.87)	(2.87)	(2.86)	(2.85)	(2.87)	(2.91)	(2.86)	(2.86)
Policy dummies											
Pre-2010 ind. policies			-6.92						-23.8		
			(10.1)						(18.8)		
Strategic Emerg. Industries				-1.80					22.3		
				(9.45)					(24.0)		
12th FYP					-5.35				-11.6		
					(9.13)				(18.8)		
Supply-side structural ref.						*-53.3			-49.1		
						(30.6)			(31.5)		

Table 8.2 (cont'd)

	Dependent variable: growth rate of investment 2012–15 in %										
Made in China 2025							**32.2 (15.7)		**38.6 (16.5)		
13th FYP								-0.74 (22.0)	-13.5 (22.8)		
NBS Strategic Em. Industries										9.27 (8.96)	
NBS High-tech											19.8 (15.2)
Intercept	*16.4 (9.61)	*30.5 (12.0)	***33.6 (12.9)	**31.3 (12.7)	**33.5 (13.1)	***32.4 (12.1)	**28.3 (12.1)	*30.5 (12.1)	***37.6 (13.3)	**26.7 (12.6)	**30.7 (12.0)
Observations	563	563	563	563	563	563	563	563	563	563	563
R²	0.063	0.075	0.076	0.075	0.064	0.080	0.071	0.075	0.092	0.078	0.078

Notes: RoA: return on assets.
Sales growth refers to main business income (*zhuying yewu shouru*).
SOSCU: State-owned and state-controlled unit; FFU: foreign-funded unit; HKMTU: Hong Kong, Macau, Taiwan unit.
FYP: Five-year plan.
NBS: National Bureau of Statistics.
Except for investment per employee, which is in CNY million per employee, all explanatory variables are expressed in %.
Investment data cover "investment, except by rural households". Industry data cover the above-norm industrial enterprises.
The sector coverage is fourth-digit sectors plus those third-digit sectors for which no fourth-digit sector data are available.
Values in parentheses are standard errors.
Significance levels: * 10%, ** 5%, *** 1%.
Sources: *Investment Statistical Yearbook 2013, 2015, 2016; Industry Statistical Yearbook 2013, 2014, 2015.*

Table 8.3: Explaining Investment Growth, 2015–17

	Dependent variable: growth rate of investment 2015–17 in %										
RoA 2015	-0.07	-0.20	-0.27	-0.20	-0.25	-0.25	-0.19	-0.23	-0.34	-0.20	-0.22
	(0.30)	(0.31)	(0.31)	(0.31)	(31.7)	(0.31)	(0.31)	(0.31)	(0.32)	(0.32)	(0.31)
Sales growth 2015	***0.48	***0.46	***0.46	***0.46	***0.46	***0.44	***0.47	***0.47	***0.44	***0.46	***0.44
	(0.06)	(0.06)	(0.06)	(0.06)	(0.06)	(0.06)	(0.06)	(0.06)	(0.06)	(0.06)	(0.06)
SOSCU 2015 share in inv.	***-0.28	***-0.28	***-0.31	***-0.28	***-0.29	***-0.27	***-0.27	**-0.24	**-0.27	***-0.29	***-0.30
	(0.10)	(0.10)	(0.10)	(0.10)	(0.10)	(0.10)	(0.10)	(0.10)	(0.11)	(0.10)	(0.10)
FFU 2015 share in investment	***1.08	***1.08	***1.11	***1.08	***1.12	***1.06	***1.18	***1.16	***0.99	***1.08	***0.88
	(0.32)	(0.32)	(0.32)	(0.33)	(0.33)	(0.32)	(0.32)	(0.32)	(0.34)	(0.32)	(0.34)
HKMTU 2015 share in inv.	*0.88	*0.88	0.79	0.88	*0.87	0.85	0.75	0.78	0.40	*0.88	0.75
	(0.52)	(0.52)	(0.52)	(0.52)	(0.52)	(0.52)	(0.52)	(0.52)	(0.53)	(0.52)	(0.52)
Investment / employee 2015	***-3.53	**-2.27	**-2.25	**-2.27	**-2.19	**-2.25	**-2.23	**-2.17	**-2.39	**-2.26	**-2.14
	(0.94)	(0.97)	(0.97)	(0.97)	(0.97)	(0.97)	(0.96)	(0.97)	(0.97)	(0.97)	(0.97)
Policy dummies											
Pre-2010 ind. policies			-5.04						***-17.4		
			(3.49)						(6.51)		
Strategic Emerg. Industries				0.30					**18.7		
				(3.25)					(8.29)		
12th FYP					-2.21				-4.83		
					(3.14)				(6.5)		
Supply-side structural ref.						*-18.0					-18.25
						(10.7)					(10.9)

Table 8.3 (*cont'd*)

	Dependent variable: growth rate of investment 2015–17 in %										
Made in China 2025							**-12.7 (5.4)		-8.55 (5.68)		
13th FYP								**-16.0 (7.61)	*-13.5 (7.82)		
NBS Strategic Em. Industries										0.22 (3.13)	
NBS High-tech											**10.5 (5.26)
Intercept	0.27 (3.11)	-1.58 (3.82)	0.56 (4.09)	-1.69 (4.03)	-0.38 (4.18)	-0.53 (3.87)	-0.92 (3.81)	-1.36 (3.81)	2.86 (4.25)	-1.68 (4.12)	-1.30 (3.81)
Observations	565	565	565	565	565	565	565	565	565	565	565
R^2	0.106	0.151	0.154	0.151	0.152	0.155	0.159	0.158	0.180	0.151	0.157

For notes see previous table.

Sources: *Investment Statistical Yearbook 2016, 2018; Industry Statistical Yearbook 2014, 2016.*

China 2025 and the 13th Five-Year Plan, both of 2015, had a (significant) negative—rather than the expected positive—impact on investment growth in 2015–17.[30]

Combining all six policies in one and the same regression attests that the pre-2010 industrial policies had a negative impact—perhaps the policies were outdated as of 2015–17—and the Strategic Emerging Industry policy of 2010 had a positive impact on investment growth in 2015–17, half a dozen years later.

The coefficient of the NBS' (2012) strategic emerging industries continued to be insignificant in the second period, while that of the NBS' (2013) high-tech sectors was newly significant, as in the case of the Strategic Emerging Industry policy of 2010.

To summarise: In the first period, profitability, market demand, ownership characteristics and capital intensity exerted an unambiguous influence on investment growth. Industrial policies in the rare instances that they matter *do so after the fact*. In the second period, the effects of market demand and ownership characteristics persisted, while the effect of capital intensity turned negative. Profitability had no effect and generally neither did industrial policies; in the few instances when they had an effect they either carried the wrong sign or the effect occurred so many years after the policy was enacted that one wonders if the effect can still be attributed to the policy.[31]

The list of sectors that the NBS in 2012 deemed to correspond to strategic emerging industries was not limited to industry. Across construction and the tertiary sector—for which detailed data, such as on profitability, are not available—investment in NBS-identified fourth-digit strategic emerging industry sectors (including those third-digit sectors that did not contain fourth-digit sectors) grew faster than in those sectors not deemed subject to industrial policy, but the difference was not statistically significant (in both the 2012–15 and 2015–17 periods). The high-tech tertiary sectors identified by the NBS in 2013 equally performed no differently than other tertiary sectors, in both periods.[32]

The findings of the regression results can be illuminated further by delving into sector, administrative subordination and ownership patterns of investment. This is done in the following three sections.

Sector Distribution of Investment

In 2015, three-quarters of FAI was concentrated in four of the 19 first-digit sectors (Figure 8.1)—manufacturing (32 per cent), real estate (24 per cent), public facilities including environment (10 per cent) and transport (9 per cent)[33]—with manufacturing, public facilities/environment and transport (half of FAI) potentially the subject of industrial policies.

In the period 2012–15, investment in mining was stagnant (indicated by the crosses in Figure 8.1), *predating* the 2015 supply-side structural reform agenda. Manufacturing investment shows little (if any) impact from the various industrial policies favouring individual manufacturing sectors promulgated in the 12th Five-Year Plan. Investment in 2012–15 grew fastest in information technology (IT), business services, health, trade and science. Growth in IT and science conforms with the 2010 strategic emerging industries policy, but IT and science each still accounted for only 1 per cent of economy-wide investment in all three years 2012, 2015 and 2017. In 2015–17, the fastest-growing sectors were public facilities, business services, education and health, none of which—except environment within public facilities—is a sector favoured by industrial policies (dots in Figure 8.1). These sectors are followed by IT and science—sectors targeted by industrial policies—but also by culture and agriculture.

Data available for the approximately 100 second-digit sectors for the subset of "urban" investment further suggest that investment growth and industrial policies are not well aligned. Examining the periods 2003–08, 2008–10, 2012–15 and 2015–17 (the choice of periods being determined by data availability, statistical breaks and policy periods), the growth rates of "urban" investment correlate with industrial policies for some sectors but not for others; many sectors with high investment growth rates are not industrial policy sectors.

Figure 8.2 graphically extracts the second-digit *industry* sectors with their 2015 shares in "urban" investment—including an ownership breakdown that is discussed below—as well as the sector growth rates in per cent between 2012 and 2015 (crosses) and between 2015 and 2017 (dots), both measured on the right-hand side axis. All mining sectors experienced significant investment declines between 2015 and 2017, including a 23 per cent fall in investment in oil and natural gas extraction, a sector *favoured* by the 13th Five-Year Plan for 2016–20. Investment in both coal and ferrous metals, key sectors targeted for reduction by the Supply-side Structural Reform Programme of 2015, already fell significantly before 2015.

In manufacturing, a broad range of light industry sectors (the approximately first dozen manufacturing sectors) experienced above-average growth rates in both periods, even though industrial policies addressed none of these sectors except for the textile industry in the 12th Five-Year Plan. The furniture industry and the manufacture of cultural goods—not industrial policy sectors—stand out with exceedingly high growth rates in both periods.

Investment growth in 2015–17 was (newly) highest for computers (including communication and other electronic equipment), an industrial

Figure 8.1: First-digit Sector Investment Shares 2015 and Growth Rates (2012–15, 2015–17)

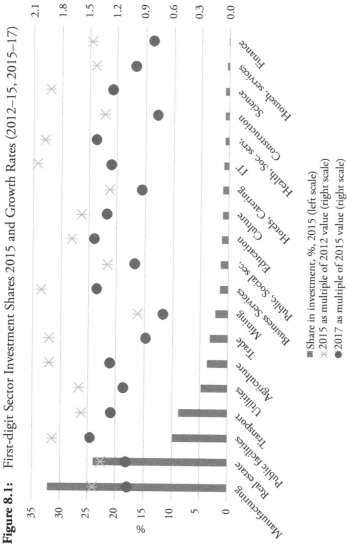

■ Share in investment, %, 2015 (left scale)
✳ 2015 as multiple of 2012 value (right scale)
● 2017 as multiple of 2015 value (right scale)

Notes: IT: Information technology (For detailed sector labels, see note to Figure 8.3, below).
Except for real estate investment and rural individual-owned investment, the minimum size of investment projects
to be included in the statistics is CNY5 million.
Source: *NBS database; Statistical Yearbook 2016, 2017, 2018* (Table 10-6).

Figure 8.2: Second-digit Industrial Sector Investment Shares 2015 and Growth Rates (2012–15, 2015–17)

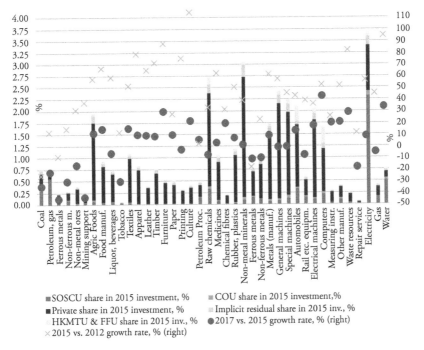

- ■ SOSCU share in 2015 investment, %
- ■ Private share in 2015 investment, %
-   HKMTU & FFU share in 2015 inv., %
- × 2015 vs. 2012 growth rate, % (right)
- ■ COU share in 2015 investment,%
-   Implicit residual share in 2015 inv., %
- ● 2017 vs. 2015 growth rate, % (right)

Notes: SOSCU: State-owned and state-controlled unit. COU: Collective-owned unit. HKMTU: Hong Kong, Macau, Taiwan unit. FFU: Foreign-funded unit.

Data coverage: Investment, except by rural households, for industry (mining, manufacturing, and utilities).

The sum of all bars across sectors (left-hand side scale) equals 39.9% of (economy-wide) "urban" investment.

In each bar, the ownership distribution begins from the bottom up. Thus, SOSCUs occupy the lowest segment of the bar, with private units the next segment up. (The shares of HKMTUs, FFUs, COUs, and of the residual tend to be relatively small and may not be easy to decipher in the chart.)

Source: *NBS database, Statistical Yearbook 2016, 2017, 2018.*

policy sector, at 43 per cent, followed by the furniture industry, not the target of industrial policy. The 18 per cent growth rate of electrical machinery and apparatuses may be in line with high-end manufacturing being promoted as a strategic emerging industry (2010) or numerical control tools and robotics being promoted by *Made in China 2025* (2015), but investment in general purpose machinery and in special purpose machinery was unchanged (negative 1 per cent and 0 per cent growth). While the Strategic Emerging Industry policy (2010) promoted the development of electric vehicles, and *Made in China 2025* the development of new energy vehicles, investment in the automobile industry rose an unremarkable 14 per cent in 2015–17 and a similarly average rate of 43 per cent in 2012–15. Overall, investment appears to grow fast in some industrial policy sectors and equally in some sectors not subject to industrial policy.

The coefficient of variation of investment growth across all second-digit sectors fell over time from 0.76 in 2003–2008 to 0.32, 0.34, and 0.25 in 2008–10, 2012–15 and 2015–17. This suggests a trend towards broad-based, economy-wide investment growth rather than any form of specialisation that could be the outcome of targeted industrial policies.

Extending the analysis to the third- and fourth-digit sector levels, changes in investment patterns across many of the sectors predate the respective industrial policies, and in some sectors concur. The fact that the 30 fastest-growing sectors together account for an ever smaller share of "urban" investment over time, by 2015 equal to only one-thirtieth of what one would expect that share to be given the average sector share, suggests that fast-growing investment in a particular sector primarily serves to develop a previously underdeveloped sector, implying a catch-up process or the completion of an industrial structure more than any kind of specialisation that would be favoured by targeted industrial policies.

Central Influence on Investment

Official statistics classify investment according to the level of government under which the investment occurs. "Central" investment denotes investment by enterprises, administrative facilities (*shiye danwei*), and administrative organs (*xingzheng danwei*)—in short, by "units"—directly subordinate to the Chinese Communist Party Central Committee, the National People's Congress, and the State Council's ministries, commissions, offices and companies.[34] All other investment is "local": all projects by enterprises, administrative facilities, and administrative organs that are directly led and administered by provincial, municipal, and county governments and their relevant departments,[35] as well as private and foreign investment that is not subordinate to any administrative tier.

The central share in FAI declined from 13.3 per cent in 2003 to a mere 4.7 per cent in 2015 and 4.1 per cent in 2017, less than one-twentieth of FAI.[36] This extremely low share of central investment means that the central government's direct impact on investment via units subordinate to it is small or near-negligible.

In the more detailed breakdown of local investment available for "urban" investment, the centre accounted for 5 per cent of investment in 2015, the provinces for 4 percent, the municipalities for 8 percent, the counties for 17 percent, and "others" for 65 per cent (Figure 8.3).[37] The centre has a relatively high investment share in mining, utilities and transport; the provinces in transport; the municipalities in transport and across all tertiary sectors; and the counties in construction, transport, public facilities, education, health and public management. These are largely public goods, not industrial policy sectors.[38]

Across sectors, central investment is highly correlated with provincial investment (Pearson correlation coefficient of 0.93), and correlated to a continuously decreasing degree with municipal, county and then "other" investment (other: 0.27). The same pattern holds for the correlation between provincial investment and municipal/county/ "other" investment, and finally municipal investment (vs. county, "other"). This gradation in correlations suggests the existence of tier-specific—rather than industrial policy— investment preferences, with some flexibility in investment assignments between adjacent tiers.

Even if the centre wanted to implement industrial policies via local government investment, implementation might not be straightforward since lower-level governments might have little interest in implementing central policies. The further removed a particular tier is from the centre, the less responsive it will likely be to central policies (while the tier's share in "urban" investment increases with the distance to the centre).

"Other" investment—principally private investment outside the control of government—is the dominant form of investment in more than half of all first-digit sectors, in particular in manufacturing (where it accounts for 87 per cent of investment) and in real estate (69 per cent), but also in agriculture, trade, business services, science and household services. The share of "other" investment is lowest in transport (29 per cent), education (34 per cent) and public management (34 per cent), namely, in public goods sectors.

Data on sources of investment funding paint a similar picture of limited direct government influence on investment. In 2017, the share of state budget appropriations in investment financing was only 6 per cent (Figure 8.4), much of which was expended on public goods projects.

Figure 8.3:   Central vs. Local Shares in "Urban" Investment, 2015 (%)

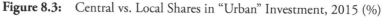
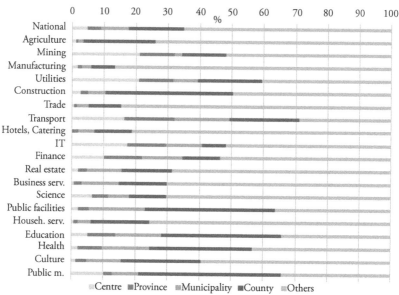

Notes: The unabbreviated sector labels are: Agriculture, Forestry, Animal Husbandry and Fishery; Mining; Manufacturing; Production and Supply of Electricity, Heat, Gas and Water; Construction; Wholesale and Retail Trade; Transport, Storage and Post; Hotels and Catering Services; Information Transmission, Software and Information Technology; Financial Intermediation; Real Estate; Business Services and Leasing; Scientific Research and Technical Services; Management of Water Conservancy, Environment and Public Facilities; Service to Households, Repair and Other Services; Education; Health and Social Services; Culture, Sports and Entertainment; Public Management, Social Security and Social Organisations.
Source: *Investment Statistical Yearbook 2016.*

Domestic loans accounted for 11 per cent of investment funding. Policy lending could target firms in industrial policy sectors and thereby increase the share of potentially policy-directed funding by a few percentage points. "Industrial guidance funds"—such as the Integrated Circuit Industry Fund, funded through the state budget, bank loans and financial contributions by various state-owned enterprises and state entities—may seem large in size but pale in comparison to overall state investment, which in turn pales in comparison to economy-wide investment.[39]

The shares of "own" and "other" funds in 2017 were 65 and 17 per cent (and that of foreign funds was 0.3 per cent). The allocation of "own" funds would seem solely at the discretion of the investing unit. One caveat, however,

Figure 8.4: Sources of Investment Funding (shares in total in %)

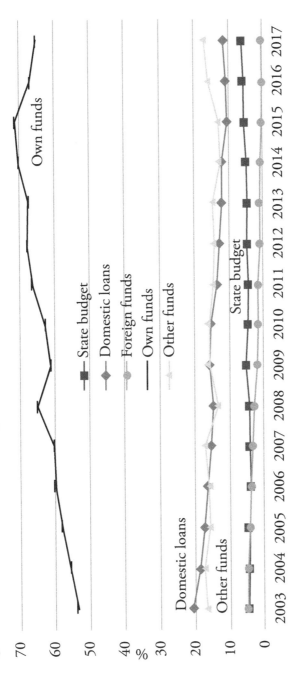

Note: The same statistical breaks as noted earlier for the years 2010-2012 apply but are ignored here since the data here represent shares in the (variably defined) totals.

Source: *Investment Statistical Yearbook 2018.*

is that "own" funds include—besides "private capital" (*ziyou zijin*) of firms and institutions (presumably retained earnings)—"funds collected from other units". Thus, some of the "own funds" could have been obtained, for example, by issuing bonds, which could be subject to government approval.

Ownership Distribution of Investment

A breakdown of investment by ownership is available for "urban" investment. A first distinction is between domestic investment vs. investment by "Hong Kong, Macau and Taiwan units" (HKMTUs) and by foreign-funded units (FFUs). Domestic investment accounted for 89 per cent of "urban" investment in 2003 and continuously increased to 96 per cent in 2017. The investment shares of HKMTUs and FFUs correspondingly decreased, from 5 per cent and 6 per cent in 2003 to 2 per cent each in 2017 (Figure 8.5).

The breakdown of domestic investment available since 2008 shows investment by private units on a steady upward trend which exceeds investment by state-owned and state-controlled units (SOSCUs) starting in 2010.[40] By 2015, private units accounted for more than half of investment (51 per cent), SOSCUs, after a phase of decline, for 32 per cent, and collective-owned units (COUs) for 4 per cent. An undefined implicit residual grew from 1 per cent in 2008 to 8 per cent in 2015. In 2016 and 2017 the SOSCU share rebounded (while the private share fell slightly), possibly due in part to reclassifications.

To graphically illustrate the principal ownership patterns across sectors, Figure 8.6 shows the ownership shares within each first-digit sector in 2015.[41] The extent of private investment in manufacturing and in real estate—the two largest sectors, together accounting for more than half of investment—is immediately apparent. Across the manufacturing sectors, key targets of industrial policies, SOSCUs in 2015 accounted for only 7 per cent of investment, while private units accounted for 78 per cent. Overall, private investment is dominant across half of all sectors, with a smaller presence in typical public goods sectors.

Investment by SOSCUs is substantial in utilities, construction, transport, information technology, finance, public facilities, education, health, culture and public management, none of which, except for information technology, is an industrial policy sector. Investment by COUs is spread across all sectors, while small shares of investment by FFUs and HKMTUs are present across two-thirds of all sectors, mostly in manufacturing, IT and real estate.

Figure 8.2 (above) includes ownership information for the second-digit *industry* sectors in 2015. SOSCUs are the dominant investors in the extraction of petroleum and natural gas, in the tobacco industry, in electricity production, and in water supply, all of which are monopoly or near-monopoly sectors.

Figure 8.5: Investment Shares by Ownership, "Urban" Investment 2003–17 (%)

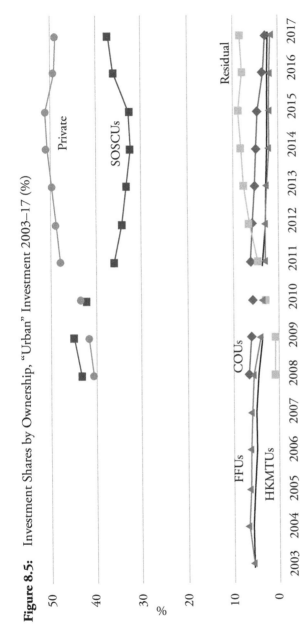

Notes: SOSCU: State-owned and state-controlled unit. COU: Collective-owned unit. HKMTU: Hong Kong, Macau, Taiwan unit. FFU: Foreign-funded unit. "Residual" is the implicit residual obtained as domestic investment less investment by SOSCUs, COUs and private units.

In 2010, the size criterion for inclusion in urban investment increased from CNY500,000 to CNY5 million (the NBS retrospectively revised the 2010 data), and in 2011 coverage switched from urban investment to "investment, except by rural households".

The HKMTU and FFU shares are indistinguishable after 2010.

Source: *NBS database, Statistical Yearbook 2018.*

Otherwise, sector by sector, private units provide the lion's share of investment. COUs play a negligible role across all sectors (barely visible in the figure), while FFUs and HKMTUs (together) play a minor role in half a dozen sectors and have a minimal presence across other sectors.[42]

Figure 8.6:   Investment (except by Rural Households) by Sector and Ownership, 2015

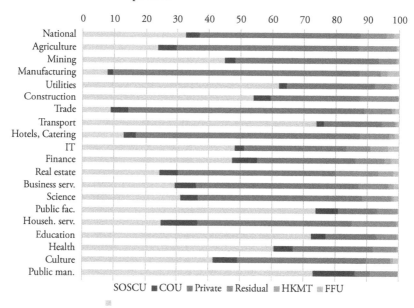

Notes: SOSCU: State-owned and state-controlled unit. COU: Collective-owned unit. HKMTU: Hong Kong, Macau, Taiwan unit. FFU: Foreign-funded unit.

For unabbreviated sector labels, see notes to Figure 8.3.

"Residual" is the implicit residual obtained as domestic investment less investment by SOSCUs, COUs, and private units.

Source: NBS database.

The distribution of private investment across sectors and its dominance in the non-public goods sectors imply that implementation of industrial policy, to a very large degree, has to rely on private entrepreneurs. Shih (2014), in a monograph on the PRC's industrial policy programmes from 1978 through 2013, concluded that industrial policy in the PRC was introduced to replace imperative planning and therefore *exclusively* targeted state-owned enterprises. The industrial policies of the last decade appear to be more inclusive and are, at least in language, not limited to state-owned enterprises. But forcing or incentivising the private entrepreneurs who account for the bulk of investment in industrial policy sectors to do the state's (policy) bidding is likely difficult.

Conclusions

Regression analysis suggests that industrial policies have little or no effect on investment outcomes in industry. At least through 2015, investment is driven primarily by profitability considerations. When industrial policies have an effect, changes in investment patterns *precede* industrial policy. Similarly, Naughton (2019: 183) in a different context finds that "policymakers are happy to pick winners after the event". And Wang (2018) argues that "China's technological success is driven by its top companies rather than government planning".[43] A caveat would be that industrial policies could have been circulated internally *well before* being formally announced.

Given that industrial policy sectors are dominated by privately owned firms, breakthroughs such as those envisaged by *Made in China 2025* may be more likely to occur if the government offers profitability-enhancing incentives. But with diverging interests between central government departments and localities and with policy documents that number in the hundreds, supporting measures could well end up supporting everything and (thereby) nothing, or be misallocated (for which there is some evidence). The sectoral patterns of investment growth over the past two decades suggest that investment grows particularly fast in underdeveloped sectors of the economy rather than in a small selection of sectors targeted by industrial policy, indicating a catch-up process and completion of a broad industrial structure.

The impression arises that different departments—each favouring projects beneficial to its mission or institutional interests—compete in issuing industrial policy document after document, filling each generation of central leaders' latest "guidance" and "strategies" with meaning, while the economy largely develops according to market principles. Industrial policies may well have some impact only when a department manages to command significant financial resources towards a particular end.[44]

The NBS' difficulty in matching policies into the sector classification system suggests that policy makers are unable or unwilling to unambiguously identify industrial policy sectors to begin with. Industrial policy appears to be not so much sector-specific as project-specific policy, accompanied by a sweeping exhortation across the five-year plans and other industrial policy documents to "upgrade" every aspect of the economy. This industrial policy is not one in the traditional sense of sector-specific policies that apply equally to all market participants. Rather, it is formed of project-targeted interventions accompanied by guidelines for bureaucrats as to what they are expected to favour by all means available to them, from development funds to various administrative measures.

The findings in this chapter contrast with evidence of the effects of the PRC's industrial policies provided elsewhere in the literature. For example, state sponsorship helped Huawei develop its 5G capabilities (via practically free 5G spectrum, research funding and state-led demand for Huawei products) and helped the China Railway Rolling Stock Corporation (CRRC) modernise and compete globally; it created the PRC's telecommunications behemoths and the PRC's solar photovoltaic panel industry; and it turned the PRC's shipbuilding industry into a global force. But at the macro level examined in this chapter, industrial policy does not have a decisive effect on resource allocation. That implies either that these examples are exceptions (highly selective cases, targeted projects) or that industrial policy in these cases was not crucial for their success to begin with.

Notes

[1] This chapter includes some (updated and expanded) earlier analysis by the author (Holz 2019).

[2] For a description of the earlier investment procedures in effect through the mid-1990s, see Huang (1996a, 1996b). On increasing encouragement of private investment in the 2000s, see Lardy (2014: 91ff.).

[3] Each set of industrial policies comprises the initial document and follow-up instructions and corresponding documents issued by central ministries as well as provincial and municipal governments. Prud'homme (2016) found more than 300 documents for the case of the 2010 Strategic Emerging Industry policy alone.

[4] Heilmann and Shih (2013) provide a list of industrial policies, here augmented and categorised.

[5] These sectors for revitalisation include, with concrete plans for 2009–11, the automobile industry, biology and medicine industry, equipment manufacturing and new energy (see China Briefing [2009]), all of which were later integrated into the Twelfth Five-Year Plan (2011–15).

[6] See section 10 of the Twelfth Five-Year Plan. Some of the subsequent sections cover aspects of the seven strategic emerging industries, though the term "strategic emerging industries" does not always appear.

[7] Articles by an "authoritative personage" in *Renmin ribao* (People's Daily) on 4 Jan. and 9 May 2016 widely promoted the supply-side structural reform agenda.

[8] The four revolutions are: water- and steam-powered mechanical manufacturing, mass production based on electric power, automation of manufacturing based on information technology, and cyber-physical systems (smart factories with embedded information technology systems).

[9] Wang (2018) argued that the PRC's success in the technology industry has been in downstream consumer goods; *Made in China 2025* is an attempt to catch up in the upstream, component-supplying sectors such as semiconductors.

[10] Explicit reference is made to "strategic emerging industries" once, as part of an introductory passage on strengthening the manufacturing capacity of the PRC.

[11] See the English-language State Council webpage that promotes *Made in China 2025* events, decisions and achievements (State Council 2020).

[12] The industry section is titled "Promote the Optimization and Upgrading of the Industrial Structure". Other sections address development of the service industry, regional balancing, and energy saving and environmental protection.

[13] The term "strategic emerging industries" does not appear in the plan. Kenderdine (2017) shows the policy consistency from "Strategic Emerging Industries" to *Made in China 2025* and the 13th Five-Year Plan.

[14] Aerospace equipment, one of the ten priority industries of *Made in China 2025*, can be matched directly with the third-digit sector "aviation and aerospace equipment manufacturing" (with further, four fourth-digit sectors). But in the investment statistics, checked for 2012–17 values, this third-digit sector is missing.

[15] The trial sector classification system was issued explicitly in response to the State Council's 10 October 2010 decision and to assist in the implementation of the 12th Five-Year Plan. An updated version of the document, adopting the new sector classification system GB2017 (replacing GB2011), was issued in 2018 (NBS 2018b). It still refers to the State Council's 2010 policy but now also refers to the 13th Five-Year Plan.

[16] As an example for the latter case, the NBS selects *all* of "agriculture" in the sector classification system to match "agricultural biotechnology applications" in the strategic emerging industries policy.

[17] Li and Alon (2019) point out that following the reactions abroad to the PRC's *Made in China 2025*, the Party has banned the media from discussing *Made in China 2025*.

[18] Most recently, Party and State Council issued "guidance" on acceleration of the development of the "Three New" (new industry, new undertakings, new commerce [*xin chanye xin yetai xin shangye*]). The NBS on 14 August 2018 then issued a circular on the sector classification of the "Three New". The matching into the sector classification system is based on the 13th Five-Year Plan, *Made in China 2025* and further listed documents.

[19] Holz (2019, 2020) provides a detailed discussion of the investment data. Key sources of investment data are the *Statistical Yearbook*, the *Investment Statistical Yearbook* and the NBS database available online.

[20] The difference between the two subsets is that the earlier excludes investment not just by rural households but also by rural non-households, that is, it excluded *all* rural investment.

[21] The three statistical breaks are: (1) In 2011, the urban-rural distinction evolved into a distinction between "investment, except by rural households" (for which detailed data are available) and "investment by rural households", accounting for 97 per cent and 3 per cent of total investment, respectively. (2) Since 2011, the new minimum urban investment size to be included in the statistics is CNY 5 million, ten times higher than the size criterion previously applied through 2010 to "urban investment", of

CNY 500,000. (3) The sector classification system was adjusted in 2012 with a switch from GB 2002 to GB 2011. For details on the transition in the classification system, statistical breaks and coverage changes over time see Holz (2013, 2020).

[22] Neither nominal nor real (inflation-adjusted) FAI data are the obviously preferred choice.

[23] Above-norm industrial enterprises are industrial enterprises with annual sales revenue from principal business above (since 2011) CNY 20 million. The data source is the *Industry Statistical Yearbook*.

[24] The availability of data coincides with the consistent use of one sector classification system (GB2011) during the period 2012–17. A new sector classification system was introduced in 2017 (GB 2017) but the published 2017 fourth-digit sector investment data still adhere to the previous classification system.

[25] Alternatively, one could use return on equity (with near-identical results).

[26] With investment growth measured for the period 2012–15, a preferred sales growth measure might cover the period 2012 vs. 2011, but 2011's fourth-digit sector industry data are not available (and data for earlier years follow the different, earlier sector classification system).

[27] The NBS sector classification systems present these third-digit sectors with two numbers: a third-digit sector number, and the same number with a zero added at the end to denote a fourth-digit sector.

[28] Ownership can also be measured by the registration-based share of different ownership forms in paid-in equity. The shares of the state and of "individuals" tend to be negative and significant, while those of FFUs and HKMTUs tend to be positive and significant. All other registration forms have no significance.

[29] The NBS identifies an additional eight *second-digit* sectors. These are not used because the NBS typically has identified a selection of fourth-digit sectors as relevant.

[30] Across all regressions involving a dummy variable for the 13th Five-Year Plan, the dummy variable was assigned the value one only for those sectors *favoured* by the 13th Five-Year Plan. Interaction terms of individual industrial policies and the investment share of SOSCUs tended to be insignificant.

[31] The explanatory power of the regressions (as measured by the R^2) was relatively low throughout. In 2015–17, variation in the explanatory variables typically explained about 15 per cent of the variation in investment growth. This suggests that other sector-specific characteristics may play an important role for investment growth.

[32] The comparison of means is based on investment growth rates across policy sectors vs. non-policy sectors.

[33] The corresponding percentages in 2012 and 2017 were similar (35/30, 26/23, 8/13, and 9/10 per cent).

[34] For the definition see the NBS (http://www.stats.gov.cn/tjsj/zbjs/201310/t20131029_449538.html, accessed 31 Jan. 2017). The website gives examples of such units, including the NBS local survey teams (directly subordinate to the NBS), the Industrial and Commercial Bank of China, China Telecom and PetroChina.

[35] Presumably, in parallel to the practice at the central level, local Party organs and people's congresses are included in the category "local".

[36] NBS database and *Investment Statistical Yearbook*.

[37] In 2017, the percentages were similar with 4, 4, 10, 20 and 62 per cent.

[38] The centre's 21 per cent share in mining may be a historical remnant, with land a key state resource, while the centre's 21 per cent share in utilities reflects ownership of the nationwide electricity grid and gas supply.

[39] On such industrial guidance funds see, for example, Naughton (2019), Wübekke et al (2016) and Zenglein and Holzmann (2019).

[40] "State-owned and state-controlled units" refers to the following units: traditional (unincorporated) state-owned units, joint state-state units, 100 per cent state-owned limited liability companies, and all other units (typically limited liability and stock companies) in which the state has an absolute or de facto controlling stake. For a discussion of the impact of the statistical breaks on the ownership shares see Holz (2019).

[41] The charts for 2012 and 2017 look very similar and a time series comparison is therefore omitted.

[42] Yet more dis-aggregated data show FFU investment to be highly concentrated in a very few sectors. But even in highest-concentration FFU sectors, such as automobile manufacturing or computer manufacturing, FFUs do not account for more than 15 per cent of investment.

[43] Wang (2018) uses Huawei as an example to show how the government in earlier years hampered the growth of a well-run company in order to boost a state-owned rival that ultimately was not successful.

[44] Reportedly, half of all of the PRC's R&D occurs in little more than 500 firms. Narrow targeting of industrial policy measures would match such a concentration of R&D.

References

Aghion, Philippe et al. 2015. "Industrial Policy and Competition", *American Economic Journal: Macroeconomics* 7, 4: 1–32.

Amsden, Alice H. 1994. "Why Isn't the Whole World Experimenting with the East Asian Model to Develop?: Review of *The East Asian Miracle*", *World Development* 22, 4: 627–33.

Ballard, Will. 2019. "Chinese Biotech: From Copycat to Innovator", *Financial Times*, 10 Oct. 2019. Available at https://www.ft.com/content/03812ddf-84a3-4540-9850-9a33cfe637d0 [accessed 7 Nov. 2019].

Barwick, Panle J., Myrto Kalouptsidi and Nahim Bin Zahur. 2019. *China's Industrial Policy: an Empirical Evaluation*. Cambridge, MA: NBER Working Paper No. 26075.

China Briefing. 2009. "Revitalization Programs Set for Five Industries". Available at https://www.china-briefing.com/news/revitalization-programs-set-for-five-industries/ [accessed 18 Nov. 2020].

Eberle, Jonathan and Philipp Boeing. 2019. *Effects of R&D Subsidies on Regional Economic Dynamics: Evidence from Chinese Provinces*. China Center for Economic Research, Working Paper Series E2019004.

Heilmann, Sebastian and Shih Lea. 2013. *The Rise of Industrial Policy in China, 1978–2012*. Harvard-Yenching Institute Working Paper Series 2013.

Holz, Carsten A. 2011. "The Unbalanced Growth Hypothesis and the Role of the State: the Case of China's State-owned Enterprises", *Journal of Development Economics* 96, 2: 220–38.

————. 2013. "Chinese Statistics: Classification Systems and Data Sources", *Eurasian Geography and Economics* 54, 5/6: 532–71.

————. 2019. "Industrial Policies and the Changing Patterns of Investment in the PRC Economy", *The China Journal* 81: 23–57.

————. 2020. "Understanding PRC Investment Statistics". *China Economic Review* 61, issue C. Available at https://www.sciencedirect.com/science/article/abs/pii/S1043951X20300584 [accessed 19 Nov. 2020].

Huang Yasheng. 1996a. "Central-local Relations in China During the Reform Era: The Economic and Institutional Dimensions", *World Development* 24, 4: 655–72.

————. 1996b. *Inflation and Investment Controls in China: The Political Economy of Central-local Relations During the Reform Era*. New York: Cambridge University Press.

Industry Statistical Yearbook. Various years. *Zhonggtuo gongye tongji nianjian* [(China) Industry Statistical Yearbook]. Beijing: Zhongguo tongji chubanshe.

Investment Statistical Yearbook. Various years. *Zhonggtuo guding zichan touzi tongji nianjian* [(China) Fixed Asset Investment Statistical Yearbook]. Beijing: Zhongguo tongji chubanshe.

Kenderdine, Tristan. 2017. "China's Industrial Policy, Strategic Emerging Industries and Space Law", *Asia & The Pacific Policy Studies* 4, 2: 325–42. [Also available at https://onlinelibrary.wiley.com/doi/epdf/10.1002/app5.177]. [accessed 7 Feb. 2021].

Lardy, Nicholas R. 2014. *Markets Over Mao: The Rise of Private Business in China*. Washington, DC: Peterson Institute for International Economics.

Li Shaomin and Ilan Alon. 2019. "China's Intellectual Property Rights Provocation: A Political Economy View", *Journal of International Business Policy*, 3 Sept. 2019. Available at https://doi.org/10.1057/s42214-019-00032-x [accessed 19 Nov. 2020].

Naughton, Barry. 2016. "Supply-side Structural Reform: Policy-makers Look for a Way Out", *China Leadership Monitor* 49 (1 March 2016). Available at https://www.hoover.org/profiles/barry-naughton [accessed 19 Nov. 2020].

————. 2019. "Financialisation of the State Sector in China", in *China's Economic Modernisation and Structural Changes: Essays in Honour of John Wong*, ed. Zheng Y. and Tong S. Y. Singapore: World Scientific, pp. 167–85.

NBS [National Bureau of Statistics]. 2011. *Guomin jingji hangye fenlei zhushi, 2011* [National economic sector classification, 2011]. Beijing: Zhongguo tongji chubanshe. Available at http://www.stats.gov.cn/tjsj/tjbz/ [accessed 14 October 2019].

————. 2012. *Zhanluexing xinxing chanye fenlei (2012) shixing* [Strategic emerging industries trial sector classification (2012)]. Available at http://www.stats.gov.cn/tjsj/tjbz/ [accessed 14 Oct. 2019].

_____. 2013a. *Gaojishu chanye (fuwuye) fenlei (2013) (shixing)).* [High tech sector trial classification (services), 2013]. Available at http://www.stats.gov.cn/tjsj/tjbz/ [accessed 14 Oct. 2019].

_____. 2013b. *Gaojishu chanye (zhizaoye) fenlei (2013).* [High tech sector classification (manufacturing), 2013]. Available at http://www.stats.gov.cn/tjsj/tjbz/ [accessed 14 Oct, 2019].

_____. 2017. *Guomin jingji hangye fenlei (2017)* [National economic sector classification, 2017]. Available at http://www.stats.gov.cn/tjsj/tjbz/ [accessed 14 Oct. 2019].

_____. 2018a. *Xin chanye xin yetai xin shangye moshi tongji fenlei (2018)* [New industry, new undertakings, new commerce (2018)]. Guo tong zi #111/2018. Available at http://www.stats.gov.cn/tjsj/tjbz/ [accessed 14 Oct. 2019].

_____. 2018b. *Zhanluexing xinxing chanye fenlei (2018).* [Strategic emerging industries sector classification (2018)]. Available at http://www.stats.gov.cn/tjsj/ tjbz/ [accessed 14 Oct. 2019].

NBS Database. National Bureau of Statistics Statistical Database. Available at http://www.stats.gov.cn.

NDRC [National Development and Reform Commission]. 2005. *Chanye jiegou tiaozheng zhidao mulu* [Guidance catalogue for adjustment of the industrial structure] (with State Council approval). Available at http://www.sdpc.gov.cn/fzgggz/fzgh/zcfg/200512/t20051222_65963.html [accessed 8 Feb. 2017].

_____. 2013. *Chanye jiegou tiaozheng zhidao mulu (2011)* [Guidance catalogue for adjustment of the industrial structure, 2011]. Available at http://www.gov.cn/gzdt/att/att/site1/20110426/001e3741a2cc0f20bacd01.pdf [accessed 19 Nov. 2020].

——. 2017. *Zhanluexing xinxing chanye zhongdian chanpin he fuwu zhidao mulu 2016* [Guiding catalogue for key products and services in the strategic emerging industries, 2016]. Available at http://www.ndrc.gov.cn/gzdt/201702/t20170204_837246. html [accessed 18 Dec. 2017].

Prud'homme, Dan. 2016. "Dynamics of China's Provincial-level Specialization in Strategic Emerging Industries", *Research Policy* 45, 8: 1586–603.

Rodrik, Dani. 2004. "Industrial Policy for the Twenty-First Century", *Mimeo* September.

Rutherford, Donald. 1992. *The Dictionary of Economics.* London: Routledge.

Shih, Lea. 2014. *Chinas Industriepolitik von 1978–2013: Programme, Prozesse und Beschränkungen* [China's industrial policy 1978–2013: programme, processes and limitations]. Wiesbaden: Springer, 2014.

Soo Zen and Meng Jing. 2019. "How China Is Still Paying the Price for Squandering Its Chance to Build a Home-grown Semiconductor Industry", *South China Morning Post*, 4 Sept. Available at https://www.scmp.com/tech/big-tech/article/3024687/how-china-still-paying-price-squandering-its-chance-build-home-grown [accessed 7 Nov. 2019].

State Council. 2004. *Decision on Reform of the Investment System. Guofa* 20/2004. Available in English at http://en.ndrc.gov.cn/policyrelease/200602/t20060207_58851.html [accessed 8 Feb. 2017].

_____. 2010. *Guanyu jiakuai peiyu he fazhan zhanluexing xinxing chanye de jueding* [Decision on accelerating cultivation and development of strategic emerging industries]. Available at http://www.gov.cn/zwgk/2010-10/18/content_1724848. htm [accessed 19 Nov. 2017]; for an English language summary of the State Council document see The US-China Business Council (2013).

_____. 2015. *Zhongguo zhizao 2025* [Made in China 2025], *Guofa* 28 / 2015. Available at http://www.gov.cn/zhengce/content/2015-05/19/content_9784.htm [accessed 19 Nov. 2020].

_____. 2020. "Made in China 2025". Available at http://english.www.gov. cn/2016special/madeinchina2025/ [accessed 18 Nov. 2020].

Statistical Yearbook. Various years. *Zhonggtuo tongji nianjian* [(China) Statistical Yearbook]. Beijing: Zhongguo tongji chubanshe.

The US-China Business Council. 2013. *China's Strategic Emerging Industries: Policy, Implementation, Challenges, & Recommendations.* Available at https://www.uschina. org/sites/default/files/sei-report.pdf [accessed 19 Nov. 2020].

Thirteenth Five-Year Plan. 2016. *Guomin jingji he shehui fazhan di shisan ge wunian guihua gangyao (quanwen)* [Outline of the thirteenth Five-Year Plan for national economic and social development (full text)]. Available at http://www.gov.cn/ xinwen/2016-03/17/content_5054992.htm [accessed 19 Nov. 2020].

Twelfth Five-Year Plan. 2011. *Guomin jingji he shehui fazhan di shi'er ge wunian guihua gangyao (quanwen)* [Outline of the twelfth Five-Year Plan for national economic and social development (full text)]. Available at http://www.gov.cn/2011lh/ content_1825838.htm [accessed 19 Nov. 2020].

Wade, Robert. 1988. "State Intervention in 'Outward-looking' Development: Neoclassical Theory and Taiwanese Practice", in *Developmental States in East Asia*, ed. Gordon White. London: MacMillan, pp. 30–67.

_____. 1990. *Governing the Market: Economic Theory and the Role of Government in East Asian Industrialization.* Princeton, NJ: Princeton University Press.

Wang Dan. 2018. "Why China Can Succeed in Tech", *Gavekal Dragonomics Ideas*, 19 Dec.

Wu Yiyun, Zhu Xiwei and Nicolaas Groenewold. 2019. "The Determinants and Effectiveness of Industrial Policy in China: A Study Based on Five-Year Plans", *China Economic Review* 53: 225–42.

Wübekke, Jost et al. 2016. *Made in China 2025: The Making of a High-tech Superpower and Consequences for Industrial Countries*, (Mercator Institute for China Studies) MERICS Papers on China No. 2, Dec. Available at https://www.merics.org/en/ papers-on-china/made-china-2025 [accessed 19 Nov. 2020].

Zenglein, Max J. and Anna Holzmann. 2019. *Evolving Made in China 2025: China's Industrial Policy in the Quest for Global Tech Leadership.* (Mercator Institute for China Studies) MERICS Papers on China No. 8, 2 July. Available at https://www.merics. org/en/papers-on-china/evolving-made-in-china-2025 [accessed 22 Oct. 2019].

9

Made in China 2025 and the Proliferation of Intangible Assets

Anton Malkin

Introduction

In 2015, *Made in China 2025* (MIC 2025) was released to much criticism. Critics claimed that this plan was a thinly veiled import substitution programme that sought to push foreign technology firms and manufacturers out of the Chinese market. The Chinese government defended it as consistent with the long-term policy objective of Reform and Opening Up, emphasising China's need to overcome the middle-income trap. The Government also pointed out that MIC 2025 called for strengthening of intellectual property (IP) law and further FDI liberalisation.

This chapter asks: How can we reconcile these dramatically opposing views? The data and analysis presented here suggest that, paradoxically, the conflicting narratives carry grains of truth, but obscure the challenges facing China's industrial economy in the near and medium term and the ways in which MIC 2025 seeks to overcome these challenges. It argues that the evolving logic of globalisation, long-standing problems of technological catch-up and economic development, reinforced by the growing importance of the intangible economy—defined by the commercialisation of, and business strategies centred around, intellectual property (IP) like patents, trademarks, copyright and data—create real tensions in China's path to catching up with advanced manufacturing economies like Japan, Germany and Korea. It briefly examines China's progress in technological standardisation and its growing portfolio of intellectual property assets and shows that despite the intrinsic contradiction in MIC 2025's insistence on both self-sufficiency and globalisation, China's continued integration into the global intangible economy creates potential tensions between China and other advanced economies.

This chapter explains that the MIC 2025 plan is inseparable from China's expanding intangible economy and is one piece of a multi-pronged strategy to move China up the global value chain hierarchy. It should be viewed alongside China's automation, standardisation and IP commercialisation strategies. These components of China's economic evolution conform to changes in patterns of globalisation, which are increasingly defined not only by the global division of labour in supply chains—a key aspect of post-Cold War trade and finance-driven globalisation—but also by the proprietorship over intangible assets like patents, data, standards and brands. In this respect, MIC 2025 tells us as much about significant changes in the global economy, as much as it tells us about the forward trend of China's industrial policy planning. This chapter explores MIC 2025 in the context of the intangible economy and explains how China's plan to transform its manufacturing sector plays out in its drive to standardise manufacturing, commercialise IP and influence Chinese firms' mergers and acquisitions (M&A) decisions and IP asset acquisitions more broadly.

An Industrial Policy for the Intangible Economy

In principle, MIC 2025 is about moving Chinese electronics manufacturers, many of which are private, up the chain of value creation. Indeed, the acceleration of the move from low-end manufacturing prompted by the trade war with the US is not an impediment to China—indeed, it reinforces MIC 2025. The plan sees China effectively abandon its role as the workshop of the world, and join the ranks of Germany, Japan and South Korea in specialising in automated, "intelligent", highly productive manufacturing activities. It also sees Chinese firms join the ranks of US multinational corporations (MNCs) in controlling the patents, brands and data that allow top global firms to generate revenues from global production without having to directly engage in physical manufacturing. In a sense, China wants to have its cake and eat it too: to create and own the technologies that go into advanced manufacturing facilities, and to engage in the physical manufacturing processes that put these technologies to work.

To be sure, many aspects of the plan are familiar to students of East Asian industrial policy. Despite the novel focus on intangible assets, MIC 2025, at its core, seeks to align government priorities with the commercial interests of its manufacturing firms, providing government funding (typically through venture capital, tax rebates and industrial park construction; see Malkin 2018). But unlike South Korea, Japan and other smaller developmental economies, MIC 2025 does not focus on export-driven rapid catch-up development. Instead, MIC 2025 is focused on the domestic economy. Critics typically assert that MIC 2025 is about displacing foreign firms globally. However, the document—with its ambitious targets of domestic supply (see Wübbeke et al. 2016)—focusses on the domestic market, projecting the global competitiveness of Chinese manufacturing brands far into the future (Table 9.1).

Table 9.1:   Timeline for Achieving MIC 2025 Goals

Step 1	
	• By 2020, consolidate manufacturing • By 2025, Information Technology will be comprehensively integrated into manufacturing (Industrial Revolution 4.0) and China will have well-known global MNCs specialising in manufacturing
Step 2	
	• By 2035, Chinese manufacturing will reach an "intermediate" level (behind Germany, Korea and Japan, but substantially ahead of middle-income economies) • China will lead global innovation in sectors where China is most competitive (i.e. MIC 2025 sectors)
Step 3	• By 2049, China will become the leader among global manufacturing powers

What, then, is MIC 2025 all about? Consider the diagnosis offered in the document of what is wrong with China's manufacturing industry. It highlights the fact that manufacturing in China is facing [a] "two-way squeeze" (双向挤压): from developed countries at the top and developing countries at the bottom. It notes that China has few world-renowned brands and that its "independent innovation capability" is weak; it also highlights that its industrial structure and service sectors are "immature". It urges the country to move from "made in China" to "created in China" (实现中国制造向中国创造的转变), putting an emphasis on R&D and brand development. Indeed, the document reads more like an innovation strategy rather than an import substitution programme.

As explained below, this framing is the result of the underlying logic of MIC 2025—the growing importance of the intangible economy in manufacturing. The intangible economy is defined as the commercialisation of, and business strategies centred around, intellectual property (IP) such as patents, trademarks, copyright, data, as well as research and proprietary knowledge. The intangible economy creates pressures not only for global economic integration—as intellectual property laws and norms in major markets increasingly converge towards more private ownership of IP assets—but by a degree of self-sufficiency as well.

As Haskel and Westlake (2018) argue, intangible assets are different from tangible, fixed asset investment in part because they are more difficult to value through traditional accounting methods, are more scalable (because they are not physical and do not have physical production constraints) and generate productivity and economic value in less predictable ways. One could also add to this collection of distinctions the problem of industry concentration. Because intangible assets are associated not with the ownership of financial or physical capital, but fundamentally concern the ownership of ideas, it is easier to exclude competitors from collecting the rents and value generated by these ideas (for example, through the legal system) than to price out competitors or create better products. Simply put, there is no such thing as a totally new idea, and increasingly, owners of "new" ideas (like owners of patents of a new technology) cannot make a new product without paying licensing fees to owners of ideas on which new inventions are built. As such, barriers to entry in industries like semiconductors and telecommunications are higher than ever before and make economic development through the import of technology and physical capital less effective than in the past. This paradox of openness begetting zero-sum gains stems from the growing importance of the rents and revenues accruing to firms and countries from owning a greater share of intangible assets that, while traded globally, are created and deployed locally.

Emerging Industries Made in China: AI, Automation and the Intangible Economy

In 2019, in response to *Made in China 2025* being featured heavily in the United States Trade Representative (USTR) 301 investigation, the Chinese authorities began to downplay the role of the plan in China's national development strategy. Needless to say, policy action and policy messaging are not one in the same. While MIC 2025 may decline in name, the sectoral catch-up goals are unlikely to be dropped from China's economic development strategy going forward.

This is because MIC 2025 is as much a descriptive outline of China's technological development strategy as it is a call to action. First, while MIC

2025 is about manufacturing at its core, observers have largely misunderstood the role of manufacturing in China's plan to climb global value chains. Simply put, manufacturing sectors' prowess should be understood as a means to an end, rather than an end itself. This is because grabbing a higher share of output in the global economy of the twenty-first century is not about making things, but about owning the brands, patents, copyrights and data that arrange how things are made, where they are made, and who collects the revenues when goods move across borders. This, in a nutshell, is the definition of the intangible economy in the context of manufacturing.

MIC 2025, in its original State Council pronouncement, was explicit about how China's manufacturing sector is seen as evolving. Automation, intelligent manufacturing (the "industrial internet of things") and standardisation are seen as the means to achieve China's value chain ascent. But the goal of manufacturing component self-sufficiency is, rather, a national security-based imperative to achieving the goal of intangible economy competitiveness.

As the International Monetary Fund (IMF) noted in their 2019 Article IV consultation on China, "China has a more advanced industrial structure than its income level would suggest. The share of high-tech in industrial value-added was 43 per cent in 2015 […], similar to the level in Belgium and Spain, where income levels are about three times higher" (IMF 2019: 13). This suggests that MIC 2025 is less trendsetting and more trend-following in its aspirations. Simply put, China has already moved a long way towards manufacturing sophistication, but its firms continue to lag in capturing the value created from this advanced structure.

In this respect, MIC 2025's sectoral self-sufficiency approach uses the wrong metrics to assess the plan's success or failure. Therefore, the stated goals of sectoral supply self-sufficiency are inappropriate measures if the goal is to see its manufacturing industry occupy a high position in global value chains (GVC). Supplying components only is a very inadequate goal, as component supply occupies the mid-range in the GVCs. As Xing explains in this volume (p. 265), "A lead firm, which manages the operation of a value chain and decides the relations between firms participating in the chain, is necessary for any meaningful GVCs".

Why is it important to have leading firms with global reach occupying the top of GVCs in their respective (or multiple) sectors? The answer has less to do with protectionism, in the classical sense of the term, and more to do with the nature of the intangible economy. It has less to do with which firms have access to China's market, or how much China exports, and more with to do with how much value Chinese firms capture from both existing and emerging technologies. In the global intangible economy, self-sufficiency in component manufacturing does not mean physically producing "core components", but rather possessing the *right* to produce these components at the exclusion of others, the ability and expertise to produce these components and the ability to earn revenues from the products they produce.

How, then, should we begin to assess China's industrial policy goals in the intangible economy? How should we interpret the tensions they create between China and other advanced economies? I propose looking specifically at the standardisation efforts and IP asset growth in China, and suggest that tracking China's IP balance of payments—the difference between payments and receipts for IP—offers a glimpse of the progress of China's intangible economy more broadly as well as its relationship with other players in the global intangible economy.[1] I suggest that while there is already a flourishing market for intangible assets in China, Chinese firms, universities, and research institutes are still substantially behind their foreign rivals in commercializing their own technology portfolios.

Standards as a Pathway to Globally Competitive Manufacturing

Standards are an important means for countries to overcome being stuck in lower tiers of GVCs. MIC 2025 offers a conflicting narrative of China's industrial upgrading strategy. While discussing the need to promote Chinese firms' standard-setting capabilities, the plan nevertheless promotes both quantitative targets for sectoral self-sufficiency in "core component" supplies and moving away from physical goods production towards intangible production.

Global value chains—broadly defined as the division of labour among firms and countries along the chain of stages of production, from basic assembly on one end through product development to branding on the other—are inherently hierarchical, with standard-setting and IP-owning firms at the top, setting prices and creating product specifications. These specifications may be open-source or proprietary, but in all cases technological standards set parameters for components manufacturers and final product assemblers that perform specialised manufacturing tasks. Standard-setting firms embed themselves in GVCs by establishing arms-length relationships with suppliers, but also by ensuring quality consistency, reliability of component and assembly manufacturing supply chains, and creating managerial consistency along these supply chains (von Hagen and Alvarez 2011). Standards are generally set behind closed doors by industry associations, governments and intergovernmental organisations.

The hierarchy in GVCs could partly be understood as a distinction between standard-makers and standard-takers. While some standard-makers like Intel, TSMC and Samsung both set standards and own manufacturing operations directly and through sub-contracting, other firms, such as Qualcomm and Intellectual Ventures focus exclusively on R&D and product standardisation. These firms often file for IPR protection for their R&D output under the category of standard-essential patents (SEP), meaning that their component design is standard-essential in that it comprises a product that is not only essential in a particular supply chain, but is also proprietary (more on this below).

The hierarchy in GVCs is defined both by productivity and by the ability to adjust to new product development and other disruptions in the existing chain of supplying global goods. Adjustment for contractors downstream in the supply chain value spectrum (for instance, factories that specialise in final assembly of various products) is typically a challenge. Small contractors involved in standardised assembly of commodified goods like fabrics, plastics and glass often have low leverage in the production cycles and final demand for their products because they are separated from the final product by multiple layers of players in the supply chain. For instance, coastal contract manufacturers in China must negotiate not only with component suppliers in Korea and Japan, which make the components that the former put together, but also with buyers in destination markets—namely, retailers, brand owners and importing firms.

By contrast, owners of global brands and firms with large quantities of standard-essential patents (SEPs) are able to command the structure of global supply chains due to their proprietorship of the intellectual property that encompasses the final goods that consumers and large organisations purchase (Schwartz 2019). Small and large manufacturing contractors, as well as manufacturers of components that feed into final assembly, must abide by the intellectual property laws and norms set in core markets if they are to maintain their supplier-buyer relationships across the global economy. Murphree and Anderson (2018: 123–36) suggest that constraints placed on firms can be explained not only by global value chain theory, but also by resource dependence theory (RDT) (see Hillman, Withers and Collins 2009: 1404–27), which was developed in international business and management literature to explain the strategic constraints placed on firms reliant on government contracts and the costs of switching business models that such constraints entail. In their study of Chinese manufacturing contractors, Murphree and Anderson showed how this concept can be applied to firms downstream from IP-owning at the top of the global value chain hierarchy. They are constrained by choices made by leading global IP owners, with adjustment burdens of novel manufacturing techniques and markets falling on the smallest players, particularly sub-contractors in China's manufacturing regions.

RDT can also be applied to standards-abiding firms at the bottom of this hierarchy. To explain how, we need to understand how standards are set and the power they confirm on standard-setting firms. Standards are set with a variety of purposes: phytosanitary precautions (for example, food safety), conformity to domestic markets (for example, different electric outlet design and driver seat placement in automobiles) and electronic component compatibility (for example, cellular phone charging cables). In manufacturing, standards define specification on everything from the design of a factory floor, to the size and weight specifications of manufactured goods. GVCs cannot function without standards. Indeed, the very process of modern globalisation could be said to be underpinned by something as simple and ubiquitous as shipping container standards, which define not only the processes and inspections that make the transit of global goods possible, but also define the size and quality of global manufactured goods (Girard 2019).

In terms of RDT, resources can be defined as the dependence of manufacturers on the specifications of the types of goods they can produce and how such goods are to be produced. Small sub-contracting manufacturers have little input over the direction of GVC structure, as technological standards are set by committees of engineers and government representatives at both the national and international levels. Moreover, the capacity to influence and create global standards does not simply benefit standard-setting firms, but also influences the capacity of the country where such firms are domiciled to adapt to the changing structures of globalisation—and to exert *relative* gains from said structures. As Girard (2019: 5) describes it, standards are more than just publicly available instructions for producers and retailers:

> Once developed, they become copyrighted documents. Standards get published and sold to users. Buyers include all players in supply chains from the producers of raw materials, those who provide parts, components and systems to the manufacturers of assembled goods, product testing laboratories and conformity assessment bodies.

In short, setting standards is profitable and reduces dependence on exogenous inputs under RDT. By contrast, MIC 2025 posits an endogenous model of component self-sufficiency. Standard-setting, by contrast, creates opportunities for Chinese firms to take proprietorship over IP assets without the necessity to own and manufacture physical products, and to have a direct stake in the functioning of a global system that increasingly depends on the protection and commercialisation of intangible assets.

Following the controversy surrounding MIC 2025, policymakers seem to have internalised these lessons and expanded on the role of standards in China's economy in a policy plan titled *China Standards 2035* (中国标准 2035). The promulgation of the government's policy guidance towards the role of standardisation in China's economy builds on an earlier State Council document, the 12 November 2013 *Decision on Major Issues Concerning the Comprehensively Deepening of Reform of the Third Plenary Session of the 18th CPC Central Committee.* This document stressed standardisation as part of the 18th CPC Central Committee's stated goals of deepening the market allocation of resources and "comprehensively deepening reform" (Hui and Cargill 2017).

This adjacent plan lays out the government's plans to promote the global promulgation of indigenous Chinese standards and their role in China's economic development. There are important, large differences between China's methods to promote standardisation and those of the US, Europe and elsewhere. In the case of the latter, standardisation relies largely on non-governmental professional associations and private firms to create national and international fora that discuss, assess, and set standards that all major global firms must rely on if they are to plug into integrated global supply chains and into global trade more broadly. These are not entirely different from financial standards that have a distinctly voluntary character (countries can receive a high rating in global financial markets if they comply) and food safety standards (which work based on market access denial for non-complying firms and jurisdictions). But, in a sense, they are more binding, due to the global reach of manufacturing supply chains.

In the Chinese case, however, technological standards see much more involvement on the part of the state. Although the role of the state in standardisation has been much critiqued and amended within China (Hui and Cargill 2017), regional governments and the central government still play an important role in the implementation of said standards. Today, it is not government bodies that propose and debate standards, per se, though government actors do set up institutions that bring together firms and professional associations (relying extensively on standardisation pilot projects) to promote indigenously developed standards and help promote them as well. As a recent work report on standardisation stipulates, the Chinese authorities have sought to bring China's standardisation practices in line with those stipulated by the International Standards Organization and other international bodies (Li 2018). By contrast, in the case of mobile telecommunications, firms like Huawei and ZTE liaise directly with global associations like the Third Generation Partnership Project (3GPP) to promote technological standards based on in-house R&D at the global level.

These developments did not come out of nowhere. Indeed, the original MIC 2025 document laid out China's standardisation goals and logic in detail and tailored these to explain how and why the manufacturing sector is undergoing changes, and the directions of the changes that Chinese authorities wish to emphasise and promote. As MIC 2025 states, China's manufacturing sector should do the following:

> Give play to the important role of enterprises in the formulation of standards, support the formation of standards-oriented industry alliances, build standards innovation research bases, and jointly promote product development and standards development. Develop enterprise group standards that meet market and innovation needs and establish self-declaration disclosure and supervision systems for corporate product and service standards. Encourage and support enterprises, research institutes, and industry organisations to *participate in the formulation of international standards and accelerate the process of internationalisation of China's standards* [emphasis added] (State Council 2015; author's translation).

Why has the central government decided to take a leading role in the promotion of China's strength in international standard-setting? In part, this speaks to the significance of the role of standards in ensuring the ascent of Chinese firms in global value chains. The analysis here highlights the importance of tracking Chinese firms' progress on the setting of standards and the globalisation of China's standards. But tracking standard-setting offers only a partial picture of the progress in China's intangible economy and its role in GVCs. This chapter proposes that there is an additional way of looking at China's progress in this regard, namely, quantitative measures of China's IP balance of payments. The rest of this section offers examples of data and brief analysis that speaks to the importance of examining IP payments as an approach to understanding how Chinese firms are progressing towards the goals of MIC 2025.

Balance of Payments in IP

The role of IP in a country's balance of payments has been documented (Neubig and Wunsch-Vincent 2017) but remains under the radar in the analysis of China's macroeconomic surpluses with the rest of the world. As China's surplus has been shrinking in recent years (Wei 2018) and trends towards either deficit or balance in the medium-term (Malkin 2018), it is important to understand the role of IP payments in this broader story. As China's economy becomes increasingly intangible-asset oriented, the pressure of the economy paying to the rest of the world more than it receives is exacerbated, in particular by the growing role of IP licensing payments.

To understand this further we need to look not only at high-tech industrial value added but at intangible asset ownership. As Figure 9.1 shows, China has become a major source of IP rents for MNCs since WTO accession. This is a product of growing IP protection and the growing importance of China as a market for global technology firms. This is due to the growing role of licensing arrangements between foreign firms and their Chinese counterparts. As Breznitz and Murphree (2013) have outlined, a significant but little-understood revolution in China's technological development strategy has been taking place, pertaining to standards and patents. Throughout the mid-late 1990s and mid 2000s, Chinese firms treated IP like a cost of doing business—something to be minimised, rather than an essential strategic asset. This all began to change following China's experience with its (by many popular accounts, unsuccessful) promotion of various domestically oriented telecommunications standards: namely, TD-SCDMA (Mobile), WAPI (Wireless LAN encryption), and AVD and CBHD (Digital disc players). While these standards had not exceeded their stature as lacklustre efforts to create a Chinese standard for China only (foreign standard-bearing components were still preferred by Chinese electronics and telecom vendors), the experience changed policymakers' and firms' understanding of IP development and commercialisation.

These efforts, along with China's growing sophistication in technological innovation more generally (see WIPO 2019), have contributed to a shifting of the extant equilibrium of the Chinese IP market. Chinese firms have gradually come to see IP as a strategic asset rather than a cost of doing business. As Breznitz and Murphree (2013: 2) put it, "In commoditised industries such as consumer electronics, licensing fees squeeze already thin profit margins. Development of low cost and potentially competitive standards for similar or identical technology niches pushes foreign standards alliances to lower royalty rates. This has been a great boon to Chinese companies". *Made in China 2025* recognises these factors and envisions Chinese firms taking a greater slice of global standardisation efforts globally, as noted above, not only to promote scientific efforts and IP commercialisation, but to help its firms' need to reverse the long-standing trend of being on the wrong side of a global intangible economy that is characterised in part by a division into IP-have and IP-have-not states.

Anton Malkin

Figure 9.1: Charges for the Use of Intellectual Property, Payments
(BoP, current US$)

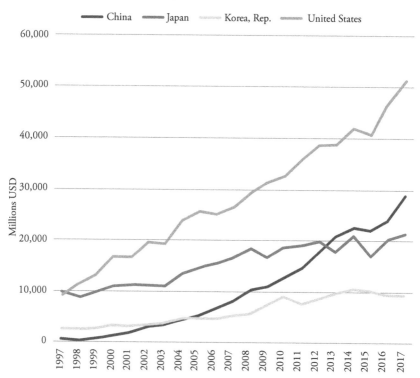

Source: World Bank.

As Figure 9.2 shows, there remains a large discrepancy between how much
Chinese firms pay for IP and how much they receive for it. The data is clear:
while China's IP commercialisation and protection have accelerated rapidly over
the past two decades (and particularly over the past five years), China remains
an IP have-not country. In the 21st century global economy, China cannot
ascend global value chains without asserting the IP rights of its companies.

But can Chinese firms be considered owners of significant quantities of
revenue-generating IP assets? This question remains contested in the literature
on China's innovation and IP development (Kennedy 2017; Malkin 2018; Yu
2018). However, from the perspective of collecting rents on patented assets, the
potential for Chinese firms to earn revenues from their IP is also growing rapidly,
as seen most vividly in China's recent foray into technological standardisation
(Murphree and Breznitz 2018: 1–55) and the growing appetite on the part of

Chinese firms to register their patents as "standard-essential"—giving them the title of standard-essential patents (SEPs) (Ernst 2017), thereby giving them rights to negotiate technology licensing arrangements with global firms that utilise technology that includes the standards they had helped set in the first place. Why is this significant? As Figure 9.3 shows, the patent grants under MIC 2025 categories have been rising, exceeding those of Japanese and Korean firms and matching (in 2017) those of the US. While it remains to be seen how many of these patents are standard essential, it is worth noting that preliminary data in the field of telecommunications technology indicates that Chinese firms (notably Huawei, and to a lesser extent ZTE) boast a significant share of SEPs in new generation mobile communications—5G (IPLytics 2019).

Figure 9.2: Charges for the Use of Intellectual Property, Receipts (BoP, current US$)

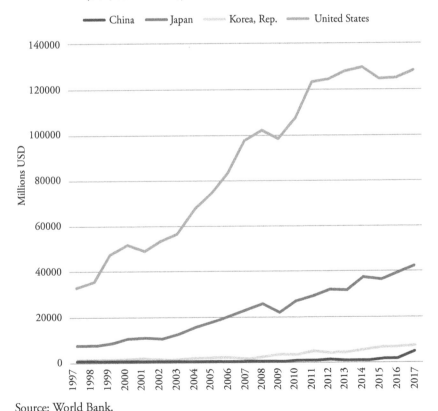

Source: World Bank.

To be sure, an IP payments deficit is not necessarily a bad thing. For instance, it highlights the growth of China as a viable market for IPRs for foreign and Chinese firms alike. Moreover, barring a detailed analysis of the specific IP assets underlying this deficit (a task beyond the scope of this chapter), it is safe to assume that many of the assets responsible for China's outgoing IP payments comprise purchases of foreign technology and consumer purchases of foreign owner brands. In principle, if the US and its allies are comfortable with American, European and Japanese technology being utilised for technological innovation in China, and if China is comfortable with this interdependent relationship as well, there is no fundamental issue with China's IP deficit.

Figure 9.3:   Patent Grants under MIC 2025 Technology Categories

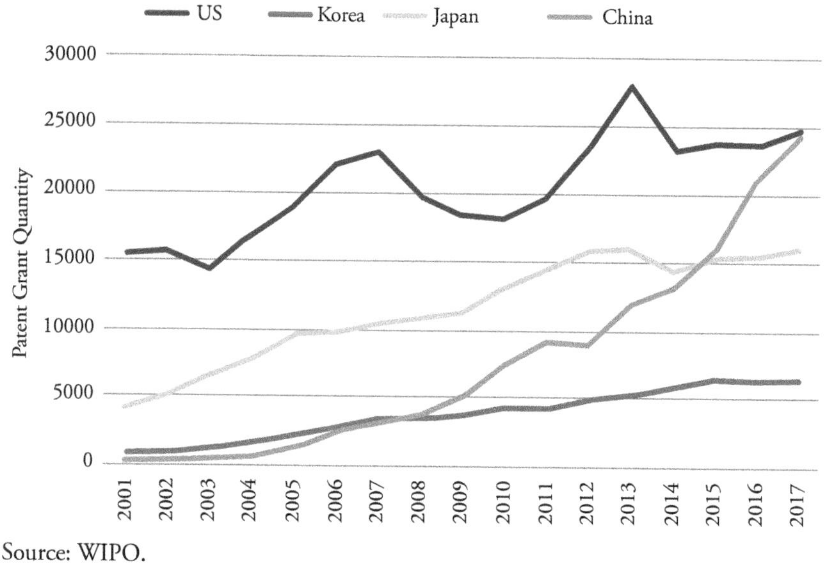

Source: WIPO.

However, much like a current account deficit, this deficit creates winners and losers. Chinese technology proprietors like Xiaomi and Huawei have spent years in Chinese and foreign courts seeking to renegotiate licensing payments demanded by foreign firms for SEP-protected technology that Chinese firms use in their finished products (Malkin 2020). This could go a long way in explaining why Chinese policymakers wish to see more manufacturing core component self-sufficiency. In simple terms, having Chinese manufacturers reduce their dependence on foreign technology would preclude the need for continued payments to foreign technology proprietors. This strategy, however, will not necessarily lower costs for Chinese manufacturers, especially if foreign-owned technology is more efficient than its Chinese counterparts and therefore earns more revenue in both domestic and global markets for Chinese firms.

Therefore, it is worth looking not only at how public policy promotes the goals of MIC 2025, but also at how Chinese firms—both state-owned and private—have been progressing towards the goals outlined in MIC 2025. As Figure 3 shows, Chinese firms have been vigorously patenting technological assets that could broadly fall under the categories outlined in MIC 2025, and they have been doing so since before the release of the plan.

The Messy Logic of Self-Sufficiency and the Role of Foreign Firms in MIC 2025

As explained above, MIC 2025 envisions China as an IP-rich manufacturing powerhouse. Where does this leave foreign, multinational firms? In other words, can the dual goals of industrial self-sufficiency and globalisation of Chinese firms be reconciled?

China's FDI regime, according to OECD standards, is among the most restricted in the world among major economies, as Figure 9.4 illustrates, and gives Chinese firms a homefield advantage in demanding technology in exchange for market access.[2] The concern stems from several factors that have historically defined China's Reform and Opening period which began in earnest in the early 1980s, but which have changed considerably over time. They include an SOE-dominated economy, where access to markets depends on contracts with these market players; a lack of intellectual property protection; a government eager to be involved in joint venture negotiations that involve important technology assets; and an active industrial policy framework involving SOEs, private firms, local governments and other actors, that aim to accelerate the process of China's technological catch-up.

However, as a McKinsey (2019) report notes, China maintains a relatively high degree of foreign MNC penetration across a range of economic sectors—much more so, in fact, than the US. However, many commentators have argued that MIC 2025 aims to change this. It is therefore worth examining policies that have accompanied and followed the promulgation of MIC 2025.

First, it is worth looking at China's long-standing joint venture (JV) law. A longstanding phenomenon in China's political economy has been that China's legislative framework has been very generous to Chinese JV partners by legislating transfer requirements directly and indirectly. Indeed, the crux of the matter boils down to the issue of technology transfers in exchange for market access, which has been the focal point of China's JV policy since the 1980s. One notable part of China's JV laws is Article 27 of the *Regulations of the People's Republic of China on the Administration of the Import and Export of Technologies,* which stipulates that any improvements made to the foreign partner's technology as part of the work conducted by the JV entity belong to the JV entity (European Commission 2018).

Figure 9.4: OECD FDI Regulatory Restrictiveness Index: Selected Economies

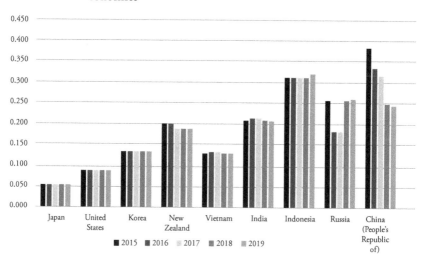

Source: OECD.

This provision, in addition to several other JV stipulations noted in the European Commission (2018) request for trade consultation with China, gave legal space to Chinese JV partners in order that they could spin off and acquire technology by using Chinese courts to secure their legal rights to said technology. It is therefore notable that this article was removed from China's JV law by the State Council on 18 March 2020, along with article item 3 of article 43. The latter limited IP protection from transferred technology to 10 years (as opposed to the twenty years typically granted to patent and copyright lifecycles). The new law also removed item 4 of article 43, which required the JV to have the right to use transferred technology by the joint venture after the termination of the period of the technology transfer agreement (Schindler 2019).

The amended law no longer includes paragraph 3 of Article 24, which indemnified the original technology owners in the transfer agreement from third party infringement claims, nor article 29, which limited the range of conditions that the tech transferring party could impose on their Chinese partner that stipulated how this technology is to be used (Schindler 2019). This latter Article stipulated specific conditions on contracts, such as licensing terms, which fall under the category of competition enforcement (State Intellectual Property Office of the People's Republic of China [SIPO] 2002). Enforcement, of course, remains an open question.

The most salient, but worst documented, change over the past decade and a half has been the declining marginal utility of China's traditional JV model as a means of technology acquisition, where foreign firms exchanged existing technology for market access. Not only are foreign firms becoming savvier about defending their technology, but China has also moved to integrate the JV model with the broader network of parallel tools of technological catch-up that relies less on importing old technology and more on domestic R&D capacity. It is therefore worth assessing how well China's JV arrangements in core MIC 2025 technology sectors like semiconductors have helped Chinese firms catch up in localising component supplies.

Semiconductors and Technological Self Sufficiency

State-owned Ziguang/Tsinghua Holdings is a technology commercialisation holding company that owns several semiconductor design, software design and financing firms, including Tsinghua Unigroup (IC design), Tsinghua Tongfang (software), Unisplendour (private equity and investment), Tus Holdings (science parks and incubator) and Tsing Capital (venture capital). This holding company was set up in 2003 by the State Council to separate management and direct ownership of these firms from Tsinghua University, the original owner of Unigroup and Tongfang.

The role of Tsinghua Holdings in China's semiconductor ecosystem can be understood to have three overarching objectives: (1) investment and commercialisation of R&D; (2) consolidation of China's IC design industry (consistent with the MIC 2025 goal of seeking to create competitive global enterprises); and (3) attracting foreign partners and domestic state funds to co-develop technology for the Chinese market (Table 9.2). Most notably, Ziguang's ventures with foreign firms represent the Chinese government's direct efforts to advance its firms' positions in the intangible economy. Ziguang, it should be noted, is not itself involved in contract manufacturing, but rather in growing China's share in the design of integrated circuit (IC) technology and ownership of its underlying IP.

Table 9.2:   Tsinghua Holdings' Sino-Foreign Partnerships

Foreign Firm	Date	Development Type or Product	Total Capital Committed ($USD)	Type of Partnership	Tsinghua Share %
Hewlett Packard	2016	High-end Server Chips	$4.5 Billion	JV: H3C Group	51
Western Digital	2016	Data Storage Centres	$300 million	JV: UNIS WDC	51
Intel	2014–2018	Cellular phone chip supply	$1.5 billion	JV: Various Ventures	55
ChipMOS and Powertech	2016	Various semiconductor design components testing	$235 million	JV: ChipMOS Shanghai	48
Microsoft and 21Vianet Group (domestic)	2016	Enterprise data centre for state-owned enterprises	Unclear	Strategic Partnership	N/A
Affymetric	2005	Medical Biochips	Unclear	Strategic Partnership	N/A
Russia-China Investment Fund, Sistema	2018	Precision medicine (biotechnology)	Unclear	Strategic Partnership	N/A
Dell	2015	Cloud computing, Mobile internet, IoT, big data, and smart cities	Unclear	Strategic Partnership	N/A
IBM	2015	Agreement to License OpenPOWER technology ecosystem	N /A	Technology Licensing	N/A

Sources: Company press releases, Chinese and English language media (cite CIGI paper Malkin 2018).

Ziguang's Unigroup boasts several joint ventures with foreign firms, as illustrated in Table 9.3. The significance of these JVs is not their novelty—JVs have been a mainstay of China's FDI regime since the start of Reform and Opening. However, over the past decade, many Sino-Foreign JVs and strategic partnerships, especially in the field of semiconductors have been formed to develop new technology, rather than to import existing technology.

With respect to consolidation, Unigroup, under the leadership of Chairman and CEO Zhao Weiguo (also chairman of Tsinghua Holdings), has undertaken several strategic acquisitions domestically and globally to consolidate China's domestic chip design capacity and to source global talent and expertise. The firm acquired private semiconductor design firms Spreadtrum and RDA in 2013 and 2014, respectively (see Feng et al. 2019).

In 2014, Unigroup began its partnership with Intel, via the latter's JV with Spreadtrum. As Zhao put it, "The strategic collaboration between Tsinghua Unigroup and Intel ranges from design and development to marketing and equity investments, which demonstrate Intel's confidence in the Chinese market and strong commitment to [sic] Chinese semiconductor industry" (Intel 2014). In 2018, Unigroup purchased French chipmaker Linxens (Wu and Chakravarti 2018). These acquisitions coincided with a Unigroup announcement that they would invest $47 billion over five years in their capacity to design high-end chips in China (Cartsen and Lee 2015).

In the same year, China announced the creation of a $31 billion semiconductor government guidance fund, which would use state capital to promote the growth of China's chip design industry (Patterson 2018). Zhao also then struck a deal with the fund to invest in Unigroup alongside Intel, which would take a 20 per cent stake in newly acquired Spreadtrum (Tan and Yue 2016). In this complex set of cross-investments of Chinese state capital, Ziguang entered into a commercial partnership with foreign firms to develop intangible assets geared towards the Chinese market.

However, as Fuller (2016) argues, Ziguang's efforts have not been without controversy and have not led to the kind of catching-up in the semiconductor design industry that the government has hoped for. Indeed, what is notable about Ziguang's experience is the extent to which it illustrates state-owned enterprises' (SOEs') focus on the domestic market, and also that top-down political projects have not borne the fruits of self-reliance to the extent that the authorities had hoped (ibid). Indeed, Zhao's ill-fated attempts to purchase multinational US and Taiwan-based IC champions have been stymied by authorities abroad and were critiqued within Chinese bureaucratic circles as well (Tan and Yue 2016). This illustrates the contradictory nature of

MIC 2025's goals and the need to ultimately adjust the strategy put forward in the plan to achieve the goals of improving China's position in the global intangible economy and, ultimately, global value chains. Maintaining the goal of self-sufficiency bodes poorly for efforts to upgrade not only China's manufacturing prowess but also its capacity to create a globally competitive semiconductor sector.

Despite three decades of restricted access for foreign firms and JV requirements for foreign entrance into the market, China's semiconductor sector remains one of the most foreign-reliant sectors outlined in MIC 2025 (*21 Shiji jingji baodao* 2019). Impressive as their efforts have been and even with the support of the central government, Ziguang continues to struggle to provide a realistic alternative to domestic technology companies, to say nothing of their ability to compete on the global stage. Moreover, looking at the emerging trends of how Chinese firms acquire foreign technology and at the reasons behind these acquisitions reveals that ramped up technology transfers and direct M&A are less significant aspects of Chinese firms' competitive efforts than commonly presumed. These changes, documented below, are a product of the development of the intangible economy in China and its integration with the global intangible economy.

The Declining Need for Foreign Technology Assets

What accounts for China's relatively solid industrial structure, as highlighted in the IMF's 2019 Article IV consultation? In part, it is the combination of the government's recent focus on intangible asset development, in combination with Chinese firms' own global acquisition strategies which are increasingly focused on three aspects of strategic acquisitions: automation and supply chain upgrading; R&D-based acquisitions; and strategic patent plays, which could specifically be described as investments in the freedom to operate in crowded markets. Table 9.1 provides some examples of these strategies and illustrates the importance of the acquisition of IP assets for Chinese firms—indeed, as it does for all competitive global technology firms.

Table 9.1 provides a limited empirical illustration of the logic of MIC 2025. Early critiques and suspicions with respect to MIC 2025 have conflated Chinese firms recent foreign M&A spree, illustrated by high profile acquisitions of German robotics firm Kuka by Chinese appliance retailer Midea Group and the firms' earlier purchase of Toshiba.[3] Ziguang's failed acquisition attempts of large US and Taiwanese semiconductor firms only reinforced the beliefs of those that looked at the plan as a thinly-veiled statement of the Chinese government's intentions to take over global tech and squeeze out foreign competitors, first from China, and then from the rest of the world (see McBride and Chatzky 2019 for an illustration).

However, if we examine developments of China's intangible economy, outbound M&A trends in the country, and the MIC 2025 document in detail, the role of foreign asset acquisition within the plan becomes far more complex than is typically portrayed. To begin, with respect to the US in particular, China's outbound M&A activity, especially in high-tech hardware and software sectors has declined steeply since 2017 and has been due in no small part to China's own actions of tightening capital controls (Hanemann et al. 2019). Not surprisingly, Beijing was unhappy with Zhao's global acquisition attempts at Ziguang, and the CEO resigned from his position in 2018.

Second, as Table 9.3 shows, understanding China's outbound tech acquisitions as limited to M&A ignores the logic of intangible asset accumulation and its impact on the strategies of Chinese firms. Simply put, acquiring foreign competitors outright is no longer the only way—or even the most effective—to gain global market share vis-à-vis their foreign competitors. An important tool available to firms in sectors ranging from telecommunications to semiconductors is the acquisition of patents from competitors, which, among other things, give firms greater room to operate and stave off IP infringement lawsuits at home and abroad.

Table 9.3:   Selected Intangible Asset-Focused Acquisitions of Overseas Assets by Chinese Firms

Acquiring Firm	Target	Type	Year	Role of Intangibles
Midea	Kuka (Germany)	M&A	2016	Automation and supply chain upgrading
	Toshiba (Japan)	M&A	2016	Branding play
Geely	Volvo (Sweden)	M&A	2010	Branding play
Ziguang	Linxens (France)	M&A	2018	R&D Play
Huawei	Caliopa NV (Belgium)	M&A	2013	R&D Play
	Amartus Ltd- Software Assets (UK)	M&A	2015	R&D Play
	Neul Ltd (UK)	M&A	2014	R&D Play

(cont'd overleaf)

Table 9.3 (*cont'd*)

Acquiring Firm	Target	Type	Year	Role of Intangibles
	Various, including Siemens, Sharp, and IBM	Patent purchases	2009–2015	Strategic patent play/ Freedom to operate
Xiaomi	Microsoft, Intel, Broadcomm	Patent purchases	2016	Strategic patent play/ Freedom to operate
Sanan Optoelectronics	Sony	Patent purchases	2017	Strategic patent play/ Freedom to operate
Oppo	Dolby, Ericsson	Patent purchases		Strategic patent play/ Freedom to operate
Alibaba	IBM	Patent Purchases	2012	Strategic patent play/ Freedom to operate

Source: Thompson-Reuters M&A Database.

As Haskel and Westlake (2018) point out, buying and selling patents is a far more subtle commercial activity than M&A. This is because the value of patents can be quite different for the transaction parties involved. Indeed, the transacting firms do not even need to be in the same industry (see examples in Table 9.3 of Chinese firms purchasing patent portfolios from foreign firms in a range of industries). Rather, patents can fit into firms' broader technological development strategy, which is in itself an intangible asset—a trade secret. Likewise, firms like Huawei have eschewed (for the most part) large overseas acquisitions and have instead invested in smaller players and in overseas R&D centres, in order to oversee organic growth in the underlying intangible value of these assets.

The MIC 2025 document describes these incentives and processes indirectly. In terms of specifics, these trends are referred to in the State Council's approach to the rapid degree of automation that is taking place in China's manufacturing sector. In a sense, automation's role in the plan illustrates all three aspects of intangible economic activity referred to here: standardisation, balance of payments and asset acquisitions. The document explicitly calls on Chinese policymakers and enterprises to

> accelerate the formulation of intelligent manufacturing technology standards, establish and improve the intelligent manufacturing and integration management standards systems […] establish intelligent manufacturing industry alliances

and jointly promote intelligent equipment and product development, system integration innovation and industrialisation. Promote the integrated integration of the industrial internet of things, cloud computing, big data in enterprise R&D and design, manufacturing, operation management, sales and service, and the entire industry supply chain (State Council 2015, author's translation).

Not only does the State Council call for the standardisation of automation and digitisation of the industrial economy, but it also asks Chinese firms to step up and standardise R&D and to commercialise it. Integrating standards effectively implies that firms need to be incentivised to have sufficient IP assets not only to allow for such integration, but also to ensure that such integration accrues revenues to Chinese firms. This would not reduce China's "dependency" on Western technology because global technological standardisation precludes any one firm (or firms from a single country) monopolising an emerging technology. Rather, if automation and industrial upgrading are more generally likely to balance China's present-day deficit in intangible payments, Chinese firms need to contribute in greater degree to global technological standardisation and ultimately grab a larger slice of intangible assets, such as patents.

To the extent that intangible asset competition is a zero-sum game where the legal boundaries demarcating the ownership of necessary but exclusive technology are set, even without explicit aims for technological self-sufficiency, the integration of Chinese firms into the global intangible economy will create tensions between China and its trading partners. A narrowing of China's IP payments deficit not only channels more IPR-related revenues into China's domestic market, but also increases the West's dependence on Chinese technology in the same way that Chinese firms are currently dependent on foreign firms. In principle, much as Chinese firms' dependence on foreign technology is not, in itself problematic, we can conclude that Western firms' increasing dependence on Chinese firms and their technology might exacerbate cross-border conflict between China and the West, but only insofar as geopolitical tensions dictate. If international tensions can be mitigated and trade tensions are managed there is no reason to presume that a global economy where Chinese firms own more IP and set global technological standards will be significantly different from that which exists today.

Concluding Discussion

This chapter has highlighted a fundamental tension between the globalising and the localising aspects of MIC 2025. It has shown that MIC 2025 displays a deep appreciation for the growing importance of the intangible economy and the need for global competitiveness and global integration associated with this trend. While this chapter has focused on China's motivations for seeking to attain the goals of MIC 2025, it did not discuss, in detail, the global economic realities which prompt such a policy.

As Schwartz (2017) has shown, the intangible economy relies less on the logic of trade in goods—less on comparative advantage and supply chain-based win-win outcomes—and more on rents accruing from the possession of IP assets like patents. This is especially true for standards-essential patents and trade secrets and other classifications of proprietary technology. The intangible economy, which includes data and standards (hence, the ubiquitous title of "intangible" assets), is not only under-theorised in political science and economics literature, but remains at an exploratory stage from an empirical perspective. But given its centrality to the current US-China trade war, the controversy over Chinese telecom giant Huawei and the ongoing discussion over "forced technology transfers" in China's JV regime, it is imperative that research across policy-oriented social sciences moves more rapidly in this direction.

It is important to identify appropriate metrics and analytical frameworks for assessing the impact of intangible investment in manufacturing, information technology, green technology and other areas. Specifically, researchers should pay closer attention to the role of asset ownership in the area of standards-essential patents, data and technology clusters such as industrial parks. It has been the intention of this chapter to highlight the importance of studying this data. To assess the successes and failures of MIC 2025 and other industrial policy frameworks in China, more accurate tools are needed to understand how countries ascend global value chains in the context of tightening intellectual property protection and how the growing investment in production networks has been underpinned by an increasing reliance on the industrial internet of things and the growing trade tensions.

To put it another way, it is possible that policies such as MIC 2025 appear to be zero sum because the intangible economy is characterised, to some extent, by zero sum gains vis-à-vis the accumulation of intangible assets by countries, firms, industrial clusters and other public and private entities. But it is also possible that that mutual gains from intangible economic development are not absent, but rather not well understood and poorly represented by the tools that policymakers and researchers rely on to measure economic development and wellbeing. As countries use time-tested policy tools and new measures to stimulate innovation, industrial upgrading and workforce transformation, researchers should use the increasingly available data on patents, standards and other intellectual property assets (proprietary and open source) to refine our understanding of the latest stage of industrial economic development.

Notes

[1] It should be mentioned that the IPRs discussed here do not provide a full exposition of an important segment of China's intangible economy, namely the role of data ownership and commercialisation. Big data commercialisation is a complex topic that goes beyond the analysis in this chapter.

[2] It should be noted that the OECD FDI Restrictiveness Index measures only formal, regulatory barriers to doing business and various informal barriers as well. National security-related barriers are not sufficiently factored into the final indexes displayed in Figure 9.4. Moreover, while New Zealand is not a major economy by GDP measures, it nonetheless stands out as an OECD member with formal restrictions that nearly match those of China, suggesting that China is neither an outlier, nor can it claim to match the restrictiveness of other middle-income economies.

[3] German media have even referred to the deal as a hostile takeover (see *Deutsche Welle* 2018). Kuka's acting CEO at the time of the deal, Till Reuter, explicitly denied this (Hack 2016).

References

21 Shiji jingji baodao [21st Century Business Herald], 2019. "Zhong bang! Zhongguo chanye lian anquan pinggu: Zhongguo zhizao ye chanye lian 60% anquan ke kong, guang ke ji, sheji fangzhen ruanjian cun 'qia bozi' duan ban" [Breaking! China's industrial supply chain security assessment: China's manufacturing industry supply chain is 60% secure and controllable, lithographic machines, design simulation software fall short, remain in "stranglehold"]. *21 Shiji jingji baodao*, 16 Oct. [accessed: 19 Oct. 2019].

Breznitz, Dan and Michael Murphree. 2013. *The Rise of China in Technology Standards: New Norms in Old Institutions*. US-China Economic and Security Review Commission. Available at https://www.uscc.gov/sites/default/files/Research/Riseof ChinainTechnologyStandards.pdf [accessed 3 Dec. 2020].

Carsten, Paul and Lee Yimou. 2015. "Exclusive: China's Tsinghua Unigroup to Invest $47 Billion to Build Chip Empire", *Reuters*, 16 November. Available at https:// www.reuters.com/article/us-china-tsinghua-m-a-idUSKCN0T50DU20151116 [accessed 3 Dec. 2020].

Chen Li. 2014. *China's Centralized Industrial Order: Industrial Reform and the Rise of Centrally Controlled Big Business*. New York: Routledge.

Deutsche Welle [DW]. 2018. "German Robot Maker Kuka's CEO to be Replaced by Chinese Owners", *Deutsche Welle*. Available at https://www.dw.com/en/german-robot-maker-kukas-ceo-to-be-replaced-by-chinese-owners/a-46440242 [accessed 15 Oct. 2019].

Ernst, Dieter. 2017. *China's Standard-Essential Patents Challenge: From Latecomer to (Almost) Equal Player?* CIGI Special Report. Centre for International Governance Innovation. Available at https://www.cigionline.org/sites/default/files/documents/China%27s%20Patents%20ChallengeWEB.pdf [accessed 3 Dec. 2020].

European Commission. 2018. *China – Certain Measures on the Transfer of Technology Request for Consultations by the European Union.* Available at https://trade.ec.europa.eu/doclib/docs/2018/december/tradoc_157591.12.20%20-%20REV%20consultation%20request%20FINAL.pdf [accessed 3 Dec. 2020].

Feng Yunhao, Wu Jinxi and He Peng. 2019. "Global M&A and the Development of the IC Industry Ecosystem in China: What Can We Learn from the Case of Tsinghua Unigroup?", *Sustainability* 11, 1: 106.

Fuller, Douglas B. 2016. *Paper Tigers, Hidden Dragons: Firms and the Political Economy of China's Technological Development.* New York: Oxford University Press.

Girard, Michel. 2019. *Big Data Analytics Need Standards to Thrive: What Standards Are and Why They Matter. Centre for International Governance Innovation.* CIGI Paper No. 209. Available at https://www.cigionline.org/sites/default/files/documents/Paper%20no.209.pdf [accessed 18 Oct. 2019].

Hack, Jens. 2016. "Kuka's CEO says Chinese Bidder Could be a Growth Driver", *Reuters.* 27 May. Available at https://www.reuters.com/article/us-kuka-m-a-midea-group/kukas-ceo-says-chinese-bidder-could-be-a-growth-driver-idUSKCN0YI10K [accessed 28 Aug. 2020].

Hanemann, Thilo, Cassie Gao, Adam Lysenko and Daniel H. Rosen. 2019. *Sidelined: US-China Investment in 1H 2019.* US-China Investment Project. Rhodium Group and National Committee on U.S.-China Relations. July. Available at https://www.ncuscr.org/sites/default/files/page_attachments/Two-Way-Street-2019-1H-Update_Report.pdf [accessed 3 Dec. 2020].

Haskel, Jonathan and Stian Westlake. 2018. *Capitalism without Capital: the Rise of the Intangible Economy.* Princeton: Princeton University Press.

Hillman, Amy J., Michael C. Withers and Brian J. Collins. 2009. "Resource Dependence Theory: A Review", *Journal of Management* 35, 6: 1404–27.

Huang Yukon and Jeremy Smith. 2019. "China's Record on Intellectual Property Rights Is Getting Better and Better", *Foreign Policy.* 16 Oct. https://foreignpolicy.com/2019/10/16/china-intellectual-property-theft-progress/ [accessed 19 Oct. 2019].

Hui Liu and Carl F. Cargill. 2017. *Setting Standards for Industry: Comparing the Emerging Chinese Standardization System and the Current US System.* East-West Center Policy Studies No. 75. Available at https://www.eastwestcenter.org/system/tdf/private/ps075.pdf?file=1&type=node&id=36156 [accessed 10 Oct. 2019].

IMF [International Monetary Fund]. 2019. *People's Republic of China: 2019 Article IV Consultation-Press Release; Staff Report; Staff Statement and Statement by the Executive Director for China.* International Monetary Fund. Country Report No. 19/266. 9 August. Available at https://www.imf.org/en/Publications/CR/Issues/2019/08/08/Peoples-Republic-of-China-2019-Article-IV-Consultation-Press-Release-Staff-Report-Staff-48576 [accessed 11 Oct. 2019].

Intel. 2014. *Intel and Tsinghua Unigroup Collaborate to Accelerate Development and Adoption of Intel-based Mobile Devices.* Intel Press Release, 26 Sept. Available at https://s21.q4cdn.com/600692695/files/doc_news/archive/INTC_News_2014_9_26_Home.pdf [accessed 10 Aug. 2020].

IPLytics, 2019. *Who is Leading the 5G Patent Race? A Patent Landscape Analysis on Declared SEPs and Standards Contributions.* Available at https://www.iplytics.com/wp-content/uploads/2019/01/Who-Leads-the-5G-Patent-Race_2019.pdf [accessed 3 Dec. 2020].

Kennedy, Scott. 2017. *The Fat Tech Dragon: Benchmarking China's Innovation Drive.* China Innovation Policy Series. Centre for Strategic and International Studies. Available at https://www.csis.org/analysis/fat-tech-dragon [accessed 3 Dec. 2020].

Li Y. 2018. *Work Report of the China Standardization Expert Committee (CSEC).* Standardization Administration of China. Report Summary Presentation [unpublished].

Malkin, Anton. 2018. *Made in China 2025 as a Challenge in Global Trade Governance: Analysis and Recommendations.* CIGI Paper No. 183. 15 August. Centre for International Governance Innovation.

_____. 2020. *Getting beyond Forced Technology Transfers: Analysis of and Recommendations on Intangible Economy Governance in China.* CIGI Paper No. 239. Centre for International Governance Innovation. Available at https://www.cigionline.org/publications/getting-beyond-forced-technology-transfers-analysis-and-recommendations-intangible [accessed 15 Aug. 2020].

McBride, James and Andrew Chatzky. 2019. *Is 'Made in China 2025' a Threat to Global Trade?* Council on Foreign Relations Backgrounder, 13 May. Available at https://www.cfr.org/backgrounder/made-china-2025-threat-global-trade [accessed 20 Aug. 2020].

McKinsey. 2019. *China and the World: Inside the Dynamics of a Changing Relationship.* McKinsey Global Institute. Available at https://www.mckinsey.com/featured-insights/china/china-and-the-world-inside-the-dynamics-of-a-changing-relationship# [accessed 3 Dec. 2020].

Murphree, Michael and John A. Anderson. 2018. "Countering Overseas Power in Global Value Chains: Information Asymmetries and Subcontracting in the Plastics Industry", *Journal of International Management* 24, 2: 123–36.

Murphree, Michael and Dan Breznitz. 2018. "Indigenous Digital Technology Standards for Development: The Case of China", *Journal of International Business Policy* 1, 3–4: 234–52.

Neubig, Thomas S. and Sacha Wunsch-Vincent. 2017. *A Missing Link in the Analysis of Global Value Chains: Cross-border Flows of Intangible Assets, Taxation and Related Measurement Implications.* World Intellectual Property Organization. Economic Research Working Paper No. 37. Available at https://www.wipo.int/edocs/pubdocs/en/wipo_pub_econstat_wp_37.pdf [accessed 10 Oct. 2019].

OECD. 2020. OECD FDI Regulatory Restrictiveness Index. *OECD.stat.* https://stats.oecd.org/Index.aspx?datasetcode=FDIINDEX# [accessed 20 Aug. 2020].

Patterson, Allan. 2018. "State-backed Fund Intends to Put China on Semiconductor Manufacturing Map". *EET Asia*. 5 March. https://www.eetasia.com/18030505-china-to-set-up-31-5-billion-semiconductor-fund/ [accessed 11 Feb. 2021].

Prud'homme, Dan and Zhang Taolue. 2019. *China's Intellectual Property Regime for Innovation*. Cham: Springer.

Reuters. 2019. "Kuka CEO says Midea Offer Not a Hostile Takeover", *Reuters*, 18 May. Available at https://www.reuters.com/article/midea-kuka-ceo-idUSL5N18F408 [accessed 18 Oct. 2019].

Schindler, Jacob. 2019. "China Budges on Much-maligned Tech Transfer Regulations", *IAM-Media*. Available at https://www.iam-media.com/law-policy/china-budges-much-maligned-tech-transfer-regulations [access to subscribers].

Schwartz, Herman Mark. 2017. "Club Goods, Intellectual Property Rights, and Profitability in the Information Economy", *Business and Politics* 19, 2: 191–214.

_____. 2019. "American Hegemony: Intellectual Property Rights, Dollar Centrality, and Infrastructural Power", *Review of International Political Economy* 26, 3: 490–519.

State Council. 2015. *Guowuyuan guanyu yinfa "zhongguo zhizao 2025" de tongzhi* [State Council Notice on the Promulgation of "Made in China 2025"] State Council Circular No. 28. 19 May. Available at http://www.gov.cn/zhengce/content/2015-05/19/content_9784.htm [accessed 10 Oct. 2019].

_____. 2017. *Waishang touzi qiye zhishi chanquan baohu xingdong fang'an* [Action Plan for the Protection of Foreign Invested Enterprises' Intellectual Property]. Available at http://www.gov.cn/xinwen/2017-09/27/5227929/files/4ebb8148d59c404db6a6f74c6ab539e0.pdf [accessed 3 Dec. 2020].

State Intellectual Property Office of the People's Republic of China [SIPO]. 2002. *Regulations on Technology Import and Export Administration of the People's Republic of China*. Available at https://wipolex.wipo.int/en/legislation/details/6585 [accessed 3 Dec. 2020].

_____. 2015. *2015 Intellectual Property Rights Protection in China*. Available at http://www.lawinfochina.com/display.aspx?id=141&lib=dbref&SearchKeyword=&SearchCKeyword=&EncodingName=big5 [accessed 11 Feb. 2021].

Tan Min and Yue Yue. 2016. "Zhao Weiguo de lianjin shu" [Zhao Weiguo's Alchemy], *Caixin wang* [Caixin Online]. Available at http://weekly.caixin.com/2016-01-08/100897387.html [accessed 3 Dec. 2020].

von Hagen, Oliver and Gabriela Alvarez. 2011. *The Impacts of Private Standards on Global Value Chains. Literature Review Series on the Impacts of Private Standards, Part I*. The International Trade Centre (ITC) Available at https://www.intracen.org/the-impacts-of-private-standards-on-global-value-chains-literature-review-series-on-the-impacts-of-private-standards/ [accessed 3 Dec. 2020].

Wei Lingling. 2018. "China's Shrinking Trade Surplus Unlikely to Impress Trump", *Wall Street Journal*, 28 July. Available at https://www.wsj.com/articles/chinas-shrinking-trade-surplus-unlikely-to-impress-trump-1532775603 [accessed 10 Oct. 2020].

WIPO. 2019. WIPO IP Statistics Data Center. *WIPO IP Portal*. Available at https://www3.wipo.int/ipstats/index.htm?tab=patent&lang=en [accessed 11 Feb. 2021].

World Bank. 2021. "Charges for the Use of Intellectual Property, Payments (BoP, current US$)", *The World Bank: Data*. Available at https://data.worldbank.org/indicator/BM.GSR.ROYL.CD [accessed 11 Feb. 2021].

Wu Kane and Prakash Chakravarti. 2018. "Chinese Chipmaker Tsinghua Unigroup to Buy France's Linxens for $2.6 Billion: Sources", *Reuters*, 25 July. Available at https://www.reuters.com/article/us-linxens-m-a-tsinghua-unigroup/chinese-chipmaker-tsinghua-unigroup-to-buy-frances-linxens-for-2-6-billion-sources-idUSKBN1KF0B1 [accessed 3 Dec. 2020].

Wübbeke, Jost et al. 2016. *Made in China 2025: The Making of a High-tech Superpower and Consequences for Industrial Countries*. Mercator Institute for China Studies (MERICS). Available at www.merics.org/ sites/default/files/2017-09/MPOC_No.2_MadeinChina2025.pdf [accessed 3 Dec. 2020].

Yu, Peter K. 2018. "When the Chinese Intellectual Property System Hits 35", *Queen Mary Journal of Intellectual Property* 8, 1: 3–14.

10

Industrial Policy and Competitive Advantage: A Comparative Study of the Cloud Computing Industry in Hangzhou and Shenzhen

Bai Gao and Yi Ru

The development of the digital economy has become a driving force behind China's economic transformation. The share of the digital economy in China's total GDP jumped from 26.1 per cent in 2014 to 34.8 per cent in 2018 (Yu and Dong 2019). The cloud computing industry, an important segment of the digital economy, grew very rapidly. Between the first quarters of 2018 and 2019, the Infrastructure as a Service (IaaS) segment of the cloud computing industry grew 74 per cent. China has become the second largest cloud computing market in the world, next only to the United States (Yiou 2019b). In 2018, four of the world's top ten companies in the cloud computing industry were Chinese, with Alibaba at number three, Tencent at number six, China Telecom at number seven, and Kingsoft at number ten (IDC 2019).

Sustained by Alibaba and Tencent, Hangzhou and Shenzhen have emerged as two powerhouses in China's cloud computing industry. Between April 2017 and the end of 2018, in the Chinese market the Ali Cloud grew 101 per cent, recorded $2.5 billion in revenue and was ranked number one (Alibaba Group 2018), while the Tencent Cloud grew 128 per cent (Yiou 2019a), recorded $1.4 billion in revenue and was ranked as number two. The Tencent Cloud's rank in the global market jumped from number eighteen in 2017 to number six in 2018 (Gartner 2019).

Despite the rapid development of cloud computing in both Hangzhou and Shenzhen, we observe some distinctive variations between these two cities. First, Shenzhen adopted its first industrial policy to support cloud computing as early as 2010, while Hangzhou did not take action until 2013. Second, even though Shenzhen adopted an official policy for cloud computing earlier than Hangzhou, the goal it set up for the industry was relatively modest. In contrast, while Hangzhou was initially slow to support the industry, its support became quite aggressive from 2014 onwards. Third, although both cities adopted industrial policies to support cloud computing's development, Shenzhen has treated it as merely one of several strategic industries while Hangzhou has regarded it as its number one priority. And indeed, in terms of market size, Hangzhou's cloud computing industry has left Shenzhen's behind.

To what extent can we use industrial policy to explain the development of the cloud computing industry in China? What kinds of industrial policy have Chinese local governments adopted to develop the digital economy? Is Chinese industrial policy different from that practised by governments in other countries? What are the implications of China's industrial policy pertaining to the digital economy for the futures of both the Chinese and international economies?

We examine the impacts of Chinese industrial policy on the digital economy in relation to private entrepreneurship through an analysis of the development of the cloud computing industry in Hangzhou and Shenzhen, focusing on Alibaba and Tencent. We first review the existing literature on industrial policy and identify four types of states differentiated by the goals of their industrial policies: the "developmental state" that focuses on promoting high value-added industries, the "social protection state" with policies oriented towards restricting competition in order to maintain political stability, the "entrepreneurial state" that shoulders the burdens of investment risks in radical frontier technologies in an effort to spur innovations, and the "market facilitating state" that emphasises building infrastructure and reducing the transaction costs for private companies. Then we present a theory of the "competitive-advantage-building state", informed by new structural economics and Michael Porter's competitive-advantage diamond diagram but at the same time transcending both of them in important ways.

Contrary to the stereotype of the heavy-handed Chinese state, we argue that the competitive-advantage-building state in the digital economy focuses on enhancing factor endowment, building infrastructure, reducing transaction costs, creating market demand, encouraging industrial clusters and promoting corporate rivalries. The primary goal of industrial policy practised by the competitive-advantage-building state is to create favourable structural and institutional conditions that empower private companies in market competition. It identifies technological frontiers and adopts industrial policies to lure private investments towards them. Instead of leading the breakthrough from 0 to 1, however, the state has emphasised pushing commercialisation forward from 1 to 100. Such an industrial policy is often informed by private entrepreneurship and constrained by the dominance of private companies in the digital economy. The policy's effectiveness is often determined by private companies' willingness to follow the state's guidance.

The Developmental State

Classical industrial policies were practised by the developmental states of Japan and South Korea during their high-speed economic growth in the 1950–70 period. The state targeted high value-added industries in which domestic companies had not yet obtained competitive advantage in an effort to obtain more trade benefits through exports. In order to nurture domestic companies' competitiveness in these industries, the state established trade barriers, both in tariff and non-tariff forms, and allocated the country's limited resources to these industries (Johnson 1982; Gao 1997). The developmental state in Japan encouraged oligopolistic competition: its rationale was that too many players in the same industry would result in "excessive competition" thereby dispersing limited resources and preventing domestic companies from becoming big players. Without competition, however, domestic companies would never become competitive in international markets. In practice, the Japanese state never controlled all industries. Rather, it cared only about the strategic ones (Gao 1997, 2001).

The Social-Protection State

The social-protection state considers political stability its major policy objective. Its industrial policy is carried out in sunset industries where domestic companies have lost comparative advantage. A major character of this type of industrial policy is its restriction on competition (Tilton 1996; Uriu 1996). For this reason, some analysts called it "competition policy". Many countries practise this type of industrial policy because, by controlling competition, it prevents massive layoffs and reduces the burden of social protection by the state. To protect jobs and slow down the decline of sunset industries, the state in both Japan and in Europe exerted various industry-based anti-competition regulations and some countries even allowed medium-size and small companies to organise cartels during recession (Gao 2001; Tilton 1996). In China, undertaking a new pattern of industrial governance after the reform started, the state often practised anti-competition policy, constraining market entry and exercising frequent administrative interventions (Chen Qingtai 2016; Wu Jinglian 2016).

The Entrepreneurial State

The entrepreneurial state is represented by the Defense Advanced Research Projects Agency (DARPA), a part of the US federal government's Department of Defense (Mazzucato 2015). Its industrial policy aims to reduce the enormous risks associated with investment in R&D in radical frontier technologies in order to spur innovation. Contrary to the conventional image of the United States in which private companies play the leading role in technological innovation, the US federal government "has provided early-stage finance where venture capital ran away, while also commissioning high-level innovative private sector activity that would not have happened without public policy goals backing a strategy and vision" (Mazzucato 2015: 79). Common practices to encourage innovation also include government subsidies and government procurements. Generally speaking, this type of industrial policy targets only frontier technologies. The state is not normally involved in the commercialisation of these technologies.

The Market-Facilitating State

The main goal of the market-facilitating state is to attract inflows of foreign direct investments in order to promote economic growth and participate in the international division of labour. Drawing upon the Chinese experience in creating the Special Economic Zones (SEZs), new structural economics considers factor endowment the most important criterion by which an economic entity chooses a path for economic growth. It maintains that an entity can enjoy comparative advantage in international trade only when it chooses to invest in industries permitted by its factor endowments in a given developmental stage, often measured by its capital-labour ratio. According to its reasoning, factor endowments do not directly represent comparative advantage because a lack of infrastructure and high transaction costs are often the primary barriers that prevent an economic entity from transforming its factor endowments into comparative advantage. In other words, comparative advantage will never be reached if one simply waits for market forces to work.

Thus, the state must step in, concentrating its limited resources to actively remove these barriers. "A capable state is the precondition for an effective market, while building an effective market is all that a capable state should do" (Lin 2013; Lin 2017). The policy practised by the market-facilitating state in China until the beginning of the 21st century, with a few exceptions, was not really industrial policy but horizontal pro-growth policy as it was driven not by technological concerns, but by a motivation to promote economic growth in the most efficient way possible.

The Competitive-Advantage-Building State

After China joined the World Trade Organisation (WTO) in 2001, and especially once the Chinese economy began to promote industrial upgrading and innovation driven by the pressures of currency value appreciation, the state started to shift its focus from comparative advantage towards competitive advantage. Competitive advantage can be characterised by a hexagon diagram, the components of which include: strengthening factor supply by upgrading the qualities and increasing the types of factor endowments; building infrastructure in order to reduce the cost of business operations; improving institutional environments to reduce companies' transaction costs; expanding market demand in an effort to create an economy of scale; developing industrial clusters for deepening the division of labour and advancing specialisation; and encouraging sector competition aiming at promoting productivity and innovation. The state treats the development of these six areas as the main goal of its industrial policy (Gao and Zhu 2020).

It may look like this hexagon diagram simply adds two components advocated by new structural economics—building infrastructure and reducing transaction costs—to Porter's diamond diagram of competitive advantage (Porter 1990). However, the hexagon diagram has altered the conceptualisations of comparative/competitive advantage in two important ways. First, it redefines the concept of factor endowment. Porter distinguishes between basic factors and advanced factors, with the former referring to the natural endowment emphasised by classical trade theory and the latter referring to those factors acquired through human effort (Porter 1990). New structural economics treats basic factors as the foundation of its reasoning, contending that an economic entity should develop only those industries permitted by its present capital-labour ratio. In contrast, we focus on the advanced factors discussed by Porter and place more emphasis on the important role of human agency in creating and enhancing factor supplies. Second, the hexagon brings the state back into the model by proposing a causal relationship between state industrial policy and competitive advantage. Although Porter acknowledges that the state is relevant to each facet of his diamond diagram, he fails to connect them with the state in his conceptualisation. In contrast, we highlight the impacts of state industrial policy on the hexagon diagram of competitive advantage and treat this policy as the determining factor that shapes the development of competitive advantage.

The competitive-advantage-building state is not a unified national model. Even among local governments in China, there is a large range of variations in practice. However, the common features we discuss above are distinctively observable in the most competitive industries of the Chinese economy, as well as in most dynamic cities in the country. Instead of leaving the fate of the digital economy to market forces, the competitive-advantage-building state actively intervenes. Nevertheless, it does not simply pick the winners, as some critics have suggested, nor does it let the state itself replace private companies. Rather, as its label suggests, the competitive-advantage-building state considers its mission to be the creation of a favourable environment at the macro and meso levels in which companies grow competitive via their own entrepreneurship and market strategies.

Data as Factor Endowment

One of the most profound industrial changes since the 1990s is that data have become an important factor endowment. As Srnicek points out, "just like oil, data are a material to be extracted, refined, and used in a variety of ways. The more data one has, the more uses one can make of them" (2017: 40). Data have profound economic implications: "they educate and give competitive advantage to algorithms; they enable the coordination and outsourcing of workers, they allow for the optimisation and flexibility of productive processes; they make possible the transformation of low-margin goods into high-margin services; and data analysis is itself generative of data, in a virtuous cycle" (Srnicek 2017: 41–2).

The development of infrastructure has bestowed China with a special competitive advantage in international competition. Internet, fibre optics, smart phones and satellites provide the most important infrastructure for data production. China is advanced in all these fields. As Table 10.1 shows, by 2018, fibre optic broadband accounted for 82 per cent of China's telecom network: the country had 600 million interfaces and 260 million users; the percentage of 4G users in the total population was more than double the global average; China had 760 million cell-phone users, the most in the world; and China, the US and Russia were the only three countries in the world with an operating global position system (Wang Jiwu 2018). In addition, China had 202 supercomputers, 43.8 per cent of the world's total, while the United States owned 116, or 23.2 per cent (Zhongguo cunchu wang 2019).

Table 10.1: Digital Infrastructure in China

Digital infrastructure	China	Global
Internet		
Fibre optic broadband households (100 million)	2.6	–
User penetration rate (%)	82	48
Mobile network users (100 million)	7.6	30.7
Global Navigation Satellite System	COMPASS	GPS(USA) GALILEO(EUR) GLONASS(RUS)
TOP 500 Supercomputers	202	accounting for 43.8% of global top 500 supercomputers

Sources: CAICT 2017, Wang Jiwu 2018, Zhongguo cunchu wang 2019.

In 2010, the Chinese government designated both Hangzhou and Shenzhen as trial cities for cloud computing, along with Beijing, Shanghai and Wuxi (National Development and Reform Commission, Ministry of Science and Technology 2010). Alibaba and Tencent, the two biggest platform companies in China, became the major players in developing both cities' cloud computing industries.

As a leading platform of e-commerce, Alibaba had already collected huge amounts of data from both buyers and sellers long before it built cloud computing capability. Different from Amazon and JD that both buy and sell merchandise, Alibaba does neither but instead provides only platforms where buyers and sellers meet for their transactions. Such platforms rely heavily upon digital eco-systems. Alibaba developed two indispensable infrastructures to support its e-commerce platforms: the payment system, Ali Pay and the logistic system, Cainiao. These infrastructures further extended Alibaba's data collection to both consumer finance and logistics. Cainiao is not a delivery company; rather, it is a logistics platform where individual consumers meet logistics service providers. Because of this, Alibaba's range of data collection reached the entire logistics industry.

Tencent started as an instant messaging tool. Its early business model saw income generated by serving as a portal, providing traffic to China Mobile and taking a share of the profits. After its cooperation with China Mobile ended in 2005, Tencent adopted an "online living" strategy (Huaerjie Jianwen 2019). In 2010, when 90 per cent of Tencent's employees still worked on PC versions of products and services, Tencent had already copied and combined every successful app in the industry into a single one-stop platform to fulfil its customers' needs through a variety of services. Even before WeChat was invented in 2011, Tencent had built multiple platforms such as QQ, QQ Space, QQ Gaming and Tencent Network. Early on, Tencent developed storage and sharing functions for its platforms with a variety of technical supports for these services (Wu Xiaobo 2017).

The Premise of the Competitive-Advantage-Building State

Producers and service providers compete with each other in market economies. When an economic entity gains extra demand as a result of the competitiveness of its products and services in non-home markets, it experiences accelerated capital accumulation, stimulating new investments, increased expendable income of its residents, improved government tax revenues and overall economic well-being for the economic entity as a whole. This in turn strengthens the legitimacy of the ruling party in the government.

However, the competitiveness of products and services does not come about in a vacuum and its development is affected by various structural and institutional conditions. Without state intervention, the hexagon diagram of competitive advantage might still evolve, sustained by market forces, but it would take a much longer time and face dire uncertainties. In the face of cross-entity competitive pressures, the competitive-advantage-building state must step in to help create structural and institutional conditions that can strengthen the competitiveness of the companies that operate within its territory. In terms of the scope of intervention, the competitive-advantage-building state does more than its intervention-state counterparts, including the developmental state, social protection state, entrepreneurial state and market-facilitating state. Nevertheless, it restricts its actions to helping companies create their own competitiveness, rather than becoming a player directly in the market.

Enhancing Factor Endowments

Developing the digital economy demands venture capital and skilled labour with a high level of specialisation in information technologies. The industrial policy practised by the competitive-advantage-building state in both Hangzhou and Shenzhen has focused on enhancing these factor endowments by luring venture capital to high-tech industries using government investment funds.

As Table 10.2 demonstrates, in Hangzhou, the government offers four types of financial aid to develop technology in the region: designated funds for specific projects, guaranteed loans, angel-stage investor funds and working capital loans.

By 2016, Hangzhou had established 47 different designated funds valued at 6.6 billion yuan, 3.3 billion of which came from the government and 2.3 billion from private investors. Of the projects that use these investments, two-thirds were conducted by local companies. 71 per cent of the investments went to start ups (Yang Zuojun 2017: 65).

In 2006, Hangzhou began offering guaranteed loans to support venture capital investment in technology. In the ten years from 2006 to 2016, Hangzhou's guaranteed loan programme financed more than 2,000 projects at a total of 7 billion yuan. Since 2012 the Hangzhou government has financed more than 5 billion yuan in loans to small tech companies to fund over 800 different projects. Specifically to help entrepreneurial college students, Hangzhou established the Risk Pool Fund worth 35 million yuan with 4 million provided by the government, 1 million by a group of ten advisors, and the remainder from various banks (Yang Zuojun 2017: 65).

By 2016, Hangzhou had established 34 joint angel-stage funds totalling 2.1 billion yuan in available money provided by the government and private capital investors. These funds had financed 184 projects with 453 million yuan from the government and 445 million yuan from private capital. Of these projects, 65 per cent were conducted by local companies accounting for 71 per cent of the invested capital (Yang Zuojun 2017: 65).

In order to support small tech companies Hangzhou has also provided working capital loans. In 2016, 100 million yuan of such loans financed 185 projects of small tech companies and the loan amount totalled 1.5 billion yuan. The average amount for each project was 8.12 million yuan, with an average length of loan borrowing of 10 days. Since 2012, when Hangzhou started this programme, it financed more than 800 projects with 5 billion yuan. 95 per cent of these projects came from small tech companies (Yang Zuojun 2017: 64–5).

Shenzhen, according to Table 10.3, established three government investment organs to finance innovation in high-tech industries. The Shenzhen Innovation Investment Group, established in 1999, has been ranked number one in China's venture capital industry over multiple years. It provides up to 30 per cent of the total investment capital for a fund, and the remaining 70–80 per cent must be raised from the market (Huang Ting 2018). A state's adopted industrial

Table 10.2: The Investment and Financing Services Provided by the Hangzhou Government

Type of investment and financing	
Hangzhou venture capital guidance fund	
Designated funds (number)	47
Fund amount (billion yuan)	6.6
Funds from the government (billion yuan)	3.3
Funds from the market (billion yuan)	2.3
Start ups' share of invested programme (%)	71
Loan guarantee for medium-sized and small tech companies	
Companies serviced in recent 10 years (times)	2000
Accumulated amount of loan guarantee (billion yuan)	7
Dandelion angel investment guidance fund	
Angel-stage fund (number)	34
Fund amount (billion yuan)	2.1
Number of projects invested	184
Funds from the government (billion yuan)	0.45
Funds from the market (billion yuan)	0.45
Hangzhou share of invested programme (%)	65
Hangzhou share of investment amount (%)	71
Working capital loan for medium-sized and small tech companies	
Working capital loan amount (billion yuan)	1.5
Companies that serviced working capital loan	185

Source: Yearbook of Hangzhou Science and Technology 2017.

Table 10.3: The Investment and Financing Services Provided by the Shenzhen Government

Type of investment and financing	
Shenzhen Venture Capital guidance fund	
Fund scale (billion yuan)	100
Number of projects invested	681
Investment amount (billion yuan)	42.8
Joint investment of social capital (billion yuan)	357
Shenzhen share of investment amount (%)	42.4
Angel investment guidance fund amount (billion yuan)	5

Source: Shenzhenshi caizheng weiyuanhui, 2018.

policy will be unlikely to succeed if it is poorly received by the market because private venture capital is not willing to gamble on risky projects. The state's 30 per cent financing alone is not enough to directly support innovation, so the state depends on private capital. At the same time, by offering 30 per cent of the capital, the state signals to the market that it supports the investment which is often enough to help convince venture capitalists to join in the investment.

The Shenzhen Investment Holding Company is 100 per cent owned by the city's State-Owned Assets Administrative Commission. It came into being as a result of the merger of three state-owned assets management companies in 2004. It has a majority share in more than 60 companies and minority shares in more than 20 companies. At the end of 2016, its assets totalled 53 million yuan (Nanfang Dushibao 2017).

The Shenzhen Angel Seed Fund was established in 2018. It provides 40 per cent of the total capital for a given project. In November 2018, the fund signed contracts with 8 private venture capital companies to provide 1.96 billion yuan on top of the 4.9 billion yuan these companies had pledged. Although the state shares the risks associated with investment, it does not share in the profits, except to recover its original investment amount (Liu Quan 2018). This practice is identical to that of the entrepreneurial state.

Human capital is another factor endowment that these two local governments have enhanced. Hangzhou began to adopt a human capital policy in 2004 (Hangzhou Municipal Communist Party Committee and Hangzhou Municipal People's Government 2004). Information technology was one of the areas of expertise listed along with journalism, culture, finance, tourism, trade, management and law. Early on, Hangzhou tried to attract both those who held PhD or Master's degrees and those without degrees who had high level skills. The government put forward a special policy to attract highly skilled workers and promoted various vocational programmes.

According to a 2017 study by LinkedIn, Hangzhou is number four in the distribution of human capital among Chinese cities in the digital economy, accounting for 3.4 per cent of the national total of skilled workers, led only by Shanghai (16.6 per cent), Beijing (15.6 per cent) and Shenzhen (6.7 per cent) (*China Digital Economy Talent Report*: 7). By September 2019, Hangzhou had attracted 55,000 university graduates from overseas with various degrees, plus 30,000 foreigners. They established 2,754 companies with 41,700 patents. Thirty-one of these companies have issued their IPO. For nine years in a row, Hangzhou has been selected as "the most attractive Chinese city for foreign talents". Since 2016, Hangzhou has been ranked number one in terms of inflow of talent, inflow of talent from overseas and inflow of talent in internet-related industries (Fu Lingbo 2019).

In 2008, the Guangdong provincial government started a programme called "Empty the cage, welcome new birds". Shenzhen announced a first-of-its-kind policy to attract senior-level talent in high-tech industries. In 2011, the year it adopted a policy to promote cloud computing, it also announced the famous "Peacock Program". By 2017, Shenzhen had successfully attracted 14 research teams, including 4,309 persons from overseas, with 35.7 per cent in artificial intelligence, 28.6 per cent in big data and the internet of things and 7.1 per cent in cloud computing (Shenzhen Technology and Innovation Commission 2018).

Shenzhen has also tried to attract young labour with higher education. In 2011–17, Shenzhen's population with local registration increased from 3.1 million to 4.4 million, with an average age of 27 (*Shenzhen Statistical Yearbook* 2018). In 2017 alone, Shenzhen attracted 174,000 college graduates, 18,307 returnees with overseas degrees ranging from a Bachelor's to PhD, 935 postdoctoral fellows, and 12 Chinese Academy of Sciences and Chinese Academy of Engineering fellows to work full-time in Shenzhen (Shenzhenshi Renli ziyuan he Shehui baozhang June 2018).

Building Infrastructure

Building infrastructure is a distinctive feature of the industrial policy adopted by the competitive-advantage-building state in China. In the digital economy era, infrastructure involves platforms of public services and hardware infrastructure that support the development of the internet of things, big data, cloud computing and artificial intelligence.

In 2016, Hangzhou opened the Qiantang Big Data Trading Center, the first trading platform for industrial data in China. Its aim is to build an effective, convenient, and open-source database for the collection, trading and service of big data that can be provided to government agencies, industrial corporations and individual users. Its services include industrial data evaluation, initial data treatment, algorithms and modelling and data application products (Hangzhou zhengfuwang 2016). The Shenzhen government has also built platforms for public services, involving the development of commonly-shared technologies, quality certification, measurement and testing, data mining, information services, shared equipment, management services and the training of skilled labour. It established the Shenzhen Industrial Design Cloud Service Platform at the National Supercomputing Center of Shenzhen in 2015.

Opening government data to the public serves as an infrastructural support for the development of cloud computing. These data help companies improve their technologies. Open data mean that companies can dispatch resources and clean data via cloud networks, improve their capabilities in business analytics, increase the value of their apps and enhance artificial intelligence training. In September 2015, the Zhejiang Provincial government publicly announced its Open Data Platform. The data came from 68 government agencies and involved eight major areas, including economy, environment and natural resources, urban development, transportation, education/science/technology, culture and leisure, civil service and other organisations (Hangzhouwang 2015). By 2018, Shenzhen had made data available to the public in 14 areas, including transportation and traffic, finance and money, culture and leisure, education and science, and ecological resources. These data involved 79 million items and 1,094 datasets from 42 government agencies (Shenzhen Shang Bao 2018).

Reducing Transaction Costs

The development of the digital economy necessitates collaboration between basic research, R&D, intellectual property right transactions and commercialisation. Improving institutional environments serves to reduce transaction costs among different players.

Hangzhou has focused on protecting intellectual property rights. Zhejiang province is a leader in intellectual property rights protection in China. In 2011–16, Zhejiang courts accepted 76,000 intellectual property rights cases, which accounted for 51.3 per cent of the total cases in the Yangzi River Delta region. The courts settled 8,364 cases that involved patents, which accounted for one-sixth of such cases settled by the Chinese courts. These cases involved 1,759 high tech/new tech companies and 720 million yuan (Pengpai Xinwen 2017). In September 2017, Hangzhou, upon the approval of China's Supreme Court, established its own Intellectual Property Rights Court. By October 2018, this court had settled 1,246 cases including 996 cases of IP rights violations and 250 cases of fake patents (Hangzhoushi Kexue Jishu Ju 2019).

Shenzhen lacks higher education institutions, and its R&D capacity has been concentrated in private companies. Its government has encouraged collaborations between academic institutions that conduct basic research and private companies that try to commercialise the outcomes of basic research. To accomplish this, the Shenzhen government made a special arrangement: when private companies build new labs jointly with universities or research institutions or upgrade old ones, the government invests up to 40 per cent of the total cost, up to five million yuan (Shenzhen Municipal Government 2011). By 2017, more than 20 labs, engineering centres, and technology centres had been established for the internet of things and 6 labs and centres had been established for artificial intelligence. In 2018, 10 such labs and centres were built specifically for big data (Shenzhen Technology and Innovation Commission 2018).

The government also started so-called "double-chain integration" projects. The two "chains" involve the chain of innovation and the chain of industry. Double-chain integration projects are driven by strong demand in the market which in turn intensifies the focuses on the basic research needed for frontier technologies, R&D for commonly shared technology and the demonstration model for commercialisation. Shenzhen pushed connections between industry and universities or research institutions by encouraging joint R&D. It provided 15 million yuan, per project, per year, for up to three years, and up to 30 per cent of the total investments (Shenzhen Jingxin Ju 2017).

Creating Market Demand

In the digital economy, size matters. The bigger the e-commerce is, the more data, and the more data, the bigger the cloud computing industry. An important role played by the competitive-advantage-building state is to create demands for new products and services for these new industries. In China, more than 300 regional-level cities have invested more than 600 billion yuan in cloud computing out of more than 3 trillion yuan pledged by these cities (Chen Jing 2018).

Hangzhou has focused on increasing application scenes, promoting government procurements and encouraging companies' transition to cloud computing. Hangzhou requested the district and county governments within its jurisdiction to purchase cloud computing services in smart transportation, smart city-rural administration, smart public security and forest-ecology security monitoring.

Encouraging private companies to shift towards cloud-based IT infrastructure has been a major focus for Hangzhou. Hangzhou announced a three-year plan in 2018. It urged government agencies to provide guidance to private companies according to the characteristics of their industries. For example, agricultural companies should focus on building a platform for cloud computing that provides applications to data-source integration, product management, supply chain management, marketing and safety tracing; companies in the manufacturing industry should develop cloud applications that help R&D, production, supply chain management and marketing; and companies in the service sector should develop cloud platforms that help marketing management, sales channels, customer service and business operations. In 2017, Hangzhou pushed more than 41,500 companies to transition to cloud computing (Zhejiangsheng Jingxin Ting 2018).

Shenzhen has focused on the smart city programme, centred around urban management and digitalisation of public administration. The former involves water, electricity, gas, sewage, telecommunications, the subway and underground pipelines (Shenzhenshi renmin zhengfu bangongting 2013). The city built a comprehensive database and unified platform, providing basic information services that were needed for the approval process of civil engineering projects and underground pipeline network management. It also set data collection standards, clarified database structure and content requirements and outlined data renewal and sharing mechanisms.

The centralisation and digitalisation of public administration data have created a huge demand for cloud computing. Shenzhen pushed the transition of the government's IT system from self-maintained to cloud, and the shift of government databases from business recording to business analytics. Between 2011 and 2018, the Shenzhen government had 175 data digitalisation projects involving 92 agencies at a cost of 15.6 billion yuan (Shenzhen Audit Bureau 2018). These projects involved information infrastructure hardware, software development, data collection, data cleaning, analytics, data application and solution design. In public services, these projects covered bureaux in charge of finances, economy and information, police, health, education, social welfare, transportation and construction.

Promoting Industrial Clusters

The spatial concentration of value chain, or industrial clusters, has been a distinctive Chinese practice over the past four decades and constitutes the basis for Chinese companies' competitiveness. In order to promote the development of the cloud computing industry, Hangzhou has focused on building ecosystems for platforms. The cloud computing industry, just like other industries in the digital economy, is characterised by numerous small companies that form varieties of ecosystems. In its 2013–15 E-commerce Plan, Hangzhou invested 313 million yuan to strengthen its e-commerce platform and related value chains. It also invested 4.8 billion yuan for 44 platforms that provided public services (Hangzhoushi Jingxin Ju 2013). Hangzhou partnered with Alibaba to create "the Yunxi Village" in 2013, the first industrial cluster in China specialising in cloud computing and big data (Fu M. 2017). By 2018, it had gathered 645 companies related to cloud computing, generating one billion yuan in annual tax revenue. The major goal of this cluster was to encourage collaboration among innovative companies in regard to business conceptualisation, production, data analytics and service supplies in support of cloud computing end users (Zhejiang Zaixian 2015).

In Shenzhen, recruiting high-tech teams, rather than individual experts, became a major strategy for enhancing human capital. Between 2011 and 2017, through its Peacock Program, Shenzhen recruited senior research teams or start-up teams in robotics and smart information technology, data management, chips, 3D sensors, natural interaction between humans and machines, visual recognition and machine learning, robotic de-escalators, and the internet of things based on 5G. Huaao Data, a company that specialised in data cleaning, had applied for 113 patents, published 82 articles in top international journals and participated in the making of 16 industrial standards, five of which became national standards (Nanfang dushibao 2016). Yunxin Yihao, a maker of chips used in cloud technologies, provides comprehensive big data products and solutions. It expanded the cloud computing industry's value chain and stimulated related industries' development. It was the fourth company in Guangdong Province, after Huawei, Tencent and ZTE, to receive big data certification from the Ministry of Industry and Information (Nanfang Ribao 2017).

Encouraging Competition

Fair competition between government agencies or state-owned enterprises and private companies has been a major issue in China. Hangzhou established a fair competition review system in 2017. It required that any regulation, administrative order, or policy adopted by government agencies or organisations that perform public functions must receive a fair competition review when they involve market access, industrial development, foreign direct investment, bidding, government procurement, business regulation or industrial standards. More importantly, it has made government agencies' performance in delivering these promises part of the evaluation system of government officials (Hangzhoushi Kexue Jishu Ju 2018).

Both cities have adopted universal criteria for the initial rounds of distribution of investment funds distribution or subsidies. So long as a company qualifies, it can receive the money. However, in order to receive funding or subsidies in subsequent rounds, a company has to meet a different set of criteria. Although the criteria for later rounds are still universal, the bar is higher with a company having to survive market competition to qualify.

The Political Economy of the Competitive-Advantage-Building State

The above analyses show that the development of both Hangzhou and Shenzhen into two cloud computing powerhouses has been supported by the industrial policy adopted by the competitive-advantage-building state. However, industrial policy alone cannot explain the different outcomes. Table 10.4 shows that in the Infrastructure as a Service (IaaS) sector of the cloud computing industry, Alibaba is number one, accounting for 45.5 per cent of the market, while Tencent is a distant number two with only a 10.3 per cent market share. In the Platform as a Service (PaaS) sector of the same industry, Alibaba is also number one, accounting for 27.3 per cent of the Chinese market while Tencent does not even appear in the top five (Yiou Zhiku 2019b). Why is Alibaba's market share in China more than four times larger than Tencent's?

Table 10.4:   The Top Five Companies in the Chinese Public Cloud Computing Market

IaaS (market share %)		PaaS (market share %)	
Alibaba Group	45.5	Alibaba Group	27.3
Tencent	10.3	Oracle	9.7
China Telecom	7.6	Amazon Web Services	9.7
Kingsoft	6.5	Microsoft	5.8
Amazon Web Services	5.4	IBM	4.5
Others	24.7	Others	43.0

Source: Yiou Zhiku 2019b: 26–7.

To answer this question, we need to examine the structural constraints on the competitive-advantage-building state: First, such a state is a product of the distribution of power in state-business relations. It tends to appear in places where private companies, either domestic or foreign, are predominant. Second, private companies' preferences are crucial to the extent to which an industrial policy gets support, and their preferences are often derived from their business models. Third, the industrial policy of the competitive-advantage-building state is often affected by those leading private companies that have succeeded in breaking through from 0 to 1. Finally, the implementation of an industrial policy creates market dynamics that often incentivise those who had been reluctant to participate to change their minds.

The Power Distribution in State-Business Relations

Why has the competitive-advantage-building state emerged in Hangzhou and Shenzhen? Part of the answer lies in the structure of corporate ownership that indicates the power distribution in state-business relations.

In both cities, private companies are predominant. Shenzhen started as a Special Economic Zone. As late as 2000, the number of foreign-invested companies, including those from Taiwan, Hong Kong and Macao, and the industrial outputs produced by these companies accounted for nearly 80 per cent of the city's total. Between 2000 and 2017, as shown in Figure 10.1, a major shift took place: the number of domestic private companies increased from 15 per cent to nearly 70 per cent, while these domestic companies' outputs grew to more than 50 per cent of the city's total. In the same period, the number of foreign-invested companies declined by one-third, and the weight of companies from Taiwan, Hong Kong and Macao declined dramatically from more than 60 per cent to less than 20 per cent while their industrial outputs also declined significantly. The share of state-owned enterprises has been negligible in Shenzhen (*Shenzhen Statistical Yearbook 2001–2018*).

Figure 10.1: The Distribution of Ownership of Industrial Enterprises[1] in Shenzhen between 2000 and 2017

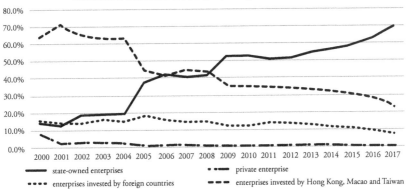

Source: *Shenzhen Statistical Yearbook 2001–18.*

In contrast to Shenzhen, with its history of a high number of foreign-invested companies, domestic private companies have always been predominant in Hangzhou. Between 2000 and 2017, as shown in Figure 10.2, the number of investments in companies by *foreign countries* and by Taiwan, Hong Kong and Macao amounted to 17 per cent of companies on average annually, while their industrial output accounted for less than 30 per cent of the city's total (*Hangzhou Statistical Yearbook 2001–2018*).

Figure 10.2: The Distribution of Ownership of Industrial Enterprises in Hangzhou between 2000 and 2017

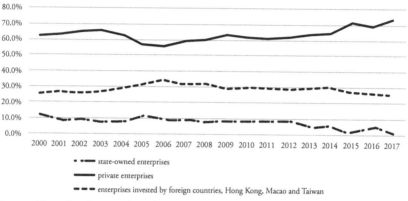

Source: *Hangzhou Statistical Yearbook 2001–18.*

As opposed to Shenzhen where private companies' production activities have been driven completely by international markets ever since the early 1980s, Hangzhou has been driven by domestic markets. In both cities, the elements and legacies of China's planned economy had been weak, making it virtually impossible for the state to take a heavy-handed approach to practise industrial policy; the government had to find a way to implement its policy, such that it would work with the market.

Business Model and Preferences of the Private Sector

Why has Hangzhou taken the lead in cloud computing while Shenzhen has been left behind? The answer is that the industrial policies in each city have been heavily affected by the preferences of the leading companies in the industry, and those preferences were often derived from their business models.

At an IT summit in March 2010, the leaders of China's big three platform companies, Baidu, Alibaba and Tencent, had a famous debate about cloud computing. Alibaba's CEO Jack Ma was very optimistic, foreseeing cloud computing to be the future direction of information technology. In contrast, both Tencent's CEO Pony Ma and Baidu's CEO Robin Li were pessimistic: the former held that the era of cloud computing would not come for another hundred years, while the latter considered cloud computing as nothing more than a "new bottle of old wine". These leaders' positions on cloud computing are largely responsible for their companies' relative positions in the industry today.

Alibaba's eagerness to develop cloud computing was driven by the bottleneck in its IT infrastructure amid the rapid growth of its e-commerce business. Before 2008, Alibaba's IT infrastructure relied heavily upon IOE, namely, IBM's servers, Oracle's database and EMC's data storage. At the time, Alibaba's business was growing by more than 30 per cent a year and its computing facilities ran at nearly full capacity every morning. An unexpected system breakdown became a lingering nightmare. Because IOE equipment was expensive, Alibaba could no longer bear the cost of upgrading its IT infrastructure. After several system breakdowns, Alibaba decided in 2008 that cloud computing was its only life-saving solution. So, even without government support, Alibaba started its R&D on cloud computing (Shi Zhong 2018).

Former deputy director of Microsoft Institute Asia and Ali Cloud CEO Wang Jian's vision plus Alibaba CEO Jack Ma's firm support played a crucial role in the development. The development process was quite bumpy. In more than three years, cloud computing was not well received within Alibaba. Subunits were not willing to try it, Wang was even called a swindler, and 80 per cent of the R&D team members quit because they had lost confidence in the project. Despite all this, Jack Ma never gave in. In fact, he proceeded to announce that Alibaba would invest one billion yuan per year for the next ten years to develop the Ali Cloud (Wei Wuji 2018). One impetus behind this effort was when, in 2009, Alibaba started to have an annual sales event on November 11th, China's "Singles' Day". This holiday has since become the most important commercial day for Chinese consumers and businesses. Future November 11th holiday sales presented great challenges to Alibaba's website because the flood of orders that pour into it each second could easily lead to a system breakdown, potentially costing the company millions. Cloud computing's promise of a solution firmed up Jack Ma's support for developing Ali Cloud.

In contrast, Tencent's journey towards cloud computing was driven by a number of circumstantial events. In 2010, the same year in which Pony Ma presented his pessimistic view about cloud computing, Qihu 360, an internet security company, launched a big lawsuit against Tencent. Although Tencent won the lawsuit in court, public opinion about Tencent was decidedly negative. Its early model of copying every successful app earned Tencent the nickname "public enemy of all industries". This forced Pony Ma to reflect (Wu Xiaobo 2017). In 2010, Tencent invented WeChat and it grew rapidly. WeChat's popularity was further enhanced by a profound shift in China's internet industry in 2012: the number of smart phone users surpassed the number of PC users. This marked the beginning of a new era in which social media would become dominant. As the digital economy became more complicated, it was no longer possible to develop everything in house. In addition, Tencent's competitors, such as Baidu, Sina and Alibaba, all adopted an open door strategy. Under the pressure of competition, Tencent was forced to open its own platforms to outsiders allowing third party companies to use its platforms. Of course, Tencent still received a share of these companies' profits by providing the gateway to the customer pool and basic infrastructural services (Liu Hongjun 2019).

Although Alibaba had the first-comer's advantage, the different perceptions and adoption models of cloud computing determined the private companies' and consequently these cities' positions in the industry. However, some puzzles still remain: why was Shenzhen left behind even after it adopted an industrial policy to support cloud computing several years earlier than Hangzhou did? And why did Shenzhen set only a moderate goal for its cloud computing industry although it quickly responded to the industrial policy adopted by the central government?

Structural Constraints and the Agency of the State

The answer is that industrial policy is often shaped by private entrepreneurship and the effectiveness of an industrial policy is often affected by the willingness of private companies to follow the state's guidance.

When the central government designated Hangzhou as one of the five trial cities for cloud computing in 2010, it provided Alibaba with 450 million yuan, while the company decided to invest 3 billion (Hangzhou Zhengfuwang 2012). Beginning in 2011, the Zhejiang provincial government provided some support for the development of the Ali Cloud but the amount of money was small. Up until 2014, Hangzhou's municipal government had essentially been taking a wait-and-see position and did not adopt a specific policy to support cloud computing.

Even by mid-2014, Hangzhou was still uncertain about the future of its economy. Before that time, Hangzhou had primarily relied on low tech, high energy consumption, cheap labour, traditional business models and small companies. This development strategy reached a bottleneck in 2012: Hangzhou ended its 21-year two-digit economic growth, recording growth of only 9 per cent, and in 2013, it dropped further to 8 per cent (Yu and Tang 2017). Although Hangzhou was one of the five trial cities designated for cloud computing and was specifically chosen by the central government to be the national centre of e-commerce, Hangzhou had never taken these designations seriously. Even after more than 190 Chinese cities launched their own smart-city programmes in 2014, Hangzhou still thought this phenomenon was merely a fad.

Ali Cloud CEO Wang Jian's advice changed government officials' minds. At a meeting in which government officials solicited advice on new industries to generate economic growth, Wang told them that Hangzhou could become China's data centre. He proposed that the digital economy represented by big data, cloud computing, the internet of things, the mobile internet and smart manufacturing could be the future direction for Hangzhou's economy (Yu and Tang 2017). Wang gave this advice with great confidence: by mid-2014 Ali Cloud had proven a big success. When the Ali Cloud was tested for the first time during the largest shopping day of the year, Singles' Day, 11 November 2012, it was able to survive a million simultaneous orders. By the following year, 11 November 2013, Alibaba's cloud computing involved more than 5,000 computers operating in a network with its cloud processing 80 per cent of 35 billion orders in a single day (Yang Xiaohe 2018).

Once the government was convinced by Wang's advice, it proposed an ambitious master plan: Hangzhou would become a major national centre for designing and planning cloud computing, building platforms for cloud computing and providing operation-maintenance services. It treated the development of the digital economy as its "number one priority" (Zhejiang Zaixian 2014). Cloud computing and big data, together with e-commerce, the internet of things, logistics, internet finance and digital content were considered a cluster of industries whose interactions would exert a positive impact on each other (Hangzhou Municipal Communist Party Committee and Hangzhou Municipal People's Government 2014).

Since 2014, Hangzhou has concentrated its resources in the digital economy. It even substantially reorganised its internal division of labour by establishing the Bureau of Cloud Computing and Big Data within its Economy and Information Commission, the first such bureau in the country. It has also made two three-year development plans for e-commerce, 2013–15 and 2015–17 (Hangzhoushi Shangwu Weiyuanhui 2015). In 2018, Hangzhou announced the next stage of development for cloud computing which will bring artificial intelligence to the centre of its future industrial upgrades (Hangzhoushi Fazhan he Gaige Weiyuanhui 2018).

For its part, Shenzhen responded to the central government's policy quickly. Only one week after it was designated one of the five trial cities for cloud computing in 2010, Shenzhen announced a cloud computing policy.

It proposed further cloud computing policies in 2011 that included various measures to support the development of the industry. Nevertheless, the goals it set for itself were rather moderate: Shenzhen would become "a center of cloud computing in South China". This lack of ambition was partly due to the fact that once a goal had been set, the performance of the local government might be evaluated accordingly. Given that the major local players, Tencent and Huawei, were less enthusiastic to embrace cloud computing technology, it was understandable that Shenzhen's government was less ambitious.

Because Tencent was the biggest platform company in China, and third-party companies operating through the Tencent Cloud could gain access to all its platforms simultaneously, one would think that the Tencent Cloud should have surpassed Ali Cloud quickly. However, the problem was that even after Tencent started its cloud computing programme, it was not serious about it until 2017. Pony Ma rejected the programme director's proposal to expand cloud computing into Tencent's major business. Within Tencent, the cloud was merely a subunit of its Social Network Group, languishing in a situation in which "no external client use[d] it while no internal unit like[d] it". Whereas Jack Ma of Alibaba forced his company's subdivisions to use Ali Cloud, the Tencent Cloud did not enjoy that kind of internal support. Tencent did not have the gene of To-B business because it had been a To-C company. In 2018, the Tencent Cloud suffered from major accidents resulting in the loss of client data and the disruption of cloud functions. Only after Tencent's profits declined by 35 per cent in the fourth quarter of the 2018 fiscal year did the company finally begin to take cloud computing seriously, after which the Tencent Cloud was upgraded to the Cloud and Smart Industry Group (AI Caijingshe 2019).

Huawei, another giant of cloud computing in Shenzhen, was in a similar situation. Huawei started its cloud computing programme in 2010. However, it took a strategy of "announcing the plan but not working hard on it". Unlike other internet platform companies, cloud computing had the potential to directly hurt Huawei's interests. According to its internal calculations, Huawei stood to make five times more profits when clients performed calculations on Huawei's servers than it would make if those clients performed the same calculations in the cloud. It was only in 2016, after Alibaba and Tencent took away nearly 60 per cent of market share in the cloud computing industry, that Huawei finally made the decision to catch up to the competition (AI Caijingshe 2019).

The agency of Shenzhen's government in implementing industrial policy for cloud computing was structurally constrained by the reluctance of two leading companies in the field. In addition, Shenzhen had been a centre of computer hardware without enough software engineers. Government officials could not do much when the private sector was not enthusiastic. At the same time, Shenzhen did not worry too much about its economic fortunes for two reasons: First, although Tencent is a major company in Shenzhen, the city has plenty of peers, such that Tencent is only one big company among many. Second, cloud computing is only one of several important industries in the city. Even as Huawei failed to actively participate in developing cloud computing, its telecom equipment and cell-phone businesses still provided the city with enormous tax revenues. So, Shenzhen did not mind if Huawei was not serious or took its time in developing its cloud computing capability.

Concluding Remarks

This study demonstrates the distinctive characteristics of the industrial policy practised by the competitive-advantage-building state in two Chinese cities. At the same time, it also shows that such a state draws upon various practices of other types of industrial policy. It shares the focuses of the developmental state in Japan, such as industrial targeting and promoting exports, but is more open to inflows of foreign capital and employs more policy tools to support private companies. When the state developed funding mechanisms to support the development of the cloud computing industry, for example, it went beyond the traditional government subsidies by creating government investment funds and also supporting private venture capital. By bearing the risks of investment in frontier technologies and by creating market demand through government procurement, the competitive-advantage-building state has also become more similar to that of the entrepreneurial state in the United States. Such a state encourages industrial rivalry in the digital economy and shows no mercy to those that fall short in competition. This is in a sharp contrast to the social protection state. Although it shares some practices of the market-facilitating state such as building infrastructure and reducing transaction costs, it is never satisfied by merely creating an effective market and always aims at helping companies that operate within its territory become more competitive. More importantly, the competitive-advantage-building state actively strengthens the factor supplies by both encouraging the development of venture capital and recruiting tech talent globally, transcending the practice of simply using the capital-labour ratio to decide which industries to target, as the market-facilitating state does.

For all other types of state intervention, industrial policy is often treated as the independent variable, which is used to explain the outcome. In contrast, our analysis extends a political economy investigation of industrial policy by turning the competitive-advantage-building state into an intervening variable. By doing so, our model reveals the impacts of both corporate ownership structure and private sector business models on state industrial policy. It demonstrates both the human agency that plays such an important role in practising state industrial policy, and the various constraints imposed by various structural conditions upon such agency.

Chinese industrial policy has often been portrayed as anti-competitive in both domestic and international debates. This may be true in cities that have relatively more state-owned enterprises in sunset industries in relation to which government policies are more similar to those practised by a social protection state. However, this is not true at the centre of China's digital economy. The reason, as this study shows, is that the dominance of private companies in the ownership structure affects the power distribution in state-business relations. In high-tech industries, it is difficult both for the state to support a monopoly of state-owned enterprises, and for private companies to build monopoly positions amid fierce competition.

Contrary to the conventional image that the state practises industrial policy in a top-down fashion, the industrial policies of Shenzhen and Hangzhou municipal governments towards high-tech industries are often affected by private companies because the giant private companies themselves take the lead in innovation and carry out the breakthrough from 0 to 1. As Ali Cloud and Hangzhou's industrial policy demonstrate, private companies' vision and knowledge often become the blueprint of state industrial policy. At the same time, Shenzhen's experience with Tencent and Huawei in cloud computing shows that the state cannot achieve its industrial policy goals when the leading private companies are not enthusiastic about them.

Note

[1] Industrial enterprises over levels refer to the industrial enterprises whose main business revenue reached the designated size, 5,000,000 yuan before 2010 and 20,000,000 yuan from 2010 to 2019.

References

AI Caijingshe [AI Finance]. 2019. *Zhongguo yunjisuan de shinian nixi* [The Return of China's Cloud Computing]. Available at https://tech.sina.com.cn/roll/2019-10-04/doc-iicezzrr0013819.shtml [accessed 23 Nov. 2020].

Alibaba. 2019. *Yin keiji, er yunxi* [Because of Science and Technology, Here Comes Yunxi]. Available at https://yunqi.youku.com/ [accessed 23 Nov. 2020].

Alibaba Group. 2018. *Alibaba jituan gongbu 2018nian 3yuedizhi jidu ji cainian yeji* [Alibaba Group Announces Quarterly and Fiscal Year Results for the End of March 2018]. Available at https://www.alibabagroup.com/cn/news/article?news=p180504 [accessed 23 Nov. 2020].

Chen Jing. 2018. *Zhihui chengshi leiji guihua touzi da 3wanyi, shuju jiazhi ying zai shenwa* [The cumulative planning investment of smart cities reaches 3 trillion, the value of data should be further digging]. *Zhongguo Jingjiwang.* Available at http://www.ce.cn/cysc/tech/gd2012/201810/10/t20181010_30470624.shtml [accessed 23 Nov. 2020].

Chen Qingtai. 2016. *Zhongguo chanye zhengce diwei zhi gao qiansuoweiyou, yi cheng zhuanxing zhangai* [China's industrial policy status is unprecedented, and it has become a barrier to transformation]. *Xinlang Caijing.* Available at http://finance.sina.com.cn/hy/hyjz/2016-11-27/doc-ifxyawmm3527483.shtml [accessed 23 Nov. 2020].

China Digital Economy Talent Report. 2017. LinkedIn Economic Graph Team. (in Chinese). Available at https://economicgraph.linkedin.com/research/china-digital-economy-talent-report [accessed 22 Feb. 2021].

Fu Lingbo. 2019. *Hangzhou jiakuai gouzhu rencai gaodi* [Hangzhou accelerates the construction of an international talent pool]. *Hangzhou Daily.* Available at https://hzdaily.hangzhou.com.cn/hzrb/2019/09/26/article_detail_1_20190926A259.html [accessed 23 Nov. 2020].

Fu M. 2017. "Yunxi xiaozhen shi zenyang liancheng de?" [How Did Yunxi Village Develop?]. *Taimeiti.* Available at http://www.sohu.com/a/205834637_116132 [accessed 23 Nov. 2020].

Gao Bai. 1997. *Economic Ideology and Japanese Industrial Policy: Developmentalism from 1931 to 1965.* New York: Cambridge University Press.

————. 2001. *Japan's Economic Dilemma: The Institutional Origins of Prosperity and Stagnation.* New York: Cambridge University Press.

Gao Bai and Zhu L. 2020. "Cong 'shijie gongchang' dao gongye hulianwang qiangguo: dazao zhineng zhizao shidai de jingzheng youshi" [From "the World Factory" to A Strong Nation of the Industrial Internet of Things: Building Competitive Advantage in the Era of Smart Manufacturing]. *Gaige* 315, 5: 429–42.

Gartner. 2019. *Market Share Analysis: IaaS and IUS, Worldwide, 2018.* Available at https://www.gartner.com/en/documents/3947169/market-share-analysis-iaas-and-ius-worldwide-2018 [accessed 23 Nov. 2020].

Guanyan Tianxia. 2019. "2019nian zhongguo yunjisuan hangye shichang guimo kuaisu zengzhang" [The Size of the Cloud Computing Industry in China Grow Rapidly in 2019]. *Zhongguo Baogaowang.* Available at http://free.chinabaogao.com/it/201908/0Q43I042019.html [accessed 23 Nov. 2020].

Hangzhou Municipal Communist Party Committee and Hangzhou Municipal People's Government. 2004. *Guanyu dali shishi rencai qiangshi zhanlve de jueding* [Decision on Vigorously Implementing the Strategy of Strengthening City with Talents]. Available at http://www.hangzhou.gov.cn/art/2004/4/21/art_809119_2306.html [accessed 23 Nov. 2020].

————. 2014. *Guanyu jiakuai fazhan xinxi jingji de ruogan yijian* [Several Opinions on Accelerating the Development of Information Economy].

Hangzhou Statistical Yearbook 2001–2018. Beijing: China Statistics Press.

Hangzhou zhengfuwang. 2012. *Dishiwujie Hangzhou guonei jingji hezuo qiatanhui* [15th Hangzhou Domestic Economic Cooperation Fair]. Available at http://www.hangzhou.gov.cn/art/2012/10/24/art_1003069_1332.html [accessed 23 Nov. 2020].

————. 2016. *Qiantang dashuju jiaoyi zhongxin shangxian* [Qiantang Big Data Trading Centre is online]. Available at http://www.hangzhou.gov.cn/art/2016/6/1/art_812262_724088.html [accessed 23 Nov. 2020].

Hangzhoushi Fazhan he Gaige Weiyuanhui [Hangzhou Development and Reform Committee]. 2018. *Guanyu yinfa Hangzhou chengshi shuju danao guihua de tongzhi* [Notice on Printing and Distributing the Planning of Hangzhou City's Data and Brain). http://www.hangzhou.gov.cn/art/2018/5/15/art_1256296_18106029.html.

Hangzhoushi Jingxin Ju. 2013. *Hangzhoushi dianzishangwu chuangxin fazhan sannian xingdong jihua (2013–2015)* [Hangzhou E-commerce Innovation and Development Three-Year Action Plan (2013–2015)]. http://www.hangzhou.gov.cn/art/2013/4/3/art_1256297_7881522.html.

————. 2018. *Hangzhoushi shenhua tuijin "Qiye shangyun" sannian xingdong jihua (2018–2020)* [Hangzhou Deepens the Three-Year Action Plan for "Enterprise cloud migration" (2018–2020)]. Available at http://www.hangzhou.gov.cn/art/2018/11/13/art_1256296_24510444.html [accessed 23 Nov. 2020].

Hangzhoushi Kexue Jishu Ju [Hangzhou Science and Technology Bureau]. 2018. *2018nian Hangzhoushi zhishichanquan zhifa weiquan gongzuo fangan* [Hangzhou Intellectual Property Rights Enforcement Plan in 2018]. http://kj.hangzhou.gov.cn/index.aspx?newsId=48351&CatalogID=767&PageGuid=4A3B6524-953E-4CA2-A5C4-0DC81BDEF4CC.

————. 2019. *2018nian hangzhoushi zhishichanquan gongzuo zongjie* [Hangzhou Summary of Intellectual Property Work of in 2018]. http://kj.hangzhou.gov.cn/index.aspx?newsId=49380&CatalogID=843&PageGuid=4A3B6524-953E-4CA2-A5C4-0DC81BDEF4CC.

Hangzhoushi Shangwu Weiyuanhui [Hangzhou Municipal Commission of Commerce]. 2015. *Hangzhoushi jianshe guoji dianzishangwu zhongxin sannian xingdong jihua (2015-2017nian)* [Three-year Plan of Action for Hangzhou to Build an International Electronic Commerce Centre]. http://sww.hangzhou.gov.cn/art/2015/9/15/art_1551501_29268679.html

Hangzhouwang. 2015. "9yue23ri Zhejiang zhengfu shuju kaifang pingtai shangxian, hangai bada lingyu 68 ge jiguo shuju" [On September 23 the Zhejiang Government put the Open Data Platform Online, which Involved Data from 68 Agencies in Eight Areas]. *Hangzhou Bendibao* http://hz.bendibao.com/news/2015924/61007.shtm.

Huaerjie Jianwen [Wall Street]. 2019. "Fu pan tengxun 20nian" [Reviewing 20 years of Tencent]. *Baijiahao.* Available at https://baijiahao.baidu.com/s?id=1626907977547660824&wfr=spider&for=pc [accessed 23 Nov. 2020].

Huang Ting. 2018. "Shenchuangtou Sun Dongsheng: Yi erji guzhi daogua shi dagailü Shijian, shouyilü kending hui zoudi" [Shenzhen Capital Group Sun Dongsheng: A valuation inversion of the new issue and security markets is a high probability event, and the yield will definitely go down]. *Lujiazui zazhi*. Available at http://www.sohu.com/a/242882819_100191015 [accessed 23 Nov. 2020].

IDC [International Data Corporation]. 2019. *2019nian yijidu, zhongguo gongyouyun shichang renao kaiju* [The First Quarter 2019, A Lively Start]. Available at https://www.idc.com/getdoc.jsp?containerId=prCHC45418919 [accessed 23 Nov. 2020].

Johnson, Chalmers A. 1982. *MITI and the Japanese Miracle : The Growth of Industrial Policy, 1925-1975*. Stanford CA: Stanford University Press.

Lin Yifu. 2013. "Zhenfu yu shichang de guanxi" [The Relationship between the Government and the Market]. *Guojia Xingzheng Xueyuan Xuebao* 6: 4–5.

_____. "Lin Yifu: Zhengfu youwei shi shichang youxiao de qianti" [Lin Yifu: Active government is the premise of effective market]. *Fenghuang Zhoukan*. https://pit.ifeng.com/a/20170504/51043072_0.shtml.

Liu Hongjun. 2019. "Tengxun kaifang zhenxiang" ["The Truth about Tencent's Opening"]. Huanqiu qiyejia. Available at http://www.gemag.com.cn/12/31479_1.html [accessed 3 Mar. 2021].

Liu Quan. 2018. "Jiemi Shenzhenshi tianshi mujijin" [Uncovering Shenzhen's Angel Fund of Funds]. *Touzijie*. November 17th. Available at https://news.pedaily.cn/201811/437894.shtml [accessed 23 Nov. 2020].

Mazzucato, Mariana. 2015. *The Entrepreneurial State: Debunking Public vs. Private Sector Myths*. New York: Public Affairs.

Nanfang Dushibao. 2016. *Huaao: Kaiken zhengfu shuju gudao* [Huaao: Reclamation government data island]. Available at http://epaper.oeeee.com/epaper/A/html/2016-10/19/content_85846.htm [accessed 23 Nov. 2020].

_____. 2017. *Duibiao Singapore danmaxi konggu shentoukong 2020nian zichan zongguimo huochao 3wanyiyuan* [Modelled on Singapore's Temasek Holdings, Shenzhen Investment Holding Company's Assets Will Reach 3 Trillion yuan in 2020]. http://www.sihc.com.cn/media_detail-3-61-1.html

Nanfang Ribao. 2017. *Qianhaixinxi xie 'Yunxin yihao' luohu baoan* [Qianhai Information Brings 'Cloud Core One' to Baoan]. Available at http://epaper.southcn.com/nfdaily/html/2017-03/28/content_7627599.htm [accessed 23 Nov. 2020].

National Development and Reform Commission and Ministry of Science and Technology. 2010. *Guojia fazhan gaigewei Gongye he xinxi huabu guanyu zuohao yunjisuan fuwu chuangxin fazhan shidian shifan gongzuo de tongzhi* [National Development and Reform Commission, Ministry of Industry and Information Technology Notice on Piloting and Demonstration of Cloud Computing Service Innovation and Development]. Available at http://www.gov.cn/zwgk/2010-10/25/content_1729805.htm [accessed 23 Nov. 2020].

Pengpai Xinwen [Breaking News]. 2017. *Hangzhou, Ningbo zhishi chanquan ting guapai, ke kuaquyu guanli zhejiang sheng nei zhongda anjian* [Hangzhou and Ningbo establish Intellectual Property Court, making the management of cross-regional major cases in the province possible]. Available at http://www.sohu.com/a/190601437_260616 [accessed 23 Nov. 2020].

Porter, Michael E. 1990. *The Competitive Advantage of Nations*. New York: The Free Press.

Shenzhen Audit Bureau. 2018. *Shenzhenshi 2018niandu jixiao shenji gongzuo baogao* [Report of Shenzhen 2018 Annual Performance Audit Work]. http://www.sz.gov. cn/sjj/qt/zyhy_1/201812/t20181225_14948279.htm.

Shenzhen Jingxin Ju. 2017. *Zhanluexing xinxing he weilai chanye fazhan zhuanxiang zijin shenqing zhinan* [Guide to applying for special funds for Strategic Emerging and Future Industries]. http://wap.sz.gov.cn/cn/xxgk/zfxxgj/tzgg/201706/t2017 0615_7126001.htm.

Shenzhen Municipal Government. 2011. *Shenzhenshi Renmin Zhengfu guanyu yinfa xinyidai xinxijishu chanye zhenxing fazhan zhengce de tongzhi* [Notice of the Shenzhen Municipal People's Government on Printing and Distributing the Policy of Promoting the Development of Shenzhen's New Generation Information Technology Industry]. Available at http://www.gov.cn/zhengce/2011-12/29/5043037/files/ 82024f082d7145b79e2995652dab79bf.pdf [accessed 23 Nov. 2020].

Shenzhen Shang Bao. 2018. *Shenzhen zhihui zhengwu zhuoyou chengxiao* [Shenzhen Smart Government has achieved fruitful results]. Available at http://szsb.sznews. com/PC/content/201812/06/content_522878.html [accessed 23 Nov. 2020].

Shenzhen Technology and Innovation Commission. 2018. *Shenzhen shi chuangxin zaiti mingdan* [List of Shenzhen innovation institutions]. Available at http://stic.sz.gov. cn/kjfw/cxzt/szscxztmd/ [accessed 21 Nov. 2020].

Shenzhenshi caizheng weiyuanhui [Shenzhen Municipal Finance Committee]. 2018.

Shenzhenshi renli ziyuan he Shehui baozhang Ju [Shenzhen Municipality Human Resources and Social Security Bureau]. 2018. *2017nian Shenzhenshi renli ziyuan baozhang gongzuo zongjie he 2018nian gongzuo bushu* [2017 Shenzhen Human Resources Guarantee Work Summary and 2018 Work Deployment]. http://www. sz.gov.cn/szrbj/xxgk/ghjh/jhjzj/201804/t20180428_11803536.htm.

Shenzhenshi renmin zhengfu bangongting [General Office of Shenzhen Municipal People's Government]. 2013. *Zhihui Shenzhen jianshe shishi fangan (2013-2015nian)* [Smart Shenzhen Construction Implementation Plan (2013–2015)]. http://zwgk. gd.gov.cn/007543382/201310/t20131025_429290.html.

Shenzhenshi tongju ju. 2001-18. *Shenzhen Statistical Yearbook*. China Statistics Press.

Shi Zhong. 2018. "Aliyun de zhequn fengzi" [Alibaba Cloud's Madmen]. *Qianhei Keji*. Available at https://yq.aliyun.com/articles/653511?spm=a2c4e.11153940 .0.0.2a60361awfKHCw [accessed 23 Nov. 2020].

Srnicek, Nick. 2017. *Platform Capitalism*. Cambridge UK: Polity.

Tilton, Mark. 1996. *Restrained Trade: Cartels in Japan's Basic Materials Industries*. Ithaca: Cornell University Press.

Uriu, Robert. 1996. *Troubled Industries: Confronting Economic Change in Japan*. Ithaca: Cornell University Press.

Wang Jiwu 2018. "Wang Jiwu lun zhongmei zhizheng: renlei diwuci kejigeming yu chanye1geming" [Wang Jiwu on the China-U.S. Competition: The Ultimate Competition in the Fifth Scientific-Technological and Industrial Revolution]. *Qidi Kungu.* http://www.sohu.com/a/255488940_465915.

Wang W., Wei W. and Hua X. 2018. *Tengxun 15nian shangye moshi bianqian* [The Transformations of Tencent's Business Models]. http://tech.ifeng.com/a/20140112 /45162067_0.shtml.

Wei Wuji. 2018. "Ta ceng 'pian' le Ma Yun 10yi, 10nian hou huanle 4500yi, cong pianzi dao dashi, ta shi ruhe Chenggong de?" [He "cheated" Jack Ma out of 1 billion yuan, and he paid back 450 billion yuan 10 years later. From cheater to master, how did he succeed?"]. *Dianshang guancha wang.* Available at http://finance.sina. com.cn/money/fund/fundzmt/2018-10-02/doc-ifxeuwws0479320.shtml [accessed 23 Nov. 2020].

Wu Jinglian. 2016. "Wu Jinglian: Chanye zhengce yizhi jingzheng, weifan gongping jingzheng yuanze" [Wu Jinglian: Industrial policy restrains competition, violates the principle of fair competition]. *Xinlang Caijing.* Available at http://finance.sina.com. cn/hy/hyjz/2016-11-27/doc-ifxyawmm3523035.shtml [accessed 23 Nov. 2020].

Wu Xiaobo. 2015. "Tengxun 17nian fazhanshi shang de 14ge guanjiandian" (The 14 Key Points in the 17 Year History of Tencent). *Tengxuwang.* 12 June. Available at https://tech.qq.com/a/20150612/019667.htm [accessed 23 Nov. 2020].

————. 2017. *Tengxun zhuan* [The History of Tencent]. Hangzhou: Zhejing Daxue Chubanshe.

Yang Xiaohe. 2018. "Zhongguo yunjisuan diedang shinian, huiwang aliyun kanke feitianlu" [Cloud Computing in China has been in Decline for Ten Years, looking back on Ali Cloud's bumpy and winding Road]. *Yi Ou.* Available at https://www. iyiou.com/p/81080.html [accessed 23 Nov. 2020].

Yang Z. 2017. *Yearbook of Hangzhou Science & Technology.* Beijing: Zhonghua Shuju.

Yiou Zhiku. 2019a. *Tengxun 2019 Q2 yeji gaozengzhang yanxu, tengxunyun zaici chengwei zengzhang yinqing* [The High-Speed Growth of Tencent's Performance has continued, Tencent Cloud became the Growth Engine Again]. Available at https:// www.iyiou.com/p/109059.html [accessed 23 Nov. 2020].

————. 2019b. *2019nian zhonggou yunjisuan hangye fazhan yanjiu baogao* [The 2019 Report on the Development of the Cloud Computing Industry in China]. Available at https://legacy.iyiou.com/intelligence/report615.html [accessed 23 Nov. 2020].

Yu J. and Dong J. 2019. "Woguo Shuzijingji gaimo da 31.3 yiyuan zhan GDP bizhong da 34.8%" [The Size of China's Digital Economy reached 31.3 Trillion Yuan and Counts for 34.8% of GDP]. *Xinhua News Agency.* Available at http://www.cac.gov. cn/2019-05/06/c_1124458275.htm [accessed 23 Nov. 2020].

Yu Xina and Tang Junyao. 2017. "Hangzhou Jingxinwei Zhuren: Cong mimang dao jianding, women zenme zhaodao fazhan zhi lu" [Director of the Hangzhou Committee of Economic and Information Technology: From Confusion to

Firmness, How can we Find the Way of Development?]. *Zhejiang News*. Available at https://zj.zjol.com.cn/news/606619.html [accessed 23 Nov. 2020].

Zhejiang Zaixian [Zhejiang Online]. 2014. *Gong Zheng: Ju quanshi zhili jiandingbuyi zhuahao 'yihao gongcheng'* [Gong Zheng: Take the strength of the whole city to firmly grasp the 'No.1 Project']. Available at http://hangzhou.zjol.com.cn/system/2014/08/23/020215484.shtml [accessed 23 Nov. 2020].

————. 2015. *Hangzhou zheng xunsu chengwei Zhongguo hulianwang chuangye chuangxin gaodi* [Hangzhou is Rapidly Becoming China's Internet Entrepreneurial Innovation Highland]. Available at http://hangzhou.zjol.com.cn/system/2015/10/15/020872798.shtml [accessed 23 Nov. 2020].

Zhejiangsheng Jingxin Ting [Economy and Information Technology Department of Zhejiang]. 2018. *Guanyu 2017 niandu 'Qiye shangyun' kaohe qingkuang de gongshi* [Announcement on the Assessment of the 'Enterprise cloud migration' in 2017]. http://www.zjjxw.gov.cn/art/2018/2/11/art_1097559_2684.html.

Zhongguo cunchu wang. 2019. *Zuixin 2019nian 6yue chaojijisuanji paiming, Top500qiang Zhongguo 219tai, dafu lingxian* [The latest supercomputer ranking in June 2019, Top500 strong China 219, a big lead]. http://www.chinastor.com/hpc-top500/061940MH019.html.

11

Global Value Chains and the Innovation of the Chinese Mobile Phone Industry

Yuqing Xing

Introduction

Innovation and new technology are primary driving forces of economic development. Constant innovation is indispensable for a developing country wishing to avoid the middle-income trap, to grow into a high-income country and eventually to become a catch-up industrialised economy. After the rapid economic growth of the last four decades, China now has a $14 trillion economy, second in size only to the US. Its GDP per capita is now about $10,000, more than ten times that when China started its revolutionary economic reform in 1978. Continuous technological innovation has contributed substantially to that economic miracle. The Global Innovation Index 2018, compiled by Cornell University, INSEAD and the World Intellectual Property Organisation, ranks China as one of the 20 most innovative economies in the world. China's aggregate investment in research and development (R&D) rose steadily as its economy grew continuously. In 2017, Chinese R&D was equivalent to 2.13 per cent of its GDP, making China the second in the world in terms of R&D investment (Atkinson and Foote 2019). Several studies (for example, Wu 2011; Iida, Shoji and Yoneyama 2018) concluded that China's R&D investment contributed substantially to the growth of the total factor productivity of the Chinese economy.

To date, China is the largest exporter not only of labour-intensive goods, such as shoes, clothes and toys, but also of personal computers, mobile phones, digital cameras and other information communication technology (ICT) products. Chinese manufacturing output has exceeded that of the US and has become the world No. 1 (West and Lansang 2018). In the world market for white goods, China's Haier Group has emerged as a leading maker of electronic appliances, to the point where Haier is now recognised as a global brand. In the global market for personal computers (PC), the Chinese company Lenovo has surpassed Hewlett-Packard and Dell to rank No.1 with 24 per cent of the global market (IDC 2018). In the global mobile phone market, home-grown Chinese brands Huawei, OPPO and Xiaomi are now three of the top five global smartphone brands (Counterpoint 2019b). Those achievements are largely the result of Chinese firms' constant endeavours to innovate.

There are many channels in which Chinese firms can innovate, thus strengthening their competitiveness in global markets and narrowing technological gaps with foreign multinational corporations (MNCs) currently leading in both technology and brands. R&D investment, foreign direct investment, innovation institutions, fiscal subsidies, learning by doing and reverse engineering are all effective tools for innovation and product enhancement. In this chapter, I focus on the role of global value chains (GVC) in facilitating both product and process innovation of Chinese firms.

With the unprecedented trade liberalisation and the modularisation of the production processes of manufactured products, in particular ICT, MNCs have reorganised their production along GVCs, where specific activities and production tasks are standardised and allocated to firms in dispersed geographic locations as a result of outsourcing or offshoring. Participating in GVCs led by MNCs having advanced technology, internationally recognised brands and global distribution networks, offers Chinese firms opportunities to learn and to access new knowledge and advanced technology, thus enhancing their innovation capacity. The expansion of GVCs has been driven by production fragmentation and the modularisation of production tasks, the two factors that have lowered technical barriers to entry into technology-intensive industrial sectors. Taking advantage of the availability of standardised technology platforms, Chinese firms have concentrated on incremental, rather than drastic innovations, and have aimed at the introduction of differentiated products and at competition with leading foreign companies in both domestic and foreign markets.

To a certain extent, Chinese firms in the ICT industry achieved their success by adopting the value chain strategy. Most of China's high-technology exports are manufactured with imported core technology components and are built on the top of technology platforms provided by foreign MNCs (Xing 2014). Assembling mobile phones for foreign vendors remains a major task for many Chinese firms. In this chapter, I will use the case of the Chinese mobile phone industry to illustrate the importance of GVCs in the facilitation of innovation, and demonstrate how Chinese firms have enhanced their innovation capacity by participating in GVCs.

GVCs, Innovation, and Upgrading

GVCs represent a new form of business operation, spanning multiple countries to create goods and deliver them to end consumers in world markets. Production fragmentation and modularisation enable production processes to disseminate ready-to-use goods, particularly ICT products, across geographically dispersed locations. Unprecedented liberalisation of trade and investment, innovation in ocean transportation and profit-seeking behaviour of MNCs have been the main drivers of the emergence of GVCs in recent decades (OECD 2013). Today, most manufacturing commodities are actually produced and traded along value chains. A typical GVC orchestrates a series of tasks necessary for delivery of a product. Ranging from conception to the delivery to end consumers, these tasks include research and development, product design, manufacture of parts and components, and assembly and distribution (Gereffi and Fernandez-Stark 2011: 4). Firms in different countries work in coordination to complete those tasks. Each firm specialises in one or more tasks in which it has comparative advantage, and contributes part of the whole value added of the final product. GVCs characterise a new division of labour—vertical specialisation across the provision of a single product. This specialisation is different from that in which firms make different products, as analysed by the British economist David Ricardo two centuries ago. Compared to conventional specialisation in different products, specialisation in tasks along value chains further refines the division of labour between nations and enhances the efficiency of resource allocation, consequently raising the productivity and economic growth of all economies involved. Three terms, GVC, supply chain and production network, refer interchangeably to the same phenomenon. Economists generally prefer the term GVC, because they are interested in the creation of value added and its distribution along value chains. Use of the terms "supply chain" and "production network" typically focuses on the production stages within value chains, the former emphasising who produces what, and the relations between upstream and downstream firms; the latter pays attention to the geographic locations of firms.

A lead firm, which manages the operation of a value chain and decides the relations between firms participating in the chain, is necessary for any meaningful GVC. If we break down the tasks contributing to the production of a product, from supply of the raw materials, to manufacture of the product and on to the eventual delivery of the product to targeted consumers, we can easily sketch a chain that superficially links all of the firms involved in the process. If the links along a value chain are not bound by binding contracts, that is if the relations are simply defined by free market transactions as buyer-seller relations, those value chains add little in terms of innovation. According to their governance structure, GVCs can be classified into producer-driven and buyer-driven. GVCs led by technology leaders in capital-intensive industries such as automobile, aircraft, computer and semiconductor, are producer-driven value chains. On the other hand, buyer-driven chains are typically organised by large retailers, branded marketers and branded manufacturers (Gereffi 1999: 41). The automobile value chains organised by Japanese auto-maker Toyota and the iPhone value chain of Apple are producer-driven GVCs. Similarly, Walmart, taking advantage of its extensive retail networks in the US and other countries, has built its buyer-driven GVC by sourcing all goods from some 60,000 contract manufacturers, 80 per cent of which are located in China.

Economists define innovation as the activities in which a firm applies new notions to the products, processes and other elements that generate increased value added. Innovation generally includes two dimensions: product innovation, the introduction of a new product; and process innovation, introduction of a new process for the manufacture or delivery of goods and services (Greenhalgh and Rogers 2010: 3ff.). It is critical to bear in mind that innovation is not a narrowly defined term referring to the creation of a drastically new product that surprises the world. To be sure, a completely new product such as the iPhone with its multi-touch screen and virtual keyboard is definitely a revolutionary innovation for the world. However, learning how to make smartphones with multi-touch screens is also an innovation for a firm imitating the iPhone. Most innovations are actually incremental achievements based on existing knowledge.

Innovations are not limited to new products, production processes or technology. New business models and marketing channels, aiming to enhance efficiency and value added, also constitute innovation. The OECD (2005) defines innovation as "the implementation of a new or significantly improved product (good or service), or process, a new marketing method, or a new organisational method in business practices, workplace organisation or external relations." For instance, using iTunes to sell songs one by one, not combined in an album (which bundles popular and less-popular songs together) is a drastic innovation that has fundamentally changed the business model of the music industry. With iTunes, an artist can achieve fame and some financial success with just one hit song (Isaacson 2011).

Along GVCs, there are many tasks with varying degrees of technical sophistication. The value added created by those tasks also varies substantially. In general, product design, R&D, branding and retailing constitute relatively high value added, while assembly and production of standardised components contribute relatively low value added.

Firms from developing countries generally start with low value-added tasks such as assembly when they join value chains governed by foreign MNCs. Many Chinese firms started with assembly of mobile phones for foreign MNCs. Innovation is imperative for firms participating in GVCs if they wish to move up the value chain ladder and reach high value added. Otherwise, they may fall into a low value-added trap (Sturgeon and Kawakami 2010). Upgrading includes product upgrading (adding additional value to products); functional upgrading, such as from pure assembly to design work; and process upgrading (making a production process more efficient) (Morrison, Pietrobelli and Rabellotti 2008). Upgrading along GVCs and entering high value-added segments result from innovation activities.

GVCs: A New Path for Innovation by the Chinese Mobile Phone Industry

In any value chain, the lead firm defines products, sets up quality standards and specifies technical parameters. All non-lead firms are obliged to follow the design rules specified by the lead firm. Intensive communication and information exchange between the lead firm and the suppliers are common, and offer a unique channel for non-lead firms to access new knowledge and production know-how. Learning mechanisms within GVCs include face-to-face interactions, knowledge transfer from lead firms, pressure to adopt international standards and training of the local workforce by lead firms (De Marchi, Giuliani and Rabellotti 2017). Gereffi (1999: 39) argued that participation in GVCs is a necessary step for industrial upgrading. Plugging into a GVC is similar to engaging in a dynamic learning curve. The transformation of some Asian suppliers from original equipment manufacturers (OEM) to original design manufacturers (ODM) in the apparel industry was significantly supported by their participation in apparel commodity chains.

China has for some time been recognised for its role as the assembly centre of major global brands. Before the emergence of smartphones, Motorola and Nokia used China as a major assembly base. Since the launch of the first generation iPhone, China has been the exclusive assembler of iPhones. At the peak, Samsung, the No. 1 mobile phone maker in the world, had 65% of its mobile phones assembled in China. The Chinese companies who assemble mobile phones for and supply components to those global mobile phone vendors are part of their value chains. The inter-firm linkages between the Chinese firms and upstream foreign buyers open the Chinese firms' access to information about technology and consumer demand, and thus facilitate their innovation activities and upgrading progress along value chains.

Upgrading along value chains step by step from low value added to high value-added tasks constitutes a linear model of innovation. For instance, a firm starts from assembling mobile phones, then enters the manufacturing of components, and eventually produces mobile phones with its own brand. This is a linear path of innovation. It refers to a sequential upgrading along value chains and differs from the "linear model" that describes the process starting with basic research and then moving into stages of applied research, development and diffusion (Godin 2006). On the other hand, sourcing core technology from foreign suppliers and jumping directly to brand building lead to a non-linear model of innovation. Chinese original brand manufacturers (OBM), such as Xiaomi, OPPO and vivo, adopted the non-linear model by taking advantage of the modularisation of mobile phone production and successfully broke the monopoly of foreign rivals in both domestic and international markets.

To a large extent, the expansion of GVCs in ICT is attributed to the development of modularity, that is, the division of the manufacture of complicated products into modules or sub-systems that can be designed and manufactured independently. Modularity allows firms to mix and match components so as to produce final products catering to various consumer preferences. By exploring modularity in the design of products, firms can improve their product innovation rate (Baldwin and Clark 2018).

Firms in developing countries typically face two challenges: a technology gap and a market gap. A "technology gap", the difficulty of accessing necessary technologies, is associated with weak innovation capacity (Schmitz 2007). Modularity creates the possibility of outsourcing essential technologies and enables firms in developing countries to specialise in value chain tasks in which they have comparative advantage. For example, a mobile phone consists of more than one thousand parts and components. The modularisation of mobile phone production has simplified the complexity of production and allowed potential entries to focus on non-core technology activities such as assembly. Given their relatively limited technology capacity in core components, say processors and memory chips, Chinese mobile phone makers entered the industry by sourcing core technological components from foreign MNCs and focusing on incremental innovations, marketing and brand building.

At the early stage of mobile phone development, their production was complicated and vertically integrated within a single firm. In that setting, a few large firms in industrialised countries (for example Nokia, Ericsson and Texas Instruments) monopolised global markets. In 2001 Wavecom, the French firm that first introduced the GSM model, developed the first module allowing handset makers to easily integrate applications into one main board. Taking advantage of this modularisation, China's TCL, an electronic appliance maker, entered the mobile phone market (Sun, Chen and Pleggenkuhle-Miles 2010).

The "turnkey" solution introduced by Media Tek (MTK), a fabless Taiwanese semiconductor firm, is a milestone in the development of the Chinese mobile phone industry. It greatly enhanced the degree of the modularity of mobile phone production, especially for small phone makers who lack the required technology capacities. The turnkey solution, an integrated solution combining hardware and software, is a single chip that combines a baseband platform and multimedia (sound and image) data processing. Using the chip, firms can easily modify product functionality to appeal to preferences of diversified consumers, thus significantly lowering entry barriers (Imai and Shiu 2010: 21). MTK's turnkey solution boosted the proliferation of "Shanzhai" mobile phone makers which had previously served as either OEMs or distributors for leading mobile phone brands. ("Shanzhai" originally meant counterfeit or imitation products.) However, a few studies have argued that Shanzai phones signified indigenous innovation products by small phone makers, and constituted good enough products at affordable prices to meet the needs of targeted customers. Shanzai phone makers gained market share not through technology innovation, but by adopting a novel business model (Hu, Wan and Zhu 2011).

In the age of smartphones, Android operating system (OS) and Qualcomm processor chipsets have become standard technology platforms. Leading Chinese smart phone makers ZTE, Xiaomi, OPPO and vivo all have adopted Android OS for their smartphones. Xiaomi and OPPO built 70 per cent of their phones on Qualcomm's platforms; ZTE and vivo used Qualcomm's platforms for 50 per cent and 60 per cent of their phones, respectively (World Bank 2019: 87). The Android OS platform has lowered technology barriers both for brand vendors, who were not capable of high-end product development, and for some handset assemblers, who were capable only of manufacturing white-box phones; this has facilitated the transformation of a few firms, OEMs, into original brand manufactures; OPPO is a noticeable example (Chen and Wen 2013: 10). The complexity of today's technology platforms and the demand for product differentiation have enhanced communication and cooperation between foreign suppliers of technology platforms and the downstream Chinese firms using those platforms, thus facilitating innovation by Chinese mobile phone makers. For instance, as the major platform supplier to leading Chinese mobile phone makers, Qualcomm welcomed the research teams of those Chinese firms to its headquarters for product development. After intensive interactions with Qualcomm and power chip provider Texas Instruments, OPPO introduced the world's first VOOC (Voltage Open Loop Multi-step Constant-Current Charging) system for smartphones (Humphrey et al. 2018).

In addition, the huge Chinese market, with a population of 1.4 billion, is conducive to marketing-focused strategies based on borrowed technology. In China a focus on the domestic market lessens the marketing gap and leads Chinese mobile phone makers towards a focus on marketing and product differentiation. Compared with leading foreign mobile phone makers, Chinese mobile phone makers have relatively more information and a better understanding of Chinese consumers. At the early stage of their development, Chinese mobile phone makers primarily adopted a low price strategy to attract consumers who could not afford expensive foreign brands, and targeted consumers in the country's third and fourth tier cities, to which foreign brand vendors had paid less attention. In addition, the Chinese makers explored niche markets, introducing a variety of peripheral functions, such as dual SIM cards, selfie applications and long life batteries.

Brandt and Thun (2010) expected that, by adopting a value chain strategy, Chinese handset makers "will be more akin to a Dell (which does little product research and design) than Tom Watson's IBM (which was highly vertically-integrated)". However, Xiaomi's MIU interface, OPPO's VOOC flashing charging technology and Huawei's Kirin processor provide clear evidence that they are technologically innovative. More importantly, by focusing on marketing and brand building, Chinese mobile phone makers have nurtured their brands, which are now recognised not only by Chinese users but also by foreign consumers. For instance, Xiaomi has surpassed both Apple and Samsung and emerged as the most popular brand in India. Brand leadership can boost sales growth, profit margin expansion and pricing power, and affords Chinese mobile phone makers the power to lead the value chains of their products and capture relatively large shares of value added. The bottom line is that brand development is an effective strategy for product innovation.

The Rise of the Chinese Mobile Phone Industry

The rise of the Chinese mobile phone industry is a GVC success story. Despite its technological dependence on foreign technology platforms, this industry has emerged as the largest mobile phone producer and exporter in the world.

Figure 11.1 outlines the trend of Chinese mobile output and exports from 2000 to 2016. At the beginning of the 21st century, the scale of China's mobile phone output and export was relatively small. In 2000, China produced 52.5 million mobile handsets, of which 22.8 million, or about 43 per cent of the total, were exported to overseas markets. Driven by the drastic growth of global demand and rapid technology innovation in the sector, the annual output of mobile phones surged to 998.3 million in 2010. Exports grew even faster, jumping to 776 million that year, making China the No.1 exporter in the world. In 2016, China produced 2.0 billion mobile phones, of which 1.3 billion were destined for foreign markets.

Figure 11.1: Chinese Output and Export of Mobile Phones (million units)

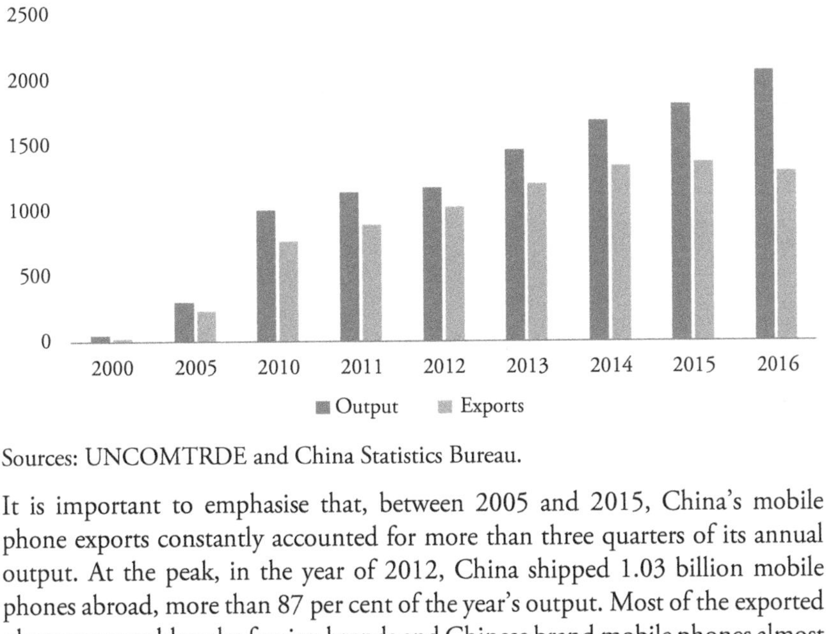

Sources: UNCOMTRDE and China Statistics Bureau.

It is important to emphasise that, between 2005 and 2015, China's mobile phone exports constantly accounted for more than three quarters of its annual output. At the peak, in the year of 2012, China shipped 1.03 billion mobile phones abroad, more than 87 per cent of the year's output. Most of the exported phones were sold under foreign brands and Chinese brand mobile phones almost did not exist in international markets. This unambiguously demonstrates that the Chinese mobile phone industry was then functioning as the assembly centre of global mobile phone production. Participation in value chains governed by leading global vendors and performing assembly tasks were the main drivers of that growth. As a segment with numerous value chains, the Chinese mobile industry simultaneously benefited from the spillover effects of innovation and marketing activities of the leading global vendors, such as Apple and Samsung, which were steadily driving the global demand for mobile phones upward.

Surging output volume represents the quantitative dimension of China's success in building its mobile phone production capacity. Another important dimension of that success is the brand development by indigenous Chinese firms. In addition to manufacturing handsets for foreign OBMs, the Chinese mobile phone industry successfully nurtured a few mobile phone brands which are competitive with foreign branded mobile phones in both China and abroad. Huawei, OPPO, vivo and Xiaomi, the most famous Chinese mobile phone brands, have successfully eroded the market share of their foreign rivals and reversed foreign domination of the sector completely in the Chinese market. Marketing research by Counterpoint (2019a) shows that in Q1 of 2019 Chinese brands captured 90 per cent of the Chinese smartphone market, led by Huawei with 34 per cent. The top four smartphone brands in terms of shipments (Huawei, vivo, OPPO and Xiaomi) together accounted for 87 per cent of the market, with Apple retaining a mere 9 per cent. The share of Samsung, the No. 1 mobile phone maker in the world, shrank to 1 per cent (Figure 11.2). Back in 2012, Samsung was the largest vendor in the Chinese market, with a 14 per cent market share, while Huawei had only 10 per cent. The market shares of OPPO, vivo and Xiaomi were negligible.

Figure 11.2: Chinese Smartphone Market Share (%)

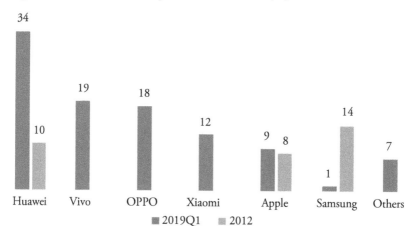

Sources: Counterpoint (2019a) and Chen and Wen (2013).

Building on their success in the home market, Chinese OBMs started to sell mobile phones with home-grown brands in international markets, gaining more and more market share, and eventually emerging as globally recognised brands. In Q1 of 2019, Huawei's global market share was 17 per cent, surpassing that of

Apple and ranking second, just 4 percentage points lower than Samsung. In fact, OPPO and vivo belong to the same company, BBK Electronics Corporation, a Chinese multinational firm. The combined market share of those two brands was 15 per cent, also exceeding that of Apple. In other words, BBK Electronics Corporation was actually the third largest mobile phone maker in the world. In 2012, Huawei's market share was about one fourth of Samsung's. OPPO, and neither vivo nor Xiaomi was known to foreign consumers. It is noteworthy that three bankrupted mobile phone makers, BlackBerry, Nokia and HTC, together accounted for 18.4 per cent of global shipments in 2012. At that time Chinese PC maker Lenovo acquired the Motorola brand. The market share of Motorola became part of the Chinese mobile phone makers' share, so together those Chinese firms accounted for 44 per cent of smartphone shipments in the global market (Figure 11.3).

Figure 11.3: Global Smartphone Market Share (%)

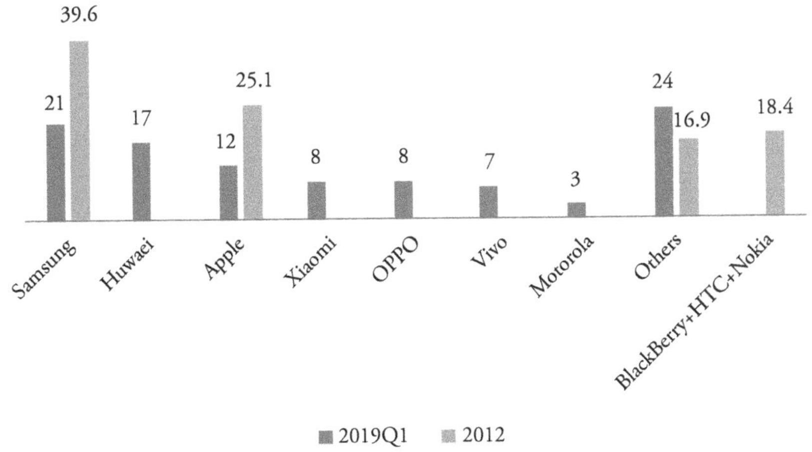

■ 2019Q1   ■ 2012

Source: Counterpoint (2019b) and Chen and Wen (2013).

Moving Up in the iPhone Value Chain

The operation of Apple is an exemplary GVC. Apple has outsourced its production to contract manufacturers in various geographic locations and has concentrated mainly on product design, R&D and the development of software for its operating systems at one tail of the smile curve and marketing and retail at the other. All Apple products, iMac, MacBook Air, iPad and iPhone, are assembled in China. The phrase, "Designed by Apple in California. Assembled in China", printed on the back of all Apple products, is a hallmark.

So far, Apple has released twelve generations of iPhones. With the introduction of the iPhone X, which carries most advanced technologies such as 3D sensing, but which comes with a $1,000 price tag, the iPhone has been transformed into a luxury high-technology gadget. China has been the exclusive assembly base for the iPhone since the first generation iPhone, iPhone 3G, was released in 2007. As the centre of the iPhone production, the Chinese mobile phone industry has benefited significantly from the popularity of the iPhone on the world market. Constantly rising global demand for it always automatically translates into demand for the services and periphery components supplied by the Chinese mobile phone industry. This has significantly promoted the growth of the Chinese sector in the last decades.

According to Xing and Detert (2010), Foxconn, a Taiwanese company with many production facilities in mainland China, received only $6.5 for assembling a ready-to-use iPhone 3G. That $6.5 accounts for 3.6 per cent of the total iPhone 3G manufacturing cost and roughly 1.3 per cent of the retail price. It consists of the whole value added captured by China in the process of manufacturing the iPhone 3G. To avoid the low-value added trap and take advantage of the learning opportunity offered by GVCs, upgrading and moving into relatively high value added segments are crucial for Chinese firms involved in the iPhone value chain. To assess this upgrading for participating Chinese firms, it is necessary to examine whether the number of Chinese firms involved in Apple's value chains has increased, whether the range of tasks performed by Chinese firms has expanded and whether the technological sophistication of the tasks has risen.

Upgrading along the iPhone value chain is highly rewarding financially. In general, future uncertainty discourages firms from engaging in innovation efforts. Once a Chinese firm joins the army of Apple supplier companies, hundreds of millions of Apple users around the world will be potential customers for that firm's products or services. The predictable and lucrative prospects motivate Chinese firms to raise the quality of their products to the standard of Apple. This is an example of innovation activities inspired by GVC participation. Grimes and Sun (2016) found that Chinese firms have played an increasingly important role in Apple's value chains. In 2014, of 198 companies in the chain, 14 were Chinese. A few supplied core components, for example displays and printed circuit boards; this suggests that Chinese firms have strengthened their presence in the value chains controlled by Apple.

The teardown data of the iPhone X are examined so that the involvement of Chinese firms in the production of the iPhone X can be assessed. The teardown data, which provide detailed information about suppliers of the iPhone X as well as prices of parts and components, show that all core components embedded in the printed circuit board assembly (PCBA), including processor, DRAM, NAND, display and camera, are supplied by Apple, Qualcomm, Broadcom, Samsung, Toshiba, Sony and other non-Chinese companies. Indigenous Chinese companies manufactured only a small portion of non-core components. It should be noted that besides the assembler Foxconn, there are 10 local Chinese companies participating in the value chain of the iPhone X. Their tasks go beyond simple assembly and spread over relatively sophisticated segments. Table 11.1 lists Chinese firms and their corresponding tasks in the production of the iPhone X.

Table 11.1:   Tasks Performed by Chinese Firms for the iPhone 3G and iPhone X

iPhone 3G (2009)	iPhone X (2018)
• Assembly (Foxconn)	• Assembly (Foxconn);
	• Function parts for Touchscreen Module (Anjie Technology);
	• Filter for 3D sensing Module (Crystal Optech);
	• Coil Module for wireless charging (Lushare Precision);
	• Printed Circuit Board (M-Flex);
	• Speakers (Goertek);
	• RF Antenna (Shenzhen Sunway);
	• Battery Pack (Sunwoda);
	• Glass cover (Lens Technology);
	• Stainless Frame (Kersen Technology);
	• Camera Module (O-Filem)

Source: Xing (2020).

Sunwoda, a leading Chinese battery maker, supplies the battery pack. Sony batteries were used in the early models of the iPhone; Sunwoda's supplanting Sony as a battery pack supplier is a significant upgrading of Sunwoda along the iPhone value chain. Kersen Technology provides the iPhone stainless frames, and Lens Technology manufactures the glass covers. The stainless frame and glass back cover together cost $53, about 13 per cent of the total manufacturing cost and more than 11 times the assembly fee of $4.5. The iPhone X is the first iPhone with a glass back cover. In addition, Chinese companies Anjie Technology and Lushare Precision are involved in manufacturing iPhone X touch screens and 3D sensing modules respectively. Touch screens and 3D sensing modules are critical technological components of the iPhone X. The former translates users' finger movements into data that can be interpreted as commands, while the latter is a key element of the facial recognition system, a new feature introduced in the iPhone X. Chinese company Dongshan Precision joined the suppliers to Apple by acquiring American company M-Flex; it now supplies the printed circuit boards for the iPhone X for $15 per unit. Chinese companies Goertek, Shenzhen Sunway, Crystal-Opetch and O-film provide functional parts: speakers, RF antennas, filters and camera modules respectively. The involvement of those Chinese firms, even though in non-core technology segments of the Phone X value chain, indicates that the Chinese mobile phone industry as a whole has moved to the upper rungs of the iPhone value chain ladder. According to the teardown data, the total bill for materials of the iPhone X is $409.25, of which the Chinese firms jointly contribute $104, about 25.4 per cent of the total manufacturing cost.

A complete value chain consists of pre-production, production and post-production activities. For estimation of the domestic value added in a country's exports, and to fairly evaluate bilateral trade balances with its trading partners, the manufacturing cost of a product can appropriately be used as a benchmark. For assessment of the value captured by Chinese firms in the whole iPhone X value chain, we should go beyond production and use retail price as a benchmark, since it proxies total value added of the iPhone X. We found that the Chinese firms together captured 10.4 per cent of the value added in the iPhone X's retail price $1,000, much higher than that for iPhone 3G (Figure 11.4).

Figure 11.4: Chinese Value Added Embedded in the iPhone 3G and iPhone X

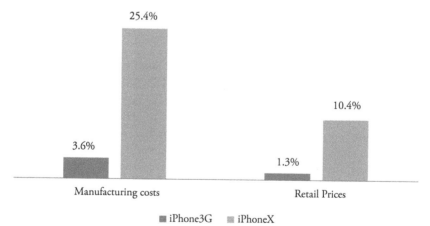

Source: Xing and Detert (2010) and the author's calculation.

Therefore, compared with the production of the iPhone 3G, more Chinese firms are involved in the production of the iPhone X and they perform more diversified tasks and capture higher value added. This implies significant upward movement by Chinese firms along the iPhone value chain. All of Apple's suppliers are required to satisfy the high quality and technology standards defined by it. The pressure to meet these standards facilitated the upgrading process of those firms and their innovation activities.

OPPO and Xiaomi: a GVC Success Story

OPPO is one of the most popular mobile phone brands in the Chinese market. In the first quarter of 2019, it ranked No. 3 after Huawei and vivo, with an 18% market share (Counterpoint 2019a). "Designed by OPPO Assembled in China" is printed on the back of OPPO phones. The statement, actually an imitation of the similar phrase on the back of the iPhone, sounds a little bit strange, as OPPO is clearly a 100 per cent Chinese company. OPPO intends to use the statement to convey a message to its users: OPPO phones use state-of-the-art technologies and China's role is limited to assembly. The statement is self-evident that OPPO phones are products of GVCs. By providing an excellent selfie experience, OPPO smartphones have achieved widespread popularity, particularly among younger consumers. OPPO actually markets its phones as camera phones in commercials, to differentiate its brand from others. The company operates a nationwide network of 200,000 stores to sell its products in China. It generally pays a much more generous commission than the industrial average to motivate its salespersons (Wang 2016). Globally, OPPO shipped 25.7 million smartphones in the first quarter of 2019 and held fifth position among leading mobile phone vendors (Counterpoint 2019b).

To understand the dependence of OPPO on foreign technology platforms, the teardown data of the OPPO R11s, a premium smartphone released in 2017 and which runs on Android OS, are used to examine the suppliers of OPPO in detail. The teardown data show that all core components were sourced from foreign suppliers. The phone is powered by Qualcomm's mid-range Snapdragon 660 processor, coupled with an embedded multi-chip package (eMCP) by Samsung. It features a 6.1-inch full screen AMOLED display by Samsung. All components embedded in the PCBA are supplied by foreign companies, particularly Qualcomm, Samsung, TDK and Muruta. SONY supplies the rear camera, Samsung the front camera for selfies. The total value added of foreign companies accounts for 83.3 per cent of the total manufacturing costs, consistent with the statement "assembled in China" (Table 11.2). A few Chinese firms provide a limited number of non-core components such as the fingerprint module (by O-film) and the battery (by Sunwoda).

Table 11.2:   Foreign Technology and Suppliers of the OPPO R11s

Component	Supplier	Total Foreign Value Added
Operating System	Android (US)	
CPU:		
Snapdragon 660	Qualcomm (US)	
Memory: eMCP	Samsung (Korea)	83.3% of the total
Display:		manufacturing cost $293.18
6.01inch, 1080x2160 pixels	Samsung (Korea)	
Dual Camera	Sony (Japan)	
Front Camera	Samsung (Korea)	

Source: Xing and He (2018).

Figure 11.5 shows the estimated distribution of value added of the OPPO R11s by country. The total bill for the phone's materials is $293.18. Korean companies Samsung and Hynix together contributed 40.3 per cent of the total manufacturing cost. The second largest source of value added is 18.5 per cent, from the US. The contribution of the Japanese companies Sony, Muruta and others is estimated at 18.4 per cent, almost the same as that of the US. The Chinese companies accounted for the smallest share of value added. However, if we take the retail price of 2999 RMB as a benchmark, the cross-country distribution of value added is dramatically different: China emerges with the largest share of total value added, about 45.3 per cent of the retail price, which shows the power of brand ownership: that significantly high share is attributed to brand value and the corresponding retail service (Figure 11.5).

Xiaomi is the 4th largest mobile phone maker in the world. It shipped 27.8 million smartphones globally in 2019 (Counterpoint 2019b). Unlike OPPO, Xiaomi is a factory-less maker and has no assembly facilities. It outsources the production of its phones to contract manufacturers. Xiaomi is the first Chinese mobile phone vendor to sell phones exclusively online. The secrets of Xiaomi's success include: selling a premium phone at about a half the price of its competitors; fast-flashing sales; and nurturing a community of users. Xiaomi's largest foreign market is India, where it surpassed Samsung to become the No.1 smartphone vendor.

Similar to OPPO smartphones, all Xiaomi phones run on Android OS and are designed based on Qualcomm chipsets. Xiaomi, however, has developed a unique MIUI interface based on Android OS and installed it on Xiaomi phones to differentiate it from other brands. The case of the flagship device MIX 2 released in the second half of 2017 demonstrates Xiaomi's reliance on foreign technology. The teardown data of the MIX2 reveal that it is powered by a top-end Qualcomm Snapdragon 835 processor, which costs $62.56, the most expensive part in the PCBA of the MIX2. It has a 6GB NAND flash memory, supplied by the Korean company Hynix, and 64GB Dynamic random access memory manufactured by Samsung. With regard to functional parts, the Xiaomi MIX 2 features a 5.99 inch 1080x2160 pixel display produced by Japan Device Inc. Sony supplies the camera embedded in the phone. Chinese companies are mainly involved in the provision of non-core components and services. For instance, BIYADI Electronics supplies the frame of the phone and the battery company SCUD provides the battery. Table 11.3 lists major foreign technology suppliers of the Xiaomi MIX 2.

Figure 11.5: Distribution of the OPPO R11s Value Added by Country (%)

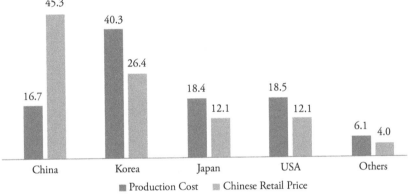

Source: Xing and He (2018).

Table 11.3: Foreign Technology and Suppliers of the Xiaomi MIX 2

Component	Supplier	Total Foreign Value Added
Operating System	Android (US)	
CPU:		
Snapdragon 835	Qualcomm (US)	
NAND 6GB	Hynix (Korea)	84.6% of the total
DRAM 64GB	Samsung (Korea)	manufacturing cost $335.98.
Display:		
5.99 inch, 1080x2160	JDI (Japan)	
Camera	SONY (Japan)	

Source: Xing and He (2018).

Foreign companies together accounted for 84.6 per cent of the value added in manufacturing the Xiaomi MIX 2 (Figure 11.6). Specifically, the US companies captured 38.6 per cent of the value added, the highest among all country groups, followed by Japanese companies with 20.3 per cent and Korean 20.0 per cent. Similar to the case of the OPPO R11s, the Chinese companies' contribution to the value added of the MIX 2 is relatively small, about 15.4 per cent of total production cost, suggesting that the involvement of Chinese companies in the value chain of Xiaomi is limited. The retail price of the MIX is 3299 RMB. If we include the value added generated by Xiaomi's brand and the retail service, the share of the Chinese value added is 41.7 per cent, significantly higher than that when only production is considered. Again, the brand ownership raises the Chinese value added.

Figure 11.6: Distribution of the Xiaomi MIX 2's Value Added (%)

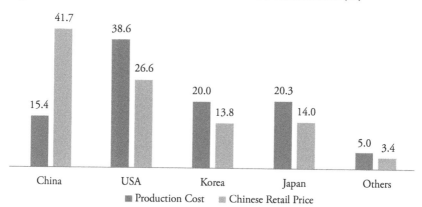

Source: Xing and He (2018).

The teardown data of the OPPO R11s and the Xiaomi MIX 2 suggest that foreign technology remains indispensable for Chinese brand mobile phones. Even though OPPO and Xiaomi have emerged as global brands, the innovations of the two companies are incremental and marginal. Instead of targeting drastic technology advancement for catching up, they emphasise product differentiation, brand building and a business model which takes advantage of the availability of the technology platforms. The successes of OPPO and Xiaomi indicate that GVCs provide non-linear models of how innovation and firms of developing countries can enter the high-tech industry and emerge as lead firms by sourcing necessary technologies.

The innovation path of Huawei differs from those of Xiaomi and OPPO. It is the largest mobile phone maker in China and the second largest in the world.

Huawei was regarded as the most innovative Chinese company. In 2018, it invested $15.3 billion in R&D and even outspent Apple (Bloomberg 2019). Compared to those by OPPO and Xiaomi, Huawei's innovations are relatively more technology-oriented. According to the teardown data of the Japanese firm Fomalhaut Techno Solution, Huawei P30 Pro is powered by the Kirin processor developed by HiSilicon, a subsidiary of Huawei, suggesting that Huawei has developed the technological capacity to design a chip set which can substitute for Qualcomm's chipsets, currently adopted by most Chinese mobile phone makers (Table 11.4). The Kirin processor marks the highest level of technological innovation by the Chinese mobile phone industry. In addition, the Huawei P30 Pro incorporates an OLED display manufactured by Chinese company BOE Technology. The OLED display is the most expensive part embedded in the Huawei P30 Pro. Because of the above two key components, the Chinese value added in the Huawei P30 Pro reached 38.1 per cent, much higher than that in the OPPO R11s and the Xiaomi MIX 2. Samsung, LG and JDI have been dominant in the OLED display market. The adoption of BOE Technology's OLED display by Huawei is a noticeable inroad into the monopoly of the foreign companies.

Table 11.4:   Technology and Suppliers of the Huawei P30 Pro

Component	Supplier	Total Foreign Value Added
Operating System	Android (US)	
CPU	HiSilicon (China)	61.9% of total manufacturing cost.
NAND	Samsung (Korea)	
DRAM	Micron Technology (US)	
Display	BOE Technology (China)	

Source: Tanaka (2019).

Concluding Remarks

The rise of the Chinese mobile industry is impressive and unique. On the one hand, China has become the largest mobile phone maker and the largest exporter in the world. Of the top five global mobile phone brands, three are Chinese: Huawei, Xiaomi and OPPO. On the other hand, all Chinese smartphones depend on foreign technology platforms. They run on the Android OS owned by Google and are powered by Qualcomm chipsets. However, that technology deficiency has not hindered the emergence of the Chinese mobile phone industry. The value chain strategy of sourcing necessary technology platforms and concentrating on product differentiation and incremental innovation explains the significant achievement of the Chinese mobile phone industry. GVCs facilitated by modularisation provide a unique path for Chinese firms to enter the industry and leapfrog technological barriers. As latecomers, Chinese firms had to begin as contract manufacturers, assembling mobile phones for foreign vendors. The emergence of home-grown brands in global markets and their upgrading along the value chain of the iPhone suggest that Chinese firms are capable of moving to upper phases of value chain work, and that their innovative activities performed a critical role in successful competition with foreign rivals.

The development of GVCs makes it possible to achieve a non-linear model of innovation, although the GVC strategy is not risk-free. All the cases presented here refer to technology platforms owned by foreign companies, mainly the American companies Google and Qualcomm. The efficiency and effectiveness of the GVC strategy are based on the assumption that Chinese firms are able to purchase necessary technologies via fair market transactions. This assumption no longer holds.

As US-China trade evolved into a technology war, Huawei was banned by the Trump administration from purchasing chipsets manufactured by American companies. Even worse, the Trump administration further strengthened the technological sanctions on Huawei and barred any companies from using American technologies to produce chipsets for Huawei. This embargo simply announced the death of Huawei's Kirin processors, which were manufactured by Taiwan Semiconductor Manufacturing Company with American technology. The technological decoupling between the US and China implies that the golden era of GVCs is over. National security has become a major obstacle for adopting GVC strategy. The Chinese mobile phone industry should invest in core mobile phone technologies and be prepared for a possible complete decoupling between the two countries.

References

Atkinson, Robert D. and Caleb Foote. 2019. *Is China Catching Up to the United States in Innovation?* Washington DC: Information Technology and Innovation Foundation. Available at http://www2.itif.org/2019-china-catching-up-innovation.pdf?_ga=2.11950839.2136986670.1612821833-635563182.1612821833 [accessed 8 Feb. 2021].

Baldwin, Carliss Y. and Kim B. Clark. 1997. "Managing in an Age of Modularity", *Harvard Business Review*, Sept.–Oct. Available at https://hbr.org/1997/09/managing-in-an-age-of-modularity [accessed 25 Nov. 2020].

Bloomberg 2019. *No Pay, No Gain: Huawei Outspends Apple on R&D for a 5G Edge.* Available at https://www.bloomberg.com/news/articles/2019-04-25/huawei-s-r-d-spending-balloons-as-u-s-tensions-flare-over-5g [accessed 18 July 2019].

Brandt, Loren and Eric Thun. 2011. "Going Mobile in China: Shifting Value Chains and Upgrading in the Mobile Telecom Sector", *International Journal of Technological Learning, Innovation and Development* 4, 1/2/3: 148–80.

Chen Shin-Horng and Wen Pei-Chang. 2013. *The Development and Evolution of China's Mobile Phone Industry.* Working paper series No. 2013–1. Taipei: Chung-Hua Institute for Economics Research.

Cornell University, INSEAD and the World Intellectual Property Organization. 2018. *The Global Innovation Index 2018: Energizing the World with Innovation.* Ithaca, Fontainebleau and Geneva.

Counterpoint. 2019a. *Chinese Smartphone Market Share by Quarter.* Available at https://www.counterpointresearch.com/china-smartphone-share/ [accessed 11 July 2019].

_____. 2019b. *Global Smartphone Market Share by Quarter.* Available at https://www.counterpointresearch.com/global-smartphone-share/ [accessed 11 July 2019].

De Marchi, Valentina, Elisa Giuliani and Roberta Rabellotti. 2018. "Do Global Value Chains Offer Developing Countries Learning and Innovation Opportunities?", *European Journal of Development Research* 30, 3: 389–407.

Gereffi, Gary. 1999. "International Trade and Industrial Upgrading in the Apparel Commodity Chain", *Journal of International Economics* 48, 1: 37–70. Available at https://www.soc.duke.edu/~ggere/web/gereffi_jie_june_1999.pdf [accessed 19 Feb. 2021].

Gereffi, Gary and Karina Fernandez-Stark. 2011. *Global Value Chain Analysis: a Primer.* Durham, NC: Duke University Center on Globalization, Governance and Competitiveness.

Godin, Benoît. 2006. "The Linear Model of Innovation: The Historical Construction of an Analytical Framework", *Science, Technology, and Human Values* 31, 6: 639–67.

Greenhalgh, Christine and Mark Rogers. 2010. *Innovation, Intellectual Property, and Economic Growth.* Princeton, NJ: Princeton University Press.

Grimes, Seamus and Sun Yutao. 2016. "China's Evolving Role in Apple's Global Value Chain", *Area Development and Policy* 1, 1: 94–112.

Hu Jin-Li, Wan Hsiang-Tzu and Zhu Hang. 2011. "The Business Model of a Shanzai Mobile Phone Firm in China", *Australian Journal of Business and Management Research* 1, 3: 53–61.

Humphrey, John et al. 2018. "Platforms, Innovation and Capability Development in the Chinese Domestic Market", *The European Journal of Development Research* 30, 3: 408–23.

IDC [International Data Corporation]. 2018. *Lenovo Reclaims the #1 Spot in PC Ranking in Q3 2018.* Available at https://www.businesswire.com/news/home/20181010005962/en/Lenovo-Reclaims-the-1-Spot-in-PC-Rankings-in-Q3-2018-According-to-IDC [accessed 8 Feb. 2021].

Iida Tomoyuki, Shoji Kanako and Yoneyama Shunichi. 2018. *What Drives China's Growth? Evidence from Micro-level Data.* Bank of Japan Working Paper Series, No.18-E-19, November.

Imai Ken and Shui Jingming. 2007. *A Divergent Path of Industrial Upgrading: Emergence and Evolution of the Mobile Handset Industry in China.* IDE Discussion paper No. 125. Chiba: Institute of Developing Economies/ Japan External Trade Organization [IDE-JETRO].

Isaacson, Walter. 2011. *Steve Jobs.* New York: Simon & Schuster.

Morrison, Andrea, Carlo Pietrobelli and Roberta Rabellotti. 2008. "Global Value Chains and Technological Capabilities: a Framework to Study Learning and Innovation in Developing Countries", *Oxford Development Studies* 36, 1: 39–58.

OECD. 2005. "The Measurement of Scientific and Technological Activities: Guidelines for Collecting and Interpreting Innovation Data: Oslo Manual, Third Edition" prepared by the Working Party of National Experts on Scientific and Technology Indicators, OECD, Paris, para. 146.

_____. 2013. *Interconnected economies: Benefiting from Global Value Chains.* Paris: Organisation for Economic Cooperation and Development. Available at https://www.oecd.org/sti/ind/interconnected-economies-GVCs-synthesis.pdf [accessed 8 Feb. 2021].

Schmitz, Hubert. 2007. "Reducing Complexity in the Industrial Policy Debate", *Development Policy Review* 25, 4: 417–28.

Sturgeon, Timothy J. and Kawakami Momoko. 2010. *Global Value Chains in the Electronics Industry:*

Sun Sunny Li, Chen Hao and Erin Pleggenkuhle-Miles. 2010. "Moving Upward in Global Value Chains: The Innovations of Mobile Phone Developers in China", *Chinese Management Studies* 4, 4: 305–21.

Tanaka, A. 2019. "Teardown of Huawei Latest Model Shows Reliance on US Souring," *Nikkei Asia*, 26 June 2019. Available at https://asia.nikkei.com/Economy/Trade-war/Teardown-of-Huawei-latest-model-shows-reliance-on-US-sourcing [accessed 2 Feb 2021].

Wang Yue. 2016. "OPPO Explained: How a Little-Known Smartphone Company Overtook Apple in China", *Forbes*, 22 July 2016. Available at https://www.forbes.com/sites/ywang/2016/07/22/oppo-explained-how-a-little-known-smartphone-company-overtook-apple-in-china/?sh=41deb5b1393c [accessed 25 Nov. 2020].

Was the Crisis a Window of Opportunity for Developing Countries? Washington DC: The World Bank Policy Research Working Paper, No. 5417. Available at https://openknowledge.worldbank.org/bitstream/handle/10986/3901/WPS5417.pdf?sequence=1&isAllowed=y [accessed 8 Feb. 2021].

West, Darrell M. and Christian Lansang. 2018. *Global Manufacturing Scorecard: How the US Compares to 18 Other Nations.* Washington DC: Brookings. Available at https://www.brookings.edu/research/global-manufacturing-scorecard-how-the-us-compares-to-18-other-nations/ [accessed 25 Nov. 2020].

World Bank. 2019. *Global Development Report 2019: Technological Innovation, Supply Chain Trade, and Workers in a Globalized World*. Washington DC: World Bank.

Wu Yanrui. 2011. "Total Factor Productivity Growth in China, a Review", *Journal of Chinese Economic and Business Studies* 9, 2: 111–26.

Xing Yuqing. 2014. "China's High-Tech Exports: The Myth and Reality", *Asian Economic Papers* 13, 1: 109–23.

_____. 2020. "How the iPhone Widens the US Trade Deficit with China: The Case of the iPhone X", *Frontiers of Economics in China* 15, 4: 642-58.

Xing Yuqing and Neal Detert. 2010. *How the iPhone Widens the US Trade Deficit with China*. Tokyo: ADB Institute Working paper 257.

Xing Yuqing and He Yuzhen. 2018. *The Domestic Value Added of Chinese Brand Mobile Phones*. Tokyo: National Graduate Institute for Policy Studies [GRIPS] Discussion Paper 18-09.

List of Contributors

Erik Baark is emeritus professor at the Division of Social Science and the Division of Environment and Sustainability, Hong Kong University of Science and Technology, Hong Kong, China; he is a former visiting research professor at the East Asian Institute, National University of Singapore, Singapore.

Cong Cao is professor at the School of Contemporary Chinese Studies, University of Nottingham Ningbo, China.

Xiaolan Fu is professor of Technology and International Development and Fellow of Green Templeton College, University of Oxford, UK.

Bai Gao is professor of Sociology at Duke University, Durham, NC, USA

Bert Hofman is director and professor at the East Asian Institute, National University of Singapore, Singapore.

Carsten A. Holz is professor in the Social Science Division at the Hong Kong University of Science & Technology, Hong Kong, China.

Gary Jefferson is Carl Marks Professor of International Trade and Finance, Brandeis University, Waltham, MA, USA.

Cintia Külzer-Sacilotto is a postdoctoral researcher at the Lee Kong Chian School of Business, Singapore Management University, Singapore.

Haibo Lin is doctor of Management at the Hong Kong Polytechnic University and adjunct lecturer at the School of Professional and Continuing Education, Hong Kong University, Shenzhen, China.

Anton Malkin is a fellow in the Centre for International Governance Innovation and assistant professor in the Department of Global Studies at the Chinese University of Hong Kong, Shenzhen, China.

Dan Prud'homme is associate professor at the EMLV School of Business at Pôle Universitaire Léonard de Vinci, Paris, France, and Kunshan Duke University, Suzhou, JS, China.

Jiwei Qian is senior research fellow at the East Asian Institute, National University of Singapore, Singapore.

Yi Ru is a China Project Research Specialist at the Domestic Think Tank Team, Institute of New Structural Economics, Peking University.

Denis Fred Simon is executive professor and senior adviser to the President for China Affairs at Duke University, Durham, NC, USA.

Yuqing Xing is professor of Economics at the National Graduate Institute for Policy Studies, Tokyo, Japan and former visiting research professor at the East Asian Institute, National University of Singapore, Singapore.

Hongru Xiong is associate research fellow (associate professor) in the Department of Innovation at the Development Research Center (DRC) of the State Council, China.

Index